"This is an enthralling account of a city on the Georgia/Alabama border that was as lawless as any place in the Wild West and of the brave warriors and decent citizens who cleaned it up. With a precise eye and marvelously readable style, this prize-winning author has scored again with a captivating book on this absorbing piece of Southern History."

— *Governor Zell Miller*
Honorable Governor of the State of Georgia

"A powerful book based on facts that defy fiction. A terrific story; meticulously researched; brilliantly written; and compellingly readable."

— *George T. Smith*
Justice of Georgia Supreme Court (retired)

"Margaret Anne Barnes has reached into the distant past to create a vivid picture of the most sensational crime story of the 1950s — the assassination of the attorney general-elect of Alabama. With the sure skill of the accomplished journalist and storyteller that she is, Ms. Barnes captures not merely "the tragedy and the triumph" of Phenix City, but the humor and pathos as well through the endless parade of bizarre characters who so vividly people this book. Although the story is nearly forgotten, the impact of the Phenix City episode on Alabama politics — and by extension on national politics — is lasting and incalculable. This makes Ms. Barnes' book both an engrossing story and a valuable contribution to history."

— *Ray Jenkins*
Former editor of the editorial page of Baltimore's Evening Sun.
As a young reporter in 1954-55, he covered the Phenix City upheaval from beginning to end for the Columbus Ledger *which won the 1995 Pulitzer prize for Public Service.*

"Even for those of us who were stationed at Ft. Benning in the early Fifties, and being young and foolish sometimes ventured across the Chattahoochee on Saturday nights, the Phenix City story is hard to believe. Perhaps nowhere in America were violence and corruption allowed to flourish so openly. "Margaret Anne Barnes's book is the best and most complete report I've ever read about crimes that shook the state of Alabama and stunned a nation; and about brave justice that eventually triumphed at a terrible price. Through patient research and skilled reporting she has recreated this story in the masterful style of her highly successful *Murder in Coweta County*"

— *Jim Minter*
Former editor, the Atlanta Journal-Constitution

"The murder of Attorney General nominee Albert Patterson in 1954 was without question one of the most dramatic and history-altering events of 20th century Alabama. For those not old enough to remember it as well as for those of us who lived through it, *The Tragedy and the Triumph of Phenix City, Alabama* is a must read. Much has been written about this event but Margaret Anne Barnes' work is the best."

— *Bob Ingram*
Political Columnist for the Montgomery Advertiser.

"Margaret Anne Barnes has written a great in-depth study of the tragedy of Phenix City, Alabama. Not since Robert Penn Warren's account of Hughey Long in *All the King's Men* has a story of such complete political control that so paralyzed a region been told. *The Tragedy and the Triumph of Phenix City, Alabama* is a highly authentic and accurate account of how it developed, the characters involved, the corruption that extended from the court house to the state house and the terrible price paid to restore justice. It is a lesson not to be forgotten."

— John Patterson

"Margaret Anne Barnes is an old pro who has done it again with *The Tragedy and the Triumph of Phenix City, Alabama*, a book that will remind readers of her earlier success with *Murder in Coweta County*.
It is the story of how a handful of brave townspeople of Phenix City stood up to an evil mob that would stop short of nothing—not bombings, not beatings, not murder—to maintain control of the town and the gambling dives and prostitution rings that once made Phenix City known far and wide as 'Sin City, USA'."

— Billy Winn
Editor of the Editorial Page
Columbus Ledger

"This is a fascinating, intriguing plot made all the more compelling by the fact of its being a true story. Margaret Anne Barnes "creates" characters and scenes that live in the imagination thereby the reader cares about what happens in this history....She allows us to know individuals in all their complexity; to understand how corruption begins and is perpetuated and to contemplate moral dimensions of human behavior under ordinary and extreme circumstances."

— Kay Beck, Ph.D.
Associate Professor Georgia State University

"In her book, *The Tragedy and the Triumph of Phenix City, Alabama*, Margaret Anne Barnes unfolds for the reader a cautionary tale. Until one has lived in a closed political system, it never occurs what the consequences might be. Barnes obviously read through miles of newspaper microfilm and mined direct quotes from official court records and criminal trials. There is a message here for a wider America: Once established, democratic freedom is hardy, yet, like a fragile plant it must be nourished. Phenix City had to water this plant with its blood.

— Harry Albert Haines
Columnist, Murfreesboro, TN

(More advanced praise for The Tragedy and the Triumph of Phenix City, Alabama *on page 321.)*

THE TRAGEDY AND THE TRIUMPH OF

PHENIX CITY, ALABAMA

by

Margaret Anne Barnes

[signature: Margaret Anne Barnes]

3rd Edition

2002

MERCER UNIVERSITY PRESS
MACON, GEORGIA

Mercer University Press
6316 Peake Road
Macon, Georgia 31210

First Edition

Third printing March 2002.

∞The paper used in this publication meets the
minimum requirements of American National
Standard for Permanence of Paper for
Printed Library Materials.

Library of Congress Cataloging-in-Publication Data

Barnes, Margaret Anne.
The tragedy and the triumph of Phenix City, Alabama, / by
Margaret Anne Barnes. — 1st edition
p. cm.
Includes bibliographical references and index.
ISBN 0-86554-613-4 (alk. paper)
1. Phenix City (Ala.) — History — 20th century.
2. Organized crime — Alabama — Phenix City —
History — 20th century.
3. Crime prevention — Alabama — Phenix City — Citizen
participation — History — 20th century.
I. Title.
F334.P45P37   1998
976.1'485 — dc21
98-27470   CIP

BOOK I: PHENIX CITY, ALABAMA

BOOK II: THE TRAGEDY

BOOK III: THE TRIUMPH

This book is dedicated to my two physicians:
Dr. Jack E. Birge and Dr. Lenora M. Ashley,
who kept me alive long enough to finish this book.

FOREWORD

This book is based on a true story as it happened in Phenix City, Alabama, 1916-1955. The main character is not a single individual but the town itself which bred conflict, controversy, killing, and crime. In the crisis which came, involving the entire state of Alabama, the town was ultimately able to heal itself.

"The Phenix City Story," as it was designated by the press received saturation reporting by the Alabama and Georgia newspapers, most notably: the *Montgomery Advertiser*, the *Birmingham News*, the *Birmingham Post-Herald*, the *Columbus Enquirer*, and the *Columbus Ledger*. The *Columbus Ledger* reported the story in detail as front page news for an entire year and for its accurate and meritorious effort for community service was awarded the 1955 Pulitzer Prize.

The story was of such significance that it attracted national notice and was published in *Time, Life, Look, Newsweek, Saturday Evening Post,* and the *London Times* (by a British correspondent sent to cover the story).

Because of the complexities, it was necessary to tell this story, not in retrospect, but as it unfolded. This fortunate avenue was made possible by the in-depth interviews with the principals and investigators who recalled their conversations and comments and made their notes and private papers available.

Direct quotations of witnesses are taken from sworn testimony, depositions, trial transcripts, and court records to reconstruct the story as it was happening. Editorial comment and daily newspaper coverage provided quotations, background, color, atmosphere, and attitude down to the smallest detail.

Insight into the gambler's activities and conversations was made available on 3 July 1954, when Hugh Bentley, head of the Russell Betterment Association, received four wire-tapped plastic discs in the mail recording earlier candid conversations between Hoyt Shepherd, Phenix City gamblers, and political figures. The sender, known only as "Mr. X," required that the recordings be played before the investigators and the press. With this done, 200 more discs wire-tapped from Hoyt Shepherd's telephone were sent to Bentley to be played in the same manner.

Private collections and preservation of the records afforded research and material for this book along with the extraordinary and unlimited assistance of Mrs. Joyce LaMont, former head, W. S. Hoole Special Collections, University of Alabama; Mrs. Linda Matthews, Head,

Special Collections, Robert W. Woodruff Library, Emory University; Mrs. Barbara Loar, former director, Decatur-DeKalb Library System; the Alabama Department of Archives and History; and Columbus State University Interlibrary loan. I am also grateful to Dr. Russell Major, former Chair of the Department of History at Emory University for appointing me Research Associate in the Department of History at Emory University.

Of special value in comprehending the background and historical events in Phenix City was the collection of stories in the 1955 book, *Phenix City*, by newsmen Ed Strickland and Gene Wortsman, the 1966 Master's Thesis by Roland Joseph Page entitled, "The *Columbus Ledger* and the Phenix City Story: On Winning a Pulitzer Prize," admission to the archives of the *Columbus Ledger* and the *Columbus Enquirer* through the courtesy of former publisher Glenn Vaughn, and the assistance of Billy Winn, editorial page editor of the *Columbus Ledger Enquirer*, in locating original photographs.

Most important of all was the generosity of the late Hugh Bentley, General Walter J. Hanna, and former Governor John Patterson in providing their recollections, views, and personal papers, as well as Bernice Bentley and Hilda Coulter.

For advice and encouragement, I am indebted to the Honorable George T. Smith, former Justice of the Georgia Supreme Court, Dr. Floyd Watkins, professor emeritus of Southern Literature at Emory University, the late Dr. George Cuttino, Professor Emeritus of Medieval History at Emory University, Dr. Fred Cerreta, University of Texas, Jim Minter, former editor of the *Atlanta Journal Constitution*, and my attorney and fellow author, Joe Beck.

I also gratefully acknowledge those who lent their expertise and encouragement to this effort:

Dean Rolin, Philip Morris, Steve Frimmer, Norman Blumenthal, John Ingersol, M. C. Whitaker, Beverly Greer, Warren Wood, Mary Lu Mitchell, Bobby Lee Cook, Dr. Peter McGuire and his son Daniel, my cardiologist Dr. E. Alan Paulk, my agent Mitch Douglas, my brother and legal advisor Billy Barnes, my sister Clare Medlin, my cousin Margaret Virginia Bryant, my dear friend Ala Boles, and my son, David J. Dukes, Ph.D.

Finally, I would like a medal struck as a special merit award for Cecil P. Staton, my overburdened editor Dr. Marc Jolley and his staff, namely Jenny Toole, Marsha Luttrell, Davina Rutland, Barbara Keene, and Amelia Barclay. Kudos!

PROLOGUE

He was an old warrior returning to his last battlefield. There were no cannon emplacements, no breastworks, no broad plain where opposing armies had clashed in bloody combat. There had been blood and killing and combat but not the kind he had experienced in his long army career and on battlefields in World War II's South Pacific.

This battlefield was a quiet Southern town perched on the curve of the Chattahoochee River which divided the state of Alabama from the state of Georgia. This was Phenix City, Alabama. Across the river was thriving Columbus, Georgia, a bustling manufacturing town and the historic site of Fort Benning, home of the United States Infantry.

He had been invited to a celebration, a recognition of sorts for deeds long since done. At 83, silver-haired, granite-jawed, a soldier's bearing still remained despite old war wounds from savage jungle fighting that now necessitated the support of a walking cane, its gold head engraved Walter J. "Crack" Hanna, Major General, a parting gift from his troops who long ago affectionately named him "Crack" for his proficiency in battle with the rifle and the bayonet. For them, he was the warrior general who gave no quarter to the enemy and whose care and defense of his troops was legend.

Joining him there that day was another combat veteran who had fought a different fight on this battlefield, but one no less deadly. His name was Hugh Bentley, a mild-mannered man, now in his seventies, whose demeanor would never suggest heroism but whose deeds and determination had begun the fight and the conflagration that engulfed the town. Hugh Bentley had been born in Phenix City, grew up there, and had suffered the outrages and injustices visited on the townspeople by the tight fist of the entrenched gamblers and home-grown Mafia. When, at last, he could endure no more, he took up arms and challenged them, exhausting every avenue of due process and being defeated in every attempt until he was joined by a man whose passion for justice matched his own.

By rights, there should have been another veteran there that day for his part in the war that was waged here in Phenix City. Albert Patterson's contribution of courage and conviction was crucial and fatal, cruelly cut down in a public assassination for his effort to restore justice. For him, they could only remember and honor the dead.

The three of them had not been comrades-in-arms as such, fighting side by side. They had confronted and fought the enemy separately and successively. As one exhausted his effort and failed, the next took up arms for the battle until at last the enemy was vanquished. But all of that had been a long time ago, thirty years in fact, when the name of Phenix City, seat of Russell County Alabama, was a name written in blood and violence.

Begun as a border town trading post in 1833, Phenix City became a 19th-century refuge from law enforcement for cutthroats, killers, and illegal traffic runners. As infamous and lawless as Dodge City, it had remained steadfastly so for 120 years. By 1940 the traffic in murder, manslaughter, gambling, illegal liquor, and white slavery was such that Secretary of War Henry L. Stimson, after inspecting the Army's classified record of Fort Benning soldiers who had been beaten, robbed, maimed, and murdered in this Alabama outlaw town declared: "Phenix City, Alabama, is the wickedest city in America."

General George C. Patton, while training his troops at Fort Benning, for what would later become their triumphant Third Army push through Europe, was so enraged by the atrocities against his soldiers in Phenix City that he publicly threatened to take his tanks across the river and mash Phenix City flat.

Lured by gambling, girls, lotteries, and illegal liquor, America's toughest fighting men were no match for the organized crime and criminals who controlled Phenix City with cunning and without conscience, using knock-out drops, knives, guns, chains, and spiked brass knuckles to tear a man's face to pieces, sometimes, disposing of their victims by dropping their weighted bodies in the muddy waters of the Chattahoochee.

But little could be done to correct this intolerable situation across the river in Alabama for Phenix City was a law unto itself. City and county police, into the pockets of the gangsters and racketeers, could never come up with any clues or evidence of crimes committed. The sheriff claimed he knew of no open gambling. The mayor saw no wrongdoing in Phenix City.

The decent, law-abiding citizens of Phenix City grieved at what they saw going on in their town, but they were no less vulnerable and victimized than were the soldiers. There was no recourse for them because the criminal element had infiltrated not only the law enforcement but the governing body and the courts as well.

What was already bad became incredibly worse. In 1954 a mortal storm was brewing that enveloped and involved the whole State of Alabama, all of its officials, and attracted the notice of the nation and the world, for in Phenix City no one was safe. The Constitutional guaranties were suspended and the basic rights of man held ransom.

The fate of this fabled city was ultimately determined by three men: Hugh Bentley, the moral leader, Albert Patterson, the political leader, and General Walter J. Hanna, the military leader, who, separately and in succession, were swept into this maelstrom of controversy and confrontation. Their convictions, actions, commitment and courage challenged and changed forever the course of events that had run rampant in Phenix City for more than 120 years.

It was for this achievement and deeds long ago done that this commemorative ceremony had been arranged by the people of Phenix City. They, too, had lived through and been drawn into the drama, some by default, some by design, some because they had just happened to be in destiny's way, each with a story of his own, weaving a thread in the tapestry of the town.

Here then is the story of Phenix City, Alabama ... the struggle, the strife, the tragedy, the ultimate triumph, and the price of its purchase.

Afterword

No requests for interviews were granted by anyone arrested, indicted, or convicted in the 1954-55 Phenix City cleanup. I did, however, receive a number of anonymous phone calls.

One man warned, "You had better not write that story about Phenix City." Another had only one question, "How would you like a pair of cement shoes?"

The only face-to-face confrontation occurred at my first autographing of the book in Scott's Book Store in Newnan, Georgia. A daughter of one of the convicted gamblers, accompanied by her husband and son, thrust the book in front of me and said, "We're gonna take this book home and read it tonight, and if we don't like it, we'll see you in the morning."

I never saw them again.

After publication in February 1999, I was invited to Phenix City for the first time by the Columbus/Chattahoochee Area Librarians to speak at the Chattahoochee Valley Community College. Considering the previously hostile environment, I was accompanied by Coweta County Deputy Buddy Barnes (no relation) and his partner, Ed Williams, since I was not sure but that I might take a bullet.

Instead, the audience was responsive and stood to tell the stories they had held secret for forty-five years. (See *Columbus Ledger/ Enquirer*, February 21, 1955, B-1.) In May 1999, I was given the key to the city of Phenix City by Mayor Peggy Martin, Russell County Historical Society president Bill Bentley, and the members of the Phenix City Commission. I accepted this honor as a tribute to those who fought and died to restore justice and law and order to Phenix City.

Hugh Bentley

Actor John McIntyre poses as Albert Patterson in the 1955 "Phenix City Story." (Courtesy of the *Columbus Ledger-Enquirer*)

Major General Walter J. "Crack" Hanna

Book I

The Town

1

THE TOWN: 1916-1941

Hugh Bentley's earliest memory was standing behind his mother's skirt, hanging on. He was only three. He could hear the words but he didn't know what they meant. All he knew was that something bad was happening. As the words grew worse, he could feel the heat of the argument, and he drew the pale gray voile of his mother's skirt with the printed black roses over his face so that he could no longer see his father's sweating red face twisted with anger and distorted by the glare of the bare light bulb hanging from the fly-specked cord in the ceiling of the store.

Even in the midst of argument, his mother was mindful of him, and reached around and cupped his head closer to her closing her soft hand over his ears.

"He killed his own son!" Minnie Bentley said.

"Well, he didn't kill him in here."

"He might just as well could have, he hangs around this store drinking, gambling, fighting, causing trouble and when they finally do lock him up, bless Jesus, if you don't go down and sign his bond."

Calvin Bentley scowled: "What I do ain't none of your affair, Minnie, and I ain't listening to another word of complaint."

"Well, I can tell you this Calvin Bentley, and you can mark it down in your book. Living over this store where all this drinking and gambling and fighting is going on is no decent place to raise children. They'll never have a chance in life ... being exposed to what's going on here."

Calvin Bentley gave his wife a long withering look. "There ain't one damn thing going on at my store that ain't going on ever place in this town. It's been that way 'nigh onto a hundred years. There ain't no way you're gonna change it, or I'm about to."

Minnie Bentley, broadened by the birth of seven sons, propped both hands on her ample hips, her heavy bosom heaving with anger. "I'm not gonna have my boys growing up in this kind of sorriness. They'll end up doing what they see happening here ... "

Calvin Bentley, crippled by rheumatoid arthritis and confined to a wicker wheelchair, had no patience with this kind of woman-talk. He enjoyed his friends and the camaraderie in his store. He liked being called "Cap'n" and getting them out of trouble for the fighting and drinking he was no longer able to do. It gave him a sense of importance and power and no damn woman was going to take it away or tell him what to do.

Calvin reared his head back and hardened his expression. "Get this straight, Minnie, and you can mark it down in *your* book: These are my friends and my customers and if they don't suit you, you can take that damned bunch of brats and get out."

The argument and the anger of that night remained with Hugh Bentley forever, for it changed his life and determined a destiny that was long in the making.

Minnie accepted her husband's challenge, packed up her seven sons, their few belongings, and her cook pots and moved down the street to an upstairs flat and began to wrestle with the problem of how to make a living for herself and her children.

৵

It was 1912 in the Alabama village of Girard, nestled on the banks of the Chattahoochee River across the bridge from the big Eagle and Phenix cotton mill in Columbus, Georgia, an era when most women dared not leave home, regardless of the circumstances. In Girard in 1912, there were only a few avenues of existence open to women: as wives, millworkers, or prostitutes.

Minnie chose to discard her role as wife because of the effect her living conditions were having on her children. She had too many children to care for to go to work in the mill, and her objection to vice and sin was what prompted her to leave home in the first place.

Untrained in anything other than domestic skills, Minnie turned to what she knew best ... cooking and sewing. Her upstairs flat was too small to take in boarders, so she cooked her meals and took them to the mill workers at the Eagle and Phenix Mill across the bridge in Columbus: three vegetables, meat, bread, and a desert for twenty-five cents, plus five cents for delivery.

All of the older boys took whatever odd jobs could be found: chopping wood, loading produce, sweeping out stores. Hugh's job was to help her deliver the meals, pulling his wooden wagon, loaded with baskets of food to the mill for the workers.

One of Minnie's first customers at the Eagle and Phenix Mill was Homer Cobb, a big raw-boned youth of nineteen, who had arrived in Phenix City the year before.

"One thing I appreciate, Miss Minnie," he told her, "is a good meal and a good place to stay, and I'd say this is the best food I've had since I got to Girard."

Even with the lint from the cotton mill clinging to him and festooning his hair, Homer Cobb had a shine to him, a sort of earnestness and enterprise that gave his plain face a glow.

"Well, I got no room in my upstairs flat ... what with seven boys ... but you can come by on Sunday and eat with us since you got no place to go."

No place to go had been a problem for Homer Cobb since he was a boy of nine when both his parents died within months of each other. After that Homer Cobb lived with relatives for a while and then began trying to shift for himself. With almost no formal education the best he could do was odd jobs and cotton milling, but one day, he planned to change all that. He had ambitions of being better than what he came from and at night after work in the cotton mill, he read books and tried to educate himself.

Minnie didn't mind squeezing one more in at the table. Homer was always pleasant and polite and paid for his meal and this helped add to the hard-earned quarters from meals to the mill and what she could take in from sewing shrouds for the dead, patches on overalls, and cutting down hand-me-downs. The biggest business was in shrouds for the dead who were laid to rest in clothes finer than they had ever owned in life, and if death had come as a result of violence, the clothes were even finer and more costly, escalating in cost with the degree of violent death as though to assuage the circumstances.

"Seems like to me, there's a brisk business in death around here," Homer told her one day as he watched her sew a fine wool suit for a man who had never owned one in life.

"Sin and killing, that's what this town's all about," Minnie said, "always has been and from the looks of it, always will be."

"Well, it seems like to me, a fellow might make a fair kind of living just building coffins."

Minnie looked up from her sewing. "You thinking about it?"

"Well, I was thinking about opening a barber shop. I've done a lot of haircutting for the men down at the mill, but it seems like to me a little business on the side of building coffins might be a good idea."

Before the year was out, Homer was back telling her: "I reckon I

3

won't be crowding your dinner table no more, Miss Minnie," his face flushed with pleasure and pride. "Looks like I'm gonna have one of my own. Miss Minnie Pearl Freeman has agreed to be my bride and I'm gonna open that barber shop and coffin company and make something of myself."

Minnie patted him approvingly on the shoulder. "I expect you will, Homer Cobb, you're a hard-working boy. This place needs a man like you."

By the time Homer left off coming for dinner, things were getting a little better for Minnie. All of the older boys had been able to find jobs that paid more than the ones they had begun with and Hugh continued helping her deliver meals to the mill in his wooden wagon.

With all of the family bending every effort, they were able to eke out an existence so that Minnie could keep them fed, clothed, in school and at church. A self-professed Christian, Minnie believed in the Will of God and the Power of the Lord. No breast-beating or public laments, just a steadying and abiding faith that gave her the strength and courage to stand for what she felt was right. Her act of independence in leaving home and objections to the wrong-doing did nothing to change the rampant vice and sin in the village of Girard, but it did change the lives of her family, for while Hugh Bentley was growing up, other forces were already at work to change Girard.

Since the turn of the century, the Women's Christian Temperance Union and the Anti-Saloon League in Alabama, supported by women, preachers, a few politicians, and moralist groups, had set upon a relentless campaign to rid Alabama of its whiskey and whiskey interests. By 1913, all the candidates for governor, whether opposed to whiskey interests or not, supported the need for a bone-dry prohibition law. After the Prohibitionists gained control of the Alabama legislature in 1914, a law was passed the following year, prohibiting the manufacture and sale of all alcoholic beverages, a full two years before the United States Congress passed the law on national prohibition.

One of the primary targets for the Alabama Prohibitionists was Russell County and its notorious village of Girard which they considered lawless, lewd, riddled by vice and sin with a history of violence that stretched all the way back to its beginning in 1833 when a visiting circuit minister, seeing the killing, the cutthroats, criminals, and renegades who sought refuge in this haven for the lawless, solemnly proclaimed: *"This is Sodom."*

The violence began with Indian massacres and retaliatory raids by white settlers who had come to share the mud flats and water falls of the Chattahoochee River with the Creek Indians. Later, when the horsepath that extended from Charleston, South Carolina, to Montgomery, Alabama, was cleared for wheel traffic and made a federal road, it became the frontier town of Girard with a few houses, a trading post and a ferry across the river to Columbus. Columbus became the crossroads of industry and trade, Girard remained the brawling bedroom community across the river throughout the founding of the State of Alabama, the Civil War, and the turn of the century with a vigilante code of conduct handed down from father to son.

Minnie had heard that the Prohibitionists planned to change all that by outlawing the whiskey and whiskey interests that fueled Girard's economy. In addition to the manufacture and traffic in illegal corn liquor, Girard had one legitimate distillery and two great whiskey warehouses used for the storage of bonded liquor that was shipped all over the Southeast, to Savannah by ship, and then on to New York with Boston as the principal market. Business from this enterprise was so profitable that a Citizen's Bank had been opened to handle the huge sums of money.

All of this was brought to a complete standstill by Alabama's 1915 Prohibition Law. Personal fortunes were lost. Family homes were put on the auction block. When those involved tried to divest themselves of their whiskey interests, the WTCU and the Anti-Saloon League thwarted every effort. As the economic knot began to strangle the economy, the citizens of Girard began an open defiance of the law. Anyone who interfered or tried to stop this defiance did so at their own peril. There were beatings, killings, houses burned, property destroyed, fine horses with their hamstrings cut, newspaper editors with their presses smashed.

The Russell County Grand Jury investigating these crimes and outrages, sometimes handed down indictments. The accused would make bond, the judge would continue the case until the next term, and when the accused failed to appear, the bond was forfeited and the case never came to trial.

This mockery of justice so enraged the WTCU and the Anti-Saloon League that they demanded that the Governor remedy this situation. When the Governor showed some reluctance, William Logan Martin, Attorney General of Alabama, decided to send a special train with forty hand-picked deputies into Russell County to seize and destroy one million dollars worth of illegal liquor.

All of this rhetoric and fighting over liquor interests meant little to Minnie Bentley and the mill workers. They had no fortunes to lose, no possessions to salvage, and little interest or energy left for any political happenings after a day's work at making a living. For the mill

5

workers, it was a dawn to dusk day at the spindle in the cotton mill, and for Minnie, longer than that, as she had increased the number she cooked for. Seven year-old Hugh could now make the food basket deliveries of meals in his wooden wagon to the mill by himself, freeing Minnie to add workers at the end of the day to eat at her dinner table.

The fight over the liquor interests meant nothing more than conversation at the table. The village of Girard was as bad as it had always been. The beatings and burnings and killings had never stopped, only the targets had changed, but at 5:30 A.M. on May 17, 1916, a special train with forty hand-picked deputies roared into Girard from the state capital in Montgomery. By 8:00 A.M., armed deputies were kicking in doors of illegal liquor establishments and hauling liquor and liquor owners out in the street.

⁊❧

Hugh Bentley, having finished his first delivery of food baskets in his wooden wagon to the mill workers at the Eagle & Phenix mill across the Fourteenth Street Bridge, watched wide-eyed at what was happening on Dillingham Street.

A crowd began to gather and grew bigger all day as the deputies seized more than one million dollars worth of liquor. By afternoon, a crowd of 4,000 people, arriving by cart, horse and car from all over the county and from across the river in Columbus gathered and watched as the deputies hauled 106 barrels of beer, 46 barrels of whiskey, and 1,000 bottles of wine, gin, and bonded liquor to Thompson's Ditch behind a warehouse on the river and smashed it, barrel by barrel, and bottle by bottle, until a rivulet of liquor ran to the river with men and boys wading in what they called "whiskey creek".

Hugh Bentley was standing transfixed at all he saw going on before him when he heard his name called.

"Hey Hugh ... Hugh ... over here."

It was red-headed "Red" Cook, one of the toughs from his school that Hugh's mama had told him to stay away from.

"Hugh," Red Cook called again, "come on over here and bring your wagon."

Hugh Bentley clutched the handle of his wooden wagon and started to move away. "I gotta go home."

Red Cook twisted his face into a taunt. "Whatsa matter, mama's little boy gotta do what mama says?"

"No. I just gotta go home."

"Then lend me your wagon. I gotta haul some of this liquor up the hill."

Red Cook was only eight but street-wise already with a confidence and a cockiness that made Hugh Bentley uneasy. He was pointing at a pile of liquor bottles that he had filled from the stream being poured out by the deputies. "Come on. We can sell this for plenty to those drunks up the hill."

Hugh Bentley lifted his chubby cheeks and tried to keep the quiver out of his voice. "I can't. My mama won't let me."

Red Cook reached over and snatched the wagon handle out of his hand. "I said I gotta have that wagon."

He piled the liquor in the wagon and walked off up the hill with Hugh Bentley running behind, worried for what his mama would say, but more worried that something would happen to his wagon for without it, he couldn't deliver the meals to the mill.

When Red Cook had sold all the liquor to the bearded men lounging around the courthouse, he flipped a quarter in the wagon and tossed the handle to Hugh. "Okay, kid, take your wagon and go home to your mama."

Hugh Bentley worried about what he would say when he got home. He knew his mother would count the quarters from delivering the baskets of food to the mill, and there was no way to explain the extra quarter unless he told her what Red Cook had done. When he did, Minnie Bentley propped her hands on her hips and said: "You mean to tell me you let him take your wagon?"

"But, Mama, he's bigger than me."

"That don't matter," Minnie said. "You gotta stand your ground with bullies ... else if you don't ... the next time, he won't just take your wagon ... he'll take it away from you."

Hugh held out the quarter in the palm of his hand. "But he gave me a quarter ...."

Minnie took the quarter and threw it through the kitchen window. "Poor as we are, we don't need tainted money."

The next day in the school yard, Red Cook came over, his hand behind him. "Hugh ...."

Hugh Bentley looked up and then saw stars as Red Cook smashed him over the head and to the ground with the brick he held in his hand.

Hugh Bentley began to cry as the blood poured down his head and onto his clean white shirt. "Why did you do that?" he cried.

Standing over him, Red Cook gave him a hard look. "For telling, that's why."

Hugh Bentley didn't even watch when the deputies put the

remaining liquor that was seized in a warehouse and put under guard by the State Militia. He didn't want any more trouble.

To make sure that the violators of the Prohibition Law were punished and no mockery was made of the law this time, the Alabama Chief Justice disqualified the Russell County courts and sent a young attorney named Hugo Black, later to become a justice on the United States Supreme Court, to act as chief prosecutor for the State of Alabama and Judge A. H. Alston to impanel a blue ribbon grand jury.

Arriving in Girard, Judge Alston was appalled at the situation he found. "It is astounding that one village should so array itself against the law. There exists in Girard a state of lawlessness that has shocked this county, this state, and this nation."

By the time Judge Alston and chief prosecutor Hugo Black finished the job they had been sent to do, the city marshal had been convicted of accepting bribes from the liquor dealers, Russell County Sheriff Pal M. Daniel was impeached, and the mayor and board of aldermen resigned "by popular demand."

After the August 1916 session of court, those who had violated the liquor laws were tried, convicted, sentenced, fined and/or sent to jail. Satisfied that the culprits had been caught and law and order restored, the Alabama Attorney General returned Judge Alston and Hugo Black to their former duties, but the liquor trade during Prohibition was too lucrative to lie dormant long. Six months later, in March 1917, the liquor runners had dug a tunnel into the river bank under the warehouse where the liquor was stored, retrieved the contraband supplies and quietly floated them down the river, resuming the operations that had been interrupted by the 1916 raid.

Despite this, the intense interest in liquor laws and the pursuit of liquor runners began to fade that spring as Alabama and the nation began to prepare for war. Across the Chattahoochee in Georgia, on the outskirts of Columbus, Camp Benning was already training soldiers and on 2 April 1917, President Woodrow Wilson told the joint Congress that with open warfare being waged on the high seas by German submarines, beginning with the *Lusitania*, that the United States could not maintain its neutrality, and four days later on 6 April 1917 the Congress declared war on Germany.

A rash of patriotism broke out with bands and banners and men lining up at the recruiting office to volunteer to go fight "Over There." Homer Cobb joined the Navy and Minnie Bentley and the other women volunteered their services to the Red Cross to roll bandages and knit socks for the troops.

Among those answering the call to battle were two other Alabama boys whose destinies would begin with the war and finally lead them to the streets of Phenix City: Albert Love Patterson born in Cowpen, Tallapoosa County, Alabama, and Walter J. Hanna, from Birmingham.

Albert Patterson was in Texas when war was declared. After finishing the seventh grade in Alabama, he had gone to Texas to work in the oil fields in search of a more profitable wage than he was able to find in Alabama. By working in the oil fields in the summer and going to school in the winter, he was able to graduate from high school with the ambition of continuing his studies and one day studying law. Twenty-years old when war was declared, he volunteered to join the Texas 36th National Guard Infantry Division as a private and wrote his sweetheart back in Alabama, asking her to marry him. In July 1917, Agnes Louise Benson traveled to Texas and became the bride of Albert Patterson before he left with the American Expeditionary Forces for fighting in France.

The Army, however, did not accept all its volunteers. There was hardly a heart in Alabama so set upon military service and defending his country as that of Walter J. Hanna. Caught up in the drum beat and patriotic fervor of World War I, he had, at fifteen, without his father's knowledge, gone down to the recruiting office in Birmingham to sign up for the defense of his country, to go "Over There," where his older brother was already serving. When the recruiter learned his age, he ran him off. "Get back in school, boy. We got no call to take kids, this is a man's war."

When his father learned what he had done, he called him out to the barn where their serious talking was done. "Walter, I appreciate your patriotic intentions, but I forbid you to do that again. You are to stay in school where you belong."

Walter Hanna braced himself for the wrath he knew his reply would invoke. "Papa, I want to join the army. I want to serve with the rest of the men."

His father answered in a voice so quiet it could scarcely be heard, the voice that meant instant, irreversible, absolute obedience. "Walter, I *forbid* you to join so much as the Boy Scouts. Is that *clearly* understood?"

"Yes, Sir. I understand."

But Walter Hanna did try it again, five more times, going to other cities, to other recruiters, hoping to pass himself off as old enough to go and fight. Finally, he tried the Marines who signed him up and then learned how old he really was. This seemed to anger the Marine recruiter more than the others.

"Get out of here, you little sawed-off-sonofabitch," the Marine sergeant yelled at him, "and stop wasting my time."

9

Angered and disappointed, red-haired Walter Hanna, just five-foot-seven, but fast with his fists and a member of the boxing team, took a swing at the big Marine sergeant and was promptly thrown down the stairs.

As the Marine sergeant ceremoniously dusted off his hands, he added: "Even the Salvation Army wouldn't take you."

With no way to quench his burning desire to be a part of the country's defense, Walter Hanna went back to Birmingham and joined the National Guard. Then it was back to the barn with his father.

"You know I ought to horsewhip you, Walter. You disobeyed my explicit order."

"Yes, Sir, but I did what I felt I had to do."

"And joined the Militia?"

"Yes, Sir, but they call it the National Guard."

His father looked at him for a long, unrelenting moment, he supposed, trying to decide on corporal punishment. And then the old man did what Walter Hanna never expected him to do. He said: "Well, you're not old enough, but you're tough enough." He paused again. "Since the time our country began, a lot of good men have joined the Militia to defend their homeland. Now that you've joined them and given them your oath, by God, go do what's right and do the best job you can."

He held his hand out to shake his son's hand, and Walter Hanna, feeling a pang of pride and joy in his father's approval wanted to hug him instead, but at fifteen, he was too old for that, being a man now, he accepted the handshake instead.

The war was over before Walter Hanna was old enough to join an active unit. Nineteen months after entering the war, the Armistice was signed on 11 November 1918, and the veterans began returning to pick up the lives they had left behind. Some, like Homer Cobb, unscathed by the war, others with health ruined by gas and their bodies broken from battlefield wounds. Albert Patterson was one of those. Shot down by German machine-gun fire in France while attacking a German strong point on the Western Front, the leg wound he received, shortened and permanently froze his right leg requiring him to use a cane to get about and making it impossible for him to ever dress himself or put on his shoes again. France awarded him the Croix de Guerre with Gilt Star for gallantry in action.

But Albert Patterson and the others took up their lives and careers and soon were immersed in the strife and struggle in their home town. The War had changed the people and the country, but not Girard or Russell County.

ॐ

Five years later, in January 1923, Sheriff Pal M. Daniel, who had been impeached for "willful neglect of duty" and possession of illegal liquor stored in his house in the cleanup of 1916, was reelected as sheriff of Russell County and what Hugh Bentley had witnessed as a child of seven, he saw happen again as a boy of fourteen.

This time, the spark that ignited the controversy was evangelist A. A. Haggard, a fiery crusading preacher who pitched his tent in the middle of Girard in April 1923 and rallied the people with the declamation: *"What's happening in Girard is a disgrace to America."*

Even though whiskey was again being sold in open defiance of the law, Girard Mayor C. M. Knowles declared he did not dare take action against the liquor interests for fear of life and property. Then, on April 21, 1923, Deputy W. T. Miller, attempting to close a place operating in violation of the Prohibition Law, was shot four times by owner, Charlie Jinnet. Girard Officer Will Hill, who was also on the scene, made no attempt to assist Deputy Miller and stood by and watched as George Davis, who had liquor interests of his own, beat the bleeding deputy. Deputy Miller and Jinnet were both taken to jail. Miller, with his wounds unattended, was locked up in a cell with three drunks. Jinnet remained in the jail corridor.

All of this was reported to Governor William W. Brandon by a group of citizens in a petition asking for his help and in response to their petition, he arrived in Girard on Sunday, April 29, 1923, to address the crowd of 8,000 people gathered at evangelist Hazzard's tent.

Minnie Bentley, hoping to hear a plan to improve the conditions in Girard went down to join the crowd and listened as the Governor called on the people to solve their problem through love.

This suggestion brought a rumble of discontent from the crowd and Minnie turned to her neighbor standing beside her and scoffed: "Love and good intentions hasn't ever solved anything yet in this town."

"Ain't it the truth!" her neighbor replied. "What we need is action, not good intentions."

The Governor, seeing that little satisfaction came from his "love" suggestion, then proposed that the village of Girard in Russell County be consolidated with the more respectable town of Phenix City just across the line in Lee County. This suggestion was met with such enthusiasm that the townspeople wanted to name the two combined areas "Brandon" in honor of the governor, but legalities prevented this, and

11

in May 1923, the rowdy village of Girard became part of the town of Phenix City with the seat in Russell County.

To remedy the situation with the illegal liquor and the trouble with the liquor runners, Governor Brandon sent Walter K. McAldory, chief of Alabama's law enforcement to supervise a clean-up. Federal agents raided twenty-six establishments and destroyed stills containing over 100 gallons of liquor and 3,400 gallons of beer, and for a while, there was a brief suspension of illegal liquor activity, but in 1925 the trouble began again with watermelon beer; in 1927, with corn liquor; and in 1931, a morphine ring, but by this time, the people of Phenix City had more to worry about than trafficking in illegal liquor and dope. The Great Depression had fallen on the nation and farmers, laborers, and people from all walks of life were migrating to the towns and cities in search of work they could no longer find on the land. The boll weevil had eaten its way across the cotton fields of Mexico, through Texas and into the Deep South damaging the cotton bolls, infesting the vegetation, and dropping the production of cotton so dramatically that it was no longer possible to make a living from the crop that had been historically the South's main source of income.

For Minnie Bentley, it was not as bad as for most. All of her seven sons were grown and established now, and Hugh, the last to leave, had found himself work at Hubbard's Hardware across the river in Columbus, had involved himself with the YMCA boxing team and had met a preacher who had convinced him to give his life to Christ. With this, Minnie felt that the goal that she had set upon twenty years before, had been accomplished, but for most of the others, and for those migrating to Phenix City, the situation went from grim to desperate.

The mill workers, when there was work to be had, were earning $450 a year, and even at that, the mill rules were so stringent that a man dared not miss work for any reason. Illness—even serious illness— was no excuse. To lose a day of work was to lose one's job with no possibility of return, and in Phenix City in 1931, the streets were filled with those in flight from hard times and hard circumstances in search of sustenance and shelter, and a dozen men waited for the job that had been vacated by another.

Among those arriving that year in search of work was a young man named Jimmie Matthews, the son of an American father and an English mother, who soon made the acquaintance of Clyde Yarborough, a seasoned Phenix City gambler, who took young Jimmie under his wing and taught him the winning ways at cards and dice.

Finding work across the river in the laundry at Camp Benning, Jimmie put this new expertise to work, gambling with the soldiers on payday, and by 1932, at age twenty-one, he had accumulated what was then a fortune—$11,000—an amount that would have taken a millworker nearly twenty-five years to earn.

Over a poker hand, he met shrewd, penniless Hoyt Shepherd, who had recently arrived in Phenix City from LaGrange, Georgia, with little more than lint in his hair and ambition on his mind. Hoyt, the son of a cotton mill worker, had little education, but an easy way with words and an innate ability to accurately figure a situation and what a man was likely to do. Together they combined their ambition and expertise and formed the S&M gambling syndicate using Jimmie's $11,000 as seed money. Besides slot machines, crooked dice and marked cards, they began a lottery, known locally as "the bug," operating out of the Ritz Cafe on Dillingham Street.

Their competitor in the lucrative lottery business was another recent arrival, C.O. (Head) Revel, whose trouble with the law had included violating the immigration laws by smuggling Chinese aliens into hidden ports in the Florida Keys, hijacking, and time on the Georgia chain gang for stealing a car. Head Revel, whose smooth good looks belied his spotted police record, joined up with short, pudgy, cigar-smoking Godwin Davis, Sr. a Phenix City resident long involved in the manufacture of illegal liquor. Together, they ran the National Lottery Company down on Dillingham Street where Godwin owned much of the property leased to honky tonks and loan sharks.

Although the lottery and gambling was against the law in Alabama, Phenix City paid no more attention to this than it ever had any statute that didn't suit what it chose to do. "The bug" operated openly attracting that part of the population that could least afford it: the poor, the unemployed, the disadvantaged, each hoping their twenty-five cent ticket would buy them the dream they cherished and catapult them out of the poverty they endured into the riches they saw the gamblers enjoying: big cars, fancy women and flashy clothes. The gambler's lifestyle, rich and rewarding, set the standard, and soon, even the school children were wagering their milk money on slot machines and "the bug" and step-stools were installed in some public establishments so that they could reach the coin deposit to play the slot machines.

This set up a great hue and cry from the preachers and the mothers in the community about the corruption of the young. A committee of concerned citizens went down to city hall to see what could be done. The city fathers, a commission of three men, one of whom served as mayor, advised this group that the revenue from gambling was essential to the survival of the city.

"But it's against the law," the preachers protested. "How can you

13

license and permit an illegal business to operate?"

"We have to," the city fathers replied, "Phenix City has no industry and no tax base and without the income from licenses and fines levied on gambling, we would have to close down the schools and every public service and the town would go into receivership."

When Minnie Bentley heard what had happened, she went straight away to see Homer Cobb. In the intervening years since his return from World War I, Homer had come up in the world. He had worked and studied and read for the law, and was now a member of the city commission.

Minnie bristled with indignation as she stomped into his office and told him: "Homer Cobb, I'm surprised at you—you of all people—and with a son of your own! How *can* you let them continue with this gambling and vice and sin that has ruined the lives of everybody who has lived here?"

"Miss Minnie," Homer Cobb tried to explain gently, "it's the best we can do. You know as well as I do that most of the folks here work in the mill in Columbus making $8.75 a week. They can't afford a tax levy. They just about can't keep their kids from being hungry. The money to run the town has got to come from somewhere and the gamblers have got it, and if we keep a tight rein on them with licenses and fines ... "

Minnie Bentley would hear no more of it. She snatched up her purse and started out the door. "Homer Cobb, you've made a deal with the devil ... and mark my words ... you'll live to rue the day." Through his window, Homer Cobb watched her stomp off down the street, the red feather in the little straw hat she wore flat on her head, like a weathervane, trembled with rage. Homer Cobb hated being the recipient of that rage and he hated the compromise he had been forced to make, but he had learned, living in Phenix City, that this was the only way to get things done. To go up against the gamblers and their interests was to insure defeat, Hoyt Shepherd had seen to that.

Since his arrival in Phenix City, Hoyt had emerged as the leader of the growing gambling community and was quick to see the need for protection and political power to insure the empire he and his partner, Jimmie Matthews, were building. Jimmie, quiet and reclusive, a genius with money and investments, managed the business while Hoyt, easygoing, friendly, and personable, spent time at the courthouse making friends with the politicians, contributing to their campaigns and then graduating to picking the candidates and running their campaigns. Buying into the courts, the law enforcement, and the governing body, Hoyt soon became so powerful that no candidate running for office could win without his backing.

An outraged citizenry could do nothing by trying to vote them out of office at the polls. Routinely, ballot boxes were stuffed with tombstone votes of those long dead. Openly, at the polls, votes were purchased for whatever price the seller would settle for. Most often, the going price was three dollars. A man making $8.75 a week at the mill, could sell his and his wife's vote for nearly a week's work, and with the worry of trying to put bread on the table, he didn't care who was in the courthouse.

If tombstone ballots and vote buying wasn't enough, then those counting the ballots took their orders from the gamblers and the vote-count totaled whatever they dictated. The hand-picked officials were installed in office and there was never a question about any problem that arose.

If a case was brought to court, it was the duty of the district attorney, then called the circuit solicitor, to present the evidence to the eighteen-man grand jury that would decide if there was sufficient evidence for an indictment in which case the Grand Jury would return a True Bill. More often than not, as concerned cases involving the gamblers and gambling activities, the circuit solicitor, whose job it was to advise the Grand Jury, would determine that there was not sufficient evidence, and following this advisement, the case would be dropped, since unlike many states, the State of Alabama did not require that the Grand Jury return a No Bill on a case with insufficient evidence to return an indictment.

If a case was so blatantly obvious that insufficient evidence could not be claimed, then there were other ways to control the outcome. One of the primary weapons and most often used was intimidation of witnesses. If a witness was foolish enough to not have any fear for himself, he was always vulnerable to the safety of his family or the security of his job.

Such a case arose in the spring of 1938, when, at noon on April 21, the worst catastrophe in the history of Phenix City took place at the Ritz Cafe on Dillingham Street. The Old Reliable Lottery, headquartered at the Ritz Cafe and operated by Hoyt Shepherd, Jimmie Matthews, and his old gambling teacher, Clyde Yarborough, had proved such an enormous success that those making wagers began to gather at the Ritz Cafe each day waiting for the winning numbers to be posted. So many people pushed into the Ritz Cafe on April 20th, that a section of the roof caved in, ten people were injured, but this did not deter the crowd that came for the daily drawing. At noon the next day, on April 21st, as more than 100 people pushed into the Ritz Cafe to see the daily posting, a steel beam supporting a wall gave way and the entire building collapsed, killing twenty-four people and injuring eighty-three. It was the greatest single disaster in numbers killed at a single time in the history of Phenix City.

An outraged citizenry demanded an investigation and families of the dead and injured threatened law suits against Hoyt Shepherd, Jimmie Matthews, and Clyde Yarborough.

Homer Cobb, Dr. Ashby Floyd, and C. L. Gullatt, members of the three-man city commission, promised an immediate investigation into the numbers racket and racketeering, but the matter never came to court. Even though more than 100 people had witnessed the tragedy, not a single witness would come forward to testify.

The oppressed and those seeking justice for their wounds had to satisfy themselves with muffled cries. It did no good whatsoever to call the police. They were in the employ of those who ran the town. It was useless to take a complaint to court. The matter had already been decided in the chambers of those who ran the town. The only solution was to try to learn to live with the situation as it was, walk the line, stay out of trouble and out of the way of those who ran the town. For those unfortunate enough to lose favor or run afoul of those who ran the town, it was just too damned bad.

Patterson became aware of this soon after moving to Phenix City. Having recovered from his war wounds, he had finished his studies, earned his degree and spent several years as a high school principal before reading for the law and coming to Phenix City to hang out his shingle.

Albert Patterson, after defending a client in a dispute over car repairs, had the jury return the verdict in favor of his client, but the judge refused to accept the verdict and directed the jury to return to the jury room and come back with a verdict in favor of the defendant.

The jury came back with the verdict that the judge had directed but added the words "done under protest." This so infuriated the judge that he threatened to charge the entire jury with contempt of court and put them all in jail unless the "done under protest" was removed from the verdict he directed. With no other options, the jury complied.

Leaving the courthouse, one of the jurymen came up to Patterson to apologize.

"I'm awful sorry about what happened in court today."

"Well, that's Phenix City for you," Patterson said with a shrug of resignation. "You did the best you could. That's all any of us can ever do."

"I just wish there could have been something more ...."

"There wasn't."

૨જ

There wasn't much anyone could do about the situation in Phenix City, even when it spilled over into the Army base across the river at Fort Benning, Georgia. Soldiers, on payday, had always sought out the sordid thrills that the Phenix City honky-tonks and gambling tables offered, but as Hitler waged war through Europe with Poland falling in 1939 and the city of Paris occupied in June of 1940, American involvement became a serious consideration as the Battle of Britain began. The population at Fort Benning swelled with the training of troops and soared with the bombing of Pearl Harbor and the declaration of War in December 1941.

In Phenix City, however, the toughest fighting men in the world were outmatched by the gamblers who waited for them with crooked dice, marked cards, knock-out drops, spiked brass knuckles and a police force that backed the establishment when a soldier complained of being cheated, robbed, rolled, and mauled. The soldier was arrested, charged with drunk and disorderly conduct, and turned over to the military police for further disciplinary action.

Operating with no restraints, the rackets continued and the outrages multiplied. Gambling establishments paid taxi cab drivers one dollar a head to deliver the soldiers to their places of business where a carnival of illegal sport and criminal intent awaited them — B-Girls who enticed them into buying them expensive drinks made of tea with a teaspoon of liquor on top, card sharks who wore infra-red croupier shades that enabled them to see the cards their customers held, roulette wheels, mechanically adjusted to pay off in favor of the house, and slot machines set to return five cents on the dollar.

If, by the end of the evening, the B-Girl and the gaming tables had not cleaned a soldier's pockets, the prostitutes did, selling their favors at a dollar a minute, a rate set by the pimps and whore-masters who ran the pleasure houses and received the lion's share of the evening's take and very often caused trouble by interrupting a man before his paid-up time was finished.

Cheated, angered, and with no court of resort, the soldiers fought their way through situations they were destined to lose. No matter how strong, agile, and adept with his fists, they were outmatched by the bully-boys' chains, gun-butts, and spiked brass knuckles that could maul a man's face beyond recognition.

It was at this point that Secretary of War Henry L. Stimson, having been informed about what was happening to the Fort Benning soldiers

17

in this outlaw Alabama town declared: *"Phenix City, Alabama, is the wickedest city in America."*

From time to time, some of the Phenix City establishments were put off-limits to the soldiers, but with a $2,000,000 a month take from the soldier's pay, enough high-level political pressure was applied to have the order rescinded and the Phenix City operation continued without interruption. A soldier would come up missing, or found floating in the muddy water of the Chattahoochee River, or on the river bottom wearing a pair of cement shoes.

Military investigations on how such a thing had happened, received a standard reply: "Hell, he was drunk and fell off the side of the bridge into the water."

Pressed further about the cement shoes: "I reckon he was so drunk he walked through fresh cement before he fell in."

General George C. Patton, while training his troops at Fort Benning for what would later become their triumphant Third Army push through Europe, became so enraged by the outrages against his soldiers that he publicly threatened to take his tanks across the river and mash Phenix City flat.

When Walter J. Hanna, now a regimental commander with the famed 31st Dixie Division training troops in Mississippi for island fighting in the Pacific, heard Patton's comment, he said: "Hell, I'll go help him. What's being done to our fighting men in Phenix City is a sin and a crime and a disgrace to the country."

Homer Cobb hated all the bad publicity that General Patton's public threat had caused and regretted the situation that had caused the comment. By now, a veteran member of the City Commission, and a staunch defender of the city he loved, Homer Cobb did what he could to enforce some restraints, and the racketeers, following their proven modus operandi, slacked off slaughter for a while until the disturbance blew over and then continued again until such time as excesses would cause another outcry.

Homer Cobb worried about what would become of Phenix City when he was no longer able to hold back the ever-increasing tide of criminal activity—when he was gone and someone else sat in the City Commission seat that now was his. Originally, his plan had been to license illegal liquor and gambling only long enough to get the city through its financial crisis and then cut the gamblers loose from their strings on the city, but it hadn't worked that way. With each passing year, the number of racketeers increased, their activities multiplied, and their attitude became more arrogant and demanding.

A hundred times over Homer Cobb had heard Minnie Bentley's

warning ringing in his ears: "You've made a deal with the devil and you'll live to rue the day."

Miss Minnie's cry against gambling and sin had been taken up now by her son, Hugh, who was only a little boy delivering meals to the mill when Homer first met him. Homer had watched him grow up and get married and start a sporting goods business of his own across the river in Columbus. For a while, he was so busy with business of his own, getting established and starting a family, that, even though he still lived in Phenix City, he didn't pay much attention to what was going until he had two sons of his own. Then, like his mother, Miss Minnie, Hugh Bentley began to object to the effects that the environment in Phenix City would have on the children. All the anger and stiff resistance that Miss Minnie had had, seemed to be born again in her son, Hugh. Active in the First Baptist Church and civic affairs, he was always trying to galvanize a group to go up against the gambling interests.

Homer Cobb knew trouble when he saw it and Hugh Bentley was trouble on its way to happen. Thirty-two years old now, quiet, soft-spoken, he didn't appear to be a potential threat, but there was a quality about him—the look in his dark brown eyes magnified by the glasses he wore that reflected no fear, only doggedness and determination. Worse yet, he knew no compromise and he never quit trying, but fortunately, his platform was primarily in the church. Like Miss Minnie, he truly believed in the Will of God, the Power of Evil, and the Protection of the Almighty. He might get people riled up and ready to do something on Sunday morning, but then, they had to face the reality of going to work on Monday and when they had to choose between Bentley or bread, they chose bread. At least, so far.

Then came that Sunday morning of 7 December 1941 and all the old arguments and antagonisms got laid aside as World War II began. In the early 1940's the nation's hearts, and minds, and efforts were riveted on recovering from the devastation at Pearl Harbor and gearing up the country and its production to win the war in Europe and the Pacific, and Homer Cobb was satisfied that if anything was to be done about Phenix City, Hugh Bentley would have to wait until the War was over.

2

HUGH BENTLEY

When the War was over, Hugh Bentley first saw Albert Fuller standing on the corner at Dillingham Street, wearing hand-tooled cowboy boots, a ten gallon white Stetson hat, and a pair of gold-plated guns, hung low on his hips, watching the girls walk by. With his thumb, Fuller pushed his hat to the back of his head and yelled at a platinum blond on the other side of the street.

"Hey, baby, I'm home."

The blonde tossed him a scornful look over the black feather boa draped across her shoulder, and minced on down the street in high-heeled black satin shoes studded with rhinestones.

Albert Fuller took one gun out of his holster and shot off the heel of one shoe, and held the second gun ready to shoot the heel off the other shoe.

The blond fell back against the store front behind her. Pulling her feather boa around her, she looked down at the shoe with the missing heel and back at Albert Fuller.

"What the hell do you think you're doing?" she demanded.

Albert Fuller grinned, pulled the white Stetson hat down to a rakish angle over his eye-brows, and ambled across the street to meet his new acquaintance.

"Trying to get your attention ... I spoke to you and you didn't answer."

"Well, you didn't have to ruin my shoe, for Christ's Sake."

Albert Fuller pulled a fistful of money from his pocket. "I'll buy you some more."

"Shoes like this aren't that easy to find," she said angrily, looking down at the black satin Baby Dolls with ankle straps and four-inch rhinestone-studded heels that caught the glitter as she walked.

Albert Fuller was losing patience. "I *said* I'd buy you some more."

The blond raked Albert Fuller's round, pudgy face and pear-shaped body with a scornful look, tossed her black boa over her shoulder and started to walk away, but Albert Fuller aimed his second gun at the heel of her other shoe.

"You want a matched pair?"

The blond swung around to face him. "Look ... who the HELL do you think you are anyway?"

Albert Fuller grinned and pushed his white Stetson back with the barrel of his gun. "I'm the new deputy, and when I speak to you ... you'd better mind what I say."

After that, Fuller was the talk of the town.

Albert Patterson, from his second floor law office in the Coulter Building, had seen Fuller swaggering down the street, picking out prey, and Patterson, being a man who kept his own counsel, made no public comments but privately he was aware that Fuller was one of the returning young Turks to watch.

Watching returning young Turks was something Hoyt Shepherd, now Phenix City's kingpin gambler, spent considerable time doing for he was fully aware that they could become a challenge. Back from the blood and battle of combat, the young Turks had not yet gotten over their thirst for conquest, but had brought it back home with them at the end of the War unwilling to settle into the acquiescence of peacetime economic and social restraints. The war had given them a taste of things they'd never had before and had raised expectations about what they could accomplish and what they could have and what they could do. Keeping control of Phenix City and what happened there had become a full time job for Hoyt Shepherd, so much so that he had made the sheriff's office in the courthouse something of an unofficial headquarters so that he could see first hand what was going on in town.

Sitting behind the sheriff's desk in the courthouse, pushed back in the sheriff's swivel chair with his feet propped on the desk, and his narrow brimmed hat pulled down over his brows in the attitude of a sleeping lion, Hoyt observed through the open window with keen interest the exchange now taking place on the courthouse steps. Sheriff Ralph Matthews, with his fat spread out on the courthouse steps, was taking the morning sun. Affable, good-natured, with a face as bland as biscuit dough, Ralph Matthews had a cordial relationship with the people of Phenix City, even when they didn't like what he did and who he worked for. The portrait of a benign public official, he sat now greeting the passers-by as they went about their day's business.

Arch Ferrell, the slim young attorney recently returned from the War in Europe to resume the law practice he had just started when the war began, walked up to the sheriff with quick, purposeful steps, propped his hands on his hips, pulling his jacket behind him and exposing a starched white shirt and a tightly tied tie. Through the open window in the sheriff's office, Hoyt heard him ask:

"Who's the new deputy?"

"You mean Albert Fuller?"

"The one who shot the girl's heel off."

The Sheriff smiled. "That's Albert, all right. He's fast with women and fast with a gun."

Arch Ferrell thrust out his lean jaw, pursed his lips in an attitude of assessment and then said:

"He must be a helluva shot."

"He's that all right. Just outa the Navy ... did shore patrol down there in Houston ... and took up all them Texas ways ... boots, cowboy hat, guns. Made him into a good shot, though. I figured he'd do all right as deputy with that fast gun of his."

Albert Fuller was a fast gun all right, but what Hoyt figured, and he hadn't figured a man wrong yet, was that Arch Ferrell was fast too—with words and actions. He had ambition written all over him and a track record that would bear out the expectations he had for himself—a brilliant law student at the University of Alabama, president of his class, then, fifty-four months with the infantry in Normandy, the Ardennes, and the Rhineland, coming out as a captain. Now, head of the Russell County American Legion Post, Hoyt was aware that Arch Ferrell was busy building a power base and that politics was the aim of his ambition. His father, old man H. A. Ferrell was the Russell County Solicitor. Hoyt figured this was what he'd aim for as soon as the old man's term was up.

With that kind of background, track record, and ambition, Hoyt figured Arch Ferrell was well worth watching and, maybe, adding him to his team one day. It never hurt to have another smart lawyer because you never knew when trouble would start or where it was coming from.

The returning young Turks were only part of the problem.

Being rightfully known as the Kingpin, the Boss, the man who ran things in Phenix City, Hoyt had the problem of territorial rights, something that took his constant vigilance and supervision. Since the beginning of the War in the forties with all the big money from Fort Benning, Phenix City was filled to overflowing with gamblers, crooks, and racketeers and little upstarts who had to be stopped before they notched themselves out a toe-hold. There were seven big lotteries run by the old timers who began back in the thirties and there was trouble and wrangling all the time between those who ran them.

Head Revel and Godwin Davis, who ran the big Metropolitan Lottery were in trouble right now with the federal government on some liquor conspiracy charge, and to make matters worse, the Feds said some soldier from Fort Benning named Johnny Frank Stringfellow who was also involved, had turned up missing. Trouble like that caused trouble for everybody because the Feds didn't fool around when it came to paying tax on money earned from illegal liquor — or anything else for that matter — that's why any gambler with any sense sure hell had better have a good bookkeeper who could keep two sets of books — in case he got caught.

And if that wasn't enough, then there was Homer Cobb, who would like to forget his beginnings and the deals that were made back during the Depression when the town was desperate for money — always agitating to keep a lid on things. Hoyt figured that making him mayor might quiet him down some, but it didn't. Instead of accepting it for the payoff that it was, Homer Cobb took it seriously. Building a high school and a hospital was all right, but when he started talking about the rackets and the reputation of Phenix City as an outlaw town — well, he had just forgot who fed him when he was hungry.

Hoyt could remind him of that and keep him quiet, but the one who could never shut his mouth for a minute was Hugh Bentley. Talking — always talking — to church groups, civic groups, veterans groups, anybody who would listen to him — trying to organize an effort to stop the gambling, stop the vice, stop the sin. If it was left up to Bentley, he would shut down every racket in town. Fortunately, Hugh Bentley had never been able to rally a crowd for long. Hoyt had seen to that. It took nothing more than threats, innuendo, and rumor to scatter his support. What Bentley realized, but refused to accept, was that most families in town were either connected to the rackets or were kin to somebody who was and a word of warning was all that was needed to stop any effort he started. But the trouble with Bentley was that he had the single-minded determination of a zealot. He wouldn't change his mind and he couldn't change the subject. He just never quit and since he did business across the river in Columbus and had a successful sporting goods store there, it wasn't that easy to put an economic squeeze on him, so Hoyt just let him rant and rave and make lists of victims with names, dates, and documented occurrences. There wasn't a damn thing he could do about it. Every once in a while he would go to the editor of the *Columbus Ledger* and some reporter would write a story, but it never amounted to a hill of beans. People had been complaining about

23

Phenix City for well over a hundred years, and they hadn't been able to seriously interrupt anything yet. But this didn't stop Bentley, he kept right on.

Hugh Bentley had now added Albert Fuller to his list of public complaints. Through the window right now, Hoyt could see him gnawing away at Sheriff Matthews.

Ralph Matthews was a good-natured fellow. Everybody called him "Sheriff" although he was actually deputy to Shannon Burch. He had been appointed sheriff by the governor when Sheriff Shannon Burch had gone off to war, then when Burch returned, he willingly gave up the position he had held and went back to being deputy sheriff.

"The last thing in this world this town needs is another fast gun," Bentley was saying. "That new deputy you've got ... that Albert Fuller ... is a menace."

A pleasant smile ringed Ralph Matthews' fat, bland face.

"Aw, now Hugh ... Albert Fuller didn't mean no harm. He's just young and frisky from being in the War and was just funning with the girls. That's all."

"Funning, my foot! Can you think what would have happened if some innocent bystander had gotten in the way of that fast gun? ... and what about the children? What kind of an example is this for the children to see ... a deputy sheriff shooting off the heel of a girl's shoe!"

Hoyt Shepherd could feel the heat of Hugh Bentley's indignation all the way through the window. Just looking at him, you'd never figure him for a fighter—short, stodgy, middle-aged, with glasses so thick that his eyes were the size of silver dollars. He looked like the Sunday School teacher that he was. What you couldn't tell, till you got up close and looked in those deep, quiet eyes, was that he was as tough and stubborn as a bull dog about what he believed and he'd keep at it till he ate your leg off if he had half of a chance.

Hoyt Shepherd watched Sheriff Matthews lean back from Bentley's anger, putting both hands behind him to prop himself up, swinging his crossed feet up and down. In the tone he used to smooth ruffled feathers, he said: "Now, Hugh. Ain't no use to get riled."

"I'm not riled, I'm outraged that you would let something like this go on ... and I tell you this, Ralph Matthews, I hold you directly responsible for what's happening in Russell County and Phenix City."

Sheriff Matthews straightened up. "Now, hold the phone, Hugh, the city ain't none of my affair. What happens in the city is up to the po-lice—and that's Pal Daniel's job. He's the Chief of Po-lice."

"You know very well, he's nothing but a figurehead who does what he's told. The one who really runs that department is that great big ape mutation named Buddy Jowers."

Sheriff Matthews shook his head back and forth slowly as though he had just received bad news.

"Now, I wouldn't go saying things like that if I was you, Hugh. Buddy Jowers is about twice your size ... six-foot-six as a matter of fact ... and he ain't got no patience with people that call him names. I seen him turn a man into a pretzel one night for a whole lot less."

"What we've got here in Phenix City and Russell County is the Mafia," Hugh Bentley said, shaking his fist at Ralph Matthews, "and one day it's going to catch up with you."

Sheriff Matthews shook his head complacently and went back to sunning himself on the courthouse wall.

Hoyt Shepherd watched Hugh Bentley storm out of sight down the street. Hugh Bentley didn't even know the half of it. Even the Mafia left Phenix City alone. Those boys knew tough when they saw it, and they respected territorial rights—which was a damn sight more than what the local talent did. Like that Fate Leebern across the river in Columbus. His real name was Fayette, but nobody local fooled with fancy French names. They called him Fate.

Hoyt figured Fate must be about fifty-one now. They had come to the area about the same time during the Depression days. Hoyt had set up shop in Phenix City and Fate had made himself rich on wholesale liquor, hotels, and real estate. Fate had his own playground over there in Columbus, but he was always trying to inch himself across the bridge into Phenix City. Hoyt had warned him that he'd better stay across the state line in Georgia, but he came across the river anyway and leased a building for a pool hall. Of course, that burned down before he ever got started, but that didn't stop Fate.

The next thing he tried was buddying up to Hoyt and his partner, Jimmie Matthews, when they got in some trouble with the Georgia Grand Jury for owning a building in Columbus that sold liquor by the drink. When the Georgia authorities arrested Hoyt and Jimmie, here comes Fate to sign their $1,000 bond. What Fate wanted was them to take it for a favor, but Hoyt knew better than that. Fate was just trying to grease his way into Phenix City with bail bond money, but Hoyt had made it plain: "If you ever cross the river again, I'll kill you."

Fate wasn't the only one Hoyt had to watch. There were all the little upstart punks who didn't have better sense and would try to poach and start something when they thought nobody was looking, or the hot-heads who got drunk and high on the power of a pistol. Phenix City

25

liked to think that all Hoyt Shepherd ever did was tell people what to do and count money.

Every time something happened the first one they blamed it on was Hoyt Shepherd. Just because he ran things, didn't mean he could control everybody. It just kept Hoyt busy all the time, keeping up with what was going on. During the war when the military population at Fort Benning had swelled to 80,000, the total take from all the rackets in Phenix City had risen to $100,000,000 a year and in this little city of 23,000 that was a lot to protect, and Hoyt Shepherd was prepared to do whatever had to be done to protect his interests in Phenix City.

⁊❧

"*Phenix City!*"

The man across the banquet table laughed so hard his face turned red and he choked as he tried to get the words out: "You are from *Phenix City, Alabama?*" He covered his mouth with his white linen napkin and shook with uncontrollable laughter.

Hugh Bentley was quite at a loss for what to say. This was his first Sporting Goods Convention and his first time in Chicago and everyone he had met since his arrival two days ago had been as nice and friendly as they could be, but the man across the banquet table was doubled up with derisive laughter. He was not drunk and he was not kidding, and Hugh Bentley was insulted.

It was one thing for him to berate Phenix City and lambaste the public officials, but it was quite another for some stranger to make fun of his hometown. He could feel the hairs on the back of his neck prickle and he drew himself up straight in his chair.

"What, Sir, do you find so funny about Phenix City?"

The tone of icy formality stopped the man's laughter. He looked surprised at Hugh Bentley's reaction.

"Why that's the worst city in the world."

"And what, Sir, brought you to that conclusion?"

"Look," the man said, trying to explain his opinion, "I was stationed at Fort Benning during the war and I never ever again saw a place as wide open and wicked as Phenix City ... not Algiers ... Rome ... Paris ... Berlin ... no place could hold a candle to the sin in Phenix City."

The man's words were embarrassing, and Hugh Bentley was trying to control his anger. "You're speaking of the gambling, of course."

"Not just the gambling. Everything's for sale in that city and they don't care who knows it or who sees them. Hell, you can go into one of those honky tonks on Saturday night and see some guy and a gal in a booth going right at it ... right in front of God and everybody ... whore houses every where ... and the damnedest thing I ever saw was what they called Mobile Units."

"I don't know what you're talking about," Hugh Bentley said stiffly.

By now the controversy had drawn the attention of the other guests and they leaned forward at the banquet table to get a better look at Hugh Bentley and to hear the wicked details of a city so wrought with sin.

"On payday, everything got pressed into service and they used pickup trucks with slat sides and a tarpaulin across the top ... like a rolling store. They would pick up a soldier, ride him around while he had his time in the back with the girl, then drop him off, cruise down the street and pick up another. It went on like that all day and all night."

It seemed to Hugh Bentley that now that the man had drawn the attention of everyone at the banquet table that he had, with relish, fallen into exaggeration, and had, by association, made him a public spectacle. Hugh Bentley was incensed. He drew himself up stiffly and let his speech fall into a formal cadence.

"Because of the company, I hesitate, Sir, to call you a liar, but I must assert, as strongly as possible, that what you are saying about Phenix City, simply is not so. I *live* there."

A smirk settled on the man's face. "Then you'd better go back and take a closer look."

৵

Bernice Bentley heard the front door open, and then, footsteps in the hall.

"Hugh? Is that you, Hugh?" Bernice called from the kitchen, taking the pie she had baked for supper out of the oven and setting it aside to cool.

When there was no answer, she untied her ruffled white apron, tossed it aside, and hurried toward the front door.

"Why, Hugh!" she exclaimed, seeing her husband standing there with the heavy suitcase he had carried to Chicago. "I thought you were still in Chicago ... I thought you were coming back tomorrow ...."

Her voice trailed off as she saw the sag of his shoulders and the glum look on his face. "You look like you're carrying around all the troubles in the world. What on earth is the matter? Didn't you have a good time in Chicago?"

Hugh Bentley set down his suitcase. "They shamed me."

A frown creased Bernice Bentley's smooth face. "What do you mean ... they shamed you?"

"They laughed at me and ridiculed me and said Phenix City was the wickedest city in the whole United States and that everybody in the country knew it, and it shamed me so bad I just went upstairs to my hotel room and packed my bags and came home."

"Why, Hugh! Phenix City isn't all that bad , is it?"

"They said it was. "

"Well, what about Chicago?" Bernice asked indignantly. "What about all those gangsters and the Mafia?"

"They said Phenix City was worse ...."

"Worse than the Mafia?"

"They said Phenix City was worse than any place anywhere and that every soldier in the country knew it was true."

Bernice could see the hurt and pain still in his eyes, and she went over and put her arms around her husband and laid her head against his shoulder. "Now don't you let those folks up there in Chicago upset you. You just forget about it ... you're home now."

Hugh kissed her on the cheek. She was a nurturing woman, soft and gentle, quick to gather up those she loved to brush away concerns and console pains and he had loved her since the moment he had seen her in her white summer dress sitting in the swing under the trees at the Sunday School picnic.

"No, I can't forget about it ... my conscience won't let me. It was like being branded with a scarlet letter ... like somebody saying something bad about your sister. I was ashamed and humiliated and angry with the man who said it ... to think that the town I call my own ... I've got to find out if what he said is really true."

Bernice pulled back out of his arms. "Hugh, you know very well this town has always had gambling and drinking and fighting ... but so have a lot of other ... "

"It was worse than that ... a whole lot worse."

Bernice Bentley could see from the resolve on his face that his mind was made up. "What are you going to do?"

"I'm going to get my buddy, Hugh Britton, and I'm going to go down to the dives on Fourteenth and Dillingham Street and find out just what's happening in this town. I've spent too many years tending my own garden ... seeing about my business, my family, my affairs."

"Now, Hugh, you know you've always been concerned."

"All I've done is give lip service to the Lord. I haven't *done* anything ... but I'm going to."

In Phenix City they were known as "the two Hughs"—Hugh Bentley and Hugh Britton—as close as kin, sharing interests, concerns and enthusiasms—and wherever one was seen, the other was most usually there also. Hugh Britton was the kind of man you could depend on. A carpenter by trade, spare and lean and hard-muscled, he was as committed to honor and decency and a better world for the children as Hugh Bentley was himself.

When Hugh Bentley told him what had happened in Chicago, Hugh Britton asked: "What are you going to do?"

"I'm going to go down to Fourteenth and Dillingham Street on Saturday night and see for myself."

Hugh Britton's voice had the tone of a pledge. "I'll go with you."

The gambling district sat on the red clay banks of the Chattahoochee River under the shadow of the twin bridges at Dillingham and Fourteenth Streets like a ragged urchin waiting for sundown. Honky tonks, cafes, gambling joints, loan companies and pawnshops crowded both sides of the street on Dillingham and Fourteenth all the way up the hill to the courthouse. The buildings housing them were cement block, and some made of weathered wood with tin roof overhangs sheltering the sidewalks. In the broad light of day it had the deserted look of an abandoned town in the old West, but when dusk fell and covered its shabbiness with darkness, brilliant neon lights sprang to life in carnival colors beckoning like a Lorelei on the riverbank to the soldiers stationed across the state line at Fort Benning, Georgia.

At the top of the hill, above the gambling district, the somber, two-story brick courthouse with a facade of white columns in the middle, turned its shoulder on the ruin below and faced the post office and the Coulter Building a block away. Beyond the courthouse, fanned out between Federal Highway 80 going west to the state capital in Montgomery and 431 going south toward Florida and Panama City, were the residences and twenty-six churches of the good people of Phenix City who turned out their lights on Saturday night and awoke to the chiming of church bells on Sunday morning. Whatever went on down by the bridges in the gambling district, they felt, was none of their affair.

"You know, that's our trouble," Hugh Bentley told Hugh Britton as they met on Saturday night to tour the gambling district. "We've been so busy disassociating ourselves with the bad influences in Phenix City that we don't even know what's really going on."

"We're going to find out tonight," Hugh Britton said, slipping in the car beside his friend.

"Let's go down to Dillingham Street and see what's happening."

The night seemed to have a thousand eyes as the twin beams of headlights in an endless caravan streamed across the high bridge over the dark water into Phenix City, coming to a stop on Dillingham Street, discharging their cargo of fresh-faced soldiers in starched khakis and combat boots, their pockets lined with a month's pay, hard-earned in the sweat and grime and killing fatigue of the training field under the relentless drive and bark of the drill sergeant. Getting out of the cars and cabs hired to bring them from Fort Benning, their eyes shone with the prospect of satiating a month's thirst for liquor, lust, excitement and entertainment.

From every direction the siren's song beckoned. The whirl of roulette wheels and the throb of music from juke boxes poured out the doors of cafes and cabarets onto streets painted harlot hues from overhead neon signs inviting the carnival crowd to the pleasures inside where bartenders in darkened caverns, busied themselves with the clink of glasses and ice and cool drinks being mixed for customers at small crowded tables. Propped at the bar in provocative and seductive attitudes were the B-Girls in slinky dresses cut hip-high on the side and down deep in the front to expose perfumed breasts that heaved with possibilities.

"Buy me a drink, soldier?"

From their perch on the barstools at the end of the bar, Hugh Bentley and Hugh Britton watched the soldier, starry-eyed and breathless, being led away while the bartender mixed a tea glass of Coke® with a splash of liquor on top and a waitress hustled it to the table.

"Ten bucks," she said, holding out her hand.

As the soldier pulled out his wallet, the B-Girl knocked over the drink that had just been served, spilling it across the table.

"That's all right," he said quickly, "I'll get you another."

"What about champagne?" the B-Girl suggested, rubbing her bare arm up against his shoulder. "It's been a long time since I met a feller as good-looking as you. I gotta celebrate."

The soldier, swept away by the flutter of long eyelashes, grinned and told the waitress: "Bring the lady some champagne."

"Twenty-five bucks before I pop the cork," the waitress said.

The soldier reached for his wallet again, taking out two more tens and a five, and when the waitress delivered it to the bartender, she said: "That's two drinks and a bottle of champagne for Martina."

The bartender marked it down on his pad behind the bar and grinned. "That girl's doing all right. That's twenty-five drinks and twelve bottles of champagne already tonight."

Then pouring the remains of several bottles of champagne into one bottle, the bartender pushed in the cork and handed it to the waitress to serve.

Hugh Britton shook his head. "The poor bastard doesn't even have a chance."

"It makes me sick just to watch," Hugh Bentley said angrily. "I'd like to go and get him out of here right now."

"No chance of that, not until every last dime he earned is gone."

Hugh Bentley slid off his bar stool. "Let's get out of here. I can't stand to watch anymore ... not and keep my mouth shut."

Outside, the crowd had grown thicker and drunker and the ladies of the evening more aggressive as they cruised up in taxi cabs and called out the window: "Looking for a good time, soldier?"

Hugh Bentley shook his head. "Just think, all this going on in the streets and Phenix City is up there on the hill asleep waiting for the church bells to chime."

"Have you seen enough?" Hugh Britton asked.

"No. I want to go that place that fellow from Chicago was talking about."

"It's likely going to be worse."

"That's what I came to find out."

The door was locked, but above it an arch of flashing lights advertised: "GIRLS! GIRLS! GIRLS!" On each side of the door, glass frames held pictures of shapely girls in sexy poses wearing little more than feathers. A small sign above a buzzer said "Ring Bell." Hugh Britton pushed the buzzer and the heavy door with brass fittings was swung open by a big, burly bouncer with a shaven head who propped one bare arm tattooed with serpents against the door frame blocking the entrance. He looked at Hugh Britton and Hugh Bentley in their windbreaker jackets and said: "Yeah?"

Hugh Bentley craned his head to see beyond the tattooed bicep at the show that was in progress inside the darkened room. On tiptoe, he could see through the smoky haze a brilliantly lit horseshoe stage with a half dozen women wearing nothing but a black lace garter and a feather headdress bouncing and grinding to the music while the circle of soldiers at the footlights reached and grabbed to put a dollar in their garter before they skillfully slipped away.

"We want to see the show," Hugh Bentley said, as the bouncer stepped back to block their view.

The bouncer scowled. "Ain't I seen you some place before?"

Hugh Bentley shook his head. "Not likely."

The bouncer looked at Hugh Britton and then back at Hugh Bentley. "I *know* I know you from someplace. What's your name, feller, and where you from?"

Hugh Bentley looked him squarely in the eye. "My name is Hugh Bentley and I live in Phenix City."

"I *knew* I knew you from someplace. You're that goddamn trouble-maker, ain't you?"

"We're not here to make trouble, we want to see the show," Hugh Bentley said, squinting through the darkness to see the booths around the rim of the room where couples were engaged in various stages of embrace.

"Well, you ain't welcome in here. We don't need your business."

"This is a public place, isn't it?" Hugh Bentley asked, taking a step forward and Hugh Britton stepping up beside him so that they were two abreast.

The bouncer tightened his grip on the door so that the serpent on his bicep rippled. "You make one more move, feller, and I'll tear your head off and hand it to you."

Hugh Bentley opened his mouth to protest, but the bouncer slammed the door shut in their faces. The word passed quickly that snoopers were out prowling and the reception was the same at Head Revel's Bridge Grocery, Clyde Yarborough's Yellow Front Cafe, Red Cook's Old Original Barbecue and Godwin Davis' Manhattan Club. At Hoyt Shepherd's Ritz Cafe, they were told: "This club's for high rollers. You ain't got the money to come in here."

"We want to watch the game," Hugh Bentley persisted.

The bouncer's beady eyes narrowed to warning slits. "Get the hell on down the road before you get somebody killin' mad."

The door slammed and Hugh Britton thrust his hands in his pockets and looked at Hugh Bentley. "Have you seen enough?"

"Enough to know that Chicago wasn't lying. It's all here, going on behind closed doors."

"Let's get the car and go home."

Hugh Bentley nodded and they turned off the lighted street toward the dark alley where the car was parked. Before they could see what was happening, they could hear the beating and the body blows. Three hefty men in the alley were taking turns knocking a soldier up against the back wall of the building. In the shadows from the bare light on the back of the building, Hugh Bentley could see that the soldier's eyes had been beaten shut and was bleeding profusely from the head and the mouth and an open gash on the side of his face.

Hugh Bentley, a light-weight boxer in his younger days, rushed forward to the rescue. "Hey you! Stop that!"

A big man with a beer belly and hate on his face whirled around and swung at Hugh Bentley with the chain in his hand. "You wanna be next?"

Hugh Britton grabbed Hugh Bentley by the arm. "Let's get the police."

They ran for the car and raced up the hill to the courthouse, swinging around behind it to the Russell County jail and rushed into the sheriff's office where Ralph Matthews was finishing the last dregs from a brown-stained coffee cup.

"They're killing a soldier down there in Shirttail Alley," Hugh Bentley said breathlessly. "You gotta get down there and stop it."

Ralph Matthews pursed his mouth, shook his head, and pushed back in his swivel chair, slapping his hands down on the arm rests. "I swear to my soul, Hugh, if you don't go minding everybody's business."

"For God's sake, man, this *is* your business."

"Ain't nobody called us."

"Who do you thinks going to call … that soldier they're beating the life out of?"

"He likely got drunk and wild … "

Hugh Bentley lurched forward. "They're killing him, I tell you. Where's that fast-gun deputy of yours … that Albert Fuller … why don't you send him?"

Ralph Matthews drew in a deep breath. "Albert's out chasing liquor runners and besides … what happens in Shirttail Alley ain't none of my affair. It ain't my jurisdiction. Now if you wanna call somebody, get Pal Daniel on the phone … the city's his jurisdiction, he's the Chief of Police."

"Give me the phone," Hugh Bentley said, snatching the receiver off the hook. "I'm going to call the Military Police at Fort Benning, at least they can come rescue him."

Ralph Matthew tossed a card across the desk. "Help yourself. There's the number right there."

On the phone the dispatcher at MP headquarters took the information and told Hugh Bentley: "We have a patrol in the area, we'll get over there right away and pick him up."

"I hope to God they get there in time," Hugh Bentley said.

Ralph Matthews lifted his bland face and smiled pleasantly. "If you ain't satisfied, Hugh, what you oughta do is go over there and see Pal Daniel at Po-lice Headquarters. See if he can help you."

"I'm going do just that," Hugh Bentley snapped, "because it's obvious to me that the Sheriff's office in this town is virtually worthless."

At Police Headquarters, Pal Daniel sat at his desk with his hat on his head. He was a man clearly overwhelmed by the demands of his job and held himself stiffly as though secretly nursing some silent pain, his eyes weary and as apprehensive as an animal expecting another blow.

"I haven't got anybody to send," he told Hugh Bentley and Hugh Britton. "I'm here by myself with a jail full of drunks and I can't leave."

"Where's Buddy Jowers?" Hugh Bentley asked. "he's supposed to be on duty at night."

"Buddy went out to the cafe to get himself something to eat. The rest of the men are on patrol."

"Well, can't you get somebody on the radio and get them down there to Shirttail Alley to see about that soldier?"

Pal Daniel's tired eyes looked defeated. "I'll have to wait 'til Buddy gets back. He takes care of those things."

Hugh Bentley was angry and frustrated but could clearly see that venting his feelings on Pal Daniel was useless. He was doing all he could do, just minding the store.

Outside, Hugh Britton asked: "What now?"

"I'm going to go home and call Homer Cobb and get him out of bed. He's mayor of this town and the police department is ultimately his responsibility."

On the phone Hugh Bentley told him: "They're down there killing a soldier in Shirttail Alley and I can't get a law officer in this town to help me. Now what are you going to do about it?"

Homer Cobb yawned. "I'm going to go back to sleep and I'll see you in church in the morning."

Hugh Bentley slammed up the phone and sank in his soft easy chair feeling defeated, wretched and at raw, ragged ends. Hugh Britton perched on the edge of the sofa opposite him, his hands resting on his long, thin legs. "You did what you could."

"Not enough." Hugh Bentley pushed himself out of his chair. "Let's go back and see if the MP's got that soldier."

Hugh Britton looked at his watch. "It's been better than forty-five minutes. They'll have gotten to him by now."

"I want to go back to the alley and see where ... "

"I tell you what, tomorrow after church, we'll get the wives and kids to go home together and I'll drive you down there myself."

It was against Hugh Bentley's nature to give up on what he started out to do, but the Westminster clock on the mantelpiece was chiming half past two. He nodded reluctantly and Hugh Britton got up, slapped him on the back and said: "See you after church tomorrow."

The churchyard was filled with ringing bells and the faithful, dressed in their Sunday best, pouring out of church, calling greetings to each other and heading home for the ritual Sunday dinner. Hugh Bentley, having finished teaching his Sunday School class of ten-year olds and serving as usher during services, was searching the crowd for Hugh Britton when a little girl in a pink pinafore with flounces of white ruffles, darted through the crowd, her warm brown hair, held back by a pink headband, bouncing on her shoulders.

"Mr. Bentley! Mr. Bentley!"

"Right here, Marjorie." Hugh Bentley held out his hand, clasping her small hand in his.

"I liked the story you told us in Sunday School this morning."

"The Good Samaritan?"

Marjorie looked up, her face full of earnestness. "Is that really your favorite story?"

Hugh Bentley nodded and smiled. "Ever since I was a boy when my mother read it to me."

"You said we should read it for ourselves. Show me where to find it."

Hugh Bentley opened the white Bible that he carried with him always to Sunday School and to church. "Right here in Luke. Chapter ten."

Marjorie bent over to see the page, smiled up at Hugh Bentley and skipped away. "See you next Sunday."

Hugh Britton walked up. "Teaching them all the way into the churchyard?"

Hugh Bentley looked off in Marjorie's direction as she joined her parents and got in the family car. "One of God's Holy Innocents — still unblemished, undamaged — full of hope and promise and faith." Hugh Bentley looked back at his friend. "We've got to find a way to protect them from all the corruption that surrounds them here in Phenix City."

Hugh Britton brushed his fist against Hugh Bentley's shoulder. "We'll do it. One way or another, we'll find a way."

From the crowd pouring out into the churchyard, three-year old Truman Bentley broke away from his brother Hughbo's hand and ran shrieking: "Daddy! Daddy!"

Hugh Bentley bent down and scooped him up in his arms, holding him on one hip and hooking the other arm around ten-year old Hughbo's neck. "How are my boys? Did you have a good lesson in Sunday School?"

Truman took his little hands, turning his father's face toward him. "Daddy, why aren't you coming home with us?"

"Daddy's got some business to do first, but I'll be there in a little while."

Bernice Bentley tugged at her husband's white jacket with a soft hand. "Now Hugh, don't you be late for dinner. Mama's coming over and that roast beef is coming out of the oven in thirty minutes and you've got to be there to carve it."

"We'll be back in no time," Hugh Bentley promised, handing Truman over to her and brushing her cheek with a kiss. Ruffling Hughbo's hair, he told him: "Help your mother until I get there," and got into the car with Hugh Britton and sighed. "I wish every day could be Sunday morning ... all the peace and good will and fellowship."

Hugh Britton nodded and turned the car toward the courthouse and the Fourteenth Street bridge. "Everything starts going to hell from here. People get back in their cars, go home, and have to face the realities of making a living on Monday morning."

"Shouldn't be that way."

"But it is." Lifting one finger off the steering wheel, he pointed down the hill. "Here is reality .... "

The heat of the noonday sun had sucked the color out of the sky and turned its harsh, unrelenting light on the gambling district exposing the ruin and the remains of last night's revelries. The littered streets were empty, the lights were off, the music gone, the doors locked against daylight's inspection.

"Reminds me of the fair grounds after the fair has gone," Hugh Bentley said.

"You want to drive down to Shirttail Alley?"

"No. Let's go down to the Dillingham Street bridge and park at the river and walk up from there."

Hugh Britton pulled off the road beside a clump of bushes and wild, tangled vines of green kudzu that ran to the river. He turned off the engine, and the moment he did, they heard the groans. Hugh Bentley laid aside the white Bible he had held in his lap and jumped out of the car, running toward the sound of the pain and the moans. In the kudzu beyond the brush, a young soldier, barefoot and bloody, was curled in the fetal position with his arms clasped around his knees, drawn up to his chest, rocking slowly to ease the pain.

"Good God!" Hugh Bentley dropped to his knees and gently tried to roll the soldier over to see what was left of his face, literally cut to ribbons as though a maddened lion had raked the flesh away with broad-blade claws from his forehead to his chin. He was bleeding from his mouth and his ear and from the caked, congealed edges of the flow, apparently had been doing so for sometime.

"I don't think that's the worst of it," Hugh Britton said, bending over what appeared to be only a boy of eighteen or nineteen. "He's wounded in the gut ... bad."

"Let's get him in the car and get him to the hospital at Fort Benning—quick."

Gently, they picked him up, Hugh Bentley holding him under his arms, Hugh Britton lifting his legs, and as they put him in the back seat of the car, he stirred and tried to talk.

"No ... no ... "

"It's all right," Hugh Bentley said, sitting on the floor beside him in the back seat while Hugh Britton spun the car back out in the road and headed toward the bridge across the river to Fort Benning. "We're going to get you to the hospital at Fort Benning and get you some help."

"No ... no ... I can't go back ... they took my boots ... my combat boots. I can't go back barefooted, my sergeant will bust my ass if he finds out my combat boots are gone."

He tried to reach toward his bare feet, but Hugh Bentley took his hand and held it. "Don't worry about the boots, I'll get you some more. Can you tell me what happened?"

His eyes were swollen shut, the lids, purple and blue and slashed, his mouth broken and bleeding, painfully he forced the words. "They took all my money ... they promised a private show after closing ... they locked the door ... and then they came after us ... with spiked brass knuckles and chains and clubs." He paused to wait for the pain to pass. "They dumped me on the riverbank and kicked me in the gut and the groin ... and then ... they took my boots ... they took my boots."

A sob wracked his body and he began to cry as though this last act had robbed him of his manhood and left him humiliated.

Hugh Britton screeched to a stop at the gate to Fort Benning. When the MP on the gate approached the car for identification, Hugh Britton told him: "We've got a soldier ... wounded bad ... call ahead to the hospital."

The MP snapped a salute in affirmative response and at the hospital, a corpsman was waiting under the portico of the emergency room. He opened the car door and looked at the broken body in the back seat. "Christ!"

Calling back over his shoulder to the nurse waiting in the doorway, the corpsman yelled: "Get a gurney quick and call the doctor. We got another one from Phenix City."

Driving back home, Hugh Britton was silent. Beside him, Hugh Bentley looked down at the boy's blood on his white Sunday suit.

That boy was somebody's son, hardly on the threshold of manhood, likely raised with love and hope, broken now by the brutality of Phenix City. Hugh Bentley felt a sick curl in his stomach. It was a feeling that went all the way back to his childhood when he stood behind his mother's skirts and listened to angry words he didn't understand about Phenix City, killing and crime, a time he could scarcely remember, only in hazy hues and vague outlines, but a feeling whose sharpness never diminished and always seized him when things were really bad and getting worse.

The sickened feeling brought it all back again—the memory of three of his closest growing-up friends killed in their adolescence by the excesses in Phenix City—Jesse Stubbs with his head shot off, Herman Elliott, knocked in the head and found floating in the river, Jimmie Hooks, stabbed in the heart. The violence of their deaths had turned him forever away from the lure that Phenix City offered youths on every corner and set him back on the path of his Mama's teachings, the path of a Christian dedicated to having the courage to do something about the spawning evil and leave the world better than he found it for those who would come after him.

There were tears in Hugh Bentley's eyes and tears in his heart and blood on his Bible—his white, pristine Bible. He couldn't take his eyes off the blood on his Bible. It was like a desecration—like a deed done to dishonor the Lord—like a guilt on his own soul—because he was part of the community that had drawn that boy's blood and put it there.

As they reached the Fourteenth Street bridge, Hugh Britton broke the silence. "What are you going to do now?"

Hugh Bentley frowned. "We got to do something, but I don't know what. Talking's not doing any good. Nobody's listening."

"What's got to happen," Hugh Britton told him, "is we got to get some control ... some political control ... get a seat on the City Council and change what's happening in Phenix City."

"We got a city election coming up in September."

"And you're the man for the job."

Hugh Bentley vigorously shook his head. "Not me. A political office is not what I want. All I want is a decent town for the children to grow up in, where they can be assured of the values everybody else takes for granted ... justice and honesty and decency."

"Then, we're gonna have to fight for it. We got to get somebody on our side on the city council."

"Well, what about Otis Taff? He's a decent fellow and he's running for City Council against the gambler's candidate, Elmer Reese. If we back Otis ...."

The decision to back Otis Taff seemed like a good one, but with this fateful decision, a chain of escalating events began, followed by a series of significant murders that each contributed to the destiny of Phenix City and brought it to its ultimate tragedy.

3

HOYT SHEPHERD

Hoyt Shepherd watched everybody, every weakness, and every strength. He took it upon himself to advise them how to correct it or improve it as he saw fit.

Elmer Reese looked like a man who had spent most of his life drinking vinegar, drawn and dried up with not enough meat on his bones to hold his britches up. But it wasn't vinegar Elmer was into, it was the pills out of his drug store where he was the pharmacist.

"You keep on with that, Elmer, and you'll be taking it in the arm," Hoyt had told him. "You better lay off them things or you'll get to where you can't even remember what I told you to do."

Elmer reached down for his belt and tugged his britches back in place trying to straighten himself up. "Now, Hoyt, just cause I got lit up on Dillingham Street and ended up in Miami ain't no use for you to think I ain't going to remember what you told me."

"Well, you listen to me now. I want you to get out there and act like a candidate for reelection to that City Council seat and not just sit on your ass and expect me to hand you that election. I want it to look like it was a landslide, like you were the overwhelming favorite of the people."

"Hoyt, I ain't gonna have no trouble running."

"What about Hugh Bentley?"

Elmer Reese wrinkled his face up into a frown. "Now, Hoyt, you ain't got no cause to go concernin' yoreself about Bentley. He's been hollering a long time about gambling and sin in Phenix City. Don't nobody take him serious."

"There's talk about him being 'a moral leader'."

"You mean that Christian Laymen's Association he organized? There ain't nothing to that. That's just church talk and preacher talk."

"No. Bentley's done started something new, a Phenix City Veteran's

League. From what I hear, he and Hugh Britton are gonna try to get all the veterans together and throw the election to Otis Taff."

Elmer Reese was suffering. The hangover made him feel like his veins had collapsed and the blood couldn't get through, and his head throbbed like it had been pierced with the spike of a barbecue spit. He felt sick and weak and not at all like trying to humor Hoyt. If Hoyt didn't have something to worry about, he would scratch around until he found something to worry about. He just busybodied all over the place, and today Elmer Reese just wasn't up to it. As best he could, he tried to keep the irritability out of his voice.

"Now, Hoyt, you know damn well we don't have nothin' to worry about with Hugh Bentley, Hugh Britton, or Otis Taff winning."

Hoyt's face was always without expression, so people couldn't tell what he was thinking or how much something meant to him. The only index was the intensity in his eyes. He fastened them now on Elmer Reese.

"Likely not, but I don't want to hear it no more. So you get out there 'mongst the people and get busy. Start shaking hands and slapping backs, and, while you're at it, get Buddy to help you."

"Buddy?" Elmer Reese repeated absently, his mind already on going home to nurse his hangover.

Hoyt was losing patience. "Don't act like you don't know who the hell I'm talking about. Buddy, Buddy Jowers, your nephew, the one we got on the Phenix City police force. Remember?"

Elmer and his nephew, Buddy Jowers, looked like the long and the short of it. Elmer was a short, wasted man of forty who looked more like fifty with a hairline that had already receded to the top of his head, leaving his face looking gaunt and peeled behind the dark rimmed glasses that magnified his eyes.

Buddy was a big, strapping giant of a man with coarse features and an eight-inch cigar that never left the corner of his mouth. Even when he was having his picture taken, the cigar was hanging from his mouth. It had become so much a part of him, that without it, it would have seemed as though part of his face was missing.

Elmer Reese looked embarrassed and tugged his britches back up again. That had taken quite a bit, getting Buddy on the police force. Buddy had gone and gotten himself in trouble. He was convicted of running liquor and received a fine and a five-year probation. It was against the law for a convicted felon to hold public office, especially in law enforcement, and it took some doing to get it done, but after pleading with a federal judge to get the probation lifted, Buddy got the job. Elmer wasn't about to forget that. He opened his mouth to tell

41

Hoyt, but Hoyt cut him off.

"I tell you, Elmer, lay off them pills and get busy with that election."

≥•

It was as bitter and hard-fought a campaign as Phenix City had seen in a long time. Every where you looked there was Hugh Bentley and Hugh Britton attacking city government and county government, Mayor Homer Cobb and the City Council and Elmer Reese. They just never let up for a minute and when election day came, they appointed themselves and some hand-picked others to be "poll-watchers" to see to it that the ballots were cast according to the law.

Hugh Bentley said that a blind man had been led from precinct to precinct and had voted five times and Hugh Britton said the ballot boxes were being stuffed with tombstone votes, but nobody outside the newspapers took much notice and when the votes were counted, Elmer Reese had won reelection to his seat on the city council by better than a two to one margin.

"Come on, boys," Hoyt Shepherd told the precinct workers, "You've done your job. We're gonna have a victory celebration." "Yahoo!" came the loyal chorus. "Where we going?"

Hoyt swung his arm in round-up fashion. "Let's go belly up to the bar over at the Southern Manor night club. All the drinks are on me."

The throng of precinct workers sprang for their cars, shooting their guns in the air. "Yahoo! Let's go get liquored up."

≥•

At the Southern Manor night club, nineteen-year old hostess Jeannette Mercer, in a shimmering green dress and a matching green plume in her upswept red curls, slid off the bar stool and took up her station at the doorway to the high dice room as soon as she saw Hoyt Shepherd's party burst through the door and head for the bar. Watching them prop themselves in various attitudes of arrogance around the bar, she could tell it was going to be a rough night and likely trouble before the night was through. They were already liquored up from the election and back at the bar pouring down more. After that, the gambling and the fighting would begin.

Hoyt Shepherd, had gathered all his old cronies around: his brother, Grady, his partner, Jimmie Matthews, and his old mentor, Clyde Yarborough who had taken him under his wing to teach when he first arrived in Phenix City.

42

"Hey, Clyde," Hoyt grinned, leaning across the bar to tap Yarborough on the chest with the back of his hand. "How 'bout that election? Right out of the textbook, wasn't it?"

Yarborough, now an old man, devastated by cancer, returned a sunken smile. "I raised you from a pup, myself!"

"Come on boys," Hoyt said, giving his round-up signal again. "Get up to the bar and get yourself a drink."

"Then let's go get old Hugh Bentley and run him out of town," one of the poll workers said.

"Hell, he ain't going nowhere till we make him," was the reply. "Let's have another drink first. This here's ole Elmer's victory celebration, ain't it, Hoyt?"

Hoyt Shepherd, leaning heavily on the bar, smiled and sloshed his drink as he tried to take another sip. "Damn shore is. Elmer won it fair and square."

The company that had gathered round the bar burst out with a shout of laughter.

"How much did you say he beat him by, Hoyt?"

Hoyt drained his glass and set it down for the bartender to refill it again. "Hell, I lost count. Whatever it was ... they made sure he beat the T-mortal hell out of Bentley's man."

"Let's go get him," the cry came again. "Let's go get Bentley and run him out of town on a rail."

"Wait a while," Hoyt said. "Elmer Reese ain't here yet."

His eye glided around the restaurant taking in those having dinner at the tables and those in the high dice room in the back.

It was then that he saw Fate Leebern, his arch rival from across the river, sitting at a table with that baby-doll Beauty Queen from Columbus, all curves and curly blond hair and giggly smiles.

"Grady." Hoyt tossed his head toward the high dice room and Grady, accustomed to following his older brother's directions, got up to follow.

Jeannette Mercer, who had been watching it all from her station near the door, caught her breath as she saw them coming. Hoyt's dead-pan face told her nothing, but he took out a black .32 caliber pistol and a round roll of bills and laid them in the middle of the dice table. Peeling off a $20 bill, he handed it to Jeannette Mercer and said: "Go buy yourself a pair of nylons."

"I'm not allowed to leave, Mr. Shepherd. I'm supposed to stay right here in the high dice room."

"Go on and do what I told you," Hoyt said, thrusting the bill in her hand.

43

Jeannette Mercer looked anxiously at Grady. "What's this all about?"

Grady shook his head. "He's just drunk. He ain't gonna kill nobody ... but you'd better do what he said."

As Jeannette Mercer turned to find her purse, she heard Hoyt tell Otis Stewart, the floor manager: "You go on and get out of here, too."

Hoyt walked back out to Fate Leebern's table, put his hand on Fate's shoulder, and Fate got up and excused himself, leaving his young companion, Edna Roye, at the table to follow Hoyt to the high dice room.

With no other preliminaries, Hoyt picked up the gun from the high dice table, turned it on Fate and said: "It's about time you and I had a showdown. You've pushed me around long enough. I told you if I ever caught you on this side of the river, I'd kill you."

Terrified, Jeannette Mercer ran for the door, but it was too late. She heard the two shots fired, heard a body hit the floor, and pushed her way through the crush of people who rushed forward to see what had happened. Jeannette Mercer ran out the door into the street, through the dark, and disappeared, and Otis Stewart was never seen again.

Inside, the door remained closed to the high dice room. The crowd that had surged forward waited five or ten minutes, then Hoyt and Jimmie Matthews walked out and left while Grady stood in the doorway with his arms folded across his chest. "There's been some trouble," he announced. "Somebody call the police."

᠗

Hugh Bentley was standing on his porch in the dark saying a prayer when he heard the sirens going out. Earlier that evening, he had received a telephone tip from the Southern Manor. Like all the dark deeds in Phenix City, the caller made no identity, there was only a voice at the end of the line saying: "They're coming to get you, Hugh, to run you out of town on a rail. You'd better go before they get there."

Hugh knew they would and he decided to station himself on the porch and meet them there so that his family would not be involved.

Waiting in the dark, he trembled and turned his face toward heaven. "Lord, I'm afraid. I'm afraid for my family and I'm afraid for myself. Protect them, Lord, and send me some help and give me the courage to do what I've got to do."

The wail of the sirens jolted him from his prayer. *Sure to God they weren't sending the police to get him.* The sirens wafted their way to the porch on the night air with their closeness and their intensity. They seemed to be coming from all directions. Hugh Bentley held his breath and waited.

The telephone rang, and a moment later, Bernice had padded through the dark to the front porch. "Hugh ... Hugh ... come quick. Somebody's on the phone; there's been a killing down at the Southern Manor."

۶

Watching violence and its aftermath was spectator sport in Phenix City. The sirens had hardly been stilled when a crowd gathered and was pushing its way inside the Southern Manor night club to see what had happened.

When Hugh Bentley and Hugh Britton got to the Southern Manor the place was all chaos and confusion. Crowds were milling about inside the high dice room where the shooting had taken place and Edna Roye, Fate Leebern's young nineteen-year old companion, kept crying and carrying on until she was allowed to ride back to Columbus in the ambulance that had been sent for him.

"Miss Roye, he's dead," the ambulance attendant tried to tell her. "He was dead as soon as he took them two slugs. Ain't nothing you can do for him now."

"I'm not going to leave him," she cried. "I'm not going to leave him."

The ambulance driver settled her in beside the dead body in the back and took off for City Hospital in Columbus, radioing ahead to the Columbus authorities to contact Leebern's only son, Donald, and notify him that his father had been killed.

Nobody seemed to know exactly what had happened. When Phenix City Police Chief Pal Daniel and Russell County Sheriff Shannon Burch arrived, only Grady remained with Fate Leebern's body collapsed against the wall in two pools of blood. People were milling about, looking at the body, looking at the blood, and looking at Grady and Clyde Yarborough standing beside him. Deputy Sheriff Dewey Chestnut, the first officer on the scene, had pocketed the .32 caliber pistol that had killed Leebern and Grady would only say: "I shot him."

"How did it happen?" the police officers wanted to know. "I'd rather not say," Grady replied.

"Do you know where Hoyt and Jimmie Matthews went to?"

Grady shook his head and fell into a sullen, tight-lipped silence, refusing to answer any further questions.

Hugh Britton turned to whisper to Hugh Bentley and said: "People who were here when it happened say Hoyt's the one who shot him, that Hoyt's the one who took Fate off into the high dice room, and that Grady didn't have any quarrel with Fate, he's just doing what Hoyt told him to do."

"Sounds just like another one of Hoyt's fast shuffles," Hugh Bentley replied, darkly watching from the sidelines as Police Chief Pal Daniel led Grady off to his squad car. "I'll be interested to see what they come up with at the preliminary hearing. That's when they determine if the right person has been charged with the crime that was committed."

"There'll be some fancy legal footwork," Hugh Britton said, "You can count on that."

At the city jail, Grady was booked on suspicion of murder and then, for no given reason, he was transferred to the Russell County jail in the custody of Sheriff Shannon Burch. After that, only bits and pieces of information eked out.

It was first learned that the witnesses in the high dice room had disappeared. Jeannette Mercer's landlady said she had left without a word, and Otis Stewart, the high dice floor manager, was no where to be found, the newspapers piling up on his front porch, a testament to his absence.

In Columbus, Edna Roye was not available for comment either. When reporters asked for an interview, her father said: "Her nerves are just tore all to pieces and I can't get her out of bed. Besides," he added, "she's under orders not to say anything."

When asked, whose orders, her father replied: "The police department."

"The police department! Why the police department?" the reporters wanted to know.

Edna Roye's father closed the door and did not answer.

Phenix City, already reeling with the sensational news of Fate Leebern's slaying at Elmer Reese's victory celebration party, was further mystified when, early Tuesday evening, twenty hours after the slaying, Clyde Yarborough, the old gambler who had taught Hoyt Shepherd all the tricks of the racketeer trade, walked into Sheriff Shannon Burch's office and laid a two and one-half inch pocket knife on his desk.

"I want to turn this knife in to you," Yarborough said. "I was one of the first in the high dice room after the shooting and I found this knife about six to eight inches from Leebern's hand."

Shannon Burch, sitting behind his desk, was genuinely surprised. Pushing his hat to the back of his head, he said: "For God's sake, Clyde, why didn't you turn it in to the deputy when you found it?"

"I'd rather not say."

"Well, I think you'd better."

"There was just so much going on," Yarborough said, "I just picked it up and absent-mindedly put it in my pocket and forgot about it."

Shannon Burch scowled. "For twenty hours?"

Clyde Yarborough shrugged and walked out.

Grady then admitted to Deputy Sheriff Ralph Matthews that Leebern had gotten into an argument over politics with Hoyt and had knocked him to the floor, and when Grady went to Hoyt's defense, then Leebern came after Grady with the knife and slashed at him.

"That's when I shot him," Grady said, showing Ralph Matthews a small three-inch gash on his chest that barely cut the skin.

Police Chief Daniel, meanwhile, was still looking for Hoyt Shepherd and Jimmie Matthews who were the only two eye witnesses, but not until Wednesday, thirty-six hours after the crime had been committed, was he able to find them and set up a meeting. Chief Daniel refused to let the reporters accompany him, and afterwards would only say: "Hoyt and Jimmie said Grady shot Leebern in self-defense."

"That's just like them," Hugh Bentley told Hugh Britton, "they're going to make up the same old sorry story of self-defense."

"From what I hear," Hugh Britton said, "it's not even a superficial wound. It's barely a scratch and didn't draw a drop of blood."

"When has that ever mattered?" Hugh Bentley asked bitterly.

The next day, Grady, somber in dark trousers and a dark blue sports shirt, was escorted by three policemen to Recorder's Court in City Hall, for arraignment before Judge Ashby Floyd, who said solemnly:

"Grady Shepherd you are charged with the murder of Fayette Leebern."

Before Grady could answer, his attorney, Roy Smith, City Attorney for Phenix City, stepped forward and replied: "I speak for the defendant and we waive preliminary hearing."

"In that case, I will not ask that bond be fixed and that the defendant be committed to the County jail for the next session of the Grand Jury on September 30."

Standing in the back of the room, Hugh Bentley whispered to Hugh Britton: "Can you believe that! Grady didn't even plead. He's going to let it go to the Grand Jury."

Hugh Britton nodded. "With Hoyt's influence, they'll probably find the usual insufficient evidence."

"This is too big a case. It's not like he knocked off some punk that nobody knows or cares about. One of the big bulls has been killed. And more than that, one of the big bulls from across the river in Columbus. Fate had considerable political clout over there and had spent a good deal of time and money trying to replace the past with a new cloak of respectability."

"Yeah, did you see yesterday's editorial in the *Columbus Ledger*? They said Leebern would be the last to deny that he derived much of his wealth and power from early dealings in liquor and gambling but that in his later years he seemed to take his greatest pride in his numerous large and legitimate businesses."

Hugh Bentley, who owned and operated a big sporting goods store in Columbus, could speak with authority. "There's no doubt about it, he's a big bull over there in Columbus. You know he owns the Cardinal Hotel and has that big wholesale wine business, and I don't think they'll let this killing get swept under the rug as they usually do in Phenix City."

"Well, the editor rather pointedly ended his editorial by saying they *assumed* the Alabama courts would establish the circumstances of Leebern's death and fix responsibility for it."

"Fat chance in Phenix City," Hugh Bentley hooted derisively. While Grady Shepherd was being returned to jail without bond in Phenix City, Fayette Leebern was being buried with considerable celebrity across the river in Columbus with the Columbus Chief of Police and the Georgia Solicitor General among the active pallbearers and a city commissioner and a judge among the honorary pallbearers. More than 1500 people tried to crowd into the Oaklawn Chapel to attend the funeral services for Fayette Leebern with the overflow standing out on the lawn. When the services were over, 175 cars formed the funeral procession, followed by five truckloads of flowers where another seventy-five cars were waiting in the cemetery.

Among those attending the funeral was Leebern's young companion, Edna Roye, who had accompanied him to the Southern Manor night club on the night he was shot. In response to reporters questions, she said: "Mr. Leebern had no premonition that he was in danger. He thought he was among friends."

After almost a week had passed since the shooting in Phenix City and the efforts of the police and sheriff's department had made little progress in their investigation, the *Columbus Ledger*, in a Sunday editorial, capsulated what people on both sides of the river were saying about Russell County and Phenix City's careless police procedure in investigating the case.

Why, they asked, did Clyde Yarborough remove the knife from the scene and turn it in 20 hours later when this could be vital evidence? Such an act would normally be considered interference with justice.

Why did it take Phenix City Police Chief Pal Daniel almost two days to find material witnesses, Hoyt Shepherd and Jimmie Matthews? Why weren't they arrested at once and held if necessary, since this was standard police procedure?

Why weren't fingerprints taken from the .32 caliber revolver that killed Fayette Leebern?

And why weren't paraffin casts made – of Grady Shepherd's hand and the hand of anyone else known to be in that room – since such casts, taken promptly, can tell unmistakably who fired the gun?

"It is the sworn duty," the *Ledger* reminded its readers, "imposed on the police, the sheriff's office, and the prosecuting attorneys to develop *the whole truth* to prove guilt or innocence without the aid of purported 'confessions'."

The next day, after a conference between Circuit Solicitor A. S. Borders and Sheriff Shannon Burch, exactly one week after the shooting, Hoyt and Jimmie Matthews were both arrested, charged with murder, and put in the same cell with Grady in the Russell County jail.

For his defense, Hoyt hired every lawyer in town: Roy Smith, the City Attorney who was also representing Grady, Jabe Brassell, William Belcher, Julius B. Hicks, Arch Ferrell, and Albert Patterson, and from Opelika, Jabe Walker.

When Hugh Bentley heard this, he went right down to the Coulter Building in Phenix City to see Albert Patterson in his office.

"I can't believe you would take on the defense of so notorious a racketeer as Hoyt Shepherd. Hoyt and his kind are what have ruined our city already."

Albert Patterson smoothed his silver hair back with one hand and pushed back in his swivel chair, resting his lame right leg on an opened drawer in his desk.

"Let me tell you something, Hugh," he said, looking over the metal rims of his glasses with dark, grave eyes, "I believe, and always have, that everyone has the right to the best defense he can hire when brought before the bar of justice. The law presumes every man innocent until proved guilty, no matter what his reputation may be."

"Hoyt and his kind are what have ruined our city and the future for our children. They aren't going to have a chance growing up with corruption like this, and if men like you, respected and admired, take on the criminal causes ... "

"Hugh, they have hired my services, not bought my soul."

"Yeah, but if the best we have, represent the worst we have, then those of us seeking justice don't have a chance."

"The State has two very able men for the prosecution of this case: Circuit Solicitor A.S. Borders and Russell County Solicitor H. A. Ferrell.

I don't think they will encounter anything they can't handle."

Only two days after Hoyt and Jimmie Matthews' arrest, Patterson, as their chief strategist, requested a preliminary hearing and Circuit Solicitor A.S. Borders, solicitor for the four-county circuit that included Russell County who would try the case was very upset. With a case of this magnitude, to call for a preliminary hearing before the State witnesses could be located and evidence could be gathered was unheard of in his Third Judicial District. It was a legal maneuver to force the State, unprepared and appearing inept, into a hearing before Jeannette Mercer and Otis Stewart, missing since the night of the murder, could be found and questioned.

At the preliminary hearing for Hoyt Shepherd and Jimmie Matthews, before Russell County Judge H. E. Randall, on Thursday, 26 September, Solicitor Borders protested vehemently.

In the courtroom, jammed with 700 spectators who had come to watch the proceedings, Solicitor Borders rose and, in a voice edged with bitterness began: "I doubt that there is a person in this courtroom who expected the State to be ready today ... they won't be disappointed."

"A week ago today, I learned for the first time about this homicide. I read it in public print. I came to Phenix City on Monday of this week to begin an investigation. My local associate, Russell County Solicitor H. A. Ferrell, was not advised by anybody for four or five days."

Solicitor Ferrell interrupted: "I haven't been notified yet."

Solicitor Borders nodded an acknowledgments and continued laying his case before the court. "It has been utterly, absolutely and humanly impossible to prepare the State's case. I was only officially notified of this case day before yesterday. My local associate, Russell County Solicitor H.A. Ferrell, has not been served yet. The State has pending investigations and witnesses who are not here, and I request that the defendants be held and a continuance granted until the Grand Jury meets on Monday of next week."

Without waiting for Judge Randall's reply, Roy Smith, Hoyt Shepherd's head defense counsel intervened: "Under the constitution of this state these two defendants are entitled to a speedy preliminary hearing to decide whether or not bond will be granted."

"Speedy?" Solicitor Borders shot back, "this is a stampede."

Appealing to Judge Randall, Solicitor Borders, referring to the editorial in the *Columbus Ledger*, said: "Phenix City has already received a great deal of unfavorable publicity about the conduct of this case, and I cannot believe that an unbiased judge seeking to do justice for the State of Alabama would take any action to lend basis to such reports. Does your Honor know of *anyone* ... ever before ... who forced the State to rush into a preliminary hearing two days after the arrests were made?"

Roy Smith was quick to answer: "We take the position that the warrants were sworn out before the Solicitor knew whether he had a case or not and that the State is holding Hoyt Shepherd and Jimmie Matthews under a charge of murder as material witnesses."

Solicitor Borders' face was stiff with rage. In a measured, deliberately controlled tone, he replied: "They were arrested on the basis of facts divulged to me by two witnesses who are not here today, but who I have reason to believe will appear, and I ask again for a continuance until these witnesses are available and the State has completed its investigation."

Judge Randall, exercising the power of the lower court judge chose to ignore Solicitor Border's urgent plea for a continuance and said: "I'm going to assess bond in this case at $7500 each."

Solicitor Borders stuffed his papers back in his briefcase and left the courtroom. Within the hour, Hoyt Shepherd and Jimmie Matthews were released and free on bond.

Not since the collapse of the Ritz Cafe in 1938 when 81 people were killed had the Phenix City been so captivated by a calamity. On every street corner, in every cafe, at every dinner table, the only topic of conversation since the night of the murder of Fate Leebern was what kind of Houdini act Hoyt would pull to get out of this one. The prosecution had already lost the first round in the legal jousting at the preliminary hearing with Judge Randall's decision to release Hoyt and Jimmie Matthews on bond.

"The State's not going to stand by and let them ramrod this through the courts," Hugh Bentley told Hugh Britton as they left the preliminary hearing with the throng of spectators who had come to watch the proceedings.

"I expect they'll up the ante," Hugh Britton replied.

The next day, Donald Leebern announced that he had hired legal lion Roderick Beddow, of Birmingham, and Atlanta's expert Fulton County Solicitor, E. E. Andrews, to assist in the prosecution of Hoyt and Grady Shepherd for the murder of his father. The first step was a permit to exhume Fayette Leebern so that an official autopsy could be performed.

"Have you seen this?" Hugh Britton said, tossing the newspaper over for Hugh Bentley to see. "Fate Leebern's only been buried for a week and now they're going to dig him back up again."

Hugh Bentley nodded his head. "I told you they weren't going to let this thing pass without a fight."

51

Meanwhile, reports of threats and intimidation of witnesses who were to appear before the Grand Jury had reached the chambers of Judge Sterling Williams, circuit court judge for the Third Judicial District of Barbour, Bullock, Dale, and Russell County. Judge Williams had been on the bench for a long time and his character was all his name implied. From a long line of distinguished forebears who had settled Alabama, fought for the Confederacy, and contributed measurably to the growth of the State, he was a seasoned jurist, appointed circuit judge in 1915 and had served Russell County for more than thirty years.

Concerned by the rumors he had heard, he carefully prepared his charge to the Russell County Grand Jury and when it met on Monday, September 30, to begin its investigation of the crimes on the docket, he made his position plain to the eighteen men who had been chosen as Grand Jurors:

"I have a genuine affection for the people of Russell County," Judge Williams told the members of the Grand Jury, "but I come to Phenix City this morning heavy-hearted. We have registered on our docket nineteen capital felonies and that is a slur on the reputation of Phenix City."

"These crimes on the docket are entitled to full consideration of this grand jury. Take as much time as you need. Review each case thoroughly and don't let any personal reasons influence you."

Without citing the Shepherd case, Judge Williams said: "Most especially of late, there have been reports of a concerted effort to undertake to influence the grand jury and terrorize and keep witnesses from telling what they have an infinite right to tell. This thing about threatening a jury, a grand jury, will not be tolerated."

"I assumed office as Circuit Judge for Russell County thirty-one years ago and decided then to do my job in keeping with the dictates of my own conscience, irrespective of persons or conditions that might arise. I *have* never and *will* never surrender myself to any group that seeks to violate the law."

"We are going to enforce the laws of the land irrespective of the character or standing of any person here or anywhere else. If you go into the grand jury room and undertake your own personal inclinations, you have simply violated the oath of office. I charge you to investigate all the crimes and bring indictments that you deem necessary. Don't let anybody escape for personal reasons." Judge Williams said again. "The solicitor and the court officers will be ready to assist you if necessary. I want to see that the people of Russell County get the proper service."

By Tuesday afternoon the case of Grady and Hoyt Shepherd and his partner, Jimmie Matthews, was brought before the Grand Jury.

Even though the Grand Jury met in secret and only they heard the testimony of witnesses, a crowd had gathered at the courthouse to count and watch the number of witnesses, waiting to see if Jeannette Mercer and Otis Stewart, the key witnesses who had been missing since the night of the murder, would appear.

By late afternoon twenty-three witnesses including the arresting officers had come forward to testify and then at the last, Jeannette Mercer surrounded and escorted by the attorneys retained as special counsel by Donald Leebern hurried her through the crowd into the grand jury room. Outside, the whispers were that Jeannette Mercer had been kept hidden for safekeeping, but Otis Stewart, the other key witness scheduled to testify, had still not been found. Two hours after Jeannette Mercer gave her testimony, the Grand Jury returned an indictment. Hoyt and Grady Shepherd were charged with first degree murder in the death of Fayette Leebern. Jimmie Matthews was not mentioned nor was he indicted. On the courthouse steps, a stir of surprise ran through the crowd that had waited all afternoon. No matter what had happened, with Hoyt Shepherd being who he was, few had expected the Grand Jury to return an indictment and on the courthouse steps wagers were being made and bets were being taken on whether the case would ever come to trial. But three days later, on Friday, October 4, when Hoyt and Grady were arraigned before Judge Sterling Williams, severance was granted and the State chose to try Hoyt Shepherd first, with Judge Williams setting trial to begin four days later on Tuesday, October 8.

"An indictment is one thing," Hugh Bentley told Hugh Britton, "but a conviction is something else. If I were a betting man I wouldn't put a penny on it."

"I hear the State's got a pretty tight case and Solicitor Borders is determined to do everything he can."

"So am I," Hugh Bentley said. "If he needs a character witness to testify against Hoyt, I'm going to volunteer."

"Good idea," Hugh Britton agreed. "I will too."

4

The Fate Leebern Murder Trial

Hugh Bentley and Hugh Britton were sequestered with the other State witnesses on Tuesday morning as seven hundred people packed the Russell County courtroom to watch the beginning of the trial of Hoyt Shepherd. Hoyt, cool, aloof, detached, immaculately dressed in a conservative blue suit, strode into court with the seven attorneys who had prepared his defense: City Attorney Roy Smith, Jabe Brassell, Julius B. Hicks, William Belcher, Arch Ferrell, Albert Patterson, and Jake Walker.

Waiting for them at the prosecution table were the seven attorneys who would present the State's case: Circuit Solicitor A.S. Borders, Russell County Solicitor H. A. Ferrell, and the five attorneys retained by Donald Leebern to assist in the prosecution: Roderick Beddow, of Birmingham, Fulton County Solicitor E. E. Andrews of Atlanta, Lawrence Andrews, of Union Springs, Alabama, and Columbus attorneys Joe Ray and Hubert Calhoun.

Directly behind the prosecution's crowded table in the first row of the courtroom, Donald Leebern, his wife, and his mother, the divorced wife of Fayette Leebern, took their seats to watch the proceedings.

The battle lines were drawn. The burden was on the State to prove that Hoyt Shepherd was guilty of the murder charge against him. His brother Grady Shepherd, having already admitted that he shot Leebern, was prepared to tell the jury a story of self-defense when Leebern, he said, came on him with a two and one-half inch pocket knife and slashed him, cutting both flesh and the pocket of his shirt. To refute the story of the knife and lay the foundation for the prosecution, Solicitor Borders called witnesses to tell the jury what they saw, what they found, and what they heard.

Trial began with the State's first witness, W. C. Weaver, the Columbus ambulance attendant who had removed Fayette Leebern's bullet-ridden body from the Southern Manor night club. When he arrived, he said, he found Leebern had been struck by two bullets and was lying slumped against the wall on the floor.

"Was there anything in either of Mr. Leebern's hands?" Solicitor Borders asked.

"No, sir," Weaver replied.

"Was there anything near the body?"

"No, sir."

Dr. C. J. Rehling, the respected State toxicologist, who had exhumed the body for autopsy on September 27, was brought to the witness stand to give his indisputable evidence. Solicitor Borders said: "Dr. Rehling, would you tell the jury what your findings were."

Dr. Rehling nodded and began. "Upon examination of the body, there was external violence in only two wounds. One was just about four inches below the shoulder, the other, three inches lower and a little forward of the first."

"A dissection of the body showed that the upper wound was that of a bullet that had entered the body there, struck a bone, curved downward, entering the chest between the third and fourth ribs and going downward through the liver and kidney."

"The second bullet entered the arm, came into the chest and penetrated the lung, shattering the eighth rib just four inches from the backbone. There was excessive hemorrhage in the lung. I dissected the neck and upper chest regions found no evidence of injury otherwise. Both bullets ranged decidedly downward in the body," Dr. Rehling told the court.

Solicitor Borders then asked: "From your examination and your experience, can you say what was the position of the right arm when the bullets were fired?"

"Yes, the arm would have had to be raised in a somewhat vertical position," Dr. Rehling replied, lifting his arm to illustrate a position that suggested a hand held shielding the body.

"It is your judgment that both bullets were fired from the same gun?"

"Yes."

"Were there powder burns on the body?" Solicitor Borders asked to establish the distance at which Grady had fired the gun and if, in fact, Leebern could have been close enough to use the alleged knife for attack when fired upon.

"No, there were not. I procured cartridges of the same size, type, and manufacture as the two .32 caliber cases given to me by Sheriff Shannon Burch to determine the distance at which a weapon of this kind would produce powder burns."

"I took the gun and fired it through white cardboard at two inch intervals ranging up to twelve inches. At two inches, the cardboard carried a distinct powder burn, at six inches the burns disappeared."

"I took the clothing, worn by Mr. Leebern and given to me by the sheriff and examined it microscopically. I was unable to find any powder burns. I examined it for unburned powder fragments. I could see none. Later, I took a scapula and scraped around the two holes for nitrates and nitrites, the substances formed when a bullet is fired. I found evidence of both. From this, I came to the conclusion that the weapon was at least a foot away from the clothes when it was fired."

Picking up the two and one-half inch pocket knife, which Clyde Yarborough had claimed he found six inches from Leebern's hand on the night of the murder and which Grady had claimed Leebern had cut him with, Solicitor Borders entered it as evidence and asked Dr. Rehling: "Did you find blood stains on this knife?"

"I was unable to find any evidence of blood stains," Dr. Relhing replied. "I also examined it for cloth, but the only thing I found were a few short cotton fibers. They were no more than would be found normally on a knife that had been carried in the pocket."

Lt. William Skytta, from the Airborne School at Fort Benning, had been at the Southern Manor on the night of the shooting seated two tables away from the door to the high dice room. On the witness stand, he said he saw four men enter the high dice room, heard the shots and saw three men come out.

"Did you go into the high dice room after the shooting?"

"Yes, sir."

"Was there anybody in the high dice room?"

"Nobody except the dead man."

"Did you see anything lying on the floor near the body in the way of a knife, gun or other weapon?"

"No, sir."

"Did any of the three men you saw leaving the high dice room have any kind of a cut, bruise, abrasion, a cut shirt or other evidence of injury?"

"Not that I could see," Lt. Skytta replied.

Turning to police procedure and investigation, Solicitor Borders called Phenix City Police Chief Pal Daniel to the stand. "Officer Dewey Chestnut was the first policeman on the scene," Pal Daniel explained, "when I arrived at the Southern Manor, Leebern's body had been removed and Hoyt Shepherd and Jimmie Matthews had already left."

"Did you make a thorough and diligent effort to locate these two eye-witnesses after the shooting on Monday night?"

"I did."

"When did you locate him?"

"Wednesday."

"And how long was this after the shooting?"

"Approximately thirty-six hours."

When Sheriff Shannon Burch was called to testify, he identified the two and one-half inch pocket knife which Clyde Yarborough had said he found near Leebern's hand shortly after the shooting.

"Did you see Clyde Yarborough at the Southern Manor on the night of the shooting?"

"Yes, sir."

"How long have you known Clyde Yarborough?"

"Twelve years."

"He knows you as the sheriff of Russell County?"

"I would imagine so."

"Did Clyde Yarborough say anything to you about this knife on the night of the murder?"

"No."

"When did Clyde Yarborough turn this knife over to you?" Solicitor Borders asked.

"The next day," Shannon Burch replied, "approximately twenty hours after the shooting."

The spectators who had come to the courthouse to hear the details of the shooting, had stayed in their seats through the noon recess for fear of losing them to the crowd that waited in the courthouse corridor. They had grown restless with the morning's meticulous details, but when afternoon came, their interest revived as the State called Edna Roye, Leebern's young companion, who had gone with him to the Southern Manor on the night of the shooting, followed by the State's key witness, nineteen-year old Jeannette Mercer. Responding to Solicitor Borders' questions, she told the jury that Hoyt had come into the high dice room, put a pistol on the table, had given her a $20 bill and told her to leave.

"When I asked Grady Shepherd what this was all about, he said: 'Hoyt's just drunk. He's not going to shoot anybody', but when Mr. Leebern came in, Mr. Shepherd cursed him and said: 'I told you if you ever came across the river I would kill you'."

"What did you do then?" Solicitor Borders asked.

"I turned to run and heard the shots and then I heard the body fall."

"Was Mr. Leebern doing anything to threaten anyone?" Solicitor Borders asked.

"No."

Walking to the defense table, Solicitor Borders said: "Your witness."

Jake Walker, skilled in cross-examination, shared chief co-counsel for defense with Roy Smith. To discredit her damaging eye-witness account, the Defense had designed questions to attack her character and integrity and were prepared to call witnesses to swear that she was not in or near the high dice room when the shots were fired. Fastening accusing eyes on Jeannette Mercer, he walked purposefully to the witness box.

"You say you heard Hoyt Shepherd curse Fayette Leebern."

"Yes, sir."

"What did he say?"

"He called him some names."

"What names?"

Embarrassed by the foul language she had heard Hoyt use, Jeannette Mercer looked out at the crowded courtroom and down at her hands twisted in her lap.

"Speak up, girl. Tell the jury what you heard."

Seeing her anguish, Judge Williams said gently, "You must repeat the words you heard said."

Jeannette Mercer drew in a deep breath, raised her head, and repeated the profanity and the obscenity that Hoyt Shepherd had used.

"You appeared before the Grand Jury on October the first, where did you go after that?"

"I went to the Cardinal Hotel in Columbus."

"You know, of course, that Mr. Leebern owned that hotel, or his son, Donald, does."

Jeannette Mercer did not answer.

Jake Walker raked Jeannette Mercer with a look that became a leer. "Who bought you that new suit you've got on there?"

"Cecil Lloyd."

"You sure it wasn't Mr. Leebern?"

"Yes."

Jake Walker gave a half-smile out of the side of his mouth. "I have no more questions. The witness may step down."

With the end of Jeannette Mercer's testimony, Solicitor Borders rose and said: "The State rests its case."

Immediately, the Defense called four character witnesses to impeach Jeannette Mercer's testimony. Two members of the Phenix City police force and two former policemen from Jeanette Mercer's home town in Dothan, Alabama, each testified that she was a woman of bad reputation and could not be believed under oath in a court of law.

Under cross examination, Beddow asked Lee B. Ray, the first witness: "Have you ever visited Mrs. Mercer at the Manhattan Inn?"

Ray grinned. "I've raided it several times."

"I didn't ask you that," Beddow snapped. "Have you ever visited her?"

"No, sir."

"You are a good friend of Grady Shepherd, aren't you?"

"I expect everybody to be a friend," Ray smiled.

"The truth is, you've been acquainted with both Hoyt and Grady Shepherd for a long time, haven't you?"

Lee B. Ray hesitated.

"Answer the question," Beddow demanded. "Yes or no?"

"Yes," Ray admitted.

"Step down," Beddow told him. "I have no more questions of this witness."

Continuing his effort to impeach Jeannette Mercer's testimony, Roy Smith called defense witness Robert Freeman, father of the owner of Southern Manor, who claimed that Hoyt Shepherd was not even in the room immediately preceding the shooting and that Jeannette Mercer had left the high dice room some time before with the comment: "Let's get out of here, there's going to be an argument."

After introducing a diagram of the floor plan at Southern Manor, Roy Smith then began calling defense witnesses who were members of the celebration party, each of whom testified that Jeannette Mercer was outside the high dice room minutes before the shots were fired, but under cross examination by Beddow, each contradicted with conflicting testimony on the time and exact spot where she was standing when the shots were fired.

Beddow's exacting and tenacious cross examination had wearied the spectators and worn the jury, and after a court session of more than ten hours, Judge Williams at 6:45 P.M., looked at the clock on the courtroom wall and said, "It's been a long day and the jury is beginning to look tired. Court is adjourned until 8:30 in the morning."

On the third day of trial, when Grady Shepherd was called as the first defense witness, Judge Williams began his instructions by telling Grady that he could refuse to testify since he was also charged with murder in the case.

Unlike Hoyt, who was closely watching the proceedings with a stolid, stone face that showed no emotion or reaction to anything around him, Grady was more volatile, quick to smile and quick to frown, quick to react to the questions put to him.

"I'll tell whatever I can," Grady smiled engagingly and began his own version of what happened at the victory celebration party at the Southern Manor the night Leebern was killed. He said he had seen

Leebern seated at a table with a young girl, walked by and spoke to him, and then entered the high dice room.

Roy Smith, the Defense attorney handling direct examination asked: "Did Hoyt come into that room?"

"Yes, sir."

"Did he lay a pistol on that table when he came in?"

"No sir, I didn't see my brother with no gun."

Shortly after Hoyt entered the room, Grady said, Leebern came in and said: "Hoyt, you are double crossing me about politics in Columbus and I don't like it at all." At that point, Grady testified that Jimmie Matthews came in and said: "Mr. Leebern please don't start nothing."

"What did Leebern do?"

"He knocked Jimmie Matthews up against the wall and then he ran his hand in his pocket and knocked my brother to his knees. Then he started advancing on me, slashing at me with his pocket knife. I told him to stop, and when he didn't, I fired twice."

Picking up the brown sports shirt Grady had worn on the night of the murder and the bottle of nose drops that were in the shirt pocket, Roy Smith asked:

"Can you identify these two items?"

"Yes, sir, that's the shirt I was wearing when Mr. Leebern cut me and the nose drops I had in my pocket. I'd been have breathing problems."

Turning to Roderick Beddow for cross-examination, Roy Smith said: "Your witness."

Beddow crossed the room like a gladiator ready for battle.

"What was your business on or before September 16?" he asked Grady.

"I was a gambler."

"Were you one of the owners and operators of the Bama Club?"

"I had a third interest."

"Were you in partnership with Hoyt Shepherd and Jimmie Matthews?"

"Yes, sir."

"How was it that you had a pistol in your pocket on the night Fayette Leebern was killed at the victory celebration for Elmer Reese at the Southern Manor night club?"

"I took it out of my glove compartment when I lent my car to a man to drive to Atlanta that night."

"How did you come into possession of this pistol?"

"I bought it from a man named James Bush."

"Did you know it had been stolen from a taxi cab parked in front of the Bama Club?"

"No, sir."

Taking the knife that Yarborough had said he found near Leebern's body, Beddow handed it to Grady: "Can you identify this knife?"

"Yes, sir. That's the knife Mr. Leebern attacked me with."

"Now, Grady, you have told the court that Leebern followed Hoyt into the high dice room and accused him of double crossing him in Columbus politics."

"Yes, sir."

"And that Jimmie Matthews came in and said: 'Mr. Leebern please don't start nothing'."

"Yes, sir."

"And that Leebern then shoved Jimmie Matthews against the wall."

"Yes, sir."

"How far did he shove him?"

"I couldn't say."

"What was the next thing that was done?"

"Mr. Leebern put his right hand in his right pocket."

"What did you do?"

"I got up and started toward them. That's when he knocked my brother to his knees and I went over and got Leebern by his left shoulder and swung him around."

"When did he open the knife?"

"He had to do it when I swung him around."

Beddow turned an aghast face to the jury and then back to Grady. "Do you mean to tell the gentlemen of this jury that he opened the knife while in motion when you were swinging him around?"

"He had to."

"How many times did he cut at you?"

"I think it was three times."

"When did you get the pistol out?"

"While he was advancing on me."

"How many times had he cut at you with this two and one-half inch pocket knife when you got your pistol out?"

"I couldn't say."

"How far was Leebern from you when you fired the first shot?"

"He was in motion. I couldn't say."

Roderick Beddow raised his great bushy eyebrows and looked down skeptically at the pocket knife he held in his hand. "It's hard for me and this jury to understand how a man in motion, being whirled around could have had the opportunity or the time to open a knife like this and use it as a deadly weapon in the time span you have describ-

ed. So that we can better understand, I would like to have a reenact-
ment of the action you have testified to."

Beddow walked over and picked up the pistol, entered in evidence
as the murder weapon, and handed it to Grady. Slipping the pocket
knife into his own pocket, he told Grady:

"Now, you put the pistol in your pocket. I will take the part of
Leebern with the knife, and as you describe the action, we will reenact
what you say happened."

Following Grady's directions, Beddow crouched with the knife,
while Grady stood beside the witness stand with the gun. When the
demonstration was done, it was clear to the court and the jury that
Leebern could not have had the opportunity or the time to open the
blade of a two and one-half inch pocket knife in the instant that it took
for Grady to whirl him around. Satisfied that the point had been taken,
Beddow took the tattered brown shirt with the slashes across the pocket
that Grady was wearing on the night of the murder.

"Now, Grady, put on this shirt and show the jury where Fayette
Leebern slashed you with his pocket knife."

When Grady put on the shirt and stood before the jury, Beddow let a
silence fall for the absurdity sink in. Then, turning to Judge Williams
he said: "I have no further questions for this witness."

To support Grady's claim, Leon Reese, a member of the party at
Southern Manor and brother of Elmer Reese, told the court that he saw
two or three cuts on Grady's shirt when he came out of the high dice
room. Under cross examination, Beddow asked: "Who was the first
person who questioned you about this case?"

"The lawyers."

"You were never interviewed by the police officers?"

"No, sir."

"You say you saw cuts on Grady's shirt. Did you see any blood?"

"No, sir."

Following Leon Reese on the stand, Defense Attorney Roy Smith
called Deputy Sheriff J.D. Harris who testified on the stand that contrary
to Police Chief Pal Daniel's testimony, that Hoyt Shepherd had come to
the Russell County jail on Tuesday, the day following the murder to
visit his brother and at that time, Harris said, he noticed that Grady had
a scratch on his chest and Hoyt had a bruised knee.

"Do you mean to tell this court," Beddow asked on cross-examination, "that all the time Chief of Police Daniel was out looking for and
unable to find Hoyt and his partner, that Hoyt was right there in the
county jail visiting his brother?"

Without blinking, J. D. Harris, his face a thin, narrow mask. replied:

"Yes, sir."

"You're sure?"

"I saw it with my own eyes," Harris said.

Beddow shook his head and said: "Step down."

Clyde Yarborough, called as a defense witness, came to the stand with a handkerchief held to the side of his face, shielding what the press called "a facial disorder," a cancer that had left him with no jaw or tongue. In response to the questions, his muffled replies had to be interpreted and transmitted to the jury by defense counsel Jake Walker.

Despite this difficulty, Yarborough told the court that he was on his way into the high dice room with Hoyt Shepherd and Jimmie Matthews when he was stopped by another guest at the party. As he stood there talking, he heard the shots. Going into the high dice room, Yarborough said, he stooped over Leebern and noticed a knife about six to eight inches from his hand. He pocketed the knife and later turned it over to Sheriff Shannon Burch and Ralph Matthews.

Roderick Beddow, on cross-examination for the State asked:

"You saw no reason for turning over the knife, you said you found, to the authorities on the night of the murder?"

"A lot was going on at the time," Yarborough said, "and I just carelessly slipped it in my pocket and didn't remember it until the next day."

Beddow bit his lower lip and nodded.

"Actually, your business is the old reliable policy ... the lottery known locally as the Bug, isn't it?"

"Partly."

"How long have you been in the Bug business?"

"About ten years."

"And Hoyt Shepherd was one of you partners?"

"Yes."

"You had another partner named Jimmie Matthews?"

"Yes."

"You and Hoyt contributed to a fund to reelect a certain commissioner in this town, didn't you?"

"No."

"Did Hoyt?"

"Not that I know of."

"When the shots were fired did you see anyone come out of the high dice room?"

"I saw Hoyt and Jimmie Matthews leave."

"What about Jeanette Mercer?"

"She had left several minutes before."

"You are sure of that?"

"Yes."

"Where was Grady?"

"He stood in the door of the high dice room and said, 'Somebody call the police'."

"Were you and Hoyt, immediately prior to this date, paying protection money to officers?"

"No, sir."

"You deny that?"

"Yes, sir."

"Did you see a single officer take names and addresses of a single person who was there?"

"No, sir."

"As a matter of fact, you know that Jimmie Matthews held the door of that room while Hoyt and Grady had a conference to decide who would claim that he shot Leebern."

"I don't know about that."

"Don't you know it's a fact that Hoyt told Grady Shepherd that he had more money and influence than Grady did and for Grady to take the rap and he would foot the bill?"

"No sir, I don't know about that."

Police Officer Dewey Chestnut, called to the stand as a defense witness said that when he arrived on the scene, he noticed that Grady's shirt was cut or torn and on later examination saw a cut "a little bigger than a pin scratch." "After Grady's arrest," Dewey said, "I took a small medicine bottle from Grady's shirt pocket, but the bottle was not mutilated nor was the label scratched."

Beddow, approaching Dewey Chestnut on the stand, asked: "How long have you been a police officer?"

"Seventeen or eighteen months."

"You know anything about fingerprints?"

"No sir."

"You do know fingerprints can be made?"

"Yes, sir."

"Did you handle the gun?"

"Yes, sir."

"Did you wrap it in a handkerchief or did you handle it with your bare hands?"

"With my bare hands," Dewey Chestnut replied.

Roderick Beddow shook his head in gravest disgust. "Step down."

The spectators in the courtroom had sat through three days of testimony just so they could hear first-hand what Hoyt Shepherd would say when he was called to the stand to testify in his own defense, but when Dewey Chestnut finished his testimony and cross-examination, Roy Smith told Judge Williams: "The defense rests."

For Hoyt not to even testify in his own defense was a shock and a surprise to those who had waited and endured hours of testimony, and a murmur of disappointment swept through the courtroom. Judge Williams, guarding the decorum of his court, smashed his gavel down and gave a warning look to the crowd.

"Are there rebuttal witnesses for the State?" he asked.

"Yes, sir." Solicitor Borders replied, "I call Wesley Claridy to the stand."

Wesley Claridy, a long-time employee of Fayette Leebern, was sworn, and Solicitor Borders asked: "Have you ever seen Mr. Leebern with a pocket knife?"

"Yes," Claridy answered.

Showing Claridy two knives, one introduced by the prosecution and another introduced by the defense, Solicitor Borders asked: "Can you identify which knife belonged to Mr. Leebern?"

"Yes, sir," Claridy said, pointing to the knife introduced by the State.

"What about this knife?" Borders asked, showing him the one introduced by the defense.

"I have never seen Mr. Leebern with that knife."

Following Claridy's testimony, Hugh Bentley, at last, was called to the witness stand and sworn.

"You are interested in good, clean and decent government, aren't you?"

"Yes, sir."

"And you, Hugh Britton, John Luttrell, and Charlie Gunter are among several men who belong to an organization called the Better Government League?"

"Yes, sir."

"You were very active in the Phenix City political election on the day of September 16, weren't you?"

"As an individual I was."

"You actively supported Otis Taff who was the candidate who was defeated?"

"Yes, sir."

"And Grady Shepherd supported Elmer Reese who was elected."

"Yes, sir."

"How long have you known Grady Shepherd?"

"More than fifteen years."

"And how is he regarded in this community?"

"Grady Shepherd is a man of bad reputation," Hugh Bentley replied, "and is not to be believed under oath in a court of law."

"Do you know Clyde Yarborough and how he is regarded in this community?"

"Yes, I've known Clyde Yarborough all my life. He is a man of bad reputation and not to be believed under oath in a court of law."

Hugh Britton, John Luttrell, and Charlie Gunter followed Hugh Bentley on the witness stand, each testifying that Grady Shepherd and Clyde Yarborough were men of bad reputation and not to be believed under oath.

When the afternoon session began, Judge Williams announced that closing arguments would be heard with attorneys on each side limited to three hours and three arguments.

Fulton County Solicitor E. E. Andrews began the State's closing argument by summarizing the testimony put before the jury.

"It was the most comical thing in the world," Andrews said, "to see those defense witnesses trying to get Jeanette Mercer as far away as possible when those shots were fired. None of them could tell you where their close friends were or anybody else, but everyone knew just where Jeanette was, although almost everyone of them placed her in a different position when the shots were fired."

"Jeanette Mercer will not profit from the verdict of you gentlemen. She has no reason on earth to come in here and testify to something that is not true. The defendant's brother, Grady Shepherd, on the other hand has every reason in the world to lie ... his life is at stake."

Roy Smith, the City Attorney for Phenix City was the first to close for the defense. Standing before the townspeople he served, he gestured with an outstretched hand toward the counsel for the State.

"I don't compare," he told the jury with feint praise, "with the experience and ability of the State's counsel, many of whom are considered the best in this part of the country."

"They can make their pleas as flowery as possible, but I intend to talk to you in a conversational tone and try to stick to the issues involved."

Centering his attack on Jeannette Mercer, Smith said: "The conspiracy that the State claims is based on one person only ... on Jeannette Mercer. As I recall, every other witness testified that she was outside that room when those shots were fired."

"Why did she have to flee from the State of Alabama, to be brought into the jurisdiction of the police of this city and county on the day of the trial if she was going to tell you the truth?"

"We think the weakness of her statement was its boldness, the way she used foul language before a packed court."

Roy Smith waited for the implication of a foul-mouthed woman to set in and then added, "It's a strange thing that in this case, that Jeannette Mercer, the only material witness for the State, was wearing a dress she said was bought for her by a man named Cecil Lloyd and that she was living in the Cardinal Hotel, owned by Fayette Leebern, before she came to this trial."

Roy Smith paused to let the implications pile up, then shrugged his shoulders and turned his attention to the allegations made against the police department.

"There've been some insinuations in this case that the State didn't have the cooperation of the police officers of Phenix City. I'd like to know where the investigation of this case began. It wasn't in the sheriff's office of Russell County ... the investigation was conducted in Columbus, Georgia."

"The trouble started, it develops, about politics in Columbus and politics in Phenix City, and it's regrettable when things get in such a condition in this community that we must have political argument aired in a murder trial."

"As for Hoyt Shepherd," Smith said, in an attempt to clear him of all blame, "It's a funny thing to me that the only people that they could get to come up here and testify against him were people who voted against him in the city election."

Solicitor Borders, the second attorney closing for the State, was solemn and serious as he stood before the twelve men in the jury box to give his closing argument. "I doubt if any of you, no matter how old you are, have ever sat on a case of more importance than this one," he told the jury, "because we have come to the crossroads in Russell County. One road leads to hoodlumism and anarchy and the other to peace and law and order."

"Mr. Smith says there has been some insinuation that the police officials have not cooperated with the State. You can call it insinuation if you want to, but what kind of cooperation do you call it when investigating officers on the scene of a crime didn't have enough sense, to put it mildly, to take the names of witnesses, make any effort whatsoever to collect evidence or to preserve fingerprints?"

"It was Hoyt Shepherd rather than this brother Grady who fired the fatal bullets," Solicitor Borders told the jury. "Even if you should decide that Grady fired the gun, Hoyt is still guilty of first degree murder because of a conspiracy between the two men and under the law of conspiracy each shares equal guilt. Hoyt is as guilty as if he held the gun in his own hand and fired the shot himself."

"Under the law of self-defense," Solicitor Borders explained, "Hoyt Shepherd was the aggressor when he approached Leebern's table and requested him to go with him into another room with conspiracy. It doesn't matter what happened after they got in that room because *they* brought it on."

"The cuts that Grady claims he received from the alleged knife he says Leebern drew were manufactured scratches and cuts. Have you heard anyone other than Grady say how they got there?"

"You can't believe what Grady said if you believe those other decent, upright citizens. You can't believe Grady anyway since he is charged with violating the same offense as his brother, Hoyt."

"Consider the defense witnesses," Solicitor Borders urged the jury. "They were either friends of the defendant, former police officers, bartenders or gamblers or both."

"Leon Reese. Who is he? About the best thing I've heard about him in this case is that he's quit drinking. He's the brother of Elmer Reese, the city commissioner whose reelection they were celebrating in the Southern Manor on the night of the shooting."

"Clyde Yarborough. Who is he? The man who heads the Bug racket in Phenix City, who is associated with Hoyt Shepherd and Jimmie Matthews. Everyone of you have heard about the Bug racket. Now, you have found out who runs it."

"The defense attorneys have tried to impeach the testimony of the State's witness, Jeannette Mercer. They upbraided that little girl for using vile language on the stand. She quoted Hoyt Shepherd word for word, and under the law, she was required to quote him word for word and it was the defense who forced her to repeat it. If anybody ruined that little girl, it was some man who did it."

"As for the defense charge that Jeanette Mercer did not stay within the jurisdiction of Russell County following the shooting," Solicitor Borders continued, "If you were a nineteen-year old girl and you had seen a man shot down in cold blood the way that girl did, do you think she would have been safe in Phenix City? Do you think she would have been living today if she had stayed here?"

He waited for the jury to answer the question in their own minds and then added: "If you ask me, she was a fool to come back when she did."

Concluding his argument, Solicitor Borders said: "I don't care what they say about Phenix City, I know you don't want it broadcast over the world that a man from a sister state can come over here and be shot down without being given a dog's chance."

Albert Patterson, silver-haired, tall, straight, cold and aloof, rose to give the second closing argument for the Defense and the last argument of the day. Using his cane to support his lame right foot, he stood before the jury.

"I have never," he told them indignantly, "heard a sheriff's department or a police department talked about as I've heard ours denounced by our circuit solicitor."

"Columbus, Georgia, nor any other town had a right to step in and take charge of the investigation. The State's investigation was conducted in Columbus and witnesses were kept in Columbus. Clothing and other articles taken at City hospital following the shooting were turned over and kept by Columbus police before being taken over by Solicitor Borders and turned over to the State toxicologist for examination."

"Phenix City is able to take care of itself and Russell county is able to take care of itself." Patterson insisted.

"One of the attorney's for the State mentioned buying influence. In answer to that I tell you it took lots of money to bring Roderick Beddow here from Birmingham to try this case, and it took lots of money to bring the honorable Mr. Andrews here from Atlanta to try this case. Beddow and Andrews stand second to none in the entire Southeast and their services come high."

"The State has mentioned the defendants ruining little girls. Fayette Leebern was a big liquor dealer and hotel owner, a man of affairs. I don't know how old he was, but he has a fine looking son here, a mature man," Patterson said, letting his eyes come to rest on Donald Leebern. Then alluding to Leebern's companion, Edna Roye, Patterson said: "It was Fate Leebern who was out there with a little girl barely grown. No one said anything about the *defendant* being out there with any little girls."

"Jeannette Mercer, the State's only material witness, testified that Hoyt Shepherd told Leebern: 'I told you that if I ever got you back across the river, I would blow your brains out'."

Raising a last doubt, Patterson leaned on his cane with both hands and studied the tip of his shoe for a while, then confronted the jury with a last challenge: "Would a man in fear of his life come back across the river where he knew he would see the man who threatened his life?" Leaving the question for the jury to answer, he turned away and took his place at the defense table.

With the conclusion of Patterson's argument, Judge Williams adjourned court until 8:30 the next morning, when the concluding arguments would be given and the case would go to the jury.

꽃

On Friday morning, the beginning of the fourth day of trial, the legal dueling over concluding arguments was left to Jake Walker for the defense and Roderick Beddow for the prosecution. Walker was the only one of Hoyt Shepherd's attorneys not from Phenix City, but being from Opelika which was in neighboring Lee County, he knew the nature of the men who sat on the jury and the prejudices they nursed, primary among them were: outsiders who came in to tell them what to do, and the evils of a bad woman with a blackened reputation. Taking these as his targets, he began his summation.

"It occurred to me that these two men from Atlanta and Birmingham were preaching to you as if they had some doubt as to the jury." Laying both hands on his chest in a gesture of earnest faith, he said earnestly, "*We* don't urge you to do your duty because you have taken an oath."

"The State's case, as you know, depends on Jeanette Mercer. If your honor instructed me to read the statement of Jeanette Mercer, I wouldn't do it because I see too many ladies in the courtroom and I see too many gentlemen of fine character to repeat such foul language."

"I say to you that her testimony is utterly impeached. Her statement is in direct contradiction to testimony of all other witnesses."

Reviewing testimony of defense witnesses, Walker pointed out that Grady Shepherd had a constitutional right not to testify since he was also charged with the murder. "But he came here anyway and he told you the truth," Walker declared.

"You know that Fate Leebern was a man of large affairs, a man drunk with power and that desperate man ... according to undisputed evidence in this case ... decided to play for high stakes that very night."

Walker leaned forward over the jury rail and in a tone disclosing a confidence, he said: "I believe they went in that high dice room and were discussing politics in Columbus and Leebern lost his temper."

Referring to the State charges that police had not cooperated in investigating the case, Walker said: "They wanted to impeach the police officials of this county, they wanted to put an indictment against the police of this city, but they couldn't. They put Chief of Police Pal Daniel on the stand to say that he couldn't find the defendant for a long time. He didn't have a warrant for his arrest."

"I say to you, gentlemen of the jury, the slur that has been made on the police department of this city is a damnable lie!"

Walker shouted, letting his face flame with fury, and then suggesting the only possible reparation to damaged reputations and false accusations, he told the jury: "In the face of this, the only action you can take is to acquit Hoyt Shepherd of the charge that has been placed against him and render a verdict of Not Guilty!"

Roderick Beddow rose from the prosecution table, his great lion head bent in thought as he walked across the room to the jury box. Placing his hands firmly on the jury rail, he looked up and confronted the twelve men sitting there.

"Are you going to let these seven men take you snipe hunting? What difference does it make if I am from Birmingham? These seven gentlemen," Beddow said, pointing out defense attorneys Jake Walker, Roy Smith, Jabe Brassell, William Belcher, Julius B. Hicks, Arch Ferrell, and Albert Patterson, "are representing a man who shows to be a rascal, an assassin."

"I am going to show you that Hoyt Shepherd is guilty of the assassination of Fayette Leebern, and I am going to tell you why Leebern was killed."

Recalling the circumstances of Elmer Reese's election, Beddow declared: "They had just elected tools they had returned to office ... they jubilantly called everybody into the Southern Manor whether he be gentleman or tramp. They said, 'Let's go out and celebrate ... our man is back in office'."

"They were full of liquor that night. Drunk on liquor and drunk on power, reckless power. "

"When Hoyt Shepherd invited Fayette Leebern into the high dice room, Mr. Leebern was a marked man. They had been wanting to kill him and they selected the night of September 16 to assassinate him because they knew their nefarious business could continue since certain individuals charged with the responsibility of law enforcement of the city had been re-elected. They had the police department under their thumbnails."

Reviewing the testimony of witnesses, Roderick Beddow told the jury: "The way Grady Shepherd described how he shot Leebern in self-defense claiming Leebern came on him with a two and one-half inch pocket knife is the most asinine thing I ever heard of."

"We could have told whether Grady Shepherd fired the fatal shots or not, if the Phenix City police department had taken that pistol and preserved it in a soft material, but no, the fingerprints were wiped out just as Fayette Leebern was wiped out."

"The police department made no attempt whatsoever to preserve fingerprints so that you would know without a doubt if the bullet was fired by Grady or Hoyt. They didn't pick up a shell, they didn't pick up the knife, they didn't get an individual thing to bring here to place before you as indisputable evidence."

"The defense counsel," Beddow said, indicating Albert Patterson with a nod of his head, "has charged that the investigation of this murder began in Columbus, Georgia. For God's sake," he shouted, smashing his fist on the jury rail, "it should have begun somewhere. It certainly didn't begin here in Russell County."

"The police officers are supposed to patrol the city of Phenix and the men on the force should have a little common sense. This man Shannon Burch who is serving this town and all of Russell County as sheriff doesn't have a chance."

"Hoyt and Grady came in this court fat and sleek with big diamonds and clothes tailored to every degree. We are treating Hoyt a lot better than he treated Leebern. They didn't give him a chance. These men would pay the jurors off if they could find a slimy one who would take the money."

"We already know that there is a close relative of Clyde Yarborough on this jury," Beddow said, letting his eyes travel the entire length of the jury box, "but, we trust him."

"I have faith in that man to do the right thing, just as I have implicit faith in all of you. I trust you men to have the same kind of courage we had to prosecute this man and render a verdict of guilty!"

Beddow let the suggestion hang in the air for a moment and then added: "Ask yourself: 'Am I going to let a gangster, a man who never made an honest dollar make a fool out of me?'"

"There is only one verdict you can render in this case," Beddow concluded with a last impassioned plea, "and that is to convict Hoyt Shepherd of murder in the first degree."

The courtroom was still filled with the emotional fallout from the closing arguments when Judge Williams began his charge to the jury.

"I want this jury to understand," Judge Williams told them, "that you are confronted with a situation that calls for honesty and uprightness. In considering the testimony that you have heard during the three and one-half days of this trial, I want you to take into consideration the fact of impeachment. Consider the impeaching testimony and whether or not a witness was impeached. This jury is exclusive and supreme where testimony is concerned."

At 12:15 P.M., the jury left the courtroom, but the crowd did not leave the courthouse. They hung around in the halls and on the steps watching the hands of the clock go around until at 4:30, the foreman notified the bailiff that they had reached a verdict, and there was a scramble to reclaim seats in the courtroom.

When Judge Williams entered, he smashed his gavel down and warned the spectators: "There will be no outburst or display of emotion tolerated in this court when the verdict is read." His eye traveled over the courtroom, packed to capacity with seven hundred people. "None."

Standing up to face the judge, Hoyt Shepherd, as he had done throughout the trial, showed no emotion, his face impassive, his eyes fixed on Judge Williams, as he listened to the foreman who stepped forward and said: "We, the jury, find the defendant, Hoyt Shepherd, not guilty."

Despite Judge Williams' warning, a loud, spontaneous gasp came from the crowd and as soon as permission was granted to leave the courtroom, they sprang from their seats and ran for the exits to collect bets and discuss the astonishing thing they had seen happen. Reporters rushed over to the defense table asking Solicitor Borders' for his comment.

"I don't have a statement to make," Solicitor Borders replied. "The jury gave one and there's nothing I can say."

"What about Grady Shepherd? When will he be tried?"

"At a special court session in November."

"Do you plan to use any of the testimony in the Hoyt Shepherd case in actions against the alleged Bug racket?" another reporter asked.

"That will come out in due time," Solicitor Borders answered.

From across the river in Columbus, the evening edition of the *Columbus Ledger* commented editorially:

"We shan't pretend any great surprise over the acquittal of Hoyt Shepherd in the Fayette Leebern slaying. That's the way the man-in-the-street thought it would be, and if the attitude was cynical ... what is anybody going to do about it?"

༜

For Hugh Bentley it was a devastating disappointment.

Realistically, he had expressed his doubts that Hoyt could be convicted, but in his heart he had hoped that this time, somehow, some way, something could be done to stop the killing, establish justice, and free the town from those who held it hostage. Everybody knew what was going on in Phenix City, but always before it happened under cover, in the dark of night. This time there were witnesses, evidence, and due process of law.

The situation he had set out to improve had failed and the legacy to be left to the children had worsened. Dismayed by the prospects for what lay ahead, Hugh Bentley, after reading the *Ledger's* editorial comment, laid the paper aside and said: "What *can* be done about it?"

Hugh Britton gave him an encouraging slap on the back. "We'll think of something."

"For the sake of the children, we've got to," Hugh Bentley replied.

Hoyt Shepherd had already thought of something. Beneath the cool, impassive exterior he had exhibited throughout the trial, he was unhappy and greatly disturbed by the disclosures and conduct of the trial. It had been a close call, too close, and he decided, as he handed out rewards to those who had helped him out of this latest trouble that it was time to reshuffle the deck and adjust the balance of power begin-nine with the circuit judge and the circuit solicitor.

Circuit judge was a powerful position, but Hoyt, expert that he was on odds, knew it was not likely that Judge Sterling Williams could be unseated in his four-county district. To Hoyt, the circuit solicitor was equally important as it was the duty of the circuit solicitor to bring evidence before the grand jury and guide them in their decision. Considering the possibility of prosecution based on Clyde Yarborough's testimony about the Bug, more important to Hoyt at the moment, was the duty of the circuit solicitor to determine whether or not there was sufficient evidence to present a case before the grand jury.

Solicitor Borders had done everything he could to hang him with that murder rap and now he was talking about investigating the Bug racket. Sheriff Shannon Burch had buckled under pressure and assisted him in every way possible. What Phenix City and Russell County needed was its own separate circuit, staffed with hand-picked elected officials who could be depended upon and appointees who knew what to do without being told.

The general election, scheduled for 5 November, was less than three weeks away. The first order of business, Hoyt decided, was to rally the big gamblers: Head Revel, Godwin Davis, Godwin's brother, George Davis, Clyde Yarborough, Red Cook and the rest of the gambling community, and begin by throwing their support behind Albert Patterson who was running for a seat in the State senate.

On that night, the cornerstone of the Phenix City Machine was laid.

5

THE MURDER OF
JOHNNY FRANK STRINGFELLOW–
1948

It was a master scheme and an incredible accomplishment.

"Father in Heaven!" Hugh Bentley exclaimed to Hugh Britton. "The county government didn't suit Hoyt Shepherd and so he changed it! Now Russell County has it's own separate circuit!"

It took some doing, but Hoyt got it done and got what he wanted. He had followed the plan he had decided on the night the Leebern trial was over. In the November 1946 general election, he had marshaled the support of the gambling community and backed Albert Patterson for state senator, Big Jim Folsom for governor, Jabe Brassell and Ben Cole for state representatives, and a slate of county officials more to his liking. All won by handsome margins and then Hoyt put in for what he wanted.

It took an act of the Alabama Legislature to cut Russell County out of the four-county Third District where Judge Sterling Williams served as circuit judge and A.S. Borders served as circuit solicitor, but after a word with Jim Folsom, the bill was written by Russell County State Senator Albert Patterson and State Representative Jabe Brassell, and introduced in the legislature by Rankin Fite, the newly-elected State senator from Marion county who served as one of the floor leaders for Big Jim Folsom's administration.

When the bill was passed in August of 1947, it caused a helluva row, but Albert Patterson, who had pushed for its passage, defended it when Governor Folsom signed it into law.

Denying rumors that the bill was passed because of an alleged "misunderstanding" among present Third District court officials and attorneys, Patterson told the press, "It was passed not on any prejudices nor personalities, but on its merits. Proponents considered the merits of the case and the service to the people."

"Russell County was made into a separate court circuit to expedite trial of cases, to give the people better service and to save the county time and expenses," Patterson insisted. "Phenix City is a segment of a huge population center and a separate court circuit is necessary to take care of the tremendous overflow of cases from Columbus and Fort Benning."

Russell County became the newly-circuited Twenty-sixth District and speculation began immediately on who would be appointed to succeed Judge Sterling Williams and Solicitor Borders as court officials. The names that had been suggested were: Phenix City Attorney Roy Smith, Julius B. Hicks, Arch Ferrell, William Belcher, Senator Albert Patterson and Representative Jabe Brassell, all of whom had defended Hoyt Shepherd in the recent unpleasantness over the Fayette Leebern murder trial.

There was no question in Hoyt Shepherd's mind who they would be, he had already decided, but, following State procedure, the appointees were recommended by the local delegates and ratified by the Governor for appointment until a general election in May of 1948 when they would stand for election with whomever else chose to run for office. On 28 August 1947, the announcement was made. Julius B. Hicks was appointed circuit judge of Russell County to replace Judge Sterling Williams and Arch Ferrell would be the new circuit solicitor to replace A.S. Borders.

"Judge Williams and Solicitor Borders," Brassell pointed out "were both from Barbour County and therefore ineligible to serve the Twenty-seventh District of Russell County."

As for the job of deputy solicitor of Russell County, held, until the re-circuiting by Arch Ferrell's father, H.A Ferrell, a bill was introduced to abolish the position.

With the separate circuit established, Hoyt then turned his attention to Phenix City, governed until then by a three-man city commission: Mayor Homer Cobb, A.L. Gullatt, and Elmer Reese. In a bill passed by the Alabama legislature in August of 1947 the commission was expanded from three to five members with the two new members appointed by the Governor until elections could be held in September. The two new appointees were Deputy Sheriff J.D. Harris, a witness in the Fayette Leebern trial, and, to many people's surprise, Otis Taff, who had been defeated by Elmer Reese in the heated election of 1946.

"I hate to see it," Hugh Bentley told Hugh Britton. "Hoyt is using his same old *modus operandi*. If you remember, Elmer Reese, years ago, started out running against the gamblers and then Hoyt offered him his support and Elmer Reese has been his boy ever since. He's going to get Otis Taff under obligation and try to corrupt him the same way."

"Maybe not," Hugh Britton said. "Otis is a pretty good old boy."

"He's already obligated. He got obligated when Hoyt had him appointed by the governor."

"Otis is pretty straight and seems determined ... "

"How many times have we started out with an organization or a candidate and had some promise of success only to have Hoyt come in, take over, corrupt and destroy whatever we tried to do?"

Hugh Britton shook his head at the record of Hoyt's success.

"As nearly as I can count, every single time."

"That's why I'm not backing Otis in the September election. This time I'm going to back Veto Walker."

"Do you think he's got a chance running against Otis and J.D. Harris?"

"Not much. The election was decided when Hoyt had the governor make the appointments. The election will just be a formality, but I'm not going to add my support to it."

When the election was held in September, J.D. Harris and Otis Taff won handily and were sworn in as the fourth and fifth members of the City Commission by Mayor Homer Cobb who congratulated the new members and said: "The commission is getting just like I want it."

Cobb's comment expressed Hoyt's sentiments exactly. The control he had set out to get had been accomplished and along the way the trouble with Grady had been tidied up too. Grady had been scheduled to go on trial for the murder of Fayette Leebern at a special court session in November of 1946 after Hoyt's acquittal in October, but when November came, Solicitor Borders had to tell Judge Williams "The State is compelled to announce *not ready* and ask for a continuance because," he said, "important witnesses, who we had expected would be here, are not here."

Jake Walker, acting as defense counsel for Grady, asked that the continuance be denied because: "The Solicitor has offered us no assurance that his witnesses ever will come into this court."

"It's a keen disappointment to me," Judge Williams told Solicitor Borders, "that the State is not ready. There has never been a case that I have been more anxious to get off the docket and off my responsibility than this one."

The State was granted a continuance, and Grady, who had been in jail since the night of the murder, was granted $7500 bail. Sheriff Shannon Burch had said that Grady would be tried at the March session of circuit court, but when Solicitor Borders came to court in March the missing witnesses were still missing and the case against Grady for the murder of Fayette Leebern was *nol-prossed*.

Along the way, Hoyt had tidied up a few other details. In the 1946 general election, Shannon Burch was taken out of the power structure by making him probate judge, and Ralph Matthews, a man Hoyt knew he could depend on, was elected Sheriff of Russell County, and then as a last final gesture, Hoyt made Lee B. Ray, a character witness against Jeannette Mercer, his personal body guard, and then the structure that Hoyt had set upon the year before was completed. The influence and power he had loosely exerted before had been crafted into a well-oiled machine.

The new set-up didn't do Head Revel and Godwin Davis much good when their trouble resurfaced in 1948 because Georgia was the jurisdiction for their case. Four years before, a federal grand jury had indicted Godwin Davis, Head Revel, and their associate, Joe Allred, on a liquor conspiracy case. Trial was set for 12 October 1944, but when the government witness, Johnny Frank Stringfellow, came up missing, the case had to be indefinitely postponed.

Davis and Revel were satisfied they would hear no more from the case, but on a warm day in March 1948, Johnny Frank Stringfellow resurfaced, a bullet through his brain, his skeleton perfectly preserved by a sack of lime that had been poured over the body to destroy it, but had, instead, done just the opposite.

Georgia Sheriff E. F. Howell in Columbus had caught up with the two hit-men hired to kill Stringfellow. Fearful of facing the electric chair, they confessed and led Sheriff Howell to the lime grave where Stringfellow had been buried. On their confession and the recovery of Stringfellow's remains, a Grand Jury indicted the two hit-men, along with Davis, Revel, and Allred, charging them with murder; and Albert Patterson, the brilliant strategist in the Fayette Leebern trial, was persuaded to represent Revel to fight his extradition to Georgia.

Sheriff Howell, a veteran law man for Muscogee County in Columbus, called the killing of the government's star witness "the most brutal I have ever seen in my eleven years in law enforcement."

Johnny Frank Stringfellow, a soldier doing time in the federal detention barracks for violating the military code, had been released from prison to become an undercover agent for the federal authorities and a government witness in the case against Davis, Revel and Allred. Reporting his findings, he had written a letter to the federal agents. Before mailing it, the letter dropped from his pocket and was found by some of the criminals in Phenix City. Immediately, the information was turned over to Revel, Davis, and Allred.

Realizing the gravity of the situation, Revel, Davis and Allred began to cast about for a reliable hit-man to get rid of Johnny Frank Stringfellow. It was important that Stringfellow not realize that his undercover role had been discovered.

After Joe Allred learned from the underground information line that Wilson McVeigh had once been a friend of Stringfellow, the decision was made to approach McVeigh and his partner, Dave Walden, with a proposition. McVeigh and Walden were two small-time hoodlums who worked in the shipyards on the coast in Brunswick, Georgia, and operated in the Phenix City area on the week-ends cracking safes to supply money and drugs for their narcotic habit.

When Walden and McVeigh came into Godwin Davis' Manhattan Cafe one night in March 1944, Joe Allred joined them at their table and approached them with the proposition.

"Head Revel, Godwin Davis, and I are in some trouble and might have to do time if the government witness testifies in federal court," he told them.

"Who's putting the heat on you?" McVeigh asked.

"A soldier whose gone undercover for the government named Johnny Frank Stringfellow."

"Hell, I know him," McVeigh said. "He used to be a friend of mine."

"I know," Allred replied, "and it would be worth something to us to make sure he never showed up for trial."

"Like how much?"

"Like $1,000 dead on delivery."

McVeigh shot his partner, Dave Walden, a glance. Walden nodded and McVeigh said: "We'll check it out and see what we can do."

"We haven't got a lot of time," Allred told him. "We gotta do something before this case comes to court on October 12."

"I'll see if I can contact Stringfellow and then I'll be in touch," McVeigh said.

Shortly thereafter, McVeigh reported that he had made contact with Johnny Frank Stringfellow and would be able to get the job done with no problem.

"Come on up to Phenix City," Allred told him, "and we'll make the final arrangements."

At a meeting with Godwin Davis, Head Revel, and Joe Allred, the fee of $1,000 was agreed upon with Davis to pay $500, and Revel and Allred, $250 each after the body was delivered to Revel in Florida.

Revel, who owned a home in Florida near St. Augustine, gave them his telephone number to call when the contract had been fulfilled.

"How come you're not doing this job yourself?" Walden asked.

"With this case coming up in federal court, he's too hot for us to handle," Revel told him.

With the promise of $1,000, McVeigh invited Stringfellow to come to Brunswick where he and Walden were roommates while working in the shipyards. On weekends they returned to Fitzgerald where McVeigh's wife, Katie, lived and from there branched out to do their burglaries. Stringfellow knew this and was not suspicious when McVeigh told him:

"We're gonna drive to Fitzgerald to Katie's house and have a party. Katie lives right there on Magnolia Street in Fitzgerald. Waits for me every week to finish work in the shipyards."

At Katie's house, Walden and McVeigh began heating up a shot of morphine over the lamp. Joining in the camaraderie, Stringfellow said: "I want a joy pop, too."

"Pretty tough stuff," McVeigh teased.

"Let me have it."

McVeigh gave him four H. M. C. tablets and fixed two grains of morphine for him to mainline. When he did, Johnny Frank Stringfellow gasped and fell over dead on the bed.

"We gotta make sure he's dead," McVeigh said. "We don't want him to suddenly come out of it and find out what we done."

"He oughta be dead," Walden said. "It's enough to kill anybody and he ain't even used to it."

"We better wait and see." McVeigh cautioned. "The deal is dead on delivery, and I wouldn't want anything to screw this deal up. We ain't dealing with no two-bit punks."

They waited. A half-hour. One hour. An hour and a half.

"Let's get outa here," Walden said, "and get the hell on down the road."

McVeigh wavered. "I can't be sure."

"Then get a glass and hold it up to his mouth to see if it makes moisture."

From the kitchen McVeigh brought a glass and held it up to Johnny Frank Stringfellow's still lips.

"See!" Walden told him. "No moisture. He's dead."

Hurriedly, they wrapped Johnny Frank Stringfellow in an old army blanket, put him in the back seat of the car and headed toward the little town of Rebecca to get on the highway to Florida. Just outside of Rebecca, McVeigh thought he heard a noise come from under the blanket in the back seat.

"Stop the car," McVeigh told Walden. "I think he may be coming around."

Walden, getting edgy and nervous with McVeigh's anxiety, swerved the car off the road. "What the hell are you going to do now?"

"I'm going to give him another shot."

McVeigh crawled into the back-seat, and pumped another shot of morphine into Johnny Frank Stringfellow's arm.

"You're sure he's dead now?" Walden asked.

"Hell yes he's dead. Let's head for Florida."

They turned south and drove to Ponte Vedra, ten miles out of St. Augustine, and in a wooded area near an airport, they pulled off the side of the road beside a palmetto swamp, and took the body out.

"I ain't satisfied," McVeigh told Walden, when they had Johnny Frank Stringfellow laid out on the ground. "He don't look dead enough to me. I think it'll look better if we was to shoot him, so when Mr. Revel comes out to inspect, he'll know he's dead."

"Then shoot him," Walden said irritably.

McVeigh took his .22 pistol out of the car, turned the blanket back and put the pistol to Stringfellow's forehead.

Walden waited, but McVeigh kept holding the gun on Johnny Frank Stringfellow until his hand began to tremble.

"What the hell is the matter?" Walden demanded.

McVeigh turned away with the pistol hanging in his hand. "I can't do it. Johnny Frank was sort of a friend of mine. He even did some time for me once, and never ever ratted on me."

Losing patience, Walden snatched the pistol out of McVeigh's limp hand. "Goddammit, give me the gun. He ain't nothing but a corpse as it is."

McVeigh watched. As Walden put the barrel against Stringfellow's forehead, his ice blue eyes never wavered once. When Walden calmly pulled the trigger and blew a hole through Johnny Frank Stringfellow's head, McVeigh figured he had an ice blue heart to match his ice blue eyes.

"Okay, Wilson, let's cover him up with some of these branches and go call Head Revel."

At a filling station in Ponte Vedra, McVeigh made the phone call, and reported back to Walden. "Mr. Revel said for us to come out to his house and lead him back to where we stashed the body. He wants to make positive identification."

When they arrived, Revel told them: "Get that shovel out of the garage so we can bury him, and I'll follow you in my car."

Arriving back at the place they had hidden Stringfellow, McVeigh pulled the blanket back. When Revel saw the bullet through his brain, he was satisfied that the witness against him had been killed and told them: "Okay, strip off all his clothes except for his shoes and start digging a grave over there in that palmetto grove. I'm going into town to get some lime to speed up decomposition."

By the time Revel returned, Walden and McVeigh had Johnny Frank Stringfellow laid out in a three-foot hole. "Throw the lime in on top of him," Revel said. "We want to make damn sure there's nothing left for anybody to find."

As the white dust covered Johnny Frank Stringfellow's naked corpse, McVeigh tried to not look at what he was doing. The job was worse than he had imagined or bargained for and he hadn't counted on getting soft-hearted about friendship, but when the dirt had been replaced and branches piled over the raw earth and the job was done, he felt better about it and turned to Revel for the money.

"There's your man. Dead on delivery. He ain't never gonna testify against anybody."

"I'm satisfied of that, " Revel said, taking a roll of bills out of his pocket and peeling off ten $100 bills. "One thousand dollars, just like the contract called for."

※

Walden took it and handed $500 to McVeigh and they headed back to Fitzgerald to finish the party. Five hundred dollars apiece would buy a lot of happy hours. Shortly thereafter, Walden and McVeigh were obliged to commit another murder, Dave Walden's bride of one week. Walden had gone and married a girl from Columbus named Patricia Ann Archer. She was pretty, tall and dark-haired, and had been married before and had two little children. Unfortunately, she began poking around and found some sacks of money and, learning of their activities, threatened to go to the authorities, if they didn't cut it out. That didn't sit well with either of them and when she and Dave Walden had been married only a week, the three of them passed a policeman as they were out driving in the car.

Continuing the argument she and Dave Walden had been having, Patricia Ann Archer said: "I ought to get out of this car right now and tell that policeman everything I know."

It was the last thing she ever said because Walden's ice blue eyes in the rear view mirror shot a look at McVeigh in the back seat and McVeigh cracked her over the head with a soft drink bottle. When they got out of view and out of town, Walden said, "We can't have no song bird hanging around."

Together, Walden and McVeigh took a siphon tube and twisted it around her neck until she choked to death, and then for good measure, crushed her skull with a tire jack.

"We gotta get rid of her," Walden said.

"Where?"

"What about the Okefenokee Swamp down by the Florida line. The Swamp swallows up everything and what it can't swallow the 'gators get."

"Let's go." McVeigh agreed.

At the Okefenokee Swamp, they stripped her body of all its clothing and watched the water and the bubbles close over her until she was gone.

"I'm sorry about your wife, Dave," McVeigh said when it was done.

Walden's ice blue eyes never flickered once. "Like I said, we cain't afford no songbirds."

In Columbus, Muscogee County Sheriff Howell, received a missing persons report from the parents of Patricia Ann Archer and inquiries from federal agents who were looking for Johnny Frank Stringfellow. Both of them seemed to have disappeared without a trace and when the government's liquor conspiracy case against Davis, Revel, and Allred was called on October 12, 1944, there were no witnesses and the case against Davis, Revel, and Allred fell to pieces.

Four years later, in March 1948, Sheriff Howell was working a burglary case when he received a tip from a Columbus man that led to the arrest of a Memphis, Tennessee, safe-cracker named Roy Williamson who had been a cell-mate of Dave Walden and Wilson McVeigh, now doing time in prison on a narcotics charge. Hoping to trade information for leniency, Williamson related to Sheriff Howell the story Walden and McVeigh had told him about the killing of Johnny Frank Stringfellow and Patricia Ann Archer. Walden was brought in from jail in Raiford, Florida, and McVeigh from prison in Georgia. Confronted with the gravity of their crimes, they each, separately, confessed, giving the details of the contract and the murder. Sheriff Howell, along with Elzie Hancock, an alcohol tax unit officer working out of Columbus with the Georgia Bureau of Investigation, took Walden and McVeigh to Ponte Vedra, Florida, where they pointed out the grave where they had buried Johnny Frank Stringfellow in the palmetto grove.

When the rotted logs were removed and the earth shoveled away, there was the skeleton of Johnny Frank Stringfellow, perfectly preserved, with the bullet hole through his forehead. One of his shoes, a portion of the army blanket, along with the body and the lime used for decomposition was exhumed for evidence.

From there they drove to the Okefenokee Swamp, where Walden and McVeigh showed the officers the spot where they had discarded Patricia Ann Archer's body. Heavy rains and sucking mud prevented the early recovery of her body, but while they waited for the weather to improve so that the swamp could be dragged, Sheriff Howell returned Walden and McVeigh to Columbus where McVeigh made out a written confession. Taken before the Ben Hill County Grand Jury, in Fitzgerald, which was the situs of the crime, they testified and told the details of the murder contract, and indictments for first degree murder were returned against Walden, McVeigh, Godwin Davis, Head Revel, and Joe Allred.

Elzie Hancock found Godwin Davis at a farm he owned in Hamilton, Georgia, arrested him and took him to the Ben Hill County jail in Fitzgerald, Georgia. Head Revel and Joe Allred in Phenix City were missing for almost a week, then turned themselves in to Russell County Deputy Sheriff Albert Fuller who told lawmen seeking them that through an arrangement with Russell County Circuit Solicitor Arch Ferrell, Revel and Allred had each posted a $5,000 bond and would fight extradition to Georgia. Right away, Revel got in touch with Albert Patterson. "I want the best lawyer I can find," he told Patterson. "I saw what you were able to do with the Fate Leebern trial."

When Hugh Bentley heard that Patterson had agreed to represent Head Revel, he told Hugh Britton: "I'm not going to say another word to him. I've already said my piece and if his conscience can let him live with it, I reckon I'll have to."

But Patterson lost his fight to prevent Revel's extradition to Georgia, and Revel, Allred and Davis were locked up in the Ben Hill County jail while their attorneys persuaded Walden and McVeigh to repudiate their confession, telling Walden, who had admitted that he had fired the shot into Johnny Frank Stringfellow's head, that he would be given $7,000 for legal fees and telling McVeigh, that his wife, Katie, would receive regular amounts of money to take care of her while he was in jail and that at the earliest time possible, they, the attorneys, would arrange for their parole.

Walden and McVeigh agreed and repudiated the confession that had been given before the Ben Hill Grand Jury. Since Georgia law required the testimony of two witnesses against a third party, the murder charges against Davis, Revel, and Allred had to be dropped. But Walden and McVeigh were tried, convicted, and given life sentences.

At McVeigh's trial, no witness appeared on his behalf, but in a statement to the jury, he denied killing Johnny Frank Stringfellow, although the prosecution had called Stringfellow's brother who identified the shoe taken from the lime grave and the suitcase found by a GBI agent in Dave Walden's bedroom.

When he tried to call into question the positive identification of the skeleton being that of Johnny Frank Stringfellow, an Army dentist, called as an expert witness, identified the dental chart, acquired by the prosecution from the permanent files at the Army Records Depot in St. Louis and entered in evidence as that of Johnny Frank Stringfellow.

Handed the skull found in the lime grave, the dentist testified: "That is the skull of Johnnie Frank Stringfellow. Comparing the treatment, cavities, and extractions in this skull with the Photostat of the dental chart, I conclude that this is the skull of Johnnie Frank Stringfellow whose serial number is 34836063."

After hearing Sheriff Howell, Elzie Hancock and the foreman of the Ben Hill County Grand Jury that had indicted McVeigh all testify to McVeigh's voluntary confession, the jury returned a verdict of guilty and when McVeigh appealed the decision to the Georgia Supreme Court, the judgment was confirmed with all justices concurring.

In handing down their opinion on McVeigh's appeal, the justices wrote: "On the general grounds of the motion for new trial this case turns upon a consideration of whether the corpus delicti was sufficiently proved. To sustain a conviction of murder, it is necessary that the corpus delicti be proved beyond a reasonable doubt."

"In defining corpus delicti," the justices pointed out in their ruling, "Wharton's Criminal Evidence says it is made up of two elements: (1) that a certain result has been produced, as that a man has died, (2) that someone is criminally responsible for the result. "

"On a charge of homicide it is necessary to prove that the person alleged in the indictment to have been killed is (1) actually dead, as by producing his dead body; (2) that his death was caused or accomplished by violence, or other criminal agency of some other human being."

"To sustain a conviction, proof of the criminal agency is as indispensable as the proof of death. The fact of death is not sufficient; it must affirmatively appear that death was not accidental, that it was not due to natural causes and that it was not due to an act of the deceased."

"Unquestionably," the justices ruled, "the first element of corpus delicti, that the person alleged to have been killed is actually dead, was sufficiently established by independent evidence."

"We think, also, that the second element of corpus delicti was sufficiently established by independent evidence. The manner of burial with no marker of any kind at the grave, the place of burial in wild country, and the condition of the body all tend to show that someone was interested in removing the deceased from society and doing away with the body in such a manner that it could never be located, and if located, in such a manner that the body would have been consumed by lime and thus rendered unrecognizable or unidentifiable. These circumstances are incompatible with the theory that the death of the deceased was accidental, or due to natural causes, or the act of the deceased."

"The confession of the accused being corroborated by sufficient independent proof to establish the corpus delicti," the justices concluded, "the evidence warranted the verdict."

Dave Walden, when tried for the murder of Johnny Frank Stringfellow, pleaded guilty and was given a life sentence, but as he waited in the Brunswick jail to be tried for the murder of his wife, Patricia Ann Archer, he persuaded a trustee to sell him a hacksaw blade for ten dollars. Sawing through the bars, he was able to squeeze his thin chest through the narrow eight-inch opening, slide down a drain pipe and escape.

Immediately, Federal Agents and police in six states were alerted to be on the look-out for the 135 pound, balding, escapee with a tattoo of the comic strip character "Jiggs" on his arm.

In Phenix City, Sheriff Ralph Matthews said his deputies had worked late at night looking for all the places where Walden might be, but could find no trace of him.

A month later, Walden was sitting under a tree beside a small pond drinking some of the liquor he had stolen in the burglary of a small store near Tallahassee when a Florida sheriff recognized him from the tattoo description in the All Points Bulletin, arrested him and returned him to Georgia for trial.

At the time of his arrest, Walden had a case of whiskey and $4,000, and offered the Florida sheriff $2,000 if he let him go free. He told the arresting officers that he had sawed his way out of jail so that he could pull a few holdups and pay off his lawyers.

"I'm the best safe-ripper in this part of the country," Walden boasted to the sheriff, "and you'd of never caught me if I hadn't gone and gotten drunk on that case of whiskey."

Walden said he was aided in his escape by Head Revel of St. Augustine who was waiting for him with a car and drove him to Florida, but when he was returned to jail in Georgia, he claimed he didn't even know a Head Revel, and in Phenix City, Head Revel claimed he knew nothing about the alleged aid in escape.

"I'm not guilty," Revel told Sheriff Matthews," but if you want me, I'll be down by the lower bridge. You won't have to send after me. I'll come in when you want me."

Revel had had enough of trouble for a while. For him, 1948 had been a bad year. There was all that involvement with the discovery of Johnny Frank Stringfellow in April and before that, he had been the centerpiece of yet another controversy, a shooting that happened after midnight on the night of 30 January 1948.

Arriving home at approximately 1:30 A.M. in the company of Clyde Yarborough's thirty-three year old wife, Mabel, who, Revel said, had driven him home from work, they were met on the sidewalk in front of the Revel home by Revel's wife, Nora. As they pulled up to the curb, Nora Revel stuck a .25 automatic pistol through the window, aimed for the heart, and shot Mabel Yarborough just below the left breast through to the right side of her back.

Mabel Yarborough, bleeding and seriously wounded, was rushed to the hospital by Revel and his wife. When the police arrived, Nora Revel became hysterical.

"I don't know why I did it," she cried. "Mabel and I were close friends. We used to go to ball games together. I was just upset and nervous."

Arriving at the hospital to sit by his young wife's side, Clyde Yarborough would only say: "It's too deep for me."

For his part, Head Revel had no comment on the shooting but turned over the .25 automatic pistol with the clip empty to Sheriff Matthews.

"It ain't nothing but a social shooting," Hoyt Shepherd told Sheriff Matthews when he heard what happened. "Just two women squabbling. It wasn't nothing serious. No money was involved."

With this decree, Sheriff Matthews went through the usual motions. Nora Revel was arrested at the hospital charged with assault with attempt to murder and taken to jail where she sat in her cell, weeping and incoherent.

When Hugh Bentley heard about the shooting, he could only despair at the turn of events. "Things have really gotten terrible when the women start shooting each other," Hugh Bentley told his wife, Bernice, at the dinner table. "Nora Revel and Mabel Yarborough were both members of our First Baptist Church."

"I know," Bernice agreed, shaking her head sadly. "It's so bad for the children. Nora was one of the teachers for our church's group of little Sunshine Girls, and Mabel has two children of her own and has always been a prominent member of the church."

always been a prominent member of the church."

"I heard the preacher went over and visited them both, Mabel, in the hospital and Nora, in jail."

"I wonder what will happen."

"Take my word for it," Hugh Bentley predicted. "Nothing."

Head Revel consulted City Attorney Roy Smith, who would make no comment for publication. Bond was arranged for Nora Revel, her case continued until the next session of court. Mabel Yarborough recovered, the gossip died down and the case joined the others gathering dust on the sheriff's desk.

Now, in the spring of 1949, the town's attention was riveted again on Walden and McVeigh. Already convicted of the murder of Johnny Frank Stringfellow, Walden and McVeigh were tried for the murder of Walden's wife, Patricia Ann Archer, whose skeletal remains were finally found in the Okefenokee Swamp three months after the search began by Sheriff Howell and Alcohol Tax Agent Elzie Hancock, the ace woodsman and tracker who had spent forty years in the field chasing moonshiners, recovering evidence, and contributing to the conviction of criminals.

Tried and convicted of both murders, Walden and McVeigh were sentenced to serve two life sentences. In prison, they waited for the promises they had been made to be kept, promises for money for Walden's legal fees and support for McVeigh's wife; but the promises were never kept and Walden and McVeigh remained in prison festering with the injustice they felt they had been dealt by Revel, Davis, and Allred.

The unkept promises, the bizarre killing of a government witness and the brutal murder of Walden's wife of one week did not sit well with Albert Patterson. His persuasion and expertise had, he felt, made him a party to an obstruction of justice and he made up his mind, then and there, that he would never again represent the criminal element who so violated his own personal code of ethics.

Two years later when Gloria Floyd Davis appealed to him to represent her in a divorce case against Godwin Davis' son, Bubber, Patterson agreed, but in the meantime, the killing never stopped.

It had spilled over into law enforcement.

6

Albert Fuller–1949

Since his sensational beginning as the deputy who shot off the heel of a girl's shoe, Albert Fuller had proved the promise he showed in the Russell County sheriff's department. After the circuiting of Russell County, when Julius B. Hicks replaced Judge Sterling Williams and Arch Ferrell replaced Circuit Solicitor A. S. Borders, Ralph Matthews replaced Shannon Burch as Sheriff and Albert Fuller was given the opportunity he was waiting for. He was promoted to Chief Deputy Sheriff. When the border war broke out between Georgia and Alabama, Albert Fuller was ready to prove his worth.

The trouble began with border crossings and illegal liquor. For years there had been a running feud between the State of Georgia and the State of Alabama over the unpaid tax on legal and illegal liquor being run across the state line from Alabama into Georgia. When Georgia revenue agents gave chase, the liquor runners ran to the sanctuary of Phenix City where Georgia agents had no jurisdiction.

By 1949, traffic in illegal liquor had become such a bustling trade that not only liquor runners, but private citizens set on saving $1 a bottle in bonded liquor, were hauling it over the bridge from Phenix City by the carload, and Georgia Governor M. E. Thompson wanted it stopped. He therefore authorized the State Revenue Department to pick their agents, best in surveillance and tracking, to cross over the bridge into Phenix City, identify those violating the liquor laws, take down license plate numbers, and arrest them as they crossed the bridge into Georgia.

This activity, known as "spotting," drew the fire of Mayor Homer Cobb since twenty percent of sales from the state-controlled liquor store came back to the city as revenue. Ever watchful of the city's coffers, he threatened to arrest anyone seen "spotting cars in Alabama." Backed by the City Council, he gave orders to Sheriff Ralph Matthews and Police Chief Pal Daniel: "Lock up anybody you see hanging around and arrest them on loitering, suspicion, or something."

"As I see it, the law officers arresting citizens in Georgia for purchasing liquor in Phenix City are violating the fundamentals of the Bill of Rights itself by depriving citizens of their property without due process of law."

Georgia's Revenue Commissioner, Charles Redwine, was quick to respond: "Transportation of out-of-state liquor into Georgia will not be tolerated. We are going to undertake to enforce the Georgia law. We will make cases against anyone bringing Alabama whiskey into Georgia. Cars used for transportation will be subject to confiscation."

And the war was on.

The Georgia Alcohol Tax agents chosen for assignment in Phenix City were Elzie Hancock and E. E. Satterfield. Hancock, with his forty years experience working with state and federal alcohol tax units, was famous throughout law enforcement for his expertise in tracking, search and seizure, and was revered by his fellow workers for his accomplishments. In 1948 alone, Hancock had been instrumental in solving two stunning cases when he assisted Muscogee County Sheriff E. F. Howell in the search for Johnny Frank Stringfellow and in April of the same year, assisting Coweta County Sheriff Lamar Potts in finding the *corpus delicti*, burned bone chips, which was all that remained of John Wallace's tenant, William Turner, after Wallace killed him, burned the body, and threw away the ashes in a nearby stream.

In addition to spotting cars, Hancock and Satterfield were specifically in search of the Hargett brothers, Guy and Pete, two small-time gamblers trying to edge in on the big time profiteering in Phenix City and running illegal liquor on the side. Before any contact was made, Hancock and Satterfield were arrested on the streets of Phenix City, charged with loitering, and locked up in jail.

When the Georgia authorities were notified, they exploded. "For Christ's sake, they've arrested Hancock and Satterfield!"

Albert Patterson, having determined a new direction after the Stringfellow case, represented Hancock and Satterfield when they were brought to Recorder's Court before Mayor Cobb where they were tried, convicted, given a three months suspended sentence and fined $50.

"This judgment is excessive," Patterson said. "We will appeal this case to Circuit Court, and demand a jury trial."

Mayor Homer Cobb supplemented his action by saying: "We just want to impress on these gentlemen that we won't stand for this policing by Georgia officers. We've been nice so far, but from now on, we're going to treat snoopers like culprits."

Georgia Attorney General Eugene Cook was notified, and on the next foray into Phenix City, four days later, the Georgia Department of Revenue got Federal Alcohol Tax Agent Grady Cook with unlimited jurisdiction to accompany two newly assigned agents to investigate the Hargett brothers. Driving up to Guy Hargett's shotgun house on the edge of town, the three revenue agents were met in the yard by the two Hargett brothers with drawn pistols and a third man, Sam Beck, who blocked the drive with his car and jumped out with a pistol in his hand.

"I'm a Federal Agent," Cook advised them.

With this warning, Sam Beck jumped back in his car and sped off. Cook and the two officers gave chase but lost him on the dusty, winding back roads in the county and then went to Phenix City to report the matter to Sheriff Matthews and request local assistance. Ralph Matthews already had his orders about the border war, but a request from a federal agent with unlimited jurisdiction was a different matter.

Federal Agent Cook told him: "I want some local help for a raid on the Hargett house. I want a deputy and the agent from Alcoholic Beverage Control."

"When?"

"Now."

Ralph Matthews' face, usually smiling and affable, sagged into sulking folds. He picked up the phone and called his chief deputy, Albert Fuller.

"Albert? I got three revenue agents in my office."

Fuller laughed. "You fixing to put them in jail again?"

"No. They got a federal agent with them this time. He wants a deputy and an ABC agent.

"To do what?"

"To accompany him on a raid out there at the Hargett house."

"Hargett? That two-bit gambler who's been trying to muscle in on the lottery?"

"Yeah. I want you to get a hold of Ben Scroggins and go out there with them to Hargett's house."

"I'll take care of it," Fuller said.

When he arrived at the sheriff's office, Fuller was wearing a grin and a pair of gold plated guns. He shook hands with Federal Agent Cook and ignored the two Georgia Agents.

"I'm Albert Fuller," he said cordially, "this here's ABC Agent Ben Scroggins."

Cook had heard about the complaints from prisoners in the Russell

County jail about big Ben Scroggins. They said Albert Fuller and Ben Scroggins roughed them up and beat them, but for now, Ben Scroggins smiled and followed Fuller's lead in shaking hands with Cook and looking right through the two Georgia agents.

"I'll lead you out there," Fuller said, "and me and Ben will act as flush men. You and your boys here station yourselves at the back door and we'll run 'em right out into your waiting arms."

At the Hargett house, when the revenue agents took their position at the back door and in the side yard. Fuller and Ben Scroggins smashed through the front door, but instead of the suspects bursting through the back door to escape, there was a burst of gunfire instead.

Cook and his two agents ran to the house and found Guy Hargett slumped in his easy chair with five bullet holes lined up in a straight row from his forehead to his belt buckle.

"What the hell happened?" Cook wanted to know.

"I had to shoot him," Fuller said.

"Five times at close range?"

Fuller shrugged. "It was his life or mine."

"Get the Sheriff," Cook snapped. "I want him out here right now."

When Sheriff Matthews arrived, he had brought Circuit Solicitor Arch Ferrell and Coroner Ralph Thornhill with him for an on the scene investigation.

ABC Agent Ben Scroggins began the explanation. "I went in just ahead of Fuller," Scroggins said. "Guy Hargett was sittin' in that chair there with a gun sticking outa his belt. As soon as he saw us he set into cussing us and went for his gun. I grabbed for him and he jumped up. I hit his gun hand, and he fired into the air. Then Fuller shot him."

Fuller stepped in. "I had to shoot him. It was him or me."

"I hate it," Fuller said, shaking his head. "Why, I've never even wounded a man before in line of duty, but when we come in the room where he was I saw him draw a gun from his belt. He fired ... it was his life or mine."

Two of the women who had been in the house at the time of the shooting began to cry and scream hysterically. "It's not true! It's not true! Guy Hargett was sitting there in his chair asleep when them two just busted through the door and pumped him full of lead."

"Hush up that squalling," Sheriff Matthews said, waving the women toward the corner of the room. "How do you expect me to get the straight of this with all that carrying on?"

"Now. What about Pete Hargett and Sam Beck?" Sheriff Matthews asked.

"We've got them both in custody," Cook answered.

"When the shooting started," Fuller continued, "Pete Hargett came from the back of the house with a gun in his hand. I started toward him. He had the gun aimed right at my belt ... why he didn't shoot me down, I'll never know ... but when I got close enough I knocked the gun out of his hand with one hand and knocked him down with the other."

"What about Sam Beck?"

"He was armed, but one of the revenue agents got him in the back room, if he hadn't, things might've been worse than they were."

After consulting with Arch Ferrell and Ralph Thornhill, Sheriff Matthews announced: "Both the solicitor and the coroner have ruled this shooting a justifiable homicide. Fuller," he said, "fired in line of duty."

෨෨

When the newspapers asked for an explanation on what had happened at the Hargett house, Sheriff Matthews said: "There was evidence of a lottery racket ... lottery tickets, an adding machine, and sacks of money were found in the house and a regular arsenal. There were five pistols, a rifle and ammunition scattered all over the house."

"Why, when they took Guy Hargett off to the funeral home," Sheriff Matthews said, "they even found a lottery ticket in his shoe."

"I arrested his brother, Pete Hargett, and Sam Beck on charges of assaulting a federal officer, interfering with officers in line of duty, and operating a lottery. In addition, they are being held by the federal officers for investigation of illegal liquor."

When word got out about what happened at the Hargett house, Albert Fuller was again the talk of the town. The spectacular shooting of Guy Hargett—five bullet holes in a row from forehead to belt buckle—gave him a celebrity status as the fastest gun in Phenix City. It was a status that Albert Fuller enjoyed and sought to improve. All he needed was another opportunity, and if there was one thing he was good at it was seeking out and finding an opportunity and turning it to his advantage. Advantage was something that had seldom been his growing up in Phenix City as a fat, funny-looking kid, ignored, left out, and laughed at by his classmates at Central High School. After graduation, he watched them join the town's power structure and go on to bigger things while he drove a bread truck. Then came World War II and Albert Fuller joined the Navy. The tough, relentless training in boot camp turned him from a pudgy apology into a fighting man who knew the power of firearms.

On shore patrol in Texas, he learned how to subdue a man and experienced the exhilaration of having another bend to his will while he wore the badge of power. In Texas, he quickly developed a taste for hand-tooled cowboy boots, wide-brimmed Stetson hats, fast women and fast guns. By the time the War was over, he was an expert, with both women and guns and had acquired a taste he wanted to continue. He wasn't about to return to Phenix City to drive the bread truck. Instead, he went into Sheriff Matthews' office and got a job as deputy. Ralph Matthews, sitting there with all sorts of potential for profit and gain, was satisfied being jolly and being sheriff. Not Albert Fuller. He didn't plan on becoming "anybody's boy". In fact, he planned on having a few "boys" of his own to run and fetch and do his bidding. He went to work right away to niche a name out for himself. Guy Hargett was just the start. Fast with a trigger and flashing guns, Albert Fuller began to come into his own without anyone realizing the potential of his power.

They may have laughed at Fat Albert before, but not anymore. Respect. Money. Power. Fame. Albert Fuller had an insatiable hunger and wanted it all. He began making friends in high places and sitting in with those who ran the town. His reputation established with the shooting of Guy Hargett, he began to emerge as the determining power in the Sheriff's department and as his power and celebrity grew, City Commissioner Elmer Reese, worried for fear of a take-over, had his big nephew, six-foot-six Buddy Jowers, appointed night police chief as a counter balance to run the city's Police Department since Pal Daniel was even more of a figurehead than Ralph Matthews. In the beginning, there was a satisfactory division of territorial rights between Albert Fuller and Buddy Jowers with Fuller providing racket protection to some of the gamblers and Buddy Jowers providing racket protection to others. Then Fuller, becoming accustomed to the rich rewards he harvested each week from lottery and gambling, decided to branch out into other endeavors.

୬

There was another whole field of exploitation that had been permitted to flourish but had not yet been organized, namely prostitution. Every bar, honky tonk, and gambling joint hired girls to lure customers into drinking themselves into insensibility, gambling their money, and losing it all before they left. Other establishments provided more extensive services where a girl's sexual favors could be bought by the minute, by the hour, or for the evening. When the heat was on and the preachers started pounding the pulpit about sin in Phenix City, a few raids were made and a few prostitutes locked up overnight until their employers bailed them out the next morning. This satisfied the preachers that sin had been swept off the streets of Phenix City, but the sex-for-sale establishments went right on with business as usual, not paying anything except the fine for the prostitute.

It occurred to Albert Fuller that what these people needed was protection. There was Ma Beachie, a frail, gray-haired, grandmotherly little woman who wore starched white uniforms and steel rimed glasses and swore that all she provided at Ma Beachie's was high-spirited good fun and a floor show. Cliff Entrekin's Fish Camp down by the river served dinner downstairs and sex upstairs, and at Frank Gullatt's Blue Bonnet Cafe, the girls he hired were tattooed, with an identification number like a thoroughbred horse, inside the lower lip, so that if they should try to run away, or if anyone tried to hire them away, the tattoo inside the lip would prove "they were one of Frank's."

The possibilities and profits from providing girls and protection was endless and Albert Fuller decided to explore and exploit this lucrative field. It was not nearly so high-risk as gambling and lottery with investigations going on all the time. There was always somebody raising hell about that. And there were always complaints about the killings, like Hugh Bentley and his present rage.

The celebrated killing of Guy Hargett started it, and as soon as Hugh Bentley heard what happened, he stormed into Mayor Homer Cobb's office. Since Hoyt Shepherd's achievement in re-circuiting Russell County with his hand-picked officials, Hugh Bentley had been powerless to do anything to change the situation in Phenix City. All he could do was continue to organize and try to urge the citizens to join him in an effort to stop the gambling and stop the crime. In the last four years, he and his small band of loyal followers had formed four organizations that had all fallen apart under outside pressure and although all his efforts had failed, Hugh Bentley was determined not to give up and give over to the reign of lawlessness that was gaining strength and growing in Phenix City.

"There's a serious deterioration of law enforcement when a killing becomes a celebrity," Hugh Bentley told Homer Cobb. "As the mayor this town, law enforcement is under your command. Now, when *will* you do something to stop the killing?"

Mayor Cobb drew in a great, weary sigh. It seemed to Homer Cobb that he had spent most of his life listening to the Bentleys' complaints about the sin and killing in Phenix City.

In the beginning it was Hugh's mother, Miss Minnie, and now Hugh, and Homer Cobb had heard all he wanted to hear but he knew better than to challenge Hugh Bentley with a reply when a platitude would do. "Hugh, I'll do what I can to stop the killing."

"How many years have you been saying that, Homer?" Hugh Bentley demanded.

"More than I'd like to remember."

"You've been on the city council for nearly twenty years."

"I'm doing what I can."

"Not enough. The killing has got to stop." Hugh Bentley huffed on his way out.

But the killing didn't stop. It continued with cab drivers and cafe owners getting away with killings they never expected they would have to account for. At one o'clock in the morning, on November 12, 1949, twenty-one year old Fort Benning Private George Outlaw was found dead behind the Hillbilly Club, run over by Cab Driver Bill Littleton.

After military police at Fort Benning were called to pick up the body, they initiated an investigation. When Chief Deputy Albert Fuller arrested Littleton, Littleton swore he knew nothing about it, but a toxicologist report showed that blood and red hair matching that of Private Outlaw were found on the bumper of his cab. Pressed by Fort Benning for prosecution, Fuller agreed to give Littleton a lie detector test. Confronted with the results of the toxicologist report, Littleton claimed, during the questioning, that he was having a heart attack and could not continue. Even though he was officially charged with first degree manslaughter, the case never came to trial.

The case of Red Cook was much the same. Red Cook had come a long way since his beginnings as a street kid hauling confiscated liquor up the hill in Hugh Bentley's wooden wagon. Allowed in the lottery by the old Phenix City gamblers, he operated the smallest of the seven big lotteries under the name of The Old Original Barbecue. In addition, he owned a cafe and gambling joint called the 601 Social Club and in a Sunday shooting in this club, he left one man dead, one man paralyzed and a bystander shot with a leg wound.

Red Cook called the Sheriff's office. "Get on over here. There's been a shooting."

When Albert Fuller and Sheriff Matthews arrived, club patrons, stepping over the pools of blood, continued drinking and playing the game machines as the investigation got under way. Cook told Fuller and Sheriff Matthews: "It was a case of shot or get shot." The dead man was John Mancil; the one paralyzed, George Rogers.

Going through the formalities, Sheriff Matthews and Fuller questioned witnesses, picked up the snub-nosed .38 used in the shooting, and then, acting as head of the department, Sheriff Matthews announced that Cook would be held without bond on a murder charge, "It will be up to the judge to decide whether bond will be allowed or not."

At the hearing before Russell County Judge Harry Randall, Cook was represented by City Attorney Roy Smith and Roy Greene, a young lawyer just two years out of law school. Prosecuting the case, Circuit Solicitor Arch Ferrell told the judge that he had gone with Chief Deputy Fuller to complete the investigation and found evidence that would uphold a verdict of conviction by a jury. "However, it is not my opinion that a verdict given under a capital penalty would stand."

Ferrell asked for a $10,000 bond on first degree murder charge and $2,000 each on assault of the other two men.

City Attorney Roy Smith, representing Cook objected. "I feel the bond is excessive and ask that it be reduced."

Judge Randall then set bond at $7,500 for the murder of John Mancil, and $1,000 each on the two counts of assault, and Red Cook was released. Sheriff Matthews said the case would be brought before the next session of the grand jury and Mayor Cobb said that the City Council would discuss the possibility of revoking the liquor license for the *601 Social Club*, but the subject was not brought up nor did Red Cook's case go before the grand jury. Cook promised to take care of George Rogers, the paralyzed man, and his family. The case never came to trial and Red Cook was satisfied he would hear no more from it.

Albert Fuller was mindful of these acts not brought to court for accounting and he let Littleton and Red Cook know he was keeping score and that they were under some obligation for the accommodation they had received, but this was small stuff compared to the next shooting. It was the opportunity that Albert Fuller had waited for ... the shooting that forever sealed his celebrity as "Top Gun."

The seed for that opportunity began with the fallout between Godwin Davis and Head Revel. Except for the lasting bond between Hoyt Shepherd and Jimmie Matthews, relationships didn't last long in Phenix City and loyalties depended on the cut and the delivery of the deal. With Godwin Davis, loyalty was limited to the members of his family. With Head Revel, loyalty was limited only to himself.

Their partnership in the lottery, run from Godwin Davis' Manhattan Cafe, began to sour when Johnny Frank Stringfellow surfaced in Florida and ended when the murder charges against them were dropped after Wilson McVeigh repudiated his confession in court, leaving McVeigh and Dave Walden with a life sentence and Revel, Davis, and Allred free of the murder charges after Judge O. T. Gowers *nol prossed* the case against them for lack of witnesses.

Free of the murder charges, Revel decided to dissolve his partnership with Davis and wanted his share of the profit from the Manhattan Club lottery. Godwin Davis, flanked by his two huge, whale-size sons, Bubba and Sonny, told him: "You've already got your share. Now get out."

Outnumbered and off his own turf, Head Revel withdrew, but shortly afterward, at 2 A.M. on the night of 9 January 1950 four men in a pickup truck backed up to Davis' Manhattan Cafe, tied up the guard and drove away with three safes. The four men were Johnny Benefield, Phenix City's master safe-cracker and two little league operators named James Rush, and Clarence Franklin Johns. The fourth man, who remained in the shadows, was thought to be Revel, but when Godwin Davis called the police in to investigate, they could find no evidence, no clues, and no arrests were made.

Later, the police found the empty safes in the woods outside Phenix City and the pickup truck used in the holdup which had been stolen, but they were unable to find any substantial evidence leading to an arrest and the case became one of the growing number of unsolved mysteries gathering dust in the sheriff's in-basket.

Revel then turned his attention to Godwin Davis' brother, George, deep into dope and a confirmed addict, who ran the big Metropolitan Lottery from a dilapidated wooden building perched on the riverbank at the end of the Dillingham Street Bridge and inappropriately called, the Bridge Grocery. Inside, there was not a can of beans, a pound of coffee, or a plug of tobacco, only gambling equipment and set ups to record and announce the day's winning lottery tickets. Taking brother George as his partner, Head Revel set about making it into a business venture that would match the size of Hoyt Shepherd and Godwin Davis' operation.

Clarence Franklin Johns, the little league operator who had helped in the heist, turned his attention to robbing the Godwin Davis' Manhattan Cafe again. Twenty-six years old and married only a month, he decided, after having been party to one successful haul, to try it again on his own with the aid of a getaway man named Clyde Gordon. At 6:50 A.M. on 2 September 1950, Clarence Franklin Johns, wearing a railroad cap and khaki pants, attempted a daring daylight holdup as customers ate their breakfast in the Manhattan Cafe. With a .38 pistol, he forced Mrs. Pearl Moore to hand over the payroll sack of money and as he ran for his getaway car parked in an alley, cafe employee, Billy Kent, grabbed a pistol laying beside the cash register and managed to shoot him in the leg before the car, driven by Clyde Gordon, sped away.

Wounded and bleeding, Clarence Franklin Johns went to a local doctor for treatment, telling him that he had been shot in a gun fight, an occurrence so common in Phenix City that this was not reported to the authorities. But Clarence Franklin Johns, fearing that the doctor might, decided to hide in the Black cemetery until dark, while his accomplice, Clyde Gordon, drove back to his barbecue stand on the outskirts of town to return at dark to collect him and the payroll sack of money.

Clyde Gordon, so unnerved by all that had gone wrong with the holdup and so fearful of what would happen should they be discovered, dropped Clarence Franklin Johns in the cemetery and drove at maniac speed on the road out of town, hitting an oncoming car with such impact that it twisted his car completely around the other vehicle, killing the Texas woman inside the car and injuring her son. Gordon, fatally wounded, died shortly after the ambulance delivered him to the hospital, but not before telling the authorities what had taken place that morning. Immediately the search began for the gunman who had robbed the Manhattan Cafe. Sheriff Matthews sent the two he could depend on: Albert Fuller and big Ben Scroggins. They caught Clarence Franklin Johns in the Black cemetery hiding behind a tombstone and emptied their guns ... shooting him thirteen times. When they reported the shoot-out to the Sheriff, Fuller told him that Clarence Franklin Johns had pointed his gun toward Ben Scroggins head. A shoot-out followed in which Clarence Franklin Johns nicked Albert Fuller in the shoulder with his .38 pistol and Albert Fuller and Ben Scroggins shot him thirteen times.

Albert Fuller basked in the glory of that shooting. It elevated him to a category all his own and sealed his celebrity forever. People came around just to take a look at him and the gun that had done the shooting and Albert noticed that there was a new respect ... almost reverence ... for someone so accomplished at killing.

Circuit Solicitor Arch Ferrell and Coroner Ralph Thornhill again ruled the killing "justifiable homicide in line of duty." The trouble came with the payroll sack of money taken from the Manhattan Cafe that morning. It was never recovered. It was not found in the wrecked car with Clyde Gordon nor in the Black cemetery with Clarence Franklin Johns.

Godwin Davis was furious. Publicly, he said it was $3,000, but those who knew said it was more like $30,000, that he didn't want to talk about for fear the IRS would come looking into how he had come by it.

Davis said it was no mystery to him who got the money, implying that Albert Fuller had made off with it, but there was nothing he could do about it. He knew better than to start trouble with Albert Fuller. Besides, he had trouble enough brewing with his youngest son, Bubber, and his daughter-in-law, Gloria Floyd Davis, who were headed for the divorce court. Godwin Davis considered himself a family man, and when one of his own was in trouble, he pulled out all the stops. From the looks of it, it was going to be a get down and get dirty divorce. But before this came to court in October, the town was again in turmoil.

❧

On a hot afternoon in August 1950, Mayor Homer Cobb stood on the pavilion at Idle Hour Park before the assembled county and city employees who had come to celebrate the third anniversary of Phenix City's Cobb Memorial Hospital with a barbecue.

Homer Cobb was in an expansive mood. He had been on the town's City Council since 1931 and had been mayor since 1944, and in that time, he had saved the city from receivership and finally, in the last three years, paid off the debts, if not the obligations. Since then he had turned the city's revenues to this fine hospital for the citizens of this town that he loved and had tried to protect as best he could with accommodations and compromise.

"Not many people realize what Phenix City is now and what it was back in 1931," he told the holiday crowd that had come to celebrate. "At that time, the city had only fifty-one employees including school teachers. Now, the city has 150 teachers alone." "We've weathered many a political storm. Back when the hospital was being built, there were folks who called it a white elephant, but everything connected with it is excellent. It's paying its bills and we have a nice cash reserve."

His speech commending the city and county police and the city and county workers for their support was glowing and when he had finished, he stepped down from the podium amidst cheers and applause and joined the throng of well-wishers in the barbecue line. In the midst of the camaraderie, Mrs. Cobb screamed. Homer Cobb, clutching his chest, had fallen to the ground.

"Get Dr. Floyd! Get Dr. Floyd! Quick!"

Phenix City's most prominent and respected physician, Dr. Seth Floyd, pushed through the crowd hovering around Homer Cobb.

Bending down and taking a look, he said: "We've got to get him to the hospital right away."

The police and sheriff's department quickly pulled cars around and

Albert Fuller, first in line, helped Mrs. Cobb, weeping and crying, into the car while Dr. Floyd held Homer Cobb in his arms as they sped to the hospital and took him into the emergency room.

Mrs. Cobb was inconsolable. "Lord have mercy," she sobbed, "what will I do without him. Doctors, please. Do something, please."

Moments later, Dr. Seth Floyd came out of the emergency room, put his arm around her and said: "Minnie Pearl, I'm sorry. He's gone."

Wild with grief, Minnie Pearl Cobb began to scream and cry and was led by her son, Homer, Jr., to a wheel chair and was taken to a hospital room to be treated for shock. Albert Fuller, who had stood by in the hospital corridor, went to the steps outside where the holiday crowd that had been celebrating Homer Cobb's achievements had come to stand in the sweltering heat and wait.

"You can go on home now," he told them. "Mayor Homer Cobb is dead."

The announcement turned the crowd of city and county employees away with shock and sadness, but in other quarters, the news of Homer Cobb's sudden death signaled an unexpected shake-up in the power-structure of Phenix City. Homer Cobb, long before he died, had feared that on the day of his death, the racketeers would move for a complete take-over of the city. Before his eulogy had ended, the fight had begun to fill the power vacuum his death had left: the office of mayor, city recorder, and his seat on the City Commission.

"I'm sorry to hear about it," Hugh Bentley said when told of Homer Cobb's death. "Homer Cobb was my political opponent for a great many years, but I still remember him from way back in beginning when he was just a boy grown tall, sitting at my mother's dinner table making plans to do bigger and better things than working at the mill. Homer's come a long way. It's just a pity that he took the wrong road."

For Albert Fuller, it appeared to be a turn in his favor. To pay the city's bills, Homer Cobb had allowed gambling and gaming but he had held out strong against prostitution. Getting that organized for protection was a project Albert Fuller had long wanted to do. Now, it seemed that the opportunity had come. There was nothing left to stand in his way.

For Hoyt Shepherd, it was time to get busy and get a man to replace Homer Cobb in order to keep his political machine running the way he wanted. The office of mayor was elected by the five members on the City Commission but three of them were up for reelection—A. L. Gullatt, the long-time commissioner who had served with Homer Cobb since 1932 and the two newest members, Deputy Sheriff J. D. Harris and Otis Taff, whose two appointments had been engineered by Hoyt

Shepherd when the city expanded from a three to a five man commission. Because of the staggered terms of city commissioners, Elmer Reese was the only member of the City Commission whose seat was not being contested.

A move to consolidate the Machine's position had already been made with Deputy J. D. Harris named to take Homer Cobb's place as mayor until the elections were held and William Belcher, one of Hoyt Shepherd's attorneys in the Leebern case, appointed as court recorder. To keep control of the city government, the political machine engineered by Hoyt Shepherd needed to win four seats in the city election. With Gullatt, J. D. Harris, and Otis Taff running for reelection only one more candidate was needed to complete the administration's ticket.

Roy Greene, the up-and-coming twenty-nine year old attorney who had assisted City Attorney Roy Smith in the defense of Red Cook and who had run the Russell County campaign for Governor-elect Gordon Persons in the May primary was persuaded to run for Homer Cobb's seat on the City Commission. Hugh Bentley, eager to wade into the competition, told his buddy, Hugh Britton, "We need to call a meeting of the Citizens Committee and survey the situation to see what can be done before the gamblers get control."

In 1954, Big Jim Folsom was finishing up his four-year term as governor and the general election, with a slate of new State officers would be held in November. City elections were scheduled for 18 September, less than four weeks away. In an attempt to wrest control, Hugh Bentley, after the meeting with the Citizens Committee, announced that they would run a slate of four candidates to oppose the administration ticket and that he would be a candidate against Roy Greene for the seat vacated by Homer Cobb. A political office was an endeavor Hugh Bentley had never wanted to undertake, but there was no one else available to run for that district seat and he waded in by announcing a platform of sweeping changes.

"We will run on an anti-administration ticket," Hugh Bentley said, "and ask all citizens to take a united stand against sin, crime, public injustices, political corruption and neglect of duty."

With the eulogies still fresh in the minds of Homer Cobb's supporters, the response came back in an attempt to smear Hugh Bentley's campaign, that Hugh Bentley was Homer Cobb's foe, saying bad things about a man barely dead.

In the conflict that followed, Hugh Bentley did not hesitate to say publicly what he had been saying to Homer Cobb all along." The late Mayor Cobb operated the city under a principle that allowed the devil to operate all his rackets, to steal money, and to sabotage lives and use that same money to give to churches and hospitals and when election time came around, to buy some candidates to continue that program."

"This not only destroys body and soul, but the respect and reputation of the entire city and leaves a blemish on every child that is born."

"I was not Homer Cobb's enemy, I was the enemy of the principle under which he operated the city because I detest that principle, and even though he is gone, the principle is still there and I am still fighting that principle and will as long as there is a drop of blood in my body."

In the fray that followed, Hoyt Shepherd let his confederates handle the conflict. A legal technicality came up that required Hugh Bentley's candidates to qualify twenty days before the election and to have a petition of 100 names from citizens from each of the districts they would represent on the City Commission. With only two days to fulfill this deadline requirement for qualifying, Hugh Bentley and his bunch scrambled and made it.

The next problem centered on Archie Funderburke, one of Bentley's anti-administration candidates. A week after the qualifying requirements were met, Mrs. Funderburke called Hugh Bentley at 11:30 P.M. worried about the whereabouts of her husband who had received a call from Elmer Reese to come to his house and had not returned.

"We'll wait for about fifteen or twenty minutes more," Hugh Bentley told her, "and if he's not home by then, we'll get up a bunch of men and go looking for him."

Before the time had passed, Archie Funderburke returned and told Hugh Bentley that Elmer Reese had offered him money if he wanted it or any of the jobs in the city he might like to have if he refused to run on the anti-administration ticket.

"I turned him down flat," Archie Funderburke said.

"Which jobs was he offering?" Hugh Bentley asked.

"City street superintendent, beer license inspector, or City clerk."

"Homer Cobb's son is City Clerk."

"Elmer Reese said that don't matter."

At the City Commission meeting on 6 September, Hugh Bentley confronted Elmer Reese. "You're trying to break us up, offering jobs to our candidates."

Elmer Reese ignored the accusation, but at the last City Commission meeting on 12 September, six days before the election, J. D. Harris, now mayor, announced that he was withholding Funderburke's name from the ballot.

"For what!" Hugh Bentley demanded.

"It appears he is not a qualified voter," Mayor Harris replied. "Mr. Funderburke has not paid his poll tax since 1937."

"Archie Funderburke has a certificate of disability that does not require him to pay poll tax. A case of infantile paralysis some years ago left him with a disability, a lame leg, and this does not disqualify him as a candidate."

"Can he produce this certificate of disability?" Mayor Harris asked.

The papers, filed thirteen years before, in 1937, had disappeared and Archie Funderburke's name was struck from the ballot.

A. L. Gullatt was the only commissioner who objected. "Otis, this is too small a thing to throw a man out on," he insisted.

"Everybody in this room thought Funderburke was a qualified voter."

Otis Taff, trying to stay out of the conflict, said: "I'll go along with whatever is right."

"I'm doing what I think is right," Mayor Harris replied, and read an opinion from the Attorney General that said a man who was not a qualified voter could not qualify as a candidate for election.

"What you're doing," Hugh Bentley said in angry accusation, "is playing the game and umpiring it too."

When election day came, the entire slate of administration candidates won and Hugh Bentley lost his bid to young Roy Greene by a two-to-one margin. The City Commissioners selected J. D. Harris to continue as mayor and chose Otis Taff as mayor pro-tem.

"We may have lost this election," Hugh Bentley said when it was over, "but we'll be back again."

No one was worried and no one was listening except for Albert Patterson who had learned something himself about losing elections. Since his involvement with Godwin Davis and Head Revel in the Stringfellow case when he had decided to sever himself from representing the crime community, he had run in the May Democratic primary for the office of lieutenant governor and lost when the support of the Machine that had elected him in 1947 as state senator was withdrawn.

Now that he had taken on the case of Gloria Floyd Davis in her divorce suit from Godwin Davis' son, Bubber, Patterson had positioned himself against the gambling community and it was an uphill fight. In trying the case, he was squarely opposed by those with whom he had served representing Hoyt Shepherd on the Fate Leebern case: Circuit Judge Julius B. Hicks, Solicitor Arch Ferrell, and City Attorney Roy Smith who would be representing Godwin Davis' son, Bubber.

He did, however, have some help of his own. John, the oldest of his four sons, an attorney who had been serving as a major in the army in Germany at the Nuremberg trials, had recently returned home to Phenix City with his family and joined him in his law practice. Now it was Patterson and Patterson, attorneys-at-law, and together they would tackle *Davis v. Davis,* a case that had all the earmarks of a landmark bloodletting.

7

THE GLORIA FLOYD DAVIS DIVORCE–1950

No one, least of all Godwin Davis and the gambling community, expected a divorce trial to put in motion a tide of events that would challenge and nearly topple their carefully crafted gambling empire. No matter how high the howls against gambling, crime, and corruption, they had always been able to see to it that there was never any solid evidence. The only real threat had come from Solicitor Borders when Clyde Yarborough testified about the Bug in the Fate Leebern trial, but Hoyt Shepherd had taken care of that when he had Russell County re-circuited and staffed with court officials whose views were more compatible with his own.

The first foundation cracks in Phenix City's open gambling began on October 20, 1950, when Gloria Floyd Davis, the twenty-three year old daughter of socially prominent, Dr. and Mrs. Seth Floyd, filed suit for divorce from her third husband, William Robert ("Bubber") Davis, son of gambling kingpin, Godwin Davis.

At first, it was largely ignored as a domestic spat between warring partners. Gloria Floyd Davis was seeking alimony, custody, and child support for their two-year old daughter. The Davis clan was set on seeing she got nothing. In her suit she had charged her husband with cruelty; he had filed a cross bill accusing her of habitual drunkenness.

Other than the families of the two in dispute, only a few courthouse spectators came to watch as the proceedings began, and they, mainly, to witness the legal jousting of two expert attorneys. Albert Patterson, representing Gloria Floyd Davis, was the silent stiletto with an instinct for the jugular and the soft underbelly, and Roy Smith, representing Bubber Davis, was one who, in an adversary position, annihilated the opposition with a broadax. Then, too, there was the opportunity to get a look at Patterson's son, John, and see what kind of lawyer he would make now that he was out of the Army and in practice with his father. Lanterned-jawed and pugnacious, John was likely as fierce a fighter as his father, but a different kind.

≥♦

The divorce hearing before Circuit Court Judge Julius B. Hicks had, by the second day of the trial, heard twenty witnesses testify on Gloria Floyd Davis' behalf, supporting her grievances and stating that a woman of her position would require $400 to $500 per month alimony and child-support to maintain her position.

Saving his stiletto for last, Albert Patterson then put Gloria Floyd Davis on the witness stand. To establish Bubber Davis' ability to pay, Patterson asked her: "What business is your husband in?"

"My husband is in business with his father and his brother. They operate the Manhattan Club, the Manhattan Cafe, and a number of other businesses where gambling is the source of income and the National Lottery Company which grosses more than one million dollars a year."

This disclosure in open court hit the courtroom like a fire bomb. Bubber Davis' face whitened as he heard the unexpected accusation. Godwin Davis, seated beside his son, chewed viciously on his unlit cigar and City Attorney Roy Smith began quickly scribbling notes on his yellow legal pad. Gloria's mother, Mrs. Alice Floyd, seated on the opposite side of the courtroom, smiled.

The stiletto had struck a main artery. The only thing Godwin Davis guarded more than his family was his money and no matter what the adversary position, those privy to the interworkings of the rackets never testified against each other in court. Honor among thieves had nothing to do with it. Self-preservation demanded it. If the interworkings began to unravel in one quarter, they could begin unraveling everywhere.

With the courtroom reeling from this unexpected disclosure, John Patterson, watched his father's icy precision with obvious admiration as the Old Man continued to press for details that would lay the whole operation bare. An Alabama newspaper once described him as "a man who could chill the Senate floor by his entrance."

"You say that your husband is in business with his father and his brother?"

"Yes," Gloria Floyd Davis replied. "He shares as equal partner with his father and his brother, and I worked as bookkeeper."

"What sort of work did you do?"

"I worked for the National Company ... the numbers racket."

"What is the National Company?"

"The Bug."

"Known as the lottery?" Patterson asked.

"Yes."

"Did your husband operate the lottery?"

"Yes."

"Is he operating a lottery now?"

"Yes. He had me keep the books and I attended to everything to see that it was working right."

"How long did you keep the books for that company?"

"For nearly two years."

"Where is the headquarters of the National Lottery Company?"

"Over the Manhattan Cafe."

"Did you see the money come in?"

"Yes."

"Did you post the entries in the books?"

"Yes."

"And your husband is a partner with his father, Godwin Davis, and his brother, Godwin Davis, Jr.?"

"Yes."

"What is the extent of operations of the Manhattan Club?"

"They have slot machines and racehorse machines with an average income of $2,000 a week."

By the time Gloria Floyd Davis had finished her testimony, word had spread around town that Albert Patterson was exposing the rackets in the courtroom. Spectators began filling up the empty seats, and Hugh Bentley and Hugh Britton, hearing what had happened, got there in time to hear the last witness, Head Revel.

Still wanting to get his licks in against the Davises, Head Revel stunned the court when he supported Gloria Floyd Davis' claim, testifying that he had earlier been in business with Davis and his sons.

On the witness stand, Patterson asked Revel: "What was the nature of that business?"

"To be frank with you," Revel answered, "we wrote numbers."

"The lottery business?"

"Yes."

"Do you have any figures of these businesses that went to Bubber Davis in the year 1947?"

"Yes, I have. The only thing I can go by is the records of income of 1947 where I paid my income tax and it shows what I received and what he received."

"Do you know whether he is in the same business this year that he was in last year?"

"As far as I know," Revel answered, "he is still operating."

Quick to act on this damaging testimony, Albert Patterson went for the soft underbelly and filed a motion asking that profit-and-loss statements, balance sheets, and income tax records for all the Davises' business enterprises for the four years of 1947-1950 be produced.

Hugh Bentley leaned over to whisper to Hugh Britton. "That would do it. It would give us the break we've been looking for."

"Papers and documents sought are necessary and material in the trial of this case," Patterson said in his motion, "and contain evidence pertinent to the issue of this trial."

But Judge Hicks, taking care of the interests that had taken care of him, denied the motion to compel the Davises to submit their income tax returns in court and adjourned court until November 6 when Roy Smith, representing Bubber Davis, astonished the courtroom with a cross bill asking that the marriage be annulled.

Gloria Floyd Davis, married twice before, filed for a divorce against her first husband in January 1946, and against her second husband in January 1947. She received her second divorce in a Georgia court after having established residence in Columbus while teaching at the Ninnette School of Dancing. Bubber contended that she had not fulfilled the Georgia requirement of twelve months residency, spending four months of that time in California, thereby making the divorce decree from her second husband "null and of no effect" and asked that he be relieved by an annulment of the marriage even though this action would bastardize his own two-year old daughter whose custody he sought.

Albert Patterson was on his feet immediately. "I object, your Honor. In the case before the court the defendant, Bubber Davis, had no interest in his wife's previous divorce and therefore cannot claim legally his present marriage to her is invalid."

Judge Hicks waved him down. "I will allow the introduction of the new testimony. If this is good, this will dispose of the whole situation ... if the contention stands, there's nothing to try." During the introduction of evidence and arguments that followed, Gloria's mother, Mrs. Alice Floyd, enraged by the accusations made against her daughter, disrupted testimony on Bubber's behalf by shouting from her seat in the courtroom: "He's a liar!"

Judge Hicks ordered her out of the courtroom for disrupting testimony, and as the bailiff escorted her, Godwin Davis, pleased to see the tables turned in this tournament to inflict deadly wounds, took his unlit cigar out of his mouth, turned around and smiled.

The testimony continued with broadax blows until Gloria Floyd Davis was reduced to tears and when the trial was done, Judge Hicks announced that he would render a decision after studying the 260 page trial transcript.

"I would have never believed," John Patterson told his father as they gathered up their papers to leave the courtroom, "that a man, seeking custody himself, would be capable of trying to bastardize his own child to win a case in court. It must surely be a landmark case."

Looking over the top of his steel rimmed glasses, Albert Patterson told his son: "Practicing law in Phenix City, you'll find they are capable of anything. There are no limits here."

"Surely, Judge Hicks won't rule in his favor."

"My boy, you will find that what we have here are not judicial rulings, but judicial slaughter and no one is immune if they are on the wrong side of the bench."

≈

When Judge Hicks handed down his decision granting Bubber Davis an annulment, Albert Patterson appealed to the Alabama Supreme Court where the justices decreed that Gloria Floyd Davis' prior Georgia divorce decree was entitled to full faith and credit, that Judge Hicks' decree of annulment was erroneous, and that the wife was entitled to a divorce plus alimony and child support.

The Supreme Court Justices, clearly surprised by Judge Hicks' decision to grant an annulment, in handing down their opinion, said: "We are much impressed that the exigencies of this case require that we exercise our discretion and render such decree on all the issues as the trial court should have rendered to end the litigation."

"The misconduct of the husband was clearly proven, indeed, not denied."

"In the prior suit of divorce in Georgia, there was no actual fraud on the court nor collusion between parties, and the Alabama court gave full faith and credit to the Georgia decree. The fact of ceremonial marriage having been admitted by the husband, the law presumes it to have been legal and that neither became guilty of the crime of bigamy."

"After the divorce decree is rendered and other marriages contracted and children born, it is against public policy to vacate the decree, as such would render innocent parties guilty of bigamy and their children illegitimate."

As for alimony and child support, "When the husband is guilty of wanton and wicked conduct toward his wife, allowance will be as liberal as the estate of the husband will permit." The court granted $300 per month plus attorneys fees.

"Considering the custody of the child," the justices continued, "the wife is living in superior surroundings with her mother and father, a well-reputed physician. The husband, in a garage apartment on his father's dwelling lot and although "there is no specific proof as to the character of this home, there is evidence that the husband and his father are engaged in business which is beyond the pale of the law. It was noted, however, that without dispute, the wife had been likewise engaged in this character of business during her marriage, and the court decrees that for the best interests of the child, a nine-month custody would be awarded to the wife, and a three-month custody to the husband."

The divorce trial of Gloria Floyd Davis had a profound effect on the community. The dissolution of a marriage and the custody fight over a little two-year old girl were the personal concerns of the two families. The real import of the issue was that organized gambling had been established in open court. No longer could the gambling charges made against the Phenix City crime syndicate be dismissed as hearsay. It was now a matter of public record and investigations were being initiated.

The Internal Revenue Service announced that they would want to study the record of the divorce trial reporting a one million dollar yearly income on illegal lottery to ascertain the amount of unpaid taxes.

Sheriff Matthews and Solicitor Arch Ferrell were being pressed to investigate and take criminal action against the gambling activities testified to in open court, and Hugh Bentley was demanding a grand jury investigation into organized gambling.

In his response, Judge Hicks bypassed the idea of a grand jury investigation, "I see no need" he said, "to cause the county the expense of a grand jury investigation as the matters under consideration are misdemeanors and indictment is not necessary to proceed. Some of the acts complained of would not be punishable because of the statue of limitations, which is a year, while others are not barred by the statute."

Instead of a grand jury investigation, Judge Hicks wrote a letter to Circuit Solicitor Arch Ferrell, in which he said: "In an equity case tried before me, the case of *Davis v. Davis*, witnesses under oath testified to facts which I feel it my duty to call to your attention."

"I will provide you with a copy of the divorce trial evidence and I suggest that you go thoroughly into this matter and proceed through your office as you deem necessary."

"I will comply with any order the judge gives me," Arch Ferrell replied. "I did not hear the trial and have not gotten the testimony of the witnesses in this case, but all persons which the testimony seems to incriminate will be proceeded against by my office."

Reporters from the *Columbus Ledger* who had come to cover the trial asked: "Will you definitely make arrests?"

"I've instructed the sheriff to be ready to make arrests when I get the evidence and draw up the warrants."

"What about the gambling places named by the witnesses. Will they be closed down?"

"Closing down places has been a problem," Arch Ferrell told them. "In the past, these places have been shifted even to dwellings. If you recall, Guy Hargett was caught and killed in a so-called shotgun shack. That gang was operating in a dwelling."

Hearing this, Hugh Britton pulled Hugh Bentley off to the side. "Arch Ferrell didn't answer the question. Guy Hargett has nothing to do with closing down the places specified in the trial testimony."

"He's just talking for the press," Hugh Bentley replied. "Neither Arch Ferrell nor Judge Hicks has any intention of prosecuting a case against the gamblers. As usual, they'll talk about it and if forced to it, maybe initiate an investigation, but nothing will ever come of it unless we do something."

"What have you got in mind?"

"United States Senator Estes Kefauver from Tennessee."

"Senator Kefauver from Washington, D.C.?"

Hugh Bentley nodded. "You know Senator Kefauver is the chairman of the newly created Special Committee to Investigate Organized Crime in Interstate Commerce. He has been appointed by the President and I've seen in the paper that he's currently accumulating evidence between crime syndicates and local political officials. What we need is to have Estes Kefauver come investigate Phenix City!"

"I thought that was for big city, big-time crime."

"Who's got bigger big-time crime than Phenix City?" Hugh Bentley replied. "Everybody in the whole country knows about Phenix City and with crime income of one hundred million dollars a year, for a city of 23,000, I think we can qualify for Senator Kefauver's attention."

Quick to seize the opportunity, Hugh Bentley called an emergency meeting of the Citizens' Committee. "We've finally got something solid to go on," Hugh Bentley told his band of loyal followers who had fought with him and stuck with him through all the failed campaigns and crusades to change Phenix City, "and we know we're not going to get any help from the court in Russell County. What we need is outside help."

When the suggestion of Senator Kefauver was met with rounds of applause, Hugh Bentley told his members: "The Committee will invite Senator Kefauver to come to Phenix City to investigate the organized crime and I want each of you to write a letter urging him to accept."

With the Kefauver Committee and the IRS interested in studying the court record and becoming involved, prudence demanded that action be taken on the local level before Federal agencies stepped in, and Godwin Davis, his two sons, his brother, George, and Head Revel were arrested by Sheriff Matthews and charged with setting up and operating a lottery.

In Russell County Court before Judge Harry E. Randall on 13 November 1950, Solicitor Arch Ferrell presented the official trial transcript in the Gloria Floyd Davis divorce trial as evidence and said: "Circuit Judge Julius B. Hicks has requested the maximum fine in each one of these cases."

City attorney Roy Smith, representing the defendants made no open plea in their defense and Judge Randall levied the maximum fine of $500 each plus court costs. That afternoon, Police Chief Pal Daniel arrested Godwin Davis, his two sons, his brother, George, and Head Revel for violating the city ordinance against gambling. In city court, they were given the maximum fine: $100 plus court costs.

"Token punishment," Hugh Bentley said. "Imagine! A five hundred dollar fine for a one million dollar a year lottery!"

Shortly thereafter, Senator Kefauver, responding to his invitation, told the Citizens' Committee that despite his interest, that due to his present heavy workload, he would be unable to come to Phenix City to investigate the situation. Having been persuaded by supporters to run for President of the United States on the Democratic ticket, he had already put on his coon skin cap and begun campaigning, but the IRS let it be known that they had no intention of abandoning their investigation of the Davises who had shared one million dollars in untaxed income from gambling.

Hugh Bentley's despair over the token punishment handed out by city and county officials was matched in the gambling community by their despair over this opening wedge into the interworkings of their underworld enterprises. The IRS was the only organization in the world that Godwin Davis and the gamblers feared. The county and city could be controlled, the IRS could not. Its pursuit of the circumstances would be thorough and relentless and for this grief, they held Albert Patterson personally responsible.

They owed him one.

8

The Ministers' War–1951

As Hugh Bentley's hope for help died in the direction of the Kefauver Committee, it came unexpectedly from another. With the evidence of open gambling made a matter of public record in the Gloria Floyd Davis divorce trial, the Phenix City Ministerial Alliance, long restrained from active participation in routing out sin and crime and restricted to sermons on the Scriptures, now felt emboldened to act and informed Hugh Bentley that they would join him and the Citizens' Committee in an all-out war against crime.

Together, they journeyed down to the Alabama capitol in Montgomery to call on Governor Gordon Persons, elected in the 1950 general election to replace Big Jim Folsom who, by law, could not succeed himself.

Acting as spokesman for the group, Hugh Bentley told the governor: "We've simply got to have some help over there in Phenix City. For five years now, ever since 1946, we've tried every way we know how to get the gambling stopped and it's beyond anything we can do by ourselves. We have got to have some State help."

Gordon Persons who had only been in office for five months asked for a review of some of the efforts and Hugh Bentley told him: "In five years, we've organized four different groups to combat crime and gambling in Phenix City. We've complained to the mayor and been to the sheriff and the chief of police. We've run for office and had the ballots bought right out from under us. Now there's a court case of record concerning the gambling and nothing has been done to close down the establishments named in the trial transcript."

"The Citizens' Committee and the Ministerial Alliance want some help and we want it now, Governor," Hugh Bentley said.

"Open gambling is against the law in Alabama," Gordon Person replied, "and I would prefer for these requests to come from the county officials."

"You won't get a request from them, Governor," Hugh Bentley said, "because they are in on it."

"In that case, I'll send a State Investigator to Phenix City to inspect."

A week later when Governor Persons' state investigator, C. L. Donaldson, arrived, Mayor J. D. Harris was waiting to escort him through the gambling district. In an all afternoon tour, they searched in vain for slot machines, dice tables, and lottery operations but nothing was found and only one incidence of gambling was discovered: six men playing cards at the Silver Dollar Cafe. Mayor Harris summoned Sheriff Matthews who ceremoniously cut the green felt of the table layout and arrested the six men whose fine was paid by the cafe owner.

Afterwards, Mayor Harris, Solicitor Arch Ferrell, and Sheriff Matthews held a long conference at the courthouse with the State Investigator and when he emerged from the meeting at the courthouse, his only reply to reporters' inquiries was: "I can't give you any statement at all."

The Reverend Roland A. Smith, the young, militant pastor of the Central Baptist Church and a member of the Ministerial Public Relations Committee, denounced the investigation as "a farce."

"The gamblers were tipped off and waiting for the state inspector. That's why he didn't find anything," Roland Smith told the *Ledger*, "but we will continue to seek State aid. We may get 400-500 people together and ride down to Montgomery to see the governor again. The only way we can win is by showing strength."

The day following the State investigator's report, the ministers, wading into the war in earnest, produced evidence that Russell County was leading in the number of slot machines in Alabama. This evidence, acquired from the Alabama Revenue Department showed that 48 licenses for gambling had been issued to Russell County residents during the fiscal year.

Although the Revenue Department could reveal the number of slot machine permits, this was not so for another racket run by the punchboard operators. Under a 1940 Alabama Code, punchboard operators paid a percentage of their gross on each board and this was interpreted by the law to be a tax return and listed as confidential.

"The records for punchboard operators are kept under lock and key," the ministers were told, "and any employee who makes the list of punchboard operators available can be fined $50 and dismissed."

As the crusade to clean-up Phenix City gathered momentum, Mayor Harris at the next meeting of the Phenix City Commission addressed the problem of a complete clean-up of illicit activities.

"If we close down the honky-tonks in this town," Mayor Harris said, echoing Homer Cobb's words, "we'll be cutting the treasury of needed funds to run the city. Right now, a legitimate business pays a license fee of $50, compared to a $2500 license for the night clubs."

Speaking for the Citizens Committee, Hugh Bentley replied: "We realize that by cutting out the rackets we will have to foot the bill for running the city and the county, but we've got to pay for it with legitimate taxes. Right now we're paying for it with the lives of our children and even at this high price, the arrangement we've got isn't paying for much. Most of the streets in Phenix City are unpaved. More sewers are needed. The schools are small and understaffed, and we need a public library."

"I don't believe the people of Phenix City are either willing or able to pick up the tab," Mayor Harris replied. "To close down all the rackets and have money to run the city and the county, we'll have to double property taxes, raise the license fees, and put an additional tax on all city services."

"That's just a smoke screen to avoid the issue of law enforcement," Hugh Bentley said, "and scare tactics to run off people who would support a clean-up."

"We'll put it in the form of a tax proposal and call a public meeting."

Afterward, at a meeting of the Citizens' Committee and the Ministerial Alliance, Hugh Bentley warned them: "Get ready. The courthouse crowd is going to do everything they can to stop our effort. They're going to say if we kill the rackets, we'll kill the town and persuade the people to go along with the status quo."

A week later, a crowd estimated at 1,000 people had been rallied to attend the meeting. A petition signed by 100 merchants, citizens, and property owners asked that the Commission refrain from any change in the present tax laws because of the demands of a small minority. The consensus was they'd rather be racket-ridden than tax-ridden.

Addressing the crowd, Mayor Harris said: "I want to get the books straight. I'm not for making any changes just because a small minority is not satisfied with the way the town is run."

Targeting Hugh Bentley's unsuccessful bid for a city commission seat, Mayor Harris said: "You folks went to the polls. You told them who you want for public officials and until you tell me something different, we're going to have Phenix City like we've always had it."

Harris supporters howled and gave him a rousing round of applause, but Edwin Moore, a man who supported the Citizens' Committee and the Ministerial Alliance, stood up and said: "We don't want the rackets in Phenix City and even if you were elected, you're not able to run the city right."

Mayor Harris, indulged in a malicious smile. "I may not be able to run the city, but I haven't had to go into the courts to get them to straighten out my family."

Moore, whose wife was suing him for divorce, shouted back: "If it wasn't for the Phenix City underworld, I wouldn't have to go to the courts with a family problem."

Turning to the Ministerial Alliance, the advocacy of the militant minister, Roland Smith, was addressed. "Now we have Brother Smith who is a fine man and pastor of the Central Baptist Church, but his taxes are paid by the people of his church who work hard in the mills."

Bill Mitchel, one of Mayor Harris supporters, rose to add his voice. "Yeah. I wish Brother Smith would take stock and find out where the money that built his church comes from. Does Reverend Smith work for a living? No! Well how does he live? It must be handed to him on a silver platter. I figure, if he doesn't like the results of the election and who's sitting on the City Commission, then what he needs to do is move out of town."

Indignant at this attack on a member of the town's clergy, Hugh Bentley fired back. "This meeting was planned to preserve the status quo. If the sentiments expressed here are a true picture of the attitude of our people, that they would rather be racket-ridden than tax-ridden, then it is now time for the governor to declare martial law as we have a complete break-down of law and order."

The next day, Hugh Bentley led a group of eight citizens back down to Montgomery to plead his case before the governor and ask again for State assistance. "We've got a complete breakdown of law and order," he told the governor. "The jury list hasn't been purged since 1931 and the Russell County grand jury has the very lowest types serving on it. It's primary use is to indict soldiers, blacks, and poor whites. It doesn't apply to dope peddlers, prostitutes, gamblers, bootleggers and others who violate the law. Gamblers openly violate the law and the Bug is like a cancer eating the heart out of Phenix City."

Gordon Persons, a short man with white hair and a florid face that grew more florid with anger, was still smarting from the remarks made by the militant minister, Roland Smith. Making an effort to restrain his anger, Gordon Persons told Hugh Bentley's group: "I'll do what I can to help you clean up the crime and corruption in Phenix City, but you'll have to let me do it my way. The last time you came to Montgomery for help, I sent a State investigator over and the next thing I know, one of your local ministers of the gospel accused me of a lack of sincerity and

117

called the investigation a farce and I don't appreciate that."

"I've been hearing about the trouble in Phenix City since I was fourteen years old, and that was thirty-six years ago. The same trouble has come before every governor that Alabama has had and you can't expect me to perform miracles. I can't send 150 highway patrolmen to Phenix City and keep them there four years, but I will try to do what I can to whittle away at gambling and other illegal operations. It may not be the methods you want, but what you want is results and that is what I will be working for."

The next day, the *Columbus Ledger* reported Governor Person's promise to clean up Phenix City in banner headlines along with Hugh Bentley's criticism of the prejudicial Russell County grand jury. Although this drew a storm of protest and verbal abuse from members who had served on the grand jury, the ministers were undeterred and renewed their pledge to clean up Phenix City, for there was further evidence that theirs was a holy cause.

In an independent survey conducted by the Phenix City Junior Chamber of Commerce, eighty percent of the graduating senior boys had listed getting into the lottery racket as their life goal and ambition. It was what Hugh Bentley had been saying all along about the effect the city would have on the children and he let the ministers take the forefront in the war against crime, supporting them and supplying information.

In an open letter to Sheriff Matthews, published in the *Columbus Ledger*, the Ministerial Alliance petitioned the sheriff to prevent the wide-open gambling and halt the illegal activities now in operation and cited an incident that took place at the Phenix City hospital when a prominent gambler accosted a member of the Ministerial Alliance and warned him to: "Lay off lobbying against gambling, or else."

Sheriff Matthews replied: "I will handle the situation to the best of my knowledge and ability." And for a few days, gambling was done in the back rooms.

Continuing their crusade, in October, the ministers went before the fall session of the Russell County Grand Jury and presented a report, compiled by Southern Investigators, a firm in Montgomery, showing that six lotteries hiring 430 Bug writers, and taking in $7,000 a day was operating in Phenix City. The Grand Jury complained that the pastors were hampering the work of the Grand Jury, that this report by an "out-of-town investigating company" did not include the tax returns for the alleged lotteries and that this would be needed by witnesses with such information.

The ministers seized upon this opportunity to inform the public of the Grand Jury's reluctance to investigate their findings and released the report to the *Columbus Ledger* and sent a copy of the report to the governor saying: "We know you will be interested in these developments."

Angered by this exposure, the Grand Jury subpoenaed the two pastors to appear before that body to answer further questions on where they got the report and how. When it was over, the ministers said they had been humiliated and embarrassed, held up to ridicule, and told to stick to their prayerbooks and go home and read them.

As for the remainder of their report, the Grand Jurors praised the work of Sheriff Matthews and his deputies, Mayor Harris, the city commissioners and their employees, and thanked Judge Hicks for his inspiring opening charge and expressed "respect for the dignity, efficiency, kindness, thoughtfulness and justice which has marked your Honor's administration."

Hugh Bentley was outraged that men of God had been subjected to such treatment, humiliated and embarrassed, and summarily dismissed. The need was for further, stronger action, but, having already tried every avenue and having exhausted all appeals, he did not know where to begin.

Unexpectedly, he got a call from Albert Patterson who had been watching the struggle and strife. "Come on over to my office, Hugh. I want to talk to you."

Having represented the racketeers twice, Albert Patterson had his own reasons. The racketeers realized they could not control him but they did figure they could count on him. After the divorce of Gloria Floyd Davis, and the damaging testimony it brought forth, they knew they couldn't, and their retaliation began.

ॐ

Retaliation was the ready weapon of the racketeers. Hugh Bentley had long known its sting, his life regularly threatened with anonymous phone calls, the new tires of his recently purchased automobile slashed to pieces while he attended Prayer Meeting at his church, but Hugh Bentley, believing in the justness of his cause and armed with faith that one day he would accomplish the mission he had set himself upon, persisted and continued.

The ministers did, too, but they fared even worse. Those who determined the dark deeds in Phenix City decided that death threats would not be an effective weapon against the ministers for they would arm themselves in "the Power of the Lord" and assume the mantle of martyrdom. So that they would never ever raise their voices again to rally dissent, it was decided to ruin them—not all of them—just a selected few to serve as primary examples of what could happen if they continued their holy war on vice and crime.

Shortly thereafter, one preacher lost his pastorate and was removed as unfit to bring the Gospel to his church. Another was accused by a young unwed girl in a paternity suit, and a third was set up, arrested and accused of rape by a woman in his own congregation.

As for Albert Patterson, he had not only exposed the syndicate's lottery operation, he worsened the situation when he represented a seventeen-year old unwed mother who had come to him for help in regaining the child that she said was taken from her shortly after its birth in Cobb Memorial Hospital.

While pregnant, the young girl, frightened by the terrible social stigma of an illegitimate birth, and urged by her mother, had agreed to give her baby up for adoption and, in the hospital, had signed a paper whose contents she was not allowed to read releasing the child. The paper was given to her by Gloria Floyd Davis' mother, Mrs. Alice Floyd, wife of the respected Dr. Seth Floyd, who, like his father before him, Dr. Ashby Floyd, was the town's most prominent physician.

After the delivery of the child, the young mother changed her mind and wanted to keep the child, but was not allowed to do so.

Mrs. Floyd told her that adoption had already been arranged by an elderly couple who had no children and that they would provide a good home for the child.

The young mother went to the Welfare Department for help, but they had no record of the child or the adoption. She then turned to Albert Patterson for help.

In court before Judge Julius B. Hicks, Mrs. Floyd was represented by Circuit Solicitor Arch Ferrell who tore into the girl's character, describing her as unfit and unable to provide a living and a home for her child, putting forth harsh facts to show the handicaps that she and her baby would face.

Undaunted, the young mother responded with pent-up fury, challenging Ferrell's facts and testified that she had in her hospital bed been required to sign a folded over paper whose contents she was not allowed to read.

In defense of her worthiness to raise her own child, she provided a witness of her own from the local Public Welfare office who testified that the child's best interests would be served by returning the child to his mother, that arrangements had been made by the mother and approved by the Welfare Department for her to live with an aunt in

Massachusetts. Even though she begged the court to return the son she was never allowed to see, Judge Hicks ruled in favor of the elderly couple who had made arrangements through Mrs. Floyd to get custody of the baby after its birth.

Attacking Judge Hicks' decision, Albert Patterson charged that Arch Ferrell, as a state solicitor had no legal right to represent Mrs. Floyd in this case and had violated the law in doing so.

Reading from the 1940 Alabama Code of Justice, he pointed out that: "All circuit solicitors shall devote their entire time to the discharge of the duties of their offices, and each and every one of such officers are prohibited from practicing law, directly or indirectly, in any court of this state or of the United States, or in any other manner or for whatsoever, except in the discharge of the official duties of their offices."

Judge Hicks waved this objection aside and decreed that adoption procedures should be carried out by the couple who had had custody of the child since its birth, and Albert Patterson, objecting to "this traffic in human life," took the case to the Alabama Supreme Court that ruled that the child should be returned to his natural mother, but years later, the case was still in litigation. As the racketeers saw it, Albert Patterson was not only trying to take away their means of livelihood by exposing the rackets, he was now attacking pillars of the community like Dr. and Mrs. Floyd, and worse yet, he was representing a black man who allegedly attacked an arresting officer and was beaten so badly he was not able to come to court.

For the aggregate of what he had done, Albert Patterson was removed from the reserved list to the endangered list and systematically stripped of every public office he held on the School Board, the Draft Board and even as a deacon of his church.

Albert Patterson was stung by this bitter retaliation and as he observed the dilemma of the ministers and Hugh Bentley, he saw his opportunity to take his turn.

In his office, he told Hugh Bentley: "I've watched you struggle for years against the crime syndicate in Phenix City, failing at every turn. I'm going to show you how to beat them, legally."

Calling Hugh Britton, Hugh Bentley told him: "Get John Luttrell and Charlie Gunter and the rest of our group together for a meeting tonight. Albert Patterson says he can show us how to beat the rackets."

On that night, 28 October 1951, the Russell Betterment Association, known thereafter as the RBA, was born. Meeting in Patterson's office in the Coulter Building, Patterson told Hugh Bentley and his group of supporters: "I believe that a board of ten strong men and true, guided by proper legal advice, can lead a movement that will eventually whip the rackets, but before it's over, gentlemen," Patterson said gravely, "I must warn you, some of us may be dead."

Outlining his plan, Patterson told them: "In the past, the criminal community has been able to divide and destroy any organization that opposed it because they knew who your members were and who to go after. In the RBA, there will be two types of membership, an open membership and a secret membership. The open membership will be the ten members of the board responsible for the actions of the RBA whose names will be known to the public. A secret membership, an underground organization, whose members will support and supply information to the RBA, will not be known to the public and not listed on the rolls. Only by this method can we circumvent the terror tactics of the gamblers and gangsters in this community."

Readily agreeing to Patterson's plan, Hugh Bentley and his group adopted his proposal and incorporation papers were filed.

The next day, the *Columbus Ledger* in a front page story announced: *Group Organizes for Phenix City Vice War.* Quoting from the certificate of incorporation, Tom Sellers, the *Ledger's* veteran reporter, reported the newly formed RBA's motivation and declared intention: "Many of our citizens," the certificate stated, "have endured so long that they have lost the will to resist the nefarious activities that are destroying the moral and spiritual fiber of our people and making us the laughing stock of the whole country."

The RBA's purpose: (1) "To uproot and drive out the destructiveness and danger of gambling or any other such organized crime and to do whatever necessary to combat it in every lawful way possible."

(2) "To keep before the general public at all times the terrible wages of crime as to its destruction of homes, morals of our boys and girls and its terrible degrading effect on our community's reputation and the public disgrace it brings to our county."

(3) "To set up temporary headquarters in the State Capitol in Montgomery or in Washington, D.C. for the purpose of lobbying and carrying on educational campaigns against organized crime."

In addition, the RBA empowered itself to arrange radio programs, advertise in newspapers, employ investigators, conduct bureaus of information, and foster educational campaigns in their war against crime. After learning of the Russell Betterment's high purpose and resolve, Howard Pennington, a tall, slim carpenter with a crew cut and a determination to add his strength to the organization to stop crime, joined the RBA as one of the ten board members that Patterson had requested.

"I decided it was time for me to do something," Pennington told Hugh Bentley and Albert Patterson, "when my boy came home from his paper route and had lost all his collection money on slot machines. When I told him what he had done was wrong, he asked: 'Then why did a policeman show me how?'"

Howard Pennington shook his head. "I'm ready to do whatever has to be done."

In other quarters, after the published announcement of the RBA's avowed purpose, whispers swept the city that a huge file was being built up: incriminations against racketeers, irregularities at polls, traffic in whiskey, narcotics, and prostitution.

For the first time, the gambling community realized that with Albert Patterson guiding the group, a serious assault was about to be made on their activities and it was time to forestall and stop it before any real damage was done. It was then that Hugh Bentley received another telephone call. This time, from Hoyt Shepherd. Hoyt wanted to see him. A meeting was arranged. Hoyt wanted to make a deal.

"Hugh, we got a mess on our hands here with you and those ministers keeping everything in a turmoil. It ain't no good for anybody. Just tell me what it is you want. You want a political office? You want to be mayor?"

"We've already got a mayor," Hugh Bentley reminded him.

"That don't matter. I'll make you mayor."

"No, Hoyt, I don't want to be mayor and I don't want a political office. I want what I've always said I wanted: a clean town and honest elections; and we're gonna get them. Before this thing is over we're gonna beat you and the rackets."

Hoyt, ever the ultimate actor, appeared to be persuaded and distressed. "Well, Hugh, I've been thinking about quitting the rackets and I guess the time has come to get out. I don't sleep so good anymore and I worry a lot. I've been shot at twice by some unidentified gunman and I know for a fact that my telephone is tapped."

Shortly thereafter, Hoyt Shepherd cashed in his chips, turning in $250,000 worth of gambling equipment and announcing that he and his partner, Jimmie Matthews were finished with gambling forever.

Hugh Bentley was ecstatic. What he had worked for all these years was at last coming true. With Hoyt Shepherd and Jimmie Matthews leading the pack, he expected that the other gamblers, seeing what they were up against, would shortly follow suit. Hoyt's quick capitulation, however, was not due to Hugh Bentley or the RBA but a federal tax increase that had been passed by Congress which included a new federal law requiring all lottery operators, nationwide, to register, buy a $50 occupational tax stamp, and pay a ten percent tax on their gross income. The law was to go into effect on the first day of November

1951 and would be enforced by the Internal Revenue Department. Any lottery operator who failed to comply faced penalties of a year in jail and a $10,000 fine. Like all the other gamblers in Phenix City, Hoyt Shepherd feared neither God nor the Devil, only the IRS. With his equipment gone, he leased his buildings and gave his full attention to politics.

For Hoyt this was easy. It was something he had been into for a long time. For the other gamblers, it was not. They had no other alternate occupation and besides that, they didn't want one. Trying to find a way around the new federal law was bad enough without Hugh Bentley and the RBA digging up evidence, exposing racketeering, reporting names, places, and volume of business. Bentley, they decided, needed to be taught a lesson. This time, a good hard lesson.

Book II

The Tragedy

Hugh Bentley's sixteen-year old son, Hughbo, standing outside his bombed-out house, marks the spot where he was thrown by the explosion from his bed to the yard outside. (Courtesy of the *Columbus Ledger-Enquirer*)

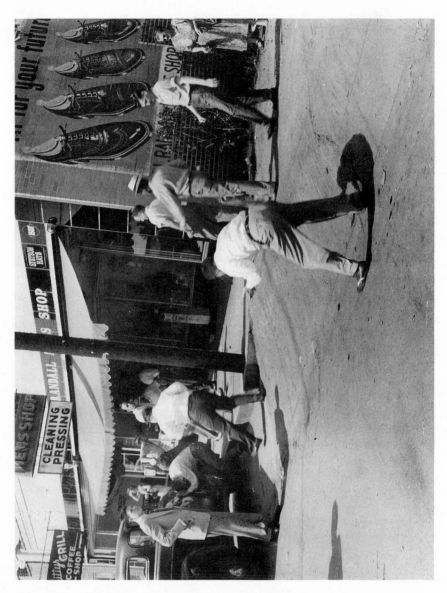

Columbus Ledger reporters and RBA members attacked by mobsters at the polls on election day 1952. Mrs. Beatrice Britton (far right), Hugh Bentley's mother-in-law, takes off her shoe to join fray in defense of her son-in-law. (Courtesy of the *Columbus Enquirer*)

Anti-vice RBA members Hugh Bentley, son Hughbo, and Hugh Britton beaten and bloodied at polling booth on election day 1952. (Courtesy of the *Columbus Ledger-Enquirer*)

Albert Patterson announces his candidacy for Alabama Attorney General on platform of "A Man Against Crime." (Courtesy of the *Columbus Ledger-Enquirer*)

Albert Patterson (with wife) checks voting returns in the 4 May 1954, primary election. (Courtesy of the *Columbus Ledger-Enquirer*)

Crowd congregates to view Patterson assassination scene 18 June 1954. Patterson's open-door car is next to building on left. (Courtesy of the *Columbus Ledger-Enquirer*)

9

BOMBING/BEATING/BURNING–1952

Hugh Bentley did not hear the explosion. In the early morning hours of 9 January 1952, at twenty-two minutes past midnight, Hugh Bentley was returning home, tired, weary, his eyes burning from having spent the day and most of the night driving across the state of Georgia to take his brother, Edwin, to the Veteran's Hospital in Augusta.

He had started out early that morning, leaving his nephew, Mike, behind with his wife, Bernice, and his own two sons, sixteen-year-old Hughbo, and ten-year-old Truman, who had the mumps.

"I'll be late getting back," Hugh Bentley told his wife, "Are you sure you'll be all right by yourself? I can get someone to come stay with you if you feel uneasy."

Bernice caught him by the lapel and kissed him on the cheek.

"Now don't you worry about us, Hugh. I've got two big boys, Hughbo and Mike, to help me if I need it, and Truman's too miserable with the mumps to be any trouble. You go on and get Edwin to the hospital. We'll be right here waiting for you when you get back."

Despite her attempts to reassure him, Hugh Bentley had worried that day about leaving her and the boys alone. Since the organization of the RBA and the controversy its activities had caused, the threatening calls had increased and he worried about the anxiety this would cause Bernice with him not at home. It was with relief that he finally finished his trip across Georgia that night and crossed the bridge into Phenix City, heading toward his quiet section of town.

Turning into his driveway, the headlights swept across his well-kept lawn and for a stunned moment, Hugh Bentley could not believe what he saw before him. His home was gone. Only the ragged edge of the roof was silhouetted against the night sky, the inside gutted and where the bedrooms had been, a smoldering pile of splintered debris. Leaping from the car in panic, he ran toward the ruin.

"Bernice! Bernice!"

From the shrubbery beside the house, he heard a low moan and a voice calling. "Daddy? Daddy?"

Rushing over, he found sixteen-year-old Hughbo, stunned and bruised, lying on the ground and gathered him in his arms.

"Hughbo! What happened?"

"I don't know. We were sleeping. Then there was this loud explosion. I was in bed, and the next thing I knew I was outside on the ground."

"Where's your mother? Where's Truman? Where's Mike?"

Hughbo rubbed his eyes and shook his head. "I don't know. It just happened."

Rushing toward the corner of the house where the bedrooms had been, Hugh Bentley began frantically pulling away beams, wallboard, ceiling, window frames and glass.

"Bernice! Bernice! Where are you?"

From beneath the debris, a weak voice responded. "Hugh, help me."

Tearing away the fallen wall, Hugh Bentley found her lying on the remains of the bed, her arm around Truman. For Hugh Bentley, the relief was so great that he wept as he held her close and kissed her. "Thank God you're alive. Is Truman all right?"

Trembling, Bernice Bentley pushed back her long dark hair that had fallen around her face. "I think so. Truman?"

Huddled in his mother's arms, his face smudged with smoke and dust, ten-year-old Truman looked at his father and began to cry. "Daddy, I'm afraid."

Reaching for his son, Hugh Bentley took him in his arms. "Don't be afraid. Everything is going to be all right."

Looking back at his wife, Hugh Bentley asked. "What happened?"

"I don't know. Hughbo and Mike were out on the sleeping porch and I had Truman in here with me. He had fallen asleep and I had too and the next thing I knew, things were falling all around me and when I looked up, the roof was gone and I could see the sky."

From outside Hughbo called. "I found Mike. He's okay."

Hugh Bentley dropped to his knees and bowed his head. The terrible fear and anguish was washed away with a flood of relief.

The family—all of them—had survived. No one was killed and no one was badly hurt, and for Hugh Bentley, what had happened here tonight was clearly one of God's miracles. Reaching out to hold all of his family in his embrace, he lifted his face toward heaven and prayed.

"Thank you, dear Lord, for sparing my family the harm that was intended in this act of violence. I accept it as a sign to continue to work diligently to do Your work to rid our town and our people of the evil that threatens us and surrounds us. Give us, Oh Lord, in this hour of peril, the strength and courage to do what has to be done."

Shivering beside her husband, Bernice Bentley whispered, "Amen", and the three boys, gathered in the family embrace each repeated after her: "Amen;" "Amen;" "Amen."

The neighbors, having been jolted from their beds by the explosion now began to gather on the lawn, the sheriff was called, and Bernice and the three boys, bruised and in shock, were taken to the hospital to be treated.

Hugh Britton, one of the first to arrive, rushed to Hugh Bentley's side. "This is the worst thing I've ever heard of. Bullying men is one thing, but bombing women and children! By God, I'd like to ..."

Hugh Bentley put his hand on his friend's arm. "We can be thankful God spared them."

"And we can get busy and find out who did it."

Sheriff Matthews arrived and walked over to Hugh Bentley. "Hugh, what in the world has happened here? Did your oil heater blow up?"

"You know damn well his oil heater didn't blow up," Hugh Britton snapped angrily. "Somebody dynamited his house."

"Well, we're sure gonna see about it," Sheriff Matthews said, kicking a piece of debris out of the way. "We gotta have an investigation."

The next morning when the governor was informed of what had happened in Phenix City, he was infuriated. "This is a terrible thing. Bombing a man's house with his wife and children inside. Phenix City has been nothing but a blight on my administration and I won't have it. We're going to get to the bottom of this thing right now and stop it, once and for all."

Arriving in Phenix City from the capital in Montgomery, Governor Persons brought with him the state's top law officer, Attorney General Silas Garrett III, the State Assistant Toxicologist, W. L. Sowell, the director from the State Department of Public Safety, a criminal investigator and a staff member from the State Fire Marshall's office.

Having been alerted to the governor's arrival, Phenix City Mayor J. D. Harris, Sheriff Matthews, Police Chief Pal Daniel and Circuit Solicitor Arch Ferrell were all on hand to join him in his inspection tour of Hugh Bentley's bombed-out house.

"I am absolutely determined," the governor told the Phenix City

127

and Russell County officials gathered in Hugh Bentley's yard to survey the damage, "that dynamiting in this state and terrorizing of the citizens is something that just isn't going to happen anymore as long as I am governor."

His face reddened with anger, his voice booming with emphasis, the governor addressed himself directly to the local law enforcement. "I want a *thorough* investigation. I want no stone left unturned. I want the culprit who committed this cowardly act caught and prosecuted. The State of Alabama will offer a $1000 reward for information leading to the arrest and conviction. Mr. Garrett, our State Attorney General, will personally check on the progress of this case and I will leave the state investigators here to assist the local authorities in getting the job done."

That afternoon, Russell County Circuit Judge Julius B. Hicks announced that he was calling the Grand Jury into special session on Friday, 11 January. "I want them to investigate this horrible explosion."

Mayor Harris requested assistance from Fort Benning's demolition squad to determine the type and amount of explosives used and said that Phenix City would add a $500 reward to that being offered by the governor. Not to be left lagging, Sheriff Matthews said he was putting up another $500 out of his own pocket.

"This is the first time in my history as a law enforcer that anything like this has happened," Sheriff Matthews told the reporters who came to interview him on what plans he had to carry out the governor's directives. "I am mighty glad that Mr. Bentley and his family were uninjured. We will do all we can to track down whoever did this awful thing and I am offering a personal reward of $500 for any information leading to the arrest and conviction of the person or persons involved, if such is the case."

As for Circuit Solicitor Arch Ferrell, he told reporters: "I have never investigated a more cowardly, sneaking, cold-blooded, vicious felony. The Alabama Code provides the death penalty as a maximum for anyone who sets off an explosion in, under, or dangerously near a building occupied by a person lodged there and I will seek the death penalty if the guilty person or persons are brought to trial."

Army ordinance experts from Fort Benning, in their preliminary investigation, said that somewhere between 24 and 48 sticks of dynamite—probably 36 sticks—had been placed beneath the porch of Hugh Bentley house. "The job was likely done by an amateur," the demolition squad determined, "because if it had been properly placed, it would have blown the Bentley's house clear out of Russell County."

The bombing of Hugh Bentley's house while his family slept inside bred a new kind of terror in Phenix City. For however bad it was, there had always remained the sanctity of a man's home and the sacredness of the family. Vengeance was now being reaped on the innocent and unsuspecting and the depth of terror was knowing that one amongst them was the terrorist. But, who? Which one?

 ?❧

Hoyt Shepherd, wanting to clear himself of any accusations, called Bernice Bentley, still shaken and under a doctor's care from the shock of the bombing.

"Mrs. Bentley, I'm mighty glad you and the children didn't get hurt bad, and I want you to know that I didn't have nothing to do with that bombing. In the past, Hugh and I have had our differences but I ain't into killing women and children."

"Then why don't you do something to stop it?" Bernice demanded.

"That ain't something that's under my control. I don't know who did it. All I can tell you is that I didn't."

"Well, something's got to be done to stop it before somebody gets killed."

From across the river, the *Columbus Ledger* expressed its concern and appealed to citizens on both sides of the river in a front page editorial:

"In the quiet stillness of Tuesday night, one or more persons with murder in their hearts crept up to the humble, suburban home of Hugh Bentley, a businessman who has waged a long and relentless fight against the racketeers and criminals in his home town. Asleep in their beds were a woman, her two sons and a nephew.

The lethal bomb which wrecked the Bentley home could have easily snuffed out the lives of the mother and children. That all escaped uninjured was the handiwork of Providence.

Violence in its crudest form has come to our community and every law abiding citizen of Columbus as well as Phenix City must awaken from their lethargy and drive the gangsters away lest their next assault result in bloodshed or death."

Hugh Britton, chairman of the publicity committee for the RBA, already had plans for awakening the citizens from their lethargy. Angry and impatient with the posturing and pronouncements of the Phenix City officials, he and RBA members John Luttrell and Charlie Gunter had called a mass meeting at the Russell County courthouse on the night following the bombing to rally public support for the RBA in fighting the crime and gambling in Phenix City.

"If there had been no gambling there would have been no bombing," Hugh Britton said. "We've invited the city and county officials and the general public to see if we can't prevent this happening again in the future."

The town turned out for the meeting at the courthouse that night. Hoyt Shepherd and Godwin Davis, city and county officials, shopkeepers, mill workers, housewives, members of the clergy and civic clubs all crowded into the courthouse filling the courtroom and corridors, standing in the aisles and hallways. Albert Patterson, sitting on the front row with members of the RBA, listened intently as the Reverend J.G.R. White, a retired Baptist minister with a white mane of hair and fiery rhetoric, began the meeting by saying: "The Russell County Circuit is the gangster circuit. What the people of Russell County want is government by law and that's exactly what they don't have." The crowd cheered and roared its approval as he continued.

"The Russell Circuit was set up by gangsters. Gangsters loaf around the courthouse, in the sheriff's office, with bodyguards and glittering guns. Neither the Circuit Court nor the County Court nor the City Court have done their sworn duty and when an official does not do what he is sworn to do, he is a perjurer and should be removed from office. Our people are tired of being held in bondage like slaves and demand that this gangster situation be cleaned up."

Following the thunderous applause for the Reverend White, members of the RBA one by one took their turn. Hugh Britton told the crowd: "Reverend White is right. We're tired of the disgusting and contemptible way some of our city and county officials kow-tow to this clique of lawless people."

Howard Pennington added his voice: "Too many men on our sheriff's force are connected with the juke joints and the rackets."

Angered by the accusations, Mayor J. D. Harris, who had been a Russell County deputy sheriff serving on Sheriff Matthews staff since the time of the Fate Leebern trial, interrupted the catalogue of grievances. "If any reference is meant to me, it's an unspeakable lie and I stand ready to defend myself."

Sheriff Matthews, eager to deny the accusations said: "I have no knowledge of any deputy on my staff owning any part of any illegal business. If proven to me any deputy does, I will immediately ask for that deputy's resignation."

Albert Fuller stood up, hands on hips, to add his denial to the others. "I don't have any connection with any kind of club or any kind of illegitimate business."

Circuit Solicitor Arch Ferrell, equally incensed by the insinuations, walked to the speaker's rostrum in quick angry steps and jutted his chin out in defiance. "I will plead guilty," he told the crowd gathered in the courthouse: "to these charges made against officials of the court if any man here can show me where I, or any of my friends in positions of trust, have intentionally failed to do their duty. Either put up or shut up."

"Yeah!" one of Ferrell's supporters yelled, "and if they don't like it, let 'em leave town, Bentley and all the rest of the RBA."

The crowd roared its disapproval, and Hugh Bentley came forward to speak from the rostrum. "This is my town and I will not quit nor will I be driven away."

The crowd cheered again and in a quiet, determined voice he began to tell his story as the crowd listened in hushed silence.

"I was born here and grew up here and I know something about the personal cost of gambling and crime. Gambling split my own family up when I was only three years old. My father, Calvin Bentley, ran a grocery where gamblers and racketeers gathered. My mother, Minnie Bentley, objecting to raising her children in this kind of environment, moved out with her seven sons and raised them alone. It was hard on us boys, growing up with no father, and it was hard on my mother, struggling to provide on what a woman could earn. If it hadn't been for gambling, we might have been a family."

Struggling to overcome emotion and the quiver in his voice, Hugh Bentley said: "Later, as a teen-ager growing up in Phenix City, I saw the terrible cost of crime. Three of my closest growing-up friends were victims. One was stabbed in the heart, another had his head shot off, and the third was knocked in the head and thrown in the river, his assailant never captured."

"Since then, gambling and crime in Phenix City has not gotten better, it has escalated and gotten worse and I hold the city, county, state and national officers responsible for the lawlessness in Phenix City. They have allowed it to operate and I will not quit until justice has been restored and democracy given back to the people of Phenix City. I urge you citizens sitting in the audience tonight to join with us in the RBA to drive out the lawlessness that has held us in servitude. We owe it to our children."

The crowd in the courthouse was on its feet applauding and Hugh Bentley held out his arm. "My sixteen-year-old son, Hughbo, who was blasted from his bed when our home was dynamited would like to speak on behalf of the children."

Hughbo, slim and shy, anxious to help yet afraid before the great assembly in the courthouse, came forward to his father's embrace. His voice trembled as he tried to get the words out. "When I woke up the other night ..." Hughbo's voice broke into sobs. "It was a terrible thing," he cried. "I just want to ask you to help my daddy and the RBA and the people of Phenix City."

Too overcome to say anymore, Hughbo left the stage weeping and Reverend White, ending the meeting, returned to the podium to demand from the people gathered in the courthouse: "Have the manhood to stand up and be counted. Drive the devils out before they drive our children away."

The next day, Circuit Court Judge Julius B. Hicks called the Russell County Grand Jury into emergency session. At the request of Governor Persons, Alabama Attorney General Silas Garrett III arrived from Montgomery to assist Circuit Solicitor Arch Ferrell and oversee the investigation of the bombing. After touring Hugh Bentley's demolished house and an hour's deliberation, Judge Hicks recessed the grand jury for lack of evidence or a suspect, and said, "The Grand Jury will be recalled if any new evidence is found."

The citizens of Phenix City and Russell County, worn out with the same old rhetoric and the same old excuses, were demanding that something be done, and Hugh Bentley went with his grievances to the *Columbus Ledger*.

"The Grand Jury was tainted," Hugh Bentley told them. From information uncovered by the RBA, it was learned that Jimmie Putnam, city clerk of Phenix City, and foreman of the Grand Jury, was a business partner of Hoyt Shepherd in a city tourist court and Lee B. Ray, who had testified in Hoyt Shepherd's defense in the Fate Leebern trial and later became Hoyt's bodyguard, was a member of the Grand Jury. When seventy-seven racehorse machines belonging to Hoyt Shepherd were found stored in the barn of Palmer Kennedy, a member of the jury commission, Hoyt and his partner, Jimmie Matthews, walked into Sheriff Matthews office and signed a waiver giving permission for them to be destroyed.

"This is it," Hoyt Shepherd told the sheriff. "We have absolutely no more gambling machines."

The federal law, enacted in November 1951 requiring registration and purchase of a gambling stamp, that had been the turning point in Hoyt Shepherd's decision to get out of gambling, had not deterred gamblers with lesser holdings in Phenix City. Searching the records, Hugh Bentley and the RBA learned that out of 270 gambling stamps issued in the state of Alabama, 230 had been purchased in Phenix City. Appearing before the Grand Jury, Hugh Bentley told them: "Here is irrefutable evidence of gambling in our community, 230 gambling stamps purchased by 230 gamblers. The sheriff and our local law enforcement say they can find no evidence of open gambling. This list gives names, places, and addresses."

The sheriff was called to the Grand Jury room, the list turned over to him, and an investigation begun into those listed as having purchased gambling stamps. Following up on the investigation, Hugh Bentley, Hugh Britton, John Luttrell and members of the RBA accompanied the sheriff on raids that netted more than 400 gambling machines valued at $500,000. Among those charged with possessing gambling equipment were Hoyt Shepherd, Jimmie Matthews, Godwin Davis, Head Revel and a score of smaller gamblers, but when the charges were brought before Russell County Judge Harry Randall, Circuit Solicitor Arch Ferrell reminded him that possession of gambling equipment was a misdemeanor and asked that each be fined $250 and court-costs.

The *Columbus Ledger*, reporting the efforts of the RBA, and supporting its cause, called for a mass resignation of all Phenix City and Russell County elected officials.

"Gambling and vice in Russell County has been permitted to expand during the years," the *Ledger* said in its 17 January editorial, "until no one knows how great is its hold on local government, nor how strong are its tentacles reaching into Montgomery and Washington."

"We therefore suggest the unprecedented action of mass resignation by every elected official so that each can extend his hands and enable the citizens to select those which are clean. If an election were fairly conducted, free of the taint of bought votes and intimidation at the polls, we've no doubt that present officials who enjoy the confidence of the public would be returned to office."

The suggestion especially angered Circuit Solicitor Arch Ferrell, and at a second meeting called by the RBA on 23 January, he and other elected officials listened as Hugh Bentley told the crowd: "The underworld has picked your public officials, corrupted your courts, contaminated your voting registration, picked your grand juries, stolen your elections and have a great deal of influence in your churches."

"The public officials have been asked to resign, but they won't do it and impeachment proceedings cost $2,000. We're asking for your support and contributions so that Russell County can rid itself of the corruption."

As the hat was passed and people began to leave, Arch Ferrell walked to the front of the room and said: "I have some facts for you if you want to stay." As the crowd continued to leave, Ferrell yelled: "The Columbus papers have sought to vilify and libel some of the most honest officials that we have in this county." The crowd jeered and continued on out the door. "If the truth hurts you, leave! Phenix City is one of the cleanest little towns in the country."

From the crowd left standing, a man yelled, "Liar!"

Sitting in the audience, Arch Ferrell's sister, Eugenia, jumped up and said: "Don't you call my brother a liar."

The man looked in Ferrell's direction again and called out: "Liar!"

Swinging her hand around, Ferrell's sister slapped the man full in the face and Ferrell leaped from the stage running toward the man as Sheriff Matthews and Lt. Smelley from the Alabama State Patrolman tried to restrain him and quiet the crowd.

"Don't you say my sister is wrong," Ferrell told him. "If you have something on your chest, I'll meet you outside."

"Get on out of here," Lt. Smelley told the man who had been slapped, "before you get trouble started."

The man walked out and Arch Ferrell swung around to the remaining crowd, aiming his words at Hugh Bentley: "If the RBA wants to try to impeach me, let 'em. I dare them to. The procedure for impeachment is not nearly so complicated as your lawyer has advised you."

Someone from the crowd yelled: "The RBA lawyer is a good one!"

"I know who he is," Ferrell replied, shooting a look at Albert Patterson, "and I'm ready to face him in any impeachment proceeding." As the controversy raged, a whisper campaign to discredit Hugh Bentley and the RBA began. Hugh Bentley, it was said, bombed his own house.

"Vicious lies," John Luttrell, one of the RBA directors adamantly insisted, "spread by the gangster rumor machine."

Hugh Bentley was not satisfied to ignore them or deny them. He felt deeply wounded that anyone would even suggest that he tried to blow up his own house with his wife and family inside.

"I am going to refute those lies once and for all," Hugh Bentley said, and to clear his name of the absurd accusations, four days later on 27 January, he voluntarily went to police headquarters in Birmingham accompanied by his pastor and Hugh Britton and took a lie detector test with State Toxicologist Dr. C.L. Rehling and Public Safety Director L.B. Sullivan looking on. After four tests and four grueling hours, the results reported what everyone already knew, that Hugh Bentley did not bomb his own house.

Physically exhausted and emotionally drained, Hugh Bentley told Hugh Britton on the way back to Phenix City: "This has been one of the worst experiences of my life and even though I know the Lord has given me this duty to do and this burden to bear, I just want to cry out: 'How long, Oh Lord, how long?' With all we've been through, we are no closer to knowing who did the bombing than we were before."

Almost three weeks had passed since the night he had found his house in ruins and his family in the rubble. The $1,000 reward offered by the governor had now grown to $9,000 with contributions coming in from all over the country as national newspapers reported the story of Hugh Bentley's struggle against crime and corruption and the midnight bombing of his family, but in Phenix City the investigation had produced no suspect and no evidence.

Governor Persons, angered by the inability of the local law enforcement to solve the crime sent ten additional State patrolmen to assist in the investigation and said: "No unsolved bombing cases will ever be marked 'closed' as long as I am in office. We will use the full facilities of our law enforcement to aid in breaking this case and in bringing the guilty parties to justice."

Calling together the members of the RBA for a meeting with Albert Patterson, Hugh Bentley told them: "I appreciate the governor's resolve, but what has always happened here before, is going to happen again and keep on happening unless we take some action ourselves."

Albert Patterson, the silent partner who advised them, listened to their discussion on more raids and more arrests and then told them: "Chasing around on raids with the sheriff is not going to do it, the arrests that are made are meaningless, the trials are useless and the fines are absurd. What we must do is concentrate a three-pronged attack on law enforcement, elections and impartial justice in the courts. We must methodically exhaust every avenue of due process."

"What we need," Patterson told them, "is a full-time intelligence officer who can coordinate the information and evidence and stay on top of it."

Hugh Britton, whose anger had never abated over the bombing of Hugh Bentley's house, volunteered for the job. "I'll take a year's leave of absence from my job and devote full-time to the RBA," Hugh Britton said. "We've been fighting for years and failing at every turn. If we can finish off crime and corruption once and for all, it'll be worth it."

The women of Phenix City and Russell County, especially the women of the church, were equally aroused and angered by the city and county officials' lingering inability to solve this crime and deeply disturbed that somewhere out there in the dark was a terrorist who knew no limits. Something, they insisted, had to be done when the escalation of violence destroyed the sanctity of a man's home and threatened the lives of innocent women and children, blasted from their beds while they slept.

Foremost among the advocates was Hilda Coulter, a petite young wife and mother of two little girls, active in church and community

135

affairs, who decided that it was time for the women to take a stand by forming the RBA Auxiliary, an organization that would act as a listening post to gather information and stand shoulder-to-shoulder with the men in their fight against crime and corruption.

Pretty and barely five feet tall, Hilda Coulter, who worked with her husband in their Phenix City florist shop, was not a woman to be dismissed. After going to Albert Patterson for advice, she had already tried her hand with getting things done by having a school lunch program instituted for the children and when this was done, she went to the governor to see about upgrading the school's geography books.

"The children can't study those books," she told the governor. "Since World War II most of the boundaries have changed. They'll learn all the wrong things. They need new books."

When this was done, she asked at the book depository what would happen to the old geography books. "We'll send them to the Black schools," she was told.

"That won't do," Hilda told them. "They need to know where Poland is just like everybody else. They'll have to have new geography books too."

Having accomplished that, she now turned her considerable energy toward the RBA Auxiliary, but the women soon found as the men and preachers had before them, that they were targets for threats and harassment — eggs thrown against their houses, trailed by unidentified cars, midnight calls with screeching tires and flashing lights — all designed to alert them to the dangers that lay ahead if they continued their work with the RBA.

When the women continued their work, the terrorist tactics escalated and a war of nerves began with anonymous phone calls threatening: "We'll get you and if you keep on, we'll get your children, too." The terror of this caused some members to drop out. For those who didn't, it was a constant watch on where the children were, what they were doing, walking them to and from school to assure their safety, never allowing them an unguarded moment.

Then on 24 February, the underworld struck again. The call came in on Sunday morning just as Hugh Bentley and his family were getting into their car to go to Sunday school.

Hugh Britton was on the line. "Somebody's set fire to Albert Patterson's office."

"How bad is it?" Hugh Bentley asked.

"I don't know. The fire department is there now."

"I'll meet you at Patterson's office."

When Hugh Bentley and Hugh Britton arrived, Albert Patterson was standing in the sodden ruins of his office, tossing debris aside with the end of his walking cane.

"What happened?" Hugh Bentley asked.

Albert Patterson's lean jaw was set, his eyes steely and steadfast. "An arsonist, obviously after the RBA files, sometime in the early morning hours climbed up to the second story roof, entered my office through the window, soaked the books, desk, filing cabinets, furniture, and floor with a low grade oil and set it afire. Fortunately, the janitor came in early to clean, found it, and called the fire department."

Hugh Britton shook his head. "I'm sure sorry about this, Mr. Patterson."

Patterson smiled a tight, grim smile. "This only means that we've really got them worried, but this attempt to burn me out will not stop our efforts. The office will be open on Monday morning as usual."

And, as was always the case in Phenix City, an investigation was begun, but no evidence could be found and no arrests were made and it was the conclusion of Police Chief Pal Daniel that the arsonist was likely an amateur who had bungled the job he had started out to do.

Disturbed by this latest travesty, the *Columbus Ledger* editorially attacked "the bastard who desecrated the Sabbath by this crime."

"The bungling punk who attempted to destroy the office of Phenix City Attorney Albert Patterson by fire Sunday," the *Ledger* said, "can now take his place on the dunce stool beside the equally inept idiot who tried to dynamite the home of Hugh Bentley several weeks ago,"

"Mr. Patterson, who serves without remuneration as attorney for the crusading Russell Betterment Association, treated with the utter contempt it deserves this latest attack on law and order by the underworld. He is hardly likely to take up his possessions and quit Phenix City at this crucial stage of the game, although no sensible person could blame him if he did. Attorney Patterson, like Hugh Bentley and other members of the RBA, is engaged in a fight to the finish with the racketeers."

"Although not as spectacular as the Bentley bombing, Sunday's arson attempt should prompt Russell County law enforcement authorities to intensify their efforts to apprehend the guilty parties. Failure over the years to control the rackets which finally grew to monstrous size and gained control of their community, places upon all governmental and law enforcement agencies of Russell County and Phenix City a measure of responsibility for what has happened there in recent weeks."

Meeting with the members of the RBA, Albert Patterson told them: "With the bombing, bootlegging, and gambling, I believe that a number of federal laws have been violated and what we must do now is take our grievances before the Middle District federal grand jury in Birmingham."

Hugh Bentley and Hugh Britton took their carefully prepared findings to the district attorney, but when the grand jury met, they reported that Phenix City and Russell County were apparently free of organized crime. "We have been unable to find any evidence of the existence of any organized criminal activities or criminal syndication anywhere in the Middle District."

Hugh Bentley and the members of the RBA were profoundly shocked. "It's inconceivable to me how the grand jury could come up with such a conclusion in view of all the evidence we turned over to them," Hugh Bentley told Albert Patterson.

"The grand jury didn't call either you or Hugh Britton as witnesses," Patterson replied. "Instead, they interviewed the very people upon whom the complaint was based." Patterson tossed the report across his desk, and Hugh Bentley picked it up and read it again as though on second reading he would see the conclusion he had hoped to find. But the words remained the same: "After interviewing and talking with local and federal officers, we found a splendid spirit of cooperation. Information is freely exchanged and they give each other mutual cooperation and active aid and support whenever necessary."

Hugh Bentley shook his head. "I still can't believe it."

Patterson, leaned back in his swivel chair and propped his lame leg on the lower drawer of his desk. "Hugh, you know very well that nothing, so far, has been able to stop the Phenix City machine. That they were able to persuade a federal grand jury is only a measure of their skill and pervasiveness."

"What in God's world is it going to take to stop the machine?"

Patterson shook his head, his eyes grave with concern. "We don't know how far nor how deep their influence goes, nor how many have been netted in their web. We can only be sure that they will bring their full force against us and fight us with every weapon in their arsenal. That's why when we began I said what we had to have was ten strong men and true, and even with that, before it's over some of us may be dead."

When Sheriff Matthews read the *Ledger's* next day's headline: *Grand Jury Reports Russell County Crime Free*, he was delighted.

"All I've got to say is that the cooperation of all state and federal agencies has been excellent and we appreciate it and hope we can continue the relationships that have worked out so successfully in the past."

While Sheriff Matthews gloated over this latest victory, Albert Patterson told the members of the RBA: "We've got to get rid of the city and county officials. Our best bet is the Democratic primary coming up on the 6th of May."

"How's that going to be different than what we've always done before?" one member asked. "We've been trying to win elections for the last six years, ever since 1946 when the Machine ran Elmer Reese against Otis Taff."

"This time," Patterson told them, "you have a better chance. You've got an aroused citizenry. People see in the bombing and burning a threat to themselves. If you can get them out to the polls to vote, their majority will make the difference. The governor has promised fair and corruption-free elections."

In an effort to secure the honest and fair elections that they sought, Hilda Coulter and the ladies of the RBA Auxiliary accompanied by Tom Sellers, the *Ledger's* six-foot-five reporter, assigned to the Phenix City beat, called on Mayor J.D. Harris at his office in City Hall. Their target: a demand that all persons who had purchased a federal gambling stamp be prohibited from working as election officials.

"We know for a fact," Hilda Coulter told Mayor Harris, "that 270 federal gambling stamps have been issued for the state of Alabama ... and 230 of those stamps have been issued to gamblers in Phenix City. We insist that none of these gamblers be allowed to work at the polling places."

Mayor Harris, a deputy sheriff working for Ralph Matthews and chairman of the Russell County Democratic Executive Committee, did not like ladies cluttering up his office with pocket books and flowered hats and he especially did not like outspoken women like Hilda Coulter who meddled in city business. The RBA Auxiliary had taken to attending meetings of the City Council and interfering with their opinions and now they were making demands about elections.

Pushing back in his swivel chair, J. D. Harris, looking down his nose at the ladies clustered around his desk, drummed his fingers impatiently and said coldly: "I'm not about to make a commitment on that, and I'm not going to let you make the rules by which to fight me."

The *Ledger* and the RBA then took up the effort calling for state supervision in the May election, and Governor Persons responded by pledging that: "Future elections will be adequately policed to assure honesty and fair play."

139

The *Ledger* was satisfied with the governor's pledge and reported on March 14th: "We don't believe that the crooks and criminals will run the risk of a term in Kilby State Prison by voting unqualified persons and falsifying the count."

Hugh Bentley and the RBA knew better and by May, the *Ledger*, on the night before the election, acknowledged in an editorial what the RBA already knew to be true: "The racketeers have made large donations to continue the machine in office, the incumbents have appointed the election officials, and their officers will patrol the balloting places maintaining whatever degree of peace suits their purposes and the machine crowd will count the ballots and keep custody of the ballot boxes."

In Phenix City, the word was out on the streets that there was likely going to be trouble at the polls when the voting began and if sensible citizens knew what was good for them, they would stay away.

"That's their way of trying to scare away honest voters and control the election," Hugh Bentley said.

To assure the public and put the racketeers on notice, the RBA ran a full page political announcement in the newspapers on the night before election announcing their intention to have qualified poll watchers at each voting booth and quoting from the Alabama Code that every person attempting to cast an illegal ballot would be promptly challenged and any person swearing to a lie would face perjury charges, the penalty on conviction, two to five years in prison.

"Under Title 17 of the Alabama Code," the RBA announcement said: "It is the duty of the Sheriff and his deputies to preserve order in all elections."

That night, the incumbents and the city and county officials held a rally and denounced the Columbus papers, Hugh Bentley and the RBA. State Representative Jabe Brassell told those who gathered to hear their denunciations: "The *Columbus Ledger* is a dirty, lying sheet, They've attacked our city and county officials, and, in an editorial cartoon, they even implied there's prostitution in Russell County."

Brassell, famous for his fiery rhetoric and support of the Phenix City and Russell County administration, shook his fist and shouted: "I want to say to that dirty, lying sheet that there is not a house of prostitution in Russell County!"

Coaxing the crowd, Solicitor Arch Ferrell told them: "Every time you put a ballot in that box, you are answering the *Columbus Ledger* and the RBA. Every man from Judge Hicks on down can stand on their records."

Adding his advice to the others, Mayor Harris urged them: "Get out there and vote. The time to stop them is tomorrow. Vote for what's good for the town and the county."

On the morning of the election, Hugh Bentley and his colleagues in the RBA and members of the RBA Auxiliary took up their positions at the ballot boxes as poll-watchers. At the downtown Fifth Avenue polling place, he, his son, Hughbo, and Hugh Britton saw the same thing happening that they had seen happen in every election held in Phenix City. Going to County Judge Harry Randall, they told him: "There are marked ballots, bought votes, and unqualified voters." When they cited the Alabama code and asked Judge Randall, who was seeking reelection, to issue warrants, he refused.

Returning to the voting booth on Fifth Avenue, Hugh Bentley found Phenix City gambler Head Revel and a bunch of toughs grinning and blocking the polling place.

"We're not going to be pushed around," Hugh Bentley said in response to their leers.

Revel spoke to the toughs gathered around the polling place and turned away. As Hugh Bentley, Hughbo, and Hugh Britton walked past the group to speak to the *Ledger* reporters, big Tom Sellers, young Ray Jenkins, and photographer Anne Robertson, who had just arrived to cover the election, one of the toughs at the polling place grabbed Hugh Britton from behind, ripping off the sleeve of his shirt. Whirling around to meet his aggressor, Hugh Britton was struck with a sledgehammer blow that sent him reeling into a plate glass window.

Hugh Bentley rushed the assailant, yelling: "You cut that out," only to double up with a battering of fists that bloodied his head while another tough struck Hughbo, knocking him to the ground where he rolled to safety under a truck. When Tom Sellers stepped in to help the reformers, he was jumped on by two men, giving as good as he got, but tall, thin Ray Jenkins, was knocked out of the fight by a hard blow to the chest.

As seven husky racketeers beat and kicked the poll-watchers and the reporters, Hugh Bentley's mother-in-law, one of the poll-watchers for the RBA Auxiliary, seeing what was happening, rushed over to a State Patrolman standing by. "Do something! Stop the beating! Help them!"

The State Patrolman shrugged. "Lady, they're not going to hurt them. They're just using their fists and feet."

The *Ledger's* Anne Robertson, quick with her camera, recorded the entire attack. The photographs of Hugh Bentley and Hugh Britton, bleeding and in blood-splattered shirts, and Hughbo with a swollen right eye, were put on the *Associated Press* wire for publication in newspapers across the country, and the disgraceful public beating at the polls became a nationwide story and symbols of the brutality in Phenix City.

Notoriety did nothing to temper Phenix City's ways. Only one of the seven men involved in the beating was arrested. This was Ernest Youngblood, operator of the infamous Diamond Horseshoe and brother to racketeer Glenn Youngblood who operated a clutch of gambling joints including the Haytag, the Oyster Bar and the Riverside Cafe where soldiers had been drugged and rolled and B-Girls bought off for prostitution.

At the hospital, Hugh Bentley lay on the gurney in the emergency room, blood and tears running down his face. Beside him, Hughbo took his hand.

"Don't cry, Daddy. The doctor's coming now to sew up your head wound."

Hugh Bentley shook his head and reached up to touch Hughbo's tender young face. Seeing his own son with his eye lid turning purple and swollen shut from the beating he had taken, all he could think about was the young soldier he and Hugh Britton had found on the river bank brutalized and beaten within an inch of his life. Now his own son had been victimized and Hugh Bentley could only wonder how many more defeats he would have to endure and how many more sacrifices would have to be made before somebody listened and something was done to solve the situation in Phenix City. And was it worth it when they tried to kill his family and beat his son? Was there any way to honorably put this burden down? Would God let him do it? In his heart, Hugh Bentley wanted to. In his soul, he knew he could not, for every time he despaired and reached the depths of despondency, faith flickered and drove him on.

Looking up at Hughbo, Hugh Bentley squeezed his hand and held it to his heart. "I'm not worried about that head wound, Hughbo. It just hurts me and cuts me to the core to see what they did to you."

"Don't worry about me, Daddy. I'm all right." The swollen smile and purple eye had twisted his face into a funny clown look. "Besides, you always said a man has to fight for things he stands for, and we did that today."

Hugh Bentley brushed away the tears. "Yes, we did, son."

Even though Hugh Bentley's head wounds required several stitches at the hospital, Ernest Youngblood was only charged with assault and battery and released on a $101.50 fine which he forfeited when he did not show up in court. As for the election, when the votes were counted, the machine candidates had all won by impressive margins.

When the RBA met to decide what action to take, Albert Patterson told them: "We tried and we lost, but we knew from the beginning that with the racketeers as entrenched as they are, that it wouldn't be easy. Now, it's time to go after the elected officials and begin impeachment proceedings."

Among the RBA members, there was disagreement on which of the county officials they should go after and take to accounting for the disgraceful conduct of county affairs. There were those who were in favor of unseating Circuit Judge Julius B. Hicks.

"He's nothing more than the judicial hand-maiden for the underworld," they said. "Look at the rulings he's handed down. Always in favor of the racketeers."

There were those who were in favor of impeaching Sheriff Matthews. "He doesn't enforce the law and it's his job to do it," they complained.

Albert Patterson was in favor of taking Arch Ferrell up on his dare and filing impeachment proceedings to unseat him as Circuit Solicitor.

"As Solicitor," Patterson said, "it's Arch Ferrell's duty to see that the law is upheld and the criminals brought to justice."

Despite Patterson's advice, the majority prevailed, and the members decided to begin by filing impeachment proceedings against Sheriff Matthews for the open gambling he permitted in the county.

Roberts Brown, of nearby Opelika, the highly respected Speaker of the Alabama House of Representative, was retained to file the impeachment proceedings on 1 July 1952, charging that: "Sheriff Matthews in his present term of office has suffered and permitted gambling to be carried on openly and notoriously in public places within Russell County."

With this done, Roberts Brown and Albert Patterson, assisting as legal advisor for the RBA, began to gather the evidence and build the case that would go before the Alabama Supreme Court. With these two notable attorneys on the case, the syndicate began to worry and Joe Allred, long notorious for his involvement in the Johnny Frank Stringfellow case, approached Roberts Brown and asked him to withdraw from the suit. When Roberts Brown refused, he received a call from an anonymous caller offering him $50,000 to drop the suit. When he refused this, he awoke on 23 October 1953, in the middle of the night to the smell of smoke. His house already in flames, he and his wife, in their night clothes, were barely able to escape through an upstairs window.

"Violence and threats are not going to stop us," Roberts Brown said. "We will continue our efforts to bring the case of impeachment before the Supreme Court."

The arsonist was never caught. No evidence was found, and this case joined the growing file of unsolved mysteries and unrestrained violence: the Bentley bombing, the Patterson fire, the public beating at the polls, and the burning of Roberts Brown's house.

Law enforcement in Phenix City had simply gone to hell. No one was safe, and no one knew who would be next.

10

THE IMPEACHMENT TRIAL–1953

Hugh Bentley and his bunch at the RBA were not the only ones saying that law enforcement in Phenix City had gone to hell. Everybody said so, including the crowd at the courthouse—Hoyt Shepherd, Godwin Davis, Elmer Reese—but theirs was for a different reason. Their grave concern was for the cavalier conduct of Chief Deputy Sheriff Albert Fuller.

While the war raged between the racketeers and the RBA over gambling and control of the courthouse, Albert Fuller had carved out an empire of his own: protection and prostitution with levies so high that there were constant complaints from the gamblers about Fuller's exorbitant fees. Godwin Davis warned Fuller that his greed and shakedowns would bring down the gambling empire, and Hoyt Shepherd warned him that his actions would get him a long prison term.

Fuller just laughed and shrugged it off. He was friends with the lead horses now, people with power, people with influence way beyond the boundary of Phenix City and Russell County, people who could do just about anything they chose to do and never once have to make an accounting for it. For the longest kind of time Hoyt Shepherd was the kingpin and called the shots, but he had lost a lot of his edge when he turned cautious and gave up gambling after the law was passed for a federal gambling stamp. His was still a heavy hand, but nothing like before.

As for Godwin Davis, Albert Fuller figured him for just a "money-grubbing, little sonofabitch" still nursing a grudge about that $3000 he lost when Clarence Franklin Johns held up the Manhattan Cafe and hid out in the Black cemetery. It wasn't enough that he and ABC agent Ben Scroggins had shot him thirteen times. Davis was still complaining about the money that was never found and mouthing around that Albert Fuller had taken it. Albert had warned him that if he kept talking about him, he'd blow his head off, and Godwin Davis sent word back that if he tried that, there would be two heads blown off.

As for Elmer Reese, he wanted to reclaim territory that had fallen into Albert Fuller's hands and had his big nephew Buddy Jowers named night police chief, ready to take over at the first unguarded moment, but Albert Fuller never let that moment go unguarded.

He was top gun and the high sheriff and they all knew it and Albert Fuller didn't give a hell what they said. He had more money than he could get in his pocket, most of it in thousand dollar bills. He had a wife and three mistresses that he kept in clothes, cars and houses and almost any woman he took a fancy to—of course, they weren't all willing—and when they weren't there were ways of persuasion or penalty which was how he kept the jail filled up and the whore houses provided with an unlimited stable of girls.

It was all so easy. Cruising around in the county, he'd see a little country girl out working in the fields, motion her over to his patrol car and ask: "What's a pretty girl like you doing out in this pig path?"

The response was always a shy smile, too shy to look him straight in the face and she'd look down at her bare feet and feel ashamed of not having shoes.

"A pretty girl like you shouldn't be barefoot out working in the fields. You ought to be in town with the bright lights and the big times."

With her hands clasped behind her she'd twist nervously and steal a glance up at him and back again at her bare feet while Albert sized up the budding young figure under her calico dress.

"Look up at me, girl. Let me see your face."

Shyly, she obeyed and Albert asked: "How old are you, girl?"

"Fourteen."

"I would have never thought it," Albert lied. "I would have taken you for eighteen."

Pleased with this mistaken maturity, she'd smile.

"How'd you like to come to work in town and have pretty clothes, bright lights, and big times?"

Twisting nervously again, she'd manage to say: "I ain't got no way to go and nowhere to stay."

"We can fix that," Albert said, peeling off a twenty dollar bill and handing it to her. "Get on the bus to Phenix City and come to the sheriff's office. Ask for Chief Deputy Sheriff Albert Fuller."

Holding the twenty dollar bill like she'd never seen one before, her eyes dazzled by the big black patrol car, the shinning silver star marked "Chief Deputy Sheriff" pinned on Albert's chest, she was breathless. "Honest? Do you mean that?"

Albert loved overcoming girls—even country girls. It gave him a high, and he pushed his white Stetson back on his head and grinned. "Sure I mean it and you'd better show up like I said."

"Oh, I will. I will," she promised.

"Don't you go running off with my twenty dollars," Albert warned, "'else I'll have to come back and get you and put you in jail for taking my money."

"I wouldn't do that."

Albert smiled a reassurance. "I know you wouldn't, that's why I'm willing to help you get out of this pig path."

Racing the motor of his big patrol car, he threw it in gear and called out the window, "See you at the courthouse."

When she showed up at the courthouse, he would tell her: "First thing we got to do is get you registered so you'll be a member of the town. Now you come over here and get your picture took and then put your finger on that ink pad and press it on this paper."

After she was mugged and fingerprinted, Albert marked it "prostitute" and put it in the file.

"Now we got you registered, we gotta go get you fitted out."

Taking her to the department store in Columbus, Albert would run up a big bill buying her clothes, shoes, pocket books and perfume, things she had never had, some, she had never seen.

"Now," Albert said, "we gotta find you a place to stay and a place to work so's you can pay for all these pretties we just bought."

"I don't know how to do much 'cept work in the fields."

Albert smiled. "You'll learn."

Looking in his little black appointment book, he would decide which place needed a new girl and take her there. By the time she realized her purpose, it was too late. If she objected and cried and said she wanted to go back home, Albert always told her: "Do you know what would happen if I took you back home and told your daddy what you been doing? He'd kill you!"

She knew it was true and she knew there was no way out, and then, like most country girls, accustomed to submission to authority, she'd turn docile as a cow with that hurt, humiliated look on her face, but she did what she was told. She had to.

Town girls were different. They had more spirit and more resistance. Like that Earlene Harper. Naive and not knowing what lay ahead, she and a friend had come to Phenix City looking for work. As soon as

147

Albert saw them walking around town, he liked the looks of Earlene Harper, long dark hair that hung in a sexy coil of curls on her shoulders and a full buxom figure that would satisfy any man.

Pulling up beside them in his patrol car, Albert got out, adjusted his big .357 magnum in it's holster and told them: "Hold it right there."

Earlene was the first to answer. "Are you talking to us?"

Albert pulled his white Stetson down to his brows and scowled as he flipped his thumb under his badge. "You're talking to an officer of the law."

"We haven't done anything," Earlene protested.

"That's just it. We got a vagrancy law that doesn't allow women walking the street with nothing to do."

"We came here looking for work."

"That's what they all say."

"It's true! Ask my friend here."

"Get in the car," Albert told her.

"What for?"

"Investigation."

At the sheriff's office, she was mugged, fingerprinted, the file marked "prostitute" and locked up in jail. Then Albert called the Youngblood brothers, Ernest and Glenn, who owned a bunch of cafes, nightclubs, and cat houses.

"I got a live one over here in jail. You might want to come take a look and see if you want her for the Diamond Horseshoe."

Glenn Youngblood came over and talked to her sweet and low and told her he would get her out of jail, that he had two nightclubs and she could come to work for him, but when he told her what he wanted her to do, Earlene Harper refused.

"That's all right," Albert told him. "We'll let her sit in jail for two or three days and she'll come around."

Albert put the word out around town that he had his eye on Earlene Harper and no one else was to hire her. After three days, he let her out of jail and warned her: "You got three days to find work, and if you don't, I'm locking you back up as a vagrant."

Earlene Harper tried every cafe in town and begged to be hired to wait tables, wash dishes, scrub floors, but no one would even talk to her and on the third day, Glenn Youngblood made his offer again.

"I don't have any money," she wept. "I can't even leave town and I don't want to go back to jail."

"You can come to work for me," Glenn Youngblood told her, and with no other alternatives, she accepted his offer.

For Albert, it was all so easy. The gamblers were willing to pay plenty for protection so that they could continue operating in back rooms with equipment hidden in secret places that the RBA raiders couldn't find, and the girls were even easier than that. All Albert had to do was make an arrest, charge them with a fine they couldn't pay, and then arrange for them work it out at whichever whore house needed a new girl. The courthouse crowd was calling it peonage, but what the hell, they'd been into peonage for years, paying a prisoner out of jail, and making him work the rest of his life to pay off a debt that the balance books never reduced.

Of course, once the girls started to work, they had to pay their dues, too, for protection to insure themselves against arrest for prostitution. With the exception of Elmer Reese, it wasn't that the courthouse crowd so much objected to prostitution, they just objected to his using one of the Russell County jail cells for that purpose when he found a soldier willing to pay for a quick trick. It was just too lucrative to quit because that meant double pay – the soldier paid for the girl and the girl paid for protection – and the money kept pyramiding and with it, power.

૨ɞ

The courthouse crowd couldn't do anything about it and they knew it. Who would stop him? His supposed-to-be boss, Ralph Matthews? Ralph Matthews might hold the title of sheriff, but all he did was wear the badge, and besides that, he had trouble enough of his own with the impeachment proceeding filed against him by the RBA. Albert had heard about that, too – the back-room whispers that said the courthouse crowd had told Ralph Matthews they would support him in his defense against impeachment *only* if he fired Albert Fuller. Fat chance. Albert's power base was too broad. He knew too much on too many people. His gun was too fast, and he didn't lose any sleep at night worrying about losing his job as Chief Deputy Sheriff. There wasn't a man in town who could take him, and only Buddy Jowers would stand up, but Albert could handle that since he and Buddy divided territory. There was plenty to go around and there was a good balance of power what with J.D. Harris being a deputy and holding the job of mayor, too.

Hugh Bentley and the RBA had no idea what was really going on in Phenix City. They could rant and rave 'til hell wouldn't have it and Albert Patterson could file every law suit he could think of and they would never be able to do anything about the gambling, the protection and the prostitution and they would never be able to beat the Machine, at least not with the way it was set up now. Every corner was covered, law enforcement, legislative and judicial. Hoyt Shepherd had seen to that years ago when he set up the machine and Albert Fuller figured the way it was now he would go on forever getting bigger and bigger, richer and richer, more and more powerful.

But then, in January 1953, the balance of power tilted. J. D. Harris suddenly died of a heart attack. Otis Taff, who along with Leonard Coulter, became a member of the city council in 1947 when the city government was changed and membership on the city council increased from three to five members, was serving as mayor *pro-tem*. On the death of J.D. Harris, Otis Taff became the Mayor of Phenix City.

For Hugh Bentley, this was the turn in fortune he had hoped for, worked for, prayed for. After all the failures, defeats and reversal since 1946, here at last was the opportunity he had waited for.

"As Mayor of Phenix City, Otis Taff is also head of the police department," Hugh Bentley told the members of the RBA. "Now we can get something done! Otis is on our side."

It was Otis Taff whom he had supported years before against Elmer Reese whose election victory celebration ended with the killing of Fate Leebern. Otis Taff was one of them. His sympathies lay with the citizens of the town demanding an end to crime and corruption and establishing justice in the courts.

Outnumbered by machine candidates on the City Council all these years, Otis Taff had been powerless to take any positive action, but now, as Mayor of Phenix City and head of the police department he listened to the complaints compiled by Hugh Bentley and the RBA and declared "a state of emergency in law enforcement." Then, on 28 April 1953, Otis organized a twenty-five man "volunteer police force," primarily members of the RBA, empowered to conduct raids and make arrests. With the authority to get the job done, Hugh Bentley, Hugh Britton, and the members of the RBA joined Otis Taff on a raid of Head Revel's Bridge Grocery.

Reaction from the status quo was quick. Russell County's State Representative, Jabe Brassell, one of the attorneys who had defended Hoyt Shepherd in the Leebern case and whose sympathies and support was allied with those opposing the RBA, was called in to defend those arrested by the Volunteer Police Force for gambling.

In Recorder's Court, he accused the Volunteer Police Force of being a private army using Gestapo tactics and on behalf of a woman named Mrs. H.E. Fuller, he filed an injunction in Judge Julius B. Hicks' Circuit Court to stop the Volunteer Police Force from further activity and nullify their appointment by Mayor Otis Taff.

Going to Albert Patterson, Hugh Bentley asked: "Who is this Mrs. Fuller? Some kin of Albert Fuller's?"

"No, there's no relation there, she's just someone they've used to file the injunction."

"What are her objections?"

"She claims in her injunction that as a taxpayer she does not want the further burden of twenty-five additional policemen, that she feels they are not needed to patrol Phenix City."

"She ought to know that the Volunteer Police Force is serving without pay and not costing her a cent."

"I'm sure she does. This is just their way of trying to stop it."

In response to the injunction, even though Otis Taff pointed out that the complaint was without grounds since the Volunteer Police Force served without pay, Judge Hicks granted the injunction, stopping the activity of the Volunteer Police Force and nullifying their appointment by Otis Taff.

The Machine and the courthouse crowd were extremely annoyed with Otis Taff's meddling in the way the town was run and his alliance with Hugh Bentley and the RBA was to cost him his job. With no election until September, it was decided to eliminate his position. To do this, Jabe Brassell and Ben Cole, Russell County's two State Representatives, acting in the interest of those who wished to replace Otis Taff, introduced a bill in the legislature declaring the five-man commission created in 1947 unconstitutional and requesting a return to the three-man commission which would include A.L. Gullatt and Elmer Reese, both of whom had been serving since the 1940's, with the place vacated by the death of J.D. Harris to be filled by appointment.

"This is another slick trick," Hugh Bentley told his group. "They're trying to get rid of Otis by ramming a bill through the legislature. We can't just let them change the government at will, every time something doesn't suit them. We've got to stop them. It's the citizens' right to have a choice in their form of government."

In an effort to stop Brassell's steamroller tactics, Otis Taff announced that he would issue a proclamation calling an election so that the voters could decide if they wanted to return to the pre-1947 three-man commission or stay with the present five-member commission. More than one thousand citizens signed the petition asking for a city-wide referendum, but before Otis Taff could set the date for an election, Jabe Brassell filed a temporary writ of injunction on behalf of his legislative colleague, Ben Cole, as the complainant charging that the 1947 act setting up the five-man city commission did not provide for the position of mayor pro-tem and that Otis Taff was assuming without authority of law the duties and powers of mayor. Judge Julius B. Hicks, acting in concert with those who wished to remove Otis Taff from office, granted the writ of injunction against Otis Taff restraining him from calling an election.

The Brassell–Cole bill ran into trouble in the legislature and before it could be brought to a vote on the floor, Judge Hicks, acting on the temporary injunction that had been filed in his court by Brassell on behalf of Ben Cole, ruled that the five-man city commission had been devised unconstitutionally in 1947 and Otis Taff and Leonard Coulter were dropped from the commission and turned out of office. Elmer Reese and A.L. Gullatt remained as commission members and by appointment, Dr. Seth Floyd, father of Gloria Floyd Davis, was made the third city commission member to fill the seat vacated by the death of J.D. Harris. When the new commission met for its first meeting, Elmer Reese was elected Mayor of Phenix City.

The *Columbus Ledger* called Brassell's legislative coup "dictatorial" and "two-bit Caesarism", and Brassell, not done with retaliatory legislation, introduced a libel bill in the legislature aimed at the *Columbus Ledger* which would allow the governing body of a city, county or town to sue and recover punitive damages from any publication which published matter concerning the population, or government of the city, county, or town. The State legislature refused to go along with such legislative restrictions and Brassell's bill died on the floor, but he had accomplished what he originally set out to do which was to turn Otis Taff out of office.

For Hugh Bentley, the promising hope of an opportunity to finally, finally take a hand in ridding the city of crime and gambling with the aid of Otis Taff as mayor was shattered. There was, however, the impeachment trial of Sheriff Matthews still ahead.

?❧

Almost a year had passed since the filing of impeachment proceedings, but on 8 June 1953, the trial opened before the Alabama Supreme Court in Montgomery with Roberts Brown assisted by Albert Patterson, representing the RBA as the complainant, and Hoyt Shepherd's two former attorneys, Jake Walker and Roy Smith, representing Sheriff Matthews as the defendant.

The case, with twenty-four specifications accusing Sheriff Matthews of gross misconduct in office, was brought before the Supreme Court under a seldom used law permitting five or more citizens to file impeachment proceedings against county and circuit officials.

"Impeachment proceedings," the Supreme Court said, "are highly penal in their nature and are governed by the same rules of law which apply in criminal cases, it will therefore be necessary that the accusers prove the sheriff's guilt beyond a reasonable doubt."

On the witness stand, Sheriff Matthews testified that there had been no open gambling in his or any previous term, but an investigator from Fort Benning's Criminal Investigation Division testified that during the period in question, he had observed open gambling in twenty-six establishments in Phenix City and Russell County including slot machines, dice tables, poker, black jack games, and horse racing machines.

Howard Pennington told of boxes stacked on the floor in front of slot machines so that children could reach the handle of "one-armed bandits" and his fourteen-year old son, James, testified that school children used their lunch money on slot machines and pinball machines that operated near the school.

Defense attorney Jake Howard hammered away in cross examination: "Even if the situation existed, the sheriff was not personally notified."

"It's the sheriff's job," Roberts Brown reminded the court, "to ferret out crime, not wait to be informed."

Attacking Sheriff Matthews' testimony that he knew of no open gambling in his term or any other, Roberts Brown introduced the court records from the Gloria Floyd Davis divorce trial, which established in open court the gambling and lottery operation run by Godwin Davis, his two sons and Head Revel. "Following the revelations at the Davis trial," Sheriff Matthews replied, "cases were made and fines were levied against Godwin Davis, his two sons, and Head Revel."

"Did you initiate raids on your own or did you wait to be told?" Roberts Brown asked.

"I instructed my deputies to be on the look-out for all violaters and make cases whenever possible."

"There have been complaints about gamblers hanging around the courthouse, specifically Hoyt Shepherd, Jimmie Matthews, Godwin Davis, and Head Revel. Can you explain this to the court?"

"Hoyt began coming by my office after he was shot at on two occasions," Matthews explained. "He said he felt safer in the courthouse."

"Did you inquire into his gambling activities?"

"I knew he wouldn't tell me nothing. When gambling was brought up, Hoyt said: 'Sheriff, I wouldn't make any statement to incriminate myself.'"

"What about Godwin Davis?"

"I asked him if he operated the Metropolitan Lottery out of the Manhattan Cafe and he said: 'Sheriff, I don't know whether I own any lottery or not.'"

"Didn't you investigate to find out if there was open gambling?"

"If I got a complaint, I made a raid. If I didn't get a complaint, I felt like the county was getting along okay."

"Did it never occur to you to go into places and look for slot machines?"

"I investigated all complaints."

"Then you didn't do anything unless you got a complaint?"

"I patrolled the county."

Defense attorney Jake Walker moved to have the charges against Sheriff Matthews dismissed. "In no case were the complaints taken directly to the sheriff."

From the Ministerial Alliance, the Rev. R. K. Jones testified before the Supreme Court that he had told the sheriff about the gambling and the large number of slot machines, and that the sheriff said he didn't know whether he would do anything about them or not.

"Later," the Rev. Jones reported, "after a concerted effort by the RBA and the Ministerial Alliance, Hoyt Shepherd and his partner turned in a large quantity of gambling machines, but they were fined and not prosecuted by the circuit solicitor."

Called to the witness stand to explain this, Circuit Solicitor Arch Ferrell, told the court that he had made an agreement with Hoyt Shepherd and his partner, Jimmie Matthews, by which they would turn over their slot machines if the solicitor would promise not to give them or people who worked for them in the past jail sentences.

"Shepherd said they had been out of the gambling business altogether for a while and out of slot machines for some months. I agreed to the proposal," Ferrell said, "on the condition that every machine be turned in to officers."

"Have you ever received any complaints that Sheriff Matthews was not doing his job?"

"I don't know that I have," Ferrell replied.

The defense called forty character witnesses on behalf of Sheriff Matthews, many of them high state and county officials: Director of the Department of Safety L.B. Sullivan, Chief of the State Highway Patrol Tom Carlisle, State Fire Marshall J.V. Kitchens, special investigator with the Department of Public Safety O.C. Hitt, and chief of the enforcement division of the Alcoholic Beverage Control Board Joe T. Burton.

The most prominent of those testifying on Sheriff Matthews' behalf was the Alabama Attorney General himself, Si Garrett, who said: "I have known almost every sheriff of Alabama since 1935 and I don't know of a better one than Ralph Matthews."

Three days later on 13 June, the Alabama Supreme Court voted unanimously to acquit Sheriff Matthews. In a nine-page opinion the court dismissed the impeachment charges.

"It has been carefully considered by the entire court and we are clear to the conclusion that there is very little, if any, evidence tending to show that bets were taken or that lotteries were played for money in public places openly and notoriously commencing in January 1951 and ending in May 1951. According to the sheriff, he promptly responded to all complaints made to him during that period of time."

"Numerous citizens appeared before this court and testified as to the good character of the respondent. This testimony must be considered along with other evidence in determining whether there was a willful neglect of duty."

They conceded however: "We would be blind to realities if we did not acknowledge the unsavory reputation, justified or not we do not say, which Phenix City has acquired because of alleged gambling operations there through years past."

Recognizing the efforts of the RBA, the court said: "We perceive that this proceeding is an outgrowth of a desire on the part of some of the citizens of Phenix City to effect a redemption of that reputation. However laudable that purpose might be, it should have no weight in determining whether the respondent is guilty or innocent."

"The citizens sought Sheriff Matthews' removal from office solely on the charge of 'willful neglect of duty'. There are twenty-four specifications under that charge, all of which broadly stated, allege that the respondent willfully neglected to perform his duty relative to the enforcement of the gambling laws of this state."

"We are not satisfied beyond a reasonable doubt from the evidence adduced that the respondent sheriff is guilty of willful neglect of official duty as is contemplated by the Constitution as grounds for impeachment and removal from office."

Quoting from an old Alabama case that defined neglect of duty, the high court was of the opinion, "that neglect of official duties, to be willful and to authorize forfeiture of office, must be characterized by a certain moral and intellectual quality different from that implied in mere intentional doing or failing to do an act."

The *Columbus Ledger* scoffed. "If we interpret the court correctly, an officer sworn to enforce the law is not to be convicted of 'willful neglect of duty' unless his thought processes can be opened to view and precise motivations involving his mentality and morality exposed. This would mean that it would be just about impossible ever to convict anyone of 'willful neglect of duty' and laws pertaining to that laxity might as well be written off the books."

Hugh Bentley and members of the RBA were in despair and at a loss for what to do next. They had appealed to the highest authority, the Alabama Supreme Court itself, and been defeated. There was nowhere else to go and nothing else to do.

Publicly, they were saying: "This is just a temporary reversal and a temporary reversal is not a defeat. If we stop now, we may just as well move out and turn our city over to gamblers. We are going to keep on keeping on. We will not stop until right and justice prevails."

Privately, sitting in Hugh Bentley's living room, Hugh Britton shook his head despondently. "We may as well write off the books anymore efforts. We've exhausted due process. There's nothing left that we haven't tried."

Hugh Bentley was sunk in his soft easy chair in a sad heap, his head propped in his hand, rubbing the wrinkles from his forehead with his fingers. "It's been seven years now," Hugh Bentley said, trying to hang onto his faith and belief, and for Hugh Bentley there was something significantly biblical about its having been seven years just as there had always been something significantly biblical to him about his being the seventh son. He believed now that his allotted time to spearhead the fight was done and that it was time to pass the torch. "We've been through hell and high water, murder, mayhem, bombing, beatings, burning, God knows how many campaigns and stolen elections and crooked court decisions. I'm satisfied we've fought the good fight and done everything there is to do, and I don't believe God is going to abandon us now. I just think maybe the time has come for us to pass the torch."

"You aren't talking about giving up?"

"No, just giving our support to someone else who can accomplish what we've been unable to."

Hugh Britton frowned, and Hugh Bentley explained.

"The most powerful law enforcement officer for the entire state is the attorney general."

"Sure to God you don't think Si Garrett is going to help us out. He's the one who witnessed for Sheriff Matthews."

"No, but election for his office will come up next year. If we run a candidate for the office of attorney general in the May 1954 election ...."

"Who did you have in mind?"

"There's only one person," Hugh Bentley said, "who could carry the torch and carry on the battle."

"Who is that?"

"Albert Patterson."

11

PATTERSON'S CAMPAIGN–1954

Albert Patterson did not want the job of attorney general.

He did not want the commitment and controversy of a campaign and a cause. Causes, he felt, were for young men and he had already had his fighting as an Infantry officer in World War I. His stiff and shortened right leg, from wounds he had received from German sniper fire, had left him, at fifty-nine, silver-haired and crippled requiring the use of a cane to get about, unable to dress himself without the help of someone to get his stiffened right leg into his trousers. That was why, when he was elected delegate to the Democratic convention in Washington in 1952 to vote for Estes Kefauver, he had taken his young son, Jack, along, not only to experience the democratic process, but to help him get into his clothes to go to the convention.

To run for office himself, the physical demands of a taxing campaign were a consideration and if he were going to submit to that kind of strenuous effort, the job he wanted was that of lieutenant-governor, the office he had run for and lost in the 1950 election.

Earlier in his career, his ambition had been to raise his four sons and impartially practice law. This was important to him because his law degree had been hard-won, financed by work on the farm, in the cotton fields and cotton mills and the oil fields of Texas and he had held to the principle that anyone brought before the bar of justice had the right to employ the best counsel available to defend their constitutional rights. Ideally, he still believed that. Realistically, he had found it could not work, not in Phenix City, not the way it was now.

After being a member of Hoyt Shepherd's defense team in the Fayette Leebern murder trial and after being counsel for Head Revel in the Johnny Frank Stringfellow case, he felt besmirched by the bending of justice. In Hoyt's case, it was the most money he had ever been paid by a client, but Hoyt expected his money and favors to buy allegiance and obedience, and his purchases had been considerable. The list of those who had succumbed to Hoyt's bounty and influence was long, but for Albert Patterson, there wasn't money enough in the world to buy his independence and his soul. Hoyt was aware of this, but continued to court Patterson's favor and consent. For the longest time Hoyt maintained a professional relationship, calling on him for legal advice, but after the sordid Stringfellow affair — the hired killing of Johnny Frank Stringfellow, the doping, shooting, and burial in a lime grave — Patterson knew he could, in good conscience, no longer ally himself nor allow himself to represent a criminal element so vicious and so unrestrained that it knew absolutely no limits.

After his decision to refuse any more representation, he was dropped from the possible list and put on the endangered list, but there was no active retaliation until his defense of Gloria Floyd Davis in her divorce from Godwin Davis' son, Bubber. Exposing the rackets drew blood, and the Mob chose the weapon that would wound him most. They had him stripped him of all his cherished civic positions — service on the school board, the draft board, even as deacon of his church. The wound was deep and bleeding and when Patterson recovered from the hurt and the loss, he was fighting mad and out to get some blood of his own. That's when he decided to join Hugh Bentley and the RBA, initially to return some licks of his own, but then, the efforts and the overwhelming defeats in every attempt they made against the racketeers and the Machine became a personal challenge to Patterson and he found himself bonded to this group of brave, decent men facing odds that were almost impossible to overcome, and their fight became his fight. As legal counsel for the RBA for the past two years, he had tried everything the law allowed, but the job of attorney general was something else again.

If the Mob was mad before, they would be murderous this time. God only knew what they would do. It would most certainly be one hell of a fight and costly, in terms more than money. But Hugh Bentley, Hugh Britton, Howard Pennington, and the members of the RBA were insistent that his winning the seat of attorney general was the only hope ever of accomplishing what they had so long tried to do in restoring justice and the rights to the people.

Patterson knew it was true. The office of the Attorney General of Alabama was that of the chief law enforcement officer in the state, empowered to go into any county and investigate any condition he saw fit, remove solicitors, and take over grand juries. If won, Patterson would have the power to crush the syndicate and correct Phenix City's incorrigible crime, vice and corruption which was far worse than anyone knew, even Hugh Bentley and the RBA.

Since taking on the job as legal counsel for the RBA and investigating the conditions to bring impeachment proceedings against Sheriff Matthews, Patterson had learned that the syndicate's tentacles of power and influence reached far beyond Phenix City out into the State and beyond with its sites ultimately on Washington, but only Patterson knew the full extent of that. It was a dangerous knowledge that he did not share with anyone for it made him a target.

Finally, after grave consideration for his family—his wife, Louise, his four sons (Jack, Maurice, Sam, and John, who had joined him in his law practice)—his finances, and his own physical limitations, Albert Patterson decided to become a candidate for the office of attorney general and once decided, he knew that nothing would be able to sway him from his decision.

❧

"All right," he told the members of the RBA. "I'll be your candidate and the platform will be *A Man Against Crime.*"

"Thank God, for that!" Hugh Bentley exclaimed, putting his hands together prayer-like. "We'll turn heaven and earth to give you our complete support."

Howard Pennington, the tall, slim carpenter with the crewcut who had joined the RBA after his young son had lost his paper route money in a Phenix City slot machine, volunteered. "I'll go with you as you stump the state."

"We'll criss-cross the state," Hugh Bentley said enthusiastically. "While you are speaking in one place, I'll be talking to them in another, spreading the word."

"I'll keep on giving them hell on the home front," Hugh Britton added.

"And I'll begin the fund raising," Charles Gunter, another RBA member, offered.

The news of Albert Patterson's candidacy came as a stunning surprise to the Phenix City political machine and they were quick to counter his campaign. Patterson's opponents in the race for attorney general would be MacDonald Gallion, a young attorney from Montgomery who represented the silk stocking trade, and Lee Porter, an attorney from Gadsden whom the Machine had chosen to back.

Lee Porter made a good appearance. A chubby thirty-seven year old attorney with thinning red hair, an attractive wife, and three children, he had established a reputation in his hometown of Gadsden as that of a family man active in civic events, the Boy Scouts, and church activities. Four years before he had made a bid for the office of attorney general and was barely beaten by the present attorney general, Si Garrett. This time, he had Si Garrett's support as well as that of his former law school classmate, Circuit Solicitor Arch Ferrell.

The quickest way to dilute Patterson's efforts, it was decided, was to destroy his credibility by insidious insinuations that Patterson, the Phenix City lawyer, was *really* the Machine's candidate, out to hoodwink the public, gather their support, and once in office, turn the power of the State's law enforcement over to the gamblers and gangsters of Phenix City. In some quarters, it was a story that people readily believed. After all, it was argued, Patterson himself had defended some of the Phenix City gamblers in two of the most notorious murders in recent Phenix City history: Hoyt Shepherd in the killing of Fayette Leebern and Head Revel in the murder of Johnny Frank Stringfellow. Why, now, should they believe this sudden change of heart, that he who had defended the gamblers was truly out to stop the crime and gambling in Phenix City?

The Columbus newspapers were much of the same mind. Even Tom Sellers and *Ledger* editor Robert Brown who had reported and supported the activities of Hugh Bentley and the RBA were not persuaded of Patterson's sincerity. Both the *Columbus Enquirer* and the *Columbus Ledger* largely ignored Patterson's uphill battle to become attorney general and turned their coverage and criticism instead on the controversial campaign of Big Jim Folsom, Alabama's seven-foot former governor who was again seeking the office of governor.

Without official sanction or financial backing, Albert Patterson went to the people with his platform. Every weekend, he and Howard Pennington pooled their money to see if they could come up with enough to buy food and gas. Then, criss-crossing the state, meeting people, speaking in country stores, shopping centers, drug stores, wherever people gathered, he introduced himself and explained his position.

"I am Albert Patterson," he told them, "from Phenix City, Alabama, a place made infamous throughout the state and nation by its historical tolerance for crime and vice. The good people of Phenix City have done all they can do to try to stop crime and the criminal element. Before it spreads further into the sovereign state of Alabama, we are coming now to the people of Alabama in a last ditch appeal for help in this battle. I ask for your vote in my campaign for Attorney General as *A Man Against Crime.*"

With each appearance, the people cheered his intentions with a standing ovation, and in each town there were volunteers who offered to manage his campaign locally.

This response caused no concern to the Machine in Phenix City. Albert Patterson had no money for a campaign, no big financial backing, little to go on but effort and a lot to overcome by his former associations with gamblers. Their man, Lee Porter, endorsed by Big Jim Folsom and Attorney General Si Garrett, kept the issue constantly before the public by referring to Patterson as "that lawyer from Phenix City," reminding them of his past association with the gamblers, and calling on them to "Beat the Phenix City Machine".

With all the campaign ritual and rhetoric, the Phenix City Machine had no worries about the outcome of the race even though every seat on the ballot for the May 4th Democratic Primary was hotly contested. They knew how to win an election. They had done it before and they would do it again.

On the night before the election, there was a near riot at a community meeting with Machine candidates and Patterson supporters hurling charges and counter charges and when the polls opened on the morning of May 4th, Hugh Bentley and RBA members Hugh Britton, Howard Pennington, John Luttrell, Charlie Gunter, and Hilda Coulter with her RBA Auxiliary members were there as poll watchers.

"Take note of all the violations and infractions," Hugh Bentley told his group. "We're not going to let them steal this election."

But, as the voting began, the violence and vote-buying began.

Albert Wade, a Phenix City mechanic, arriving at the polls to vote, was confronted by a man named Ernest Allen who wanted to buy his vote.

"Damn a man who would sell his vote," Albert Wade replied, and as he shouldered past Ernest Allen, he was struck from behind with a blow so powerful that he was knocked semiconscious to the sidewalk. As he lay there on the ground, trying to regain his sensibilities, the voting officials took no notice, and Albert Wade was finally able to struggle to his feet and leave the polling place without voting.

Mrs. Edna Norris found when she went to the polls to cast her ballot that someone else had already voted in her name. "What do you mean," she demanded, "that someone has voted in my name?"

"That's all right," the election officials told her. "You can vote anyway."

Hilda Coulter, having seen a woman cast her ballot once, saw her return to vote again under the name of Mrs. Revel.

"Haven't you already voted once?" Hilda Coulter asked.

The woman gave her a hostile look, hastily turned on her heel and left.

RBA member John Luttrell, took note of Godwin Davis palming money into the hands of voters after casting their ballots and Red Cook marking ballots for them. Angered by poll-watcher John Henry East's note-taking, Red Cook grabbed the next voter's ballot out of his hand, marked it, and put it in the ballot box.

"Now! How do you like that?" Red Cook snarled.

Albert Fuller was making no pretense of his participation in the voting. Wearing guns and holsters, he was photographed by news cameraman Glen Brougham from Columbus TV station WBBL, openly marking ballots.

Questioned about this, Albert Fuller grinned. "The man's blind. I'm just helping him out."

Keeping account of all the illegalities, Hugh Bentley told Hugh Britton, "It's the worst I've ever seen. They're openly and arrogantly stealing the election right in front of our eyes."

But when the ballots were counted in the state-wide election, Albert Patterson won in the three-way race between MacDonald Gallion and Lee Porter by a 70,000 vote margin, forcing him into a run-off election with Lee Porter scheduled for 1 June.

Patterson's victory over machine candidate, Lee Porter, shocked and galvanized the criminal community, and an intense, all-out effort began to win the June 1st runoff election. Attorney General Si Garrett personally took over the direction of Porter's campaign sending out letters from his office over his signature urging the support of Porter in the June runoff election. To further strengthen Porter's position on the upcoming contest for attorney general, he called a meeting of all the state solicitors, ostensibly to discuss the United States Supreme Court's recent ruling on segregation, but used the time instead to lambaste Patterson and urge the support of Lee Porter.

From the head table, Garrett told them: "I know all you solicitors are interested in and will be effected by the attorney general's race. It is imperative that you get out there and work for our man, Lee Porter."

Adding his voice to the support, Arch Ferrell told the group:

"There's all this talk about cleaning up Phenix City. I want to clean up Phenix City, but Albert Patterson is tied to the rackets and he won't let me. Mr. Garrett and I are set on seeing that Albert Patterson never becomes attorney general of this state and I ask for your support in signing a petition supporting our candidate, Lee Porter."

Meanwhile, in Phenix City, another turmoil, largely overlooked and ignored, was brewing. When the votes were counted on the night of May 4th, Porter and his supporters were not the only ones who were shocked and surprised. Incumbent State Representatives Jabe Brassell and Ben Cole, running for reelection to Alabama House Seat #1 and #2 had also been defeated. Brassell, who had previously been backed by the Machine, who supported their position, and who had so vehemently fought for their causes on the floor of the legislature, had had a falling out with the syndicate. He had insisted on their support for Ben Cole and when they refused, he and Cole were defeated by young Phenix City attorney V. Cecil Curtis and William Belcher, one of the Hoyt Shepherd's team of defense lawyers in the Fayette Leebern trial.

Brassell was furious, after all his years of allegiance, he had no intention of accepting the election results which gave his office to a young upstart lawyer half his age. Stung and unappeasably angry by the defeat, he, along with Ben Cole, immediately filed a complaint with the Democratic Executive Committee charging their opponents with wholesale fraud and vote buying. In response, Chairman Ben Ray appointed a three-man subcommittee to look into Brassell and Cole's complaint in Phenix City beginning 3 June, two days after the runoff election.

This upcoming action was largely ignored by the public and dismissed as sour grapes by the victors. The routine complaint about vote fraud and vote buying in Phenix City had been made so many times that it had become virtually meaningless and almost no one took notice of this small storm that was brewing. Everyone's attention was riveted on the race for Attorney General.

MacDonald Gallion, who had lost in the three-way race for attorney general, threw his support behind Albert Patterson. Jim Folsom, who had won his nomination as Democratic nominee to governor, endorsed Patterson's opponent, Lee Porter, and Attorney General Si Garrett and Russell County Circuit Solicitor Arch Ferrell, lent every support to Porter with Ferrell introducing Porter to the Phenix City crime syndicate and wringing from them $23,000 in campaign funds to insure Porter's victory over Patterson.

Patterson was feeling the pressure. Warnings and threats began to arrive. Always the same. Always anonymous.

Hugh Bentley was worried. "I think we'd better try to get you some protection."

Albert Patterson shook his head. "You know we can't afford that, Hugh. The RBA is doing all it can to try to finance the expense of this runoff election."

"Then at least carry a gun so that you can protect yourself."

Albert Patterson's face was gray and grim. "That won't do any good. If they decide to kill me, they'll pick the time and the place and nothing will stop them ... no amount of protection or guns. The only thing we can do about threats is ignore them. I've had warnings and threats before, just like you have. I'm committed to this cause and I have no intention of giving way now."

For Albert Patterson, the possibility of nomination for attorney general, once remote, was now within grasp. With election to that post, he could make an historic difference, he could restore meaning to the words in the Constitution, he could clean out the everlasting crime and corruption that had festered in Phenix City for over 100 years and bring justice and meaningful due process back to the courts. It was a goal worthy of a man's efforts and a man's life. If the risks for attaining these things were inordinately high, so was the proportionate glory and gains, and he and his friends and supporters in the RBA redoubled their campaign efforts as they struggled toward the June 1st runoff election.

When the ballots were counted on the night of June 1st, Patterson, by the slimmest margin—874 out of 400,000 votes cast—won again. Hugh Bentley was ecstatic, and while he and the members of the RBA celebrated this signal victory, the crime syndicate, stunned beyond belief that in the buying, not enough votes had been bought, swung into action, dispatching three car loads of satchelmen with $30,000 in cash to criss-cross the state and buy a better count of the ballots before the official count was turned in at the State capitol in Montgomery on June 10th.

Attorney General Si Garrett, who had been so adamant in his support of Lee Porter, did not plan to rely solely on these efforts for he had already masterminded a scheme that would tip the scales and take the election. Very simply, if they couldn't buy the election, they would steal it. Taking Russell County Solicitor Arch Ferrell along, Garrett decided to set his sites on big, industrial Birmingham, the seat of Jefferson County, and use his considerable influence and position to persuade young, ambitious Lamar Reid to change the vote totals received by Porter. As chairman of the Jefferson County Democratic Executive Committee in Birmingham, Reid was responsible for the official vote count there. To make a 2,000 vote alteration in Lee Porter's favor, it would be a simple matter of changing 0's to 9's and 1's to 6's on the tally sheets.

Three days after the runoff election, on Friday, June 4th, Garrett had his secretary call Lamar Reid in Birmingham and tell him: "The Attorney General wants to see you."

12

THE VOTE FRAUD–1954

Silas Comer Garrett III was a man accustomed to having his own way. He was from a prominent and distinguished family of attorneys. His father was a probate judge, his two brothers, Broox and T. Watrous, were lawyers, and he himself was Attorney General for the State of Alabama. His ambition was to become a great deal more. Power and its trappings suited him, and from a look back at his record, the indications were that he had all the qualities to achieve what he wanted.

At the University of Alabama Law School, he had achieved a brilliant record, and immediately upon graduation was taken as an assistant in the attorney general's office where he remained for fifteen years, learning the expertise of politics. Then, at thirty-seven, he made his bid for the office of attorney general barely beating out his virtually unknown opponent, Lee Porter. This less than stunning victory had surprised him and depressed him, for this slim margin of victory cast serious doubts on any higher ambitions. It was at this time that his colleagues first became aware of his erratic behavior, absent from the office for days at a time, then returning with fanatic fervor to get things done. It was first attributed to his heavy drinking, but then, on promises to his family, he gave this up, substituting prodigious amounts of burgundy, and finally replacing that with seltzer water which he drank by the case.

Everyone knew of Si Garrett's brilliance, but only the family was aware of the thin line between that and the dark side of the manic-depressive. When he sought an appointment to the State Supreme Court, his own father persuaded the Governor not to name him. Stung by this, Si Garrett redoubled his efforts to procure the power he sought and disprove his family's dark doubts.

Foremost among his qualities was master persuasion. Tall, almost handsome, with liquid, dark eyes, he had the ability to mesmerize his subject and overwhelm his opposition. He could dazzle them with brilliance and baffle them with prodigious assorted facts, case citations, and documents which he drew from his satchel-sized briefcase and threw around the room in a virtuoso performance so filled with passion that it rivaled theater and left his opponents bereft of opposition.

His success at so articulately seducing his subject had given him a self-confidence that had escalated to a swagger. This was further embellished by his trademark: a broad-brimmed Texas-style white hat which he wore squarely on his head like Winged-Victory, an oversized, almost frock-length jacket that flapped along with his purposeful strides, and his bulging brown briefcase which he intimated held the answer to everything.

By any standard, Si Garrett had a presence that was overwhelming, and on that Friday morning of 4 June 1954, as he set out from Montgomery for Birmingham to see Lamar Reid, he was certain that none of these powerful reserves would be necessary. In fact, persuading Reid to change the vote totals in Jefferson County to favor Lee Porter would be a piece of cake.

Lamar Reid was a baby-faced twenty-eight year old kid, brand new at his job as chairman of the Jefferson County Democratic Executive Committee in Birmingham, ambitious, eager to please and acquit the confidence placed in him by the uncle who had raised him, the father-in-law who had made him a partner in the family's prestigious law firm, and the uncle-by-marriage who had helped secure his job as chairman of the Committee.

Reid was just beginning to learn the way of the world of politics. His recent defeat for an office in the May Primary was a good lesson in the necessity of favors, stored up as collateral to be called on in times of trouble or when support was needed. If Reid was as smart as he was supposed to be, Si Garrett didn't expect it to take any more than an inflection in his voice to get him to change the Jefferson County vote totals by 2,000 votes in order for Lee Porter to wrest away the seat of attorney general from Albert Patterson who had won the runoff election by 854 votes. Of course, the correct count had already been announced and published in the paper, but the totals would not be official until they were certified by the State Committee in Montgomery on 10 June.

As county chairman, Reid had in his custody the tabulation sheets for Jefferson County and it would be his job to turn over and certify the results to the State chairman. The deadline, by state law, was noon on Friday, 4 June, but when Garrett had called and said he wanted to see the tabulation sheets before turning them in, Reid did not hesitate to accommodate the attorney general's request. He had been instructed to bring them with him to Room 804 in the Molton Hotel in Birmingham at 2:00 P.M., two hours past the state deadline.

෯

Joy. Unrestrained joy. That was the only word in the world Lamar Reid could think of to adequately describe the way he felt that Friday afternoon of 4 June 1954, as he left his office in the Title Building in Birmingham with the three copies of the tabulation sheets, the box-by-box count of the attorney general's race for Jefferson County. He was on his way to the eighth floor of the Molton Hotel to meet Silas Comer Garrett III, the sitting attorney general for the State of Alabama. *The attorney general!*

The most influential and powerful attorney in the whole state had called *him*, A. Lamar Reid, to a meeting in his hotel room. Not his office, but his *hotel* room.

Talk about being singled out! He had only met the attorney general once, and this, in a group, and had no idea that Silas Garrett had remembered him, his name, or who he was until his phone rang at 4:30 in the morning on the day after the runoff election and Si Garrett himself was on the phone asking what the results were in the sixty-four Jefferson County boxes in the race for attorney general.

Well, the results were not yet in. Neither were they complete when he called again at ten that morning, but by four in the afternoon, with Leroy Simms from the Associated Press and Ed Strickland from the *Birmingham News* looking on and keeping a count of their own, the official canvas and the tabulation for the voting in Jefferson County was complete. Lamar Reid was quick to announce the official results for he knew Si Garrett was anxious to know: Patterson–23,854; Porter–23,060.

Lamar Reid knew Si Garrett would not be too pleased *with* the results for his declared and open support of Lee Porter had been strenuous, but he was sure Si Garrett would be pleased to finally *get* the results, and he rolled the three tabulation sheets up and hurried to his office to call the attorney general and tell him that the job was done.

When he got Si Garrett on the line, he didn't seem dismayed at all that Patterson had beaten his candidate by nearly 800 votes. Instead, he said: "Porter's won the race and will make an announcement soon. You can tell the 'close supporters' up there in Birmingham that there's been a Porter victory."

That's not what the newspapers were saying the next day. At first, they said the race, statewide, was too close to call, and then they said that Patterson had won by a bare 1404 votes in the runoff after a 70,000 vote plurality in the primary election. There was a lot of comment and controversy about that, and from Phenix City that day, at the opening of the Brassell-Curtis hearing on vote fraud and vote buying in the May 4th Primary, charges were being made that there was also vote fraud and vote buying for Porter in the runoff election for attorney general.

Si Garrett called again that night. "Patterson has claimed victory on the unofficial returns, Lamar, but I feel *certain* ..." his voice boomed over the phone line, "that 1700 votes have been changed in Patterson's favor in Randolph and Tallapoosa Counties ... *and* ..." the phone trembled with emphasis, "it looks like a contest will have to be filed in that election."

Lamar Reid could feel the power and intensity in the attorney general's voice from a hundred miles away and he was weak with relief that he had found no such discrepancies in the Jefferson County totals, but then he was saying: "What about Jefferson County, Lamar? Do any of the election results there bear looking into?"

"Oh, no sir," Lamar Reid was quick to say. "The count here is correct. Leroy Simms from the Associated Press and Ed Strickland from the *Birmingham News* made independent counts and they came up with the same totals that we got: 23,858 for Patterson and 23,060 for Porter."

There was a silence like the phone had gone dead, and then Si Garrett was saying: "I heard that some of the boxes in Jefferson County came in late."

"No, sir ..." Lamar Reid began timorously, trying to think of a way to gentle his words so that it would not seem he was contradicting the attorney general.

"Well, in any case, I'll want to get with you this weekend and discuss with you the filing of a statewide contest."

WOW! Imagine that! The attorney general wanted him, A. Lamar Reid, to help with a statewide contest! The trip to Florida for a family vacation scheduled to begin on the weekend would just have to be delayed a few days until the meeting with the attorney general was done. After all ...

The next morning, Friday, June 4th, the attorney general's secretary called from the State capital in Montgomery and said Mr. Garrett would like him to come to a meeting at the Molton Hotel in Birmingham at two o'clock and he should bring the three tabulation sheets with him. This latter request presented something of a problem. By state law, he, Lamar Reid, as chairman of the Jefferson County Democratic Executive Committee, was required to turn over the official canvas of votes by noon on Friday to the sheriff who was the custodian of the vote count. When he got there, Sheriff Holt McDaniel, sitting behind his desk glanced up at the wall clock.

"Yes, sir, Mr. Reid," the sheriff began cordially. "You got the tabulation sheets for me?"

"Not yet ..." Lamar Reid began. He had planned to tell the sheriff that the results would be late, past the deadline, and if there was any static about that, he would simply say 'the attorney general wants to see them,' but something in the sheriff's stern demeanor stopped him, and he said instead: "There's a new form for filing ..."

The sheriff reached in his desk and handed him the paper and then pointed to the clock with its hands at eleven o'clock and said: "You've got just one hour."

Officious bastard. If he only knew that the delay was at the request of the attorney general, he would crawl over to the Molton Hotel to give it to him. After all, the attorney general was the top law enforcement officer for the entire state. He could suspend a sheriff, replace a solicitor, and step into a situation anywhere in the state and impose his inquiry into any matter he felt warranted it. So, if the sheriff knew what was good for him, he would do what he was told and keep his mouth shut. He should have been in politics long enough to know that.

By 2:00 P.M., Lamar Reid had gotten over his miff with the sheriff and was on his way over to the attorney general's hotel room in the Molton Hotel, overcome with unmitigated joy. He could only imagine the outcome of this all-important meeting. Perhaps he had been singled out because Garrett had been told that he was a bright and coming young lawyer. Perhaps he knew that he had taken his recent loss in the May primary manfully and had not kicked up the mess and row presently going on in Phenix City between Jabe Brassell and V. Cecil Curtis over House Seat #2 in the legislature. Maybe he had found another more important place in the party for him. Maybe—it was just too delicious to anticipate anymore. He could only think that this was a wonderful, memorable, special day, and as he arrived outside Room 804 in the Molton Hotel, he paused before knocking on the attorney general's door to suck in his breath and try to swallow some of his excitement. He had no idea what was waiting on the other side of that door, but as he raised his hand to knock, he only knew that he would never, ever, forget the fourth of June 1954.

He had barely drawn his hand back from knocking when the door swung wide and Si Garrett was there filling the door frame, shaking his hand, and drawing him inside with an arm around his shoulder.

"*Good* to see you again, Lamar," Si Garrett was saying. "Let's take a look at those tabulation sheets."

The hotel suite was strewn with papers and Si Garrett's satchel-sized briefcase was open and bulging with more. Clearing away those on the coffee table, Garrett said: "Roll them out here."

Doing as he was directed, Lamar Reid stood by and watched the attorney general bend over the tabulation sheets and study intently the box-by-box count while he basked in the glory of being in the attorney general's presence on such an important mission.

He had barely had his fill of this when the door to the adjoining room opened and another man, shorter and slimmer than Si Garrett, but with dark eyes and the same intense expression walked into the room. Garrett glanced up, and with a wave of his hand said: "Lamar, this is Arch Ferrell, my good friend, who's the solicitor down there in Russell County."

Lamar Reid did not need to be told who he was. Even though they had never met, he *knew* who Arch Ferrell was, a power in politics and the political kingpin down in Phenix City.

With a tight smile and no change in the intensity of his dark eyes, Arch Ferrell walked over and shook hands, a hard, dry handshake that had no more warmth than a newspaper.

"How do you do, Sir?" Lamar Reid responded, unable to keep the reverence out of his voice, for he was now even more profoundly impressed by his inclusion at this high-level meeting. It really was true. They really did have plans for him. He could no longer even speculate on what they might be for Ferrell had joined Garrett at the coffee table pouring over the tabulation sheets with the same amount of concentration. Then they began to talk about the totals in Randolph and Tallapoosa County and how some of the boxes had come in late, particularly Randolph County where there had been a big increase in Patterson's totals.

"Yeah," Garrett said, looking up to include Lamar Reid in what he was saying, "it looks like we're going to have to contest the runoff election." He paused, letting the statement settle, then: "Lamar, didn't you tell me on the phone that the newspapers got the same totals for Jefferson County as you've got listed here on the tabulation sheets?"

"Yes, Sir."

"Then, how 'bout running over there to the newspaper office and getting them to give you a copy of their statewide totals."

Lamar Reid made the trip as quickly as possible, going to the *Birmingham News* office and getting the totals from Leroy Simms at the Associated Press desk. When he returned, the meeting had gotten even bigger. Lee Porter, the candidate that Ferrell and Garrett had so ferociously backed in his race against Albert Patterson for attorney general, was there with his stunning, dark-haired wife, Martha. After introductions and an exchange of pleasantries, Garrett told the Porters, "You'll have to leave now. We got some business to attend to on this election contest."

Porter looked embarrassed, his round fat face reddening all the way to the edge of his receding hairline, and he took his wife's arm to guide her out.

"Go see a picture show," Garrett told them. "There's a good one down at the Grand with Ray Milland and Grace Kelley. "It's called 'Dial M for Murder.'"

The Porters obediently left the room and Ferrell followed them out, leaving Lamar Reid alone with Garrett, who picked up the state totals and began a long, silent concentration on the figures. The time stretched out and the silence deepened. Lamar Reid began to feel uncomfortable and ill-at-ease, not knowing what to do with himself, but Garrett took no notice, his eyes, magnified by his steel-rimmed glasses were fastened on the state totals he was studying.

Finally, after what seemed an eternity to Lamar Reid, Garrett got up and tossed the papers aside. "You know, Lamar, I worked long and hard on this election," he said, striding about the room, "in fact, I got up out of a sick bed to do it mostly at Arch Ferrell's request. Arch." His voice dropped a decibel in describing his feelings. "I love him like a brother."

While Lamar Reid was digesting this confidence, Garrett continued his pacing up and down the room. Getting ever more agitated as he did so, he slid his hands into the back pockets of his pants, his coat bunched up and bobbing behind him. Lamar Reid watched, not knowing what to say.

Garrett swung around and slammed his fist down on the dresser as he passed.

"It's just a dirty, damned shame!" Garrett bellowed.

"What's that, Sir?" Reid asked timidly, afraid the question would be an intrusion on Garrett's great anguish.

"Patterson's people have stolen the election!" He snatched up the papers on the coffee table and hit them with the back of his hand. "Seventeen hundred votes in Randolph and Talapoosa Counties; we're gonna have to contest the election!"

The fact seemed to sadden him. His face was long and drawn. "And it's gonna cost a lot of money to contest." Tragedy edged into his voice as he confided: "and I'm not sure my health will hold out."

Lamar Reid was shocked by this disclosure. The strong, vibrant man of a moment ago had become a frail shadow of what he had been and Lamar Reid was struck with sympathy for this wounded giant. "I'll be glad to do whatever I can to help."

This seemed to lighten the load. Hope visibly flickered in Si Garrett's eyes. "Well, Lamar, as chairman of the county Democratic Executive Committee, you, more than anyone are in a position to help Porter win the election."

"Me!"

Garrett sat down beside him on the sofa, leaned back, closed his eyes and nodded his head.

"How?"

The door opened and Ferrell came back in the room. Lamar Reid looked up, then back at Garrett and asked again: "How?"

"Have you rechecked the Jefferson County vote totals?"

"No, Sir, not since the night of the election when we took the final count down at the courthouse."

"I think you would be remiss in your duties if you did not recheck the totals before they are sent to Montgomery as official figures for Jefferson County."

Lamar Reid bobbed his head in agreement, and Si Garrett pressed him further: "You never did run a tape on the adding machine?"

"No, Sir."

"Well, you'd be doing your duty to run a tape. You wouldn't want someone you're interested in to lose an election just because you didn't recheck the figures. Why, very often you'll find that 3's have been put down for 5's, 7's for 9's—you might find that count off by 2,000 votes."

Lamar Reid was so shocked by this suggestion he didn't even pause for caution. "That's impossible! There's no way we could have miscounted by 2,000 votes. Besides, the totals have already been announced in the newspapers and they would spot that in a minute."

Arch Ferrell, who had been leaning against the door he had entered, his hands behind him on the door knob, listening to Garrett's pitch and assessing Reid's reaction, stepped forward to enter the arena of conversation. "Two thousand votes is too rough for your young friend here to handle," he advised. "I think there's a smoother way to do it."

Garrett considered the suggestion for a moment. His great, liquid dark eyes turned for a moment from their mesmerization of Lamar Reid.

Taking his cue from Ferrell, Garrett got up from his place on the sofa beside Lamar Reid, rising to his full height in the stance of a pronouncement. "You're right, Arch. I've got most of my Birmingham staff checking on the vote frauds in Randolph and Tallapoosa Counties. It is entirely possible that they will uncover enough votes so that nothing further will need to be done."

Lamar Reid knew he was being dismissed, and he stood up to take his leave, but as he started to gather up his tabulation sheets from the coffee table, Garrett said: "You can leave those here for now, Lamar. Arch and I will want to go over them."

"I've got to turn them into the Chairman of the State Executive Committee. Today is the deadline. In fact, they were supposed to be in the sheriff's office by noon."

"That's not necessary," Garrett said, edging his voice with authority and annoyance, "for Ben Ray or the sheriff to get those tabulation sheets immediately. The only real necessity is that they be in Montgomery by next Thursday, the tenth of June, for the official statewide canvass. By that time, we'll have this thing straightened out."

Seeing the stricken look on Lamar Reid's face, Garrett softened his voice, smiled, and slapped him on the back. "You worry too much, young fellow, when you got nothing to worry about." Garrett had him by the elbow, guided him to the door and opened it. "We'll discuss this some more tomorrow."

Back at his office in the Title Building, Lamar Reid set into full time worrying. It was already four o'clock. Four hours past deadline. Friday afternoon with only an hour to go before all the offices closed down for the weekend, and then he would be not just hours past the State deadline, but days overdue, and how would he be able to explain it? What would he be able to tell Chairman Ben Ray was the reason for his not fulfilling his duty. It was no longer possible to throw around the attorney general's name, because what the attorney general was up to would not bear looking at.

The vacation to Florida. He could say that the details for leaving for Laguna Beach had so claimed his attention that he passed the deadline without being aware of it, and when realization came, it was too late to get the tabulation sheets in by Friday. That would make him only seem irresponsible and unworthy of the office he had been appointed to, a posture he would not like to assume, but far better than the alternative of deliberately aiding and abetting a change in the official vote count.

The clock was ticking and time was running out. The day that had begun with joy and promise was ending in anguish and indecision, but now it was past five and he would have to go with the operative of being irresponsible and inefficient, unworthy and all of that. When he got the tabulation sheets back from Si Garrett in the morning, he would sign the official canvas form and leave a note for his secretary with instructions to deliver the tabulation sheets on Monday. By that time, he would be in Florida, and hopefully, with his mind on no more than water-skiing.

Not a good solution, but at this point, the only solution. There was left now only to put his desk in order and go home to the party his wife had planned to kick off their vacation.

At 5:30 P.M., everyone else in the office was gone and Lamar Reid was picking up his briefcase to leave too when, without a word or warning, the attorney general burst through his office door, followed shortly thereafter by the Russell County Solicitor, Arch Ferrell.

"We got a proposition for you, Lamar," Si Garrett said, taking papers out of his briefcase and spreading them all over Lamar Reid's freshly straightened desk.

"Arch and I have been going over your figures in Jefferson County. I got the hotel to send up an adding machine and we ran a tape on the total. We're not going to need as many votes as we first thought, nothing like 2,000, more like 700."

He let the suggestion hang in the air, and when Lamar Reid hesitated, Garrett in full possession of all his persuasive powers, leaned across the desk and yelled: "Hell, boy! Patterson and his pack of crooks have stolen the election. We gotta steal it back. Think of what will happen to Alabama and all its honest citizens if Patterson and that pack of racketeers and criminals from Phenix City get hold of the courts and the law enforcement in this state. Why there'll be blood in the streets and no recourse in the courts. Why do you think I've got Arch Ferrell here with me now?"

Garrett didn't wait for an answer but continued with his barrage. "*Because*, because he *knows* what the situation is down there in Phenix City and Russell County. He *knows* Patterson is tied in with those crooks and criminals, has been for years."

Lamar Reid stood perfectly still behind his desk, still clutching his briefcase. It didn't make sense. Patterson had won his race for attorney general running against the crime and criminals in Phenix City on the platform of "A Man Against Crime."

"But, Mr. Patterson ran *against* them ..." Lamar Reid began.

Si Garrett let a smile smirk at the corner of his lip and he exchanged a look of amused contempt with Arch Ferrell who responded with a tight little smile of his own.

"Lamar, you're just a kid. You haven't even got your feet wet yet in the political waters, but if you're going to stay in the game, you gotta quit being so politically naive."

Garrett drew in a deep breath to show his exasperation. "Don't you know that Patterson carried on his campaign against the racketeers in Phenix City to mask his secret support of them and all their doings? Where do you think he got all that money to run his campaign and buy all those votes? *From the gamblers in Phenix City!* The very ones he's going to protect when he gets in office! The very ones who'll be setting the policy and running this state!"

Lamar Reid stifled the gasp that came to his throat. "I can't believe ...."

"That anyone could be so devious?" Garrett's liquid dark eyes were burning with an intensity that Lamar Reid had never ever seen in eyes before. "Well, you'd better. Patterson's been pussyfooting around this state promising to bring down crime and criminals. What he's really going to do is bring down law and order, honor and decency, and it's up to us to stop him no matter what has to be done."

Garrett paused, consumed by his passion, his face pale and sweating. "Now, are you with us? Are you going to help us save the State, or are you going to stand by like some scared school kid, too awed and addled to act before it's too late? Too late for the people of this great State who have put their faith and trust in a conniving, scheming, two-faced sonofabitch who's ready to sell them down the river the moment he takes office?"

Lamar Reid was overcome. He had heard what the attorney general was like in the courtroom when he had an attack of passion, but he had never seen it. He could only respond meekly, " I had no idea Mr. Patterson ..."

"Of course, you didn't. Patterson's a pro, as smooth and slick as they come — talking about crime and planning corruption, posing as a Christian while he's planning criminal acts — can't you see his evil scheme? Are you just going to stand by and do nothing and allow it to happen?"

Lamar Reid broke away from the hammer-lock of Garrett's mesmerizing liquid-dark eyes and looked over at Arch Ferrell, still standing by the door, still silent, still resting against the door frame, his hands behind him, his face impassive, his eyes passing judgment. Waiting.

What Garrett was saying was just too much for him to take in all at once. It was a scheme so awesome, so evil as to be unbelievable, and yet, here was the Attorney General of Alabama, the top law enforcement officer of the State, and the Circuit Solicitor of Russell County; it had to be true.

Lamar Reid felt his latest doubts being swept away and a return to his earlier euphoria of being included in something important.

"Well, Lamar, how about it? Are you going to join us in our effort to save the State?"

How could he refuse? It was a call to arms, an invitation to an heroic act, a case of being singled out and selected as a silent partner and standard bearer to save the State from an insidious pretender.

"The plan has the approval of those higher up in State affairs," Garrett confided.

For Lamar Reid, it was a proud moment to know that he had been trusted to share this confidence, to participate in this grand and heroic effort. A lump rose in his throat. He was so overcome with emotion, he could hardly speak. "I'm with you, Sir, all the way."

Si Garrett's face glowed with triumph. "I knew we could count on you, Lamar." He glanced over at Ferrell. "Didn't I tell you this boy's heart was in the right place? That he was full of promise and headed for a bright future?"

Arch Ferrell, still standing silently against the door, nodded his head.

"All he needed was to know what was going on, and I *know* ..." he fixed Lamar Reid with another mesmerizing look, his dark-liquid eyes glowing, "that we can trust you not to say *anything* to *anyone*. Patterson has infiltrated every level of government. He has listening posts everywhere. If word were to leak out..." He shook his head sadly, "our mission would fail, he would see to it."

Feeling like the good and trusted soldier, Lamar Reid said: "You can count on me, Sir."

Si Garrett reached across the desk and shook his hand, covering their handclasp with his left hand in a seal of solemn vow and conspiracy. "Good boy."

Garrett smiled and the room radiated with good will and he began gathering his papers scattered across Lamar Reid's desk and stuffing them back in his satchel-sized briefcase.

"We'll get together on the details in the morning."

Lamar Reid wanted to mention that his plans were to leave for Florida in the morning, but he looked at his watch. Six o'clock. It was enough that he was going to get to go home in time for his party which was already in progress.

As they started out of his office door, Si Garrett stopped abruptly as though he had suddenly been reminded of something. "We'd better not leave together." His eyes darted about looking to see if anyone else was lurking in the hall. "Arch, you take the elevator first. We'll follow later."

Driving home, Lamar Reid had a chill of anticipation. Talk about top drawer! Talk about high-level power plays! It was going to be a real cloak-and-dagger operation and the mission was control of the State. He was bursting with the secret confidence that had been placed in him, but he dared not tell. Anyone.

❧

The next morning at ten o'clock when Lamar Reid arrived for his appointed meeting in the attorney general's hotel room, Si Garrett was alone. Yesterday's prevailing air of partnership was gone, replaced now by impatience and an obvious attempt to make short work of what had to be done followed by an early dismissal. Si Garrett's attitude was underlined by a cold countenance and a great flurry of activity, throwing clothes into his suitcase and papers into his briefcase.

Si Garrett looked up momentarily from his packing and waved his hand casually toward the tabulation sheets on the coffee table. "You can take those now, Lamar, and turn them in to Ben Ray for the State-wide canvas in Montgomery on Thursday. Certify the total now shown on your tabulation sheets."

"What total is that?"

"For Patterson: 23,858. For Porter: 23,660. We only needed 600 votes instead of 700. The necessary changes have already been made."

Lamar Reid was aghast. *"Where?"*

Si Garrett threw down the shirt he was folding in his suitcase. His face was etched with annoyance. With impressive strides he bounded over to the coffee table and poked his finger in the places where the changes had been made.

Lamar Reid looked at the total and the alterations and his heart stopped. Without any consultation, without so much as 'by your leave,' they had changed the vote total to favor Porter by an additional 600 votes. When the discovery was made—and it would be—the responsibility of what had been done would be his.

He had been raped, used, exploited, and the worst of it was that *he* had let it happen. He had wanted to see inside high stakes politics. He had wanted to be a part, a partner. A fool.

He felt a sickness, a sudden shutdown of energy with all the promise and purpose of yesterday flowing down his body to his feet which seemed to be nailed to the floor unable to move. He had not been chosen for a mission. He had been picked for a patsy, tricked, duped, and dazzled by a master manipulator, his soul and services bought without a promise or a penny.

Standing there in the attorney general's hotel room, he stared at the altered tabulation sheets, not knowing what to do, how to protest the dishonor of this deception, or how to reclaim the integrity that only yesterday was his.

"Mr. Garrett..."

The attorney general fixed him with a riveting stare, a demand to get out and be gone. The room was filled with his aggravation and annoyance. He remained in stony silence, making no response.

"Mr. Garrett, I'm uneasy about these changes on the tabulation sheets. There's no way that it will go unnoticed. I've got to know what is going to happen to me, and how I'll be taken care of in this matter."

"I told you, Lamar, not to worry. If the vote totals are contested, you'll be in good hands."

Fear had made him bold and Lamar Reid stepped forward and insisted: "I've got to know more about what's going on."

Briefly, Garrett returned to his solicitous ways. He walked across the room and draped his arm over Lamar Reid's shoulders, all the while walking him toward the door.

"I want to get with you and explain this thing," he said, beaming stress and sincerity, "but I've got to go see Arch Ferrell and do some other things," implying a more important mission.

Lamar Reid wanted to resist, but he was locked in Garrett's bear-embrace standing in the hotel hall.

"I tell you what, Lamar. Come to Arch Ferrell's room tonight over at the Bankhead Hotel. Maybe we'll have time then."

Si Garrett closed the door to his hotel room and Lamar Reid found himself standing alone in the hallway, bereft even of the opportunity to protest.

That night at eight o'clock, Lamar Reid arrived at the Bankhead Hotel and knocked on the door of Room 706. Ferrell was there. Garrett was not. With Ferrell in room 706 were Neal Metcalf, of Cullman, and John Drinkard, the driver for Governor-elect Jim Folsom. With these two present, the conversation was general, concerning politics and the election.

Twenty minutes later, Garrett arrived with his satchel-sized suitcase, dismissed Metcalf and John Drinkard, then turned to Lamar Reid and took two file folders out, threw them across the bed and said: "There you are, Lamar. These files will give you a good idea what kind of a sorry sonofabitch we're dealing with."

Papers fell out of the fat folders and slid across the bed, papers concerning Patterson, statements by investigators, criminals in and out of prison, some concerning Hoyt Shepherd and the Phenix City machine, and Patterson's connection with the Fayette Leebern case, the Johnny Frank Stringfellow murder and Patterson's representation of Head Revel.

"You see, Lamar. It's what I've been telling you all along.

Patterson's in with them, represented them, fought for them, saw to it that they got off and didn't serve time for murders that were committed, bent the bar of justice!"

It was all there, just as Garrett said. Lamar Reid was appalled. He looked up and Garrett had his liquid brown eyes fastened on him, gauging his reaction. "I could have used that during the campaign," Garrett told him, "and it would have been devastating, but *I* kept Porter from using it."

He drew himself up into the posture of the Attorney General to explain his commendable actions. "I felt the campaign for this high office should be conducted on a high level, but now, now that Patterson has stolen an honest man's victory, I am prepared to use it."

Lamar Reid nodded his head and looked back at the bed-full of documents, but Garrett was not prepared to let the matter rest or be prolonged. Flinging his hand toward the files he had brought, Garrett demanded sternly, "So what does it take to convince you, Lamar? Sure to God ..." He stopped and glanced at the door through which Metcalf and Drinkard had so recently departed. "The others are pretty quick to catch on, to understand the situation and what has to be done. So what is your problem?"

Lamar Reid felt overwhelmed and embarrassed that he had so taken the Attorney General to task. "I just wanted to know ..."

"Arch will tell you what the details are," Garrett said impatiently, turning on his heel with a flap of his coattails and going into the adjoining room of Ferrell's suite.

Ferrell stepped forward with the papers showing the state-wide totals, and it was clear to see that he was not about to go to the effort of courting that the attorney general had.

"The whole matter concerning the vote changes has been arranged," he announced. "We've contacted various people over the state, and fifty votes in Walker County will be deducted from Patterson's total and fifty added to Porter's for a net gain of 100 votes. As Si told you this morning, 600 votes have been added to Porter's total in Jefferson County on your tabulation sheets and another 500 will be changed in Geneva County. We're on our way down there tonight with the man to do it. Any questions?"

The Circuit Solicitor made it plain that there was no margin for discussion or disagreement. What had been done was a *fait accompli* and yet Lamar Reid felt pressed to find out what would happen if the vote change was discovered, no matter how forbidding Ferrell made this presumption seem.

"Well, Sir, I would like to know what would happen if there was an investigation into the vote change in Jefferson County."

Arch Ferrell's answer came through lips stretched tight as though he were about to whistle. "First of all, what we're doing is the right thing to do. Every political faction is behind it, including Governor-elect Jim Folsom and he is the one who is going to see to it that this transaction gets closed out."

"I can appreciate that, Sir, but if there's an investigation?"

"There's no need for concern because any committee formed to investigate would not investigate the tally sheets, and besides, I already know the subcommittee members who would handle such matters if a question were raised."

Garrett bustled back into the room, all business and impatience. "Okay, Lamar, you're going to have to run on now. Arch and I have to get on down the road to take care of this other business." Taking hold of Lamar Reid's arm, he led him to the door saying: "Like I told you this morning, you're in good hands. Go on to Florida and enjoy your vacation, and if anything comes up, all you have to do is call either me or Arch."

The audience was over and Lamar Reid found himself again, alone in the hotel hallway. Going down on the elevator, the swift descent only added to the sinking feeling that had settled in the pit of his stomach.

Lamar Reid went to his office and signed a blank certificate of results with instructions to his secretary to type in the results that Si Garrett had given him.

The next morning, he turned toward Florida and tried to forget.

13

THE KILLING

When Lamar Reid drove off to Florida for a family vacation at Laguna Beach, he had hoped to leave the concerns over the election and the anxieties over the changes in the tally sheets behind him. They not only followed him, they eventually drove him back to Birmingham to what became a fire storm.

By Monday, 7 June, Ben F. Ray, chairman of the State Democratic Executive Committee, received a telegram from RBA President Howard Pennington stating that as much as $30,000 had been offered to county election officials across the state to change their tally sheets in favor of Lee Porter before the official canvas in Montgomery on June 10th.

On Tuesday, 8 June, Leroy Simms, bureau chief of the *Associated Press* in Birmingham at his desk in the offices of the *Birmingham News* received an anonymous phone call. The male voice on the end of the line said: "Check the tally totals for Jefferson County. You'll find that 600 votes have been added to Porter's total since the official count was taken on election night."

A call to Chairman Ben Ray's office verified that the total for Porter in Jefferson County now stood at 23,660 votes. Leroy Simms' own notes, taken on election night, stood at 23,060. He called Ed Strickland, the political reporter for the *Birmingham News* who had been there in the courthouse Tuesday night when the vote was counted.

"Hey, Ed, what was your count for Porter on election night?"

Ed Strickland squinted pale blue eyes against the gray curl of cigarette smoke and turned back to his notes. "I got 23,060."

"Me, too. The vote count now stands at 23,660. Somebody called and says there's been a vote change of 600 votes. I called Ben Ray and he says the certificate of results he received from Lamar Reid yesterday says 23,660."

"What does Reid say?" Strickland asked.

"I called his office and they say he's off on vacation in Florida."

To Ed Strickland, long acquainted with the way of politics, it sounded like mischief afoot. "Let's jump on it and find out."

The next morning in the Wednesday edition of the *Birmingham News*, a front page story announced: "It was discovered today that the results certified to Ben Ray, chairman of the State Democratic Executive Committee, were not the same as those announced last Wednesday after the official vote count." When Albert Rosenthal, a Birmingham attorney, who had been campaign manager for Albert Patterson in Jefferson County, read the report, he was enraged, furious and fighting mad. He called Ed Strickland at the *Birmingham News*, Ben Ray at his office, and then Emmett Perry, the circuit solicitor of Jefferson County.

"Goddammit, Emmett, I want a Grand Jury investigation and I want it *right now*."

"Fortunately, the Grand Jury, as you may know, is now in session, but they are just about to wrap up their work and adjourn for the June session. When do you want to bring this before the Grand Jury?"

"Today!"

"How about tomorrow? I can't get it on the docket before then."

"Okay, tomorrow."

On Thursday, 10 June, while Albert Rosenthal was presenting his grievance before the Jefferson County Grand Jury, the official state canvas was being conducted in Montgomery. Albert Patterson, surrounded by friends, sat in the Senate chamber and watched the proceedings. When it was over, he had won his race for attorney general by a mere 854 votes out of a total of 400,000 that had been cast statewide in the runoff election.

Afterwards, Albert Patterson said: "Large sums of money were collected and used against me in this race by the Phenix City gamblers in an attempt to take over the election machinery of the State. Organized crime is a threat to the welfare of the people and must be stamped out."

Meanwhile, in Birmingham, the Jefferson County Grand Jury was trying to determine what happened in the vote tally change, who did it, and why. And in Florida, the mounting pressure of the day-by-day events was too much for Lamar Reid. The situation had gone from critical to crisis. He called Si Garrett and a meeting was arranged for the next night in Selma, Alabama, at the Albert Hotel. Accompanied by his brother-in-law, Bruce White, Lamar Reid, following Garrett's direction, registered at the Albert Hotel under the name of "Frank Long." This was the code name Garrett and his associates used when they wanted to contact each other on a matter of importance. Frank Long, in point of fact, was a young lawyer, recently graduated from the University of Alabama Law School and president of the Alabama League of Young Democrats, who had traveled the state and vigorously supported Jim Folsom in his race for governor. Garrett simply appropriated his name as a password.

When Garrett met Reid in Selma, Garrett assured him that there was nothing to worry about, that challenges like this came up all the time, and they always came to nothing. He tried to impress on Reid the powers available to him as attorney general.

"If things get too hot, I can, as attorney general, dismiss the Jefferson County Grand Jury and dismiss Solicitor Emmett Perry."

Garrett waited to see the effect of this on Reid. Not satisfied with what he saw, he added for emphasis: "Hell, I can send Emmett Perry somewhere else on a five dollar cattle theft charge and take over the investigation into the vote fraud myself."

Impatient with the amount of persuasion it was taking, Garrett added: "Now try to have a little backbone, Lamar, and don't fall over with the first wind to give rise."

Lamar Reid was no longer impressed with Garrett's bloated promises, but that is all he got. When he got a summons to appear before the Jefferson County Grand Jury on Monday, 14 June, he packed up his family and came back to Birmingham to testify.

In the car, following his meeting with Garrett, Reid had asked his brother-in-law, an attorney in the family firm, "What must I do?"

Without a moment's hesitation, Bruce White had replied: "Cover your own ass."

Before the facts could be gathered and the witnesses subpoenaed to appear before the Jefferson County Grand Jury in Birmingham, the hearing into the charges of vote fraud in Phenix City, brought by Jabe Brassell, had gotten underway.

Brassell, charging malconduct and fraud, also charged that election officials were largely composed of professional gamblers, ex-convicts, racketeers and other underworld characters whose reputations were generally known and that black voters were herded into the courthouse and required to vote in the sheriff's office in front of armed men who intimidated them. Brassell, who had previously spent considerable energy and effort denouncing the RBA and their cleanup efforts, now turned to Hugh Bentley for help asking that he and his poll-watchers who had witnessed the violations at the polls appear as witnesses before the subcommittee hearing looking into the vote fraud during the 4 May primary.

Discussing the request with Howard Pennington, who had succeeded him as RBA president, Hugh Bentley said: "Jabe Brassell has fought us every foot of the way, and now that he has been thrown out by the Machine, he's ready to switch sides."

"If he's ready now to stand for law and order," Pennington said, "I'll testify. At least the violations will get on the official record."

Originally scheduled to begin on 3 June, the hearing had been delayed until 14 June by a Writ of Prohibition to stop the election contest, filed by Brassell's opponent, V. C. Curtis, and granted by Circuit Judge Julius B. Hicks on the grounds that Brassell had not put up surety to cover the cost. Brassell had taken the matter to the Alabama Supreme Court where Judge Hicks' decision was overturned when the high court by a Writ of Mandamus directed Judge Hicks to set aside his restraining order and prohibited him from further action in the matter, ruling that contestants are not required to post security costs for a primary election, only for the contest of a general election. Beginning 14 June, for four days, thirty-five witnesses testified about the flagrant and criminal violations in the voting on the May 4th primary. Day after day, witness after witness came forward with damaging testimony that exploded into black headlines across the state.

To substantiate Jabe Brassell's charge that ex-convicts, racketeers, gamblers, and other underworld characters were among the election officials when he was defeated in the 4 May Primary, Brassell provided numerous documents introduced as evidence showing that Night Police Chief Buddy Jowers had been convicted of violating the federal liquor law on 12 April 1941, and that Conrad Thompson, in charge of ballot box #11B, had been convicted of burglary and was still on parole even though he had sworn he had never been convicted of a crime. Another witness, John Henry East, had testified that gambler E. L. "Red" Cook had forcibly marked one voter's ballot and election official Billy Walls was drinking beer while officiating at the polls. Albert Wade described his encounter at the polls when he refused to sell his vote and was knocked to the ground semi-conscious.

"This was at the polling place?" the Sub Committee asked.

"Yes, right in full view of the election officials."

"What did they do?"

"Nothing," Wade replied. "They went right on with their business."

"Did you report this to the authorities?"

"What good would that do?" Wade said bitterly. "They were busy buying votes." Poll-watcher Floyd Foster then testified that Buddy Jowers was the satchelman who delivered and doled out the money, taking it out of his pocket to pay off voters and RBA member, John

Luttrell, described slot-machine king Godwin Davis' payoff technique. "The way it happened," Luttrell explained, "a voter would enter the voting place to mark his ballot and an election official would go in with him. Then when the voter left, the election official would give a wink or a nod to Godwin Davis and Davis would come forward, shake hands with the voter, putting the money in the voter's palm."

"How many votes do you think were sold in Russell County at the 4 May Primary?" the committee asked.

"I'd estimate at least thirty percent," Luttrell replied.

Hugh Bentley told of Chief Deputy Sheriff Albert Fuller constantly scanning the register of official voters for names of those who had not voted and bringing carloads of women from the honky tonks to vote under an assigned name and others arriving in taxi cabs, one calling back as she got out of the taxi: "What did you say my name was?"

RBA Auxiliary President Hilda Coulter testified that she had seen Chief Deputy Sheriff Albert Fuller marking ballots and to substantiate this charge, the picture taken by the Columbus TV station on election day was offered in evidence.

Hugh Britton told of premarked sample ballots that were passed out and the payoffs that followed. Jabe Brassell's son, Jack, who had served as poll-watcher for his father testified to vote stealing. He reported that officials stopped counting votes at one point, saying: "We'd better go slow, we don't know how many votes we will have to steal."

A.C. Stewart, another poll-watcher, told the subcommittee that at 1:00 A.M., Albert Fuller came to where the votes were being counted and said: "The boss said hurry this thing up."

"Who," the subcommittee asked, "is the boss?"

Hugh Bentley took the stand to answer that question and testified that gambling czar Hoyt Shepherd was the one who controlled the Phenix City elections and recounted Shepherd's offer to make him mayor if he would stop the gambling raids. But it was for RBA president, Howard Pennington, to make the most shocking accusation of all.

"There are always two tickets on election day in Russell County," Pennington explained, "one is the gamblers' ticket and the other is the cleanup ticket."

"Who makes up the gamblers' ticket?" Judge Mayhall asked.

"There's Head Revel, Buddy Jowers, Red Cook, and the Youngblood brothers—Ernest and Glenn—they are the trouble shooters when things get rough. These are the people who are behind the Machine, but Hoyt Shepherd is the head of the Machine, and Arch Ferrell is the brains behind the Machine."

Judge Roy Mayhall, chairman of the subcommittee was so appalled by this accusation, that he asked Pennington to repeat what he had said. "Do you mean to say that Arch Ferrell, the Solicitor of Russell County Circuit, is 'the brains' behind the Phenix City political machine?"

"Yes, Sir," Pennington replied calmly.

Arch Ferrell was not present at the hearing, and Judge Mayhall asked: "Would you be willing to accuse those you have mentioned if they were in the courtroom this morning?"

"Yes, Sir."

That night the *Columbus Ledger* and the *Birmingham News* repeated Pennington's accusation in banner headlines across the front page of their newspapers.

In Birmingham, the unreeling revelations taking place in Phenix City were being closely watched by the Jefferson County Grand Jury investigating the vote tally change. When Lamar Reid testified and told that secret body of his meeting and acquiescence to the wishes of Si Garrett and Arch Ferrell, tough, hard-hitting Jefferson County Circuit Solicitor Emmett Perry immediately *invited* Si Garrett to appear before the Grand Jury, a delicate point of law which would allow Garrett to make an unsworn statement instead of being challenged with a subpoena which might provoke him to take over the Grand Jury.

On Wednesday, June 16th, in response to Emmett Perry's invitation, Si Garrett told him: "I'm taking a much needed vacation on my cattle farm in Grove Hill right now, Emmett, but I will be in Birmingham to go before the Grand Jury on Friday, the eighteenth."

In Phenix City, on Thursday, 17 June, the subcommittee after four days of hearings into the conspiracy, malconduct and vote fraud of the 4 May Primary, had heard the thirty-five witnesses describe an appalling situation that had violated every election law on the books.

With more witnesses yet to be heard, Judge Mayhall said: "We are not going to cut off any legitimate testimony that will throw light on the conditions that existed in Russell County during the voting at the May 4th Primary, but because of prior legal commitments of this sub committee, the hearings will have to be adjourned until June 28th."

෯

Albert Patterson had sat in the courtroom in Phenix City and closely followed the hearings and it was clear that the situation was becoming explosive. Even though he had been confirmed as the winner in the attorney general race at the official canvass in Montgomery on 10 June, there were rumblings from the opposition camp about a recount, and as the investigations into vote fraud in Phenix City and Birmingham accelerated, the death threats against Albert Patterson increased.

Leon Sanders, a friend of Patterson's on the Phenix City police force, passed the word to Patterson's son, John, "Things are looking pretty bad. There're a lot of comings and goings from out-of-state hit-men. You'd better tell your daddy he should get some protection."

Patterson was aware that the danger could no longer be dismissed or taken lightly and in an address to the Methodist Men's Club on Thursday night, 17 June, he told the group: "My chances of living to take office are about 100 to one."

The gathering assumed he meant some technical reversal that would interminably tie up the vote count, but Patterson had confided his concern to his friend, RBA president Howard Pennington, who had also been threatened.

"If anything happens to me," Patterson told Pennington that Thursday night, "don't let them get away with it."

"I promise I won't," Pennington pledged, "and I want you to do the same for me in case they get me first."

They sealed their pact with a handshake and the next morning, Patterson went to his office in the Coulter Building to catch up with some pressing work left undone during the rigors of the campaign.

When he got a call from attorney Reuben Newton asking him to appear with him that morning at a disbarment proceeding against him in Montgomery, Patterson at first refused.

"Look," Newton said, "they're after me too."

"I've got commitments I've got to keep," Patterson told him. "There's just no way I can get away today."

Patterson had barely hung up the phone when he changed his mind and told his secretary he was leaving for Montgomery. "When a friend calls who's in trouble, there's nothing to do but go to his assistance."

That morning of 18 June, as Patterson was driving to Montgomery to appear at Newton's disbarment hearing, Attorney General Si Garrett was driving to Birmingham to appear before the Jefferson County Grand Jury looking into the vote tally change.

Garrett, casual and confident, arrived at the Jefferson County Courthouse carrying his bulging briefcase and wearing his wide-brimmed floppy hat. He reminded the Grand Jurors that he was not under subpoena, that his appearance was voluntary and he had come at the invitation of Solicitor Emmett Perry. He wished first to make a statement as attorney general and then he would try to shed some light on the statement made by Lamar Reid.

Even though Emmett Perry reminded him that his would be an unsworn statement, Garrett insisted that his participation in this inquiry was so impeccable that he insisted on its being a sworn statement and the Clerk of Court duly took it all down for the record, pages and pages and pages of it.

For an hour and a half he told the Grand Jurors about his background, his father's background, his relatives who served in high places, and earlier attorney generals he had served under beginning in 1935 as an assistant attorney general.

"I've been in the attorney general's office for nineteen years," Garrett told them. "The state of Alabama is the only client I ever had. Now some of you may not be familiar with the responsibilities of the attorney general's office so I would like to read for the record from the Code of Alabama Section 234, 235, and 236."

Garrett read from the code making it perfectly plain that at his discretion, he had the power to supersede Solicitor Emmett Perry and dissolve the Grand Jury if he so chose.

When he had finished, Emmett Perry asked: "Does that conclude what you have designated as your official statement?"

"Yes, except that I want to repeat again that my purpose was solely for advising the Grand Jury as to my authority, power, and duty as Attorney General, not because I have ever at any time had the slightest idea of coming up here and attempting to supersede you in this matter."

Following this, Garrett launched into another four hours of testimony concerning Lamar Reid and the discrepancy in the Jefferson County vote tally, telling the Grand Jury that he only knew what he had read in the newspapers, finishing at last at five o'clock in the afternoon.

While Garrett was doing this, Albert Patterson in Montgomery made an astonishing tactical move. Patterson, characteristically a very private man who never disclosed his intentions, decided that day to make it known to everyone he talked with in the state capitol that on Monday he planned to go before the Jefferson County Grand Jury and tell all he knew about the vote fraud in Birmingham and the concerted effort that had been made to cheat him of the election by changing the vote totals.

At the disbarment hearing for Reuben Newton, Patterson told him: "I've got the goods on Si Garrett and Arch Ferrell and on Monday I'm going to tell the Grand Jury all I know."

When Patterson had finished his rounds of the offices where he had business, he ran into Jabe Brassell in the Exchange Hotel who was also in Montgomery that day on business and as they sat in the lobby waiting out a rain storm, he told Jabe Brassell the same thing.

"I've been sitting in on the hearings in Phenix City and keeping up with the Grand Jury investigation in Birmingham and I have never heard of such crookedness in all my life. If God lets me live, I'm going to clean it up."

"What do you mean 'if God lets you live'?" Brassell asked.

"They're threatening me now," Patterson said, "and on Monday I'm going to go before the Jefferson County Grand Jury in Birmingham and explode the whole thing. I've got the goods on them, and I'm going to ruin them."

Then, as Brassell left for his appointment, Patterson headed back to Phenix City stopping along the way at a drive-in for a raw egg and vanilla milk shake and then driving straight to his office in the Coulter Building to resume the work he had left behind that morning.

Sometime after eight o'clock that evening, his friend, Leland Jones, walked into his office.

"I saw the light on in your office and thought I'd drop by and see if you'd like to join me and my wife for dinner. We're just on our way."

"No thank you, Leland," Patterson told him. "I've been in Montgomery all day and I just came by the office to catch up on some thank-you notes to those people who worked so hard in my campaign."

"Did you see the editorial in today's paper?"

"No, I haven't."

Leland pulled the paper out of his pocket and began to read, but Patterson seemed not to be listening.

"You seem distracted," Leland told him. "Are you worried about something?"

Patterson pulled off his steel-rimmed glasses and rubbed his tired eyes. "No, just tired. It's been a long day and I'm going to finish up here and go home."

Leland got up to go. "Then I'll go on and take the missus to dinner and leave you to your work."

Shortly after nine o'clock, Patterson picked up his cane, turned off his office light and clumped down the stairs to where his car was parked in an alley behind the Coulter Building.

At that hour in Phenix City on the night of 18 June, the business district was still crowded with Friday night shoppers finishing their weekend buying. Quinnie Kelley, the courthouse janitor, was locking up the courthouse after the conclusion of a Boy Scout Honors Court that had taken place there earlier.

Johnny Dees, a jailer at the Russell County Jail, was threading his way through the crowded sidewalk on his way to Smitty's Cafe to buy an ice cream cone to take the edge off the hot, humid June evening.

189

Circuit Solicitor Arch Ferrell was in his second floor office in the courthouse talking long distance to Attorney General Si Garrett who had gathered some of his young supporters around him and was hosting a post-Grand Jury appearance party at the Redmont Hotel in Birmingham.

Ed Strickland was bent over his phone at his desk at the *Birmingham News*. Having heard of Patterson's intention to appear before the Jefferson County Grand Jury on Monday, he was trying to get a long distance call through to Patterson to confirm the rumors he had heard.

In Columbus, cab driver James Radius Taylor, had picked up a fare, an Army lieutenant, whose destination was a Phenix City night spot called Chad's Rose Room. As Taylor stopped for a traffic light a block from the Russell County Courthouse, three shots rang out. The lieutenant in the back of Taylor's cab said: "Well, I know we're in Phenix City now."

A block away, Patterson, mortally wounded, staggered out of the alley, around the corner and fell dead on the sidewalk in front of a dress shop, his keys still clutched in his hand. He had been shot three times: in the chest, in the arm and in the mouth, the acknowledged death-mark for informers.

Ed Strickland, finally able to get his call through, told the long distance operator: "I want to speak to Albert Patterson."

The operator gasped: "Haven't you heard? Mr. Patterson's just been shot."

Ed Strickland dropped the phone, and yelled to his photographer: "Grab your camera quick. We gotta go."

"Where to?"

"Phenix City. Somebody's just shot Albert Patterson!"

Hugh Bentley was closing his sporting goods store in Columbus when Hugh Britton called. The words were so devastating that for several moments Hugh Bentley could not get his breath to answer. "Oh, God," he moaned at last, "I never thought it would come to this. I never believed they would really kill an attorney general-elect."

"We're going to call an emergency meeting of the RBA. We're going to get up a bunch of men and go looking ..."

"No ... no ... we musn't," Hugh Bentley insisted. "Law and order and due process is what we've fought for and Albert Patterson stood for. We musn't let this make us vigilantes too."

"Folks are tore all to pieces about this thing, Hugh. They're killin' mad."

"I know. I feel that way, too, but we musn't let mob violence take over."

Hugh Britton's tone was grim. "I don't know if we can stop them now."

The news of Albert Patterson's ambush slaying flashed like lightning across Alabama. At the State Capitol in Montgomery when the governor was informed, his first words were: "Get me "Crack" Hanna in Birmingham."

The governor's aide scurried to the phone to call Walter J. Hanna, Adjutant General of the State of Alabama and Commanding General of Alabama's National Guard, known by everyone since his early army days as "Crack" because of the records he had established during his Army career.

Returning moments later, the aide reported: "Mrs. Hanna says he's not at home, that he's on his way back from dedicating an armory in Gadsden."

Gordon Persons, with only six months left in office as governor of the State of Alabama, was acutely aware of the powerful passions and potential powder keg in Phenix City, the shooting, killing and retaliation that was likely to occur as a result of this shocking slaying of the attorney general-elect. "Put out an All Points Bulletin," the governor said. "I want "Crack" Hanna to get to Phenix City immediately, before the shooting starts."

BOOK III

THE TRIUMPH

Alabama National Guard ordered by Governor patrols Phenix City gambling district on 14th Street following Patterson's murder. (Courtesy of the *Columbus Ledger-Enquirer*)

July 1954 *Columbus Enquirer* front page editorial cartoon depicts General "Crack" Hanna's beginning Martial Rule.

General Hanna with Alabama National Guard troops uncovers hidden gambling evidence for vice trials. (Courtesy of the *Columbus Ledger-Enquirer*)

General Hanna reads *Columbus Ledger* reports of National Guard's clean-up blitz. (Photo: Albert Kraus, Montgomery, Alabama)

General Hanna in 1984 interview with author Margaret Anne Barnes recounts Phenix City Clean-up. (Photo: Lauri Shaw-Wood)

14

CHAOS AND CONCEALMENT

On that night of 18 June 1954, Walter J. Hanna, Adjutant General of the State of Alabama and Commanding General of Alabama's National Guard, known since his early army days as "Crack" because of the record he established for expert proficiency with the rifle and bayonet, was hurtling down a dark, narrow road across Alabama with his driver, Lieutenant Colonel Tony Jannett. They were returning to Birmingham after activating the 225th Radio Relay Squadron at the newly opened National Guard Armory in Gadsden, Alabama, when he heard the APB on the police band on his car radio.

Jannett was driving the general's specially equipped, souped-up green Lincoln at the general's normal cruising speed of eighty miles per hour with the car radio turned low to the Alabama State Patrol band. Hearing his name mentioned, General Hanna picked up the car mike to respond, but the broadcaster refused to relinquish the air.

At fifty-two, Crack Hanna's life had been one of controversy, conflict, and combat. In thirty-five years, he had risen through the ranks as a citizen soldier from private to major-general. Silver-haired and granite-jawed, the stern look in his green eyes could hold a man at attention without ever giving the command to do so. The one thing he was accustomed to was instant response to command. The broadcaster on the line was yammering away about a code number.

"Goddammit!" Hanna yelled, "give me the line!"

"Don't you know what Code 7 is!" the broadcaster snapped back.

Then over the airwaves came the message: "Emergency! All cars call in! General Walter J. Hanna. Call home immediately!"

Hurtling through the dark night down the deserted road, General Hanna and Jannett pulled into the little town of Springville. Although only just past 8:30 P.M. central standard time, the town was already closed down and asleep. The only telephone, in a booth beside the road, was an ancient crank model. When General Hanna reached home, his wife, Vera, answered.

"Vera. What the hell's happened?"

"Albert Patterson has been killed."

"Be goddammed! Where?"

"Phenix City. The Governor wants you to come on in and contact him immediately."

Back in the car, Jannett asked: "What's up, General?"

"Albert Patterson's been killed. We got to get to Birmingham in a helluva hurry so get on it."

Jannett swung the big green Lincoln back onto the road and pressed the accelerator until the speedometer was throbbing at 100 miles per hour.

General Hanna leaned over to take a look. "We're not going to a garden party, Jannett, the Governor's got an emergency. Get on down the road."

Jannett gripped the wheel and pressed the accelerator to the floor. Outside of Birmingham, a police car with siren screaming and lights flashing raced to catch up with them.

"You want me to outrun him?" Jannett asked.

"No. Just tell him to get the hell out of the way so we can get on down the road."

Jannett pulled over, and before the police officer could say anything, Jannett told him: "I've got General Hanna and the Governor wants him."

"I'll escort you through town," the police officer replied.

General Hanna leaned over to the opened window on the driver's side. "We don't need an escort. Just get the hell out of the way."

"Yes, Sir, General!" the officer answered with a salute.

When he got home, he got the Governor on the phone. "Gordon, what the hell happened?"

"We don't know yet. Somebody shot and killed Patterson in Phenix City about nine o'clock Eastern time."

"Any idea who did it?"

"Not yet, but I want you to get down there right away to see what the situation is. Bring in whatever you need in men and equipment, and just make damn sure they don't start shooting and killing each other or anybody else."

"Count on it."

General Hanna's next call was to Birmingham police lieutenant, Jack Warren, the senior military police officer in the National Guard. "Get in your uniform and get down to the Armory. We may have to pull men into Phenix City."

"*Phenix City!*"

"Somebody shot and killed Albert Patterson tonight. We're going to go down to make damn sure there's no more shooting."

"Yes, sir!" Warren replied, the snap of a salute in his voice. "I'll be there in ten minutes."

When the phone calls were finished, General Hanna turned back to his family that had gathered round, waiting expectantly for what would come next.

"Crack, how long do you think you'll be gone?" Vera asked.

"No way to tell right now. We don't even know what the situation is."

Seventeen-year old Pete pressed forward. "Let me go, too, Dad."

Vera, a pretty, petite blonde, turned on him with flashing blue eyes. "Now, Pete, you've got no business down there."

"Hell, Vera, he's already a private in the Guard. He can go and be my driver, and he'll likely do a damn sight better than Jannett did getting me here tonight."

Pete looked at his mother, seeking approval. "Mom?"

General Hanna knew he wanted to go and he knew Vera wouldn't stop him, so he turned to Pete and said: "Get into uniform, soldier."

Pete grinned, wheeled out the door and was gone to change from saddle shoes to combat boots.

Vera scowled at this disregard for her wishes and asked her husband again: "How long will you be gone?"

"Til the job gets done."

"That's no answer!"

"It's the only one I've got now."

With a kiss and an embrace he was gone.

❧

On the road to Phenix City, Pete pushed the big green Lincoln to its limit. In the back seat, Jack Warren closed his eyes. If they were about to be hurled into eternity—and it was likely at the speed they were going—then he didn't want to see it coming. In the front seat beside Pete, General Hanna puffed his cigar, his eyes set on the destination and the duty ahead. Jack Warren had seen the process before. How many times? How many places? How to count thirty years? Strikes. Riots. Floods. Civil unrest. War.

Like most of the members of his unit, Jack Warren had grown from boyhood to manhood under Crack Hanna's command. He was only sixteen years old when he joined then-Captain Hanna's command in the National Guard and learned right away that "the old man "didn't put up with a damn thing. The night before the Inspector General's inspection, Crack Hanna had had him arrested and put in jail.

"What the hell is the matter with you, boy?" Crack Hanna had demanded. "Don't you know you don't get drunk *before* the IG inspection? You get drunk *after* the inspection."

Tough? By God, he was tough like Patton was tough. In combat he gave no quarter, in principle, he knew no compromise, and personal cost was no consideration. His concern was for the mission and the safety of his men and the confidence this inspired rallied them to whatever challenge arose.

In the savage jungle warfare at Morotai, he achieved a military record in cost to the enemy: for every battalion casualty, eighty enemy dead. And during the eighty-nine days of heavy Japanese bombardment he was wounded with a percussion bomb that left him with two broken vertebrae, shattered knees and a broken nose. He demanded that the battalion surgeon bandage him up and continued fighting until the battle was over.

His conduct in combat, his code of never asking a soldier to do what he himself did not do first, earned him the admiration of his troops and the ultimate acclaim: "a soldier's soldier" and "the warrior general."

But he was more than the warrior general, he chose the role of defender and protector and if advantage was being taken of the defenseless and unprotected, they had to face Crack Hanna's fists first. There was hell to pay if anyone took advantage of a woman or one of his soldiers, but God save the soldier who broke ranks and disobeyed an order. Like that time back in the thirties when a black man had brutally raped and killed a young white mother and her baby. The man was tried and sentenced to die, but the anger and tension of the town was such that to insure his safety against lynching, the National Guard was called to escort him by train to Kilby Prison.

On the train trip down, the man, belligerent and bragging, told the troops who guarded him: "Yeah, I killed her and her baby too and I'd do it again 'cause I got what I always wanted–a piece of that white meat."

The guardsmen were enraged, and one man lunged toward the prisoner. "Goddam you sonofabitch, I'm going to kill you now."

Others rose to join in. Crack Hanna drew his gun. "If just one of you lays a hand on that man, I'll shoot you myself. He's been tried and convicted, and the law, *BY GOD*, is going to carry out the sentence."

And that's the way it was. They arrived with the prisoner at Kilby Prison, turned him over to the warden, and due process was served.

It was hard for Jack Warren to imagine what due process would be in Phenix City, or what lay ahead. He only knew that whatever the challenge, there would be hell to pay.

"What's that, Warren?"

Jack Warren leaned forward to respond. "Sorry, General Hanna. I must have been thinking out loud. I just said, 'there'll be hell to pay.'"

In the front seat, "Crack" Hanna squinted at the dark road ahead. There was going to be hell to pay all right. This time Phenix City had gone too far. This time, the racketeers, the Mob, the rats' nests, all would have to be cleaned out for good and forever.

Thinking back, Crack Hanna could not remember a time when Phenix City was not a blight on the border of Alabama, always a law unto itself with no enforceable restraints and no regard whatever for human life. People used to say it was worse than Dodge City, but Dodge City had come and gone. Phenix City, with its vigilante code and frontier ways, remained the same right into the middle of the twentieth century with no administration either able or willing to tackle the task of taming the outlaw town. Gordon Persons had done more than most but he himself had said that he could not, in his four-year administration as governor, change what had been allowed to flourish for more than 100 years. Well, now he would have to, the ambush killing of the attorney general-elect would demand it.

~

In Phenix City, all was chaos and confusion. From the moment the shots were fired, the streets began filling up with spectators, onlookers, and speculators. As word was flashed on the radio and across TV screens, people poured out of their homes and into the streets to hurry to the downtown spot where Patterson was slain, and then to the hospital where Patterson's family had gathered and where the mayor, the sheriff, and all the law enforcement had come to look under the white sheet covering Patterson's shattered body.

At the other end of town, at the foot of the bridge across the Chattahoochee on Dillingham Street, pandemonium had gripped the criminal fringe; the petty peddlers of crime and vice, the prostitutes, pimps, card sharks, and small-time crooks were crowding into every conveyance, car, truck, and taxi cab, trying to get out of town in advance of the biggest trouble Phenix City had seen in thirty years. The word had already come down, the Guard and the Governor were on the way.

Albert Fuller, quick to protect his interests, had already alerted the gamblers and gambling houses under his protection, and Buddy Jowers had done the same, sending members of the Phenix City police department to make the rounds of the favored houses who paid for his protection, instructing them to put up and put away all gambling paraphernalia because the governor was sending General "Crack" Hanna and the National Guard to patrol the city. They knew "Crack" Hanna's reputation as did everyone else in Alabama—tough, determined, relentless—a veteran of savage jungle warfare in the Pacific who spared no one and no effort to get a job done, but Phenix City would be ready for him when he arrived, Albert Fuller and Buddy Jowers had seen to that.

For the others, the warning was plain: to talk, give information, or assistance to those coming to investigate Phenix City and what had happened there would be done at one's own peril.

For the big-time gamblers and the governing establishment, it was time to lay low and wait until it all blew over. It always had. It would again. It was just a matter of waiting out the storm.

≈

Across the Chattahoochee River in Columbus, Georgia, Robert Brown, editor of the evening *Columbus Ledger*, was at home listening to the radio when the program was interrupted to announce the violent slaying of Albert Patterson. Realizing the import of this event and its possible explosive complications, he immediately called an emergency meeting of his staff and put veteran reporter and editor, Carlton Johnson in charge of "the Phenix City desk."

Taking personal charge of the assignments, Brown dispatched reporters and photographers to leave immediately to begin their coverage. With seasoned reporter Tom Sellers away on duty at a Georgia National Guard summer camp, he chose young Ray Jenkins, who along with Hugh Bentley had been attacked at the polling place in the 1952 elections, to follow the preliminary investigation in Phenix City.

This done, he sat down to write a front page editorial headlined: "Alabama Must Avenge the Murder of Albert Patterson," ending with the editorial demand: "Let martial law be declared and then let the State move in with all of the power at its command, not only to investigate the cruel murder of Albert Patterson, but to find out why the legally constituted local authorities have allowed the atmosphere for murder to be built up."

While Robert Brown bent over his editorial in the offices of the *Columbus Ledger*, across town, Columbus cab driver James Radius Taylor anguished over being in the wrong place at the wrong time. Shaken by what he had seen and frightened by what he had said, he had given up taking fares for the night and went home vowing not to say another word, ever. As he had stopped at the traffic light in Phenix City shortly after 9:00 P.M. when the shots rang out, he had looked to his left and recognized a man running from the scene. As he was driving back over the bridge to Columbus after letting his fare out at Chad's Rose Room, the dispatcher, over the cab radio said: "Albert Patterson's been shot!" Another cabbie came back: "Who did it?" Before he thought of what he was doing, James Radius Taylor spontaneously said the name of the man he had seen. "Who said that?" the dispatcher wanted to know, but James Radius Taylor, thoroughly frightened by what he had done, never opened his mouth again and went home vowing silence forever.

In Phenix City, another vow of silence was being taken by cab driver Bill Littleton. Moments before the shots rang out, he had driven his cab past the courthouse, recognized two men standing there and had thrown up his hand in greeting. Minutes later, the shots rang out and Patterson was dead. To his bitter regret he had mentioned this to his girlfriend and her boss at the cafe where she worked, and now, fearful of what might happen should anyone learn what he had seen, he took a solemn oath never to mention it again, for Bill Littleton knew what trouble was. Back in 1950 he had been charged with the murder of Private Outlaw, but he had kept his mouth shut and nothing had ever come of the charges. Having learned the value of silence once, he planned to keep his mouth shut again. With the slaying of Albert Patterson and the Guard and the Governor on the way, it was safe to say, all hell was about to break loose.

❧

Arriving in Phenix City less than an hour after leaving Birmingham, General Hanna looked at his watch and tapped his son on the shoulder, "Good work, Pete."

At the top of the hill near the Russell County Courthouse and the Coulter Building, all was chaos and confusion. Spectators, onlookers and speculators were standing in knots in the street and in the alley behind the Coulter Building where Patterson's bloodstained car still stood with the door open and a bullet hole piercing the right front window.

General Hanna pulled down the gold braided brim of his cap, and tossed away his cigar. "Stop here, Pete, and stay with the car. I want to see what the situation is. Warren, you come with me."

As he stepped out of the car and headed toward the snarl of people standing on the sidewalk and in the street, a tall, thin, dark-haired man with a receding hairline, stepped out of the crowd, his hand extended.

"General Hanna? Ed Strickland, *Birmingham News.*"

"Yeah, Ed. How'd you newspaper boys get here so fast?"

"I was on my way while they were still looking for you. We were told that the Governor is sending in the National Guard. What will its role be?"

"To keep the peace and close down the gambling joints."

"What do you anticipate?" The question came from the young, bespectacled reporter who had joined them. Seeing that General Hanna did not recognize him, he said: "Ray Jenkins, sir, *Columbus Ledger.*"

General Hanna held up his hand to stop him. "I'll let you boys know as soon as I find out what the hell is going on here. Where is the sheriff? Who is the officer in charge? Why haven't they set up any police lines?"

"Damnedest thing I ever saw," Ed Strickland answered, looking back over his shoulder. "No one seems to be in charge. The sheriff has gone off to the hospital, various deputies come and go, but no attempt has been made to rope off the murder scene."

"Where is the chief deputy Albert Fuller?"

Ed Strickland shook his head. "He was here a while ago, wearing an empty holster."

"Empty holster? You mean no gun? Why?"

"I asked him. He said he'd been getting a lot of criticism lately about his guns, so he just decided to leave off carrying them for a while."

"That's a helluva thing to do on a night like this," General Hanna said, walking toward the alley behind the Coulter Building where Patterson's blue Plymouth was parked. The right front window was pierced with a bullet hole, the door still open, the seats splattered with blood. Patterson's walking cane, essential to him in getting about, was on the back seat. Around the corner in front of the dress shop where Patterson had fallen and died, a press of people stood around the puddle of blood that had settled into a dark, gritty stain on the sidewalk.

General Hanna looked back over his shoulder. "Come on, Warren, let's go find the sheriff."

Outside Cobb Memorial Hospital, another group of people kept a vigil outside on the lawn. Inside, Hugh Bentley and Hugh Britton, withdrawn and bereft, waited in the hallway. Their suffering was obvious. Hugh Bentley's face was stiff with pain, grief and extreme remorse for persuading his friend to pick up the flag that ultimately cost that friend his life. With the greatest amount of effort, Hugh Bentley restrained the tears that welled up inside, trying to hold up in front of those who relied on him. Then, recognizing General Hanna, Hugh Bentley stepped forward, his face, momentarily relieved of its worry.

"Thank God, you've come, General Hanna." Hugh said, shaking hands. "This terrible tragedy, this awful deed, it's just beyond us."

"We'll get to the bottom of it," General Hanna said, giving him a firm handshake.

"If there's anything I or the RBA can do ..."

General Hanna gave him a warm clap on the shoulder. "I'll call."

In the hallway up ahead, outside the emergency room door, Mrs. Patterson, frail and drawn, clutched the lace collar of her dress and clung to her eldest son, John, "I want the State Toxicologist Dr. Rehling to do the autopsy," she told the hospital administrator.

John Patterson, a tall dark-haired young man, jutted out a determined steel jaw. "See to it that my mother's wishes are carried out."

"Well, Sir, we got a call into Dr. Rehling, but nobody's located him yet. Dr. Sowell, his assistant, is on the way."

Seeing General Hanna, Mrs. Patterson attempted a brave smile and held out her frail hand. "Thank you for coming, General Hanna."

General Hanna took her hand in both of his. "I can't tell you how sorry I was to hear what happened."

Her eyes clouded and she turned her face into her son's shoulder.

"John ..." General Hanna clasped his hand, "we're here to help in whatever way we can." John Patterson nodded, his eyes full of pain, his face full of controlled anger. "They shot him down like a dog. Go take a look for yourself. He's up there in the emergency room."

Inside the emergency room, heavy with heat and humidity, there was the smell of antiseptics. From the onlookers came the smell of sweat and sour liquor that had been drunk hours before. Under the white glare of the overhead lights, Sheriff Matthews, Arch Ferrell, and Mayor Reese were waiting beside the sheet-draped gurney on which Albert Patterson's body had been lain.

General Hanna nodded an acknowledgment and as he lifted the sheet covering Patterson's shattered body, Arch Ferrell, silent and red-eyed, left the room.

"Arch ain't got no stomach for this," Sheriff Matthews said, sopping away the sweat that popped out on his face like rain drops.

away the sweat that popped out on his face like rain drops.

General Hanna turned the sheet back. Patterson wasn't just shot, he was executed, three bullets at close range, in the arm, in the chest and in the mouth—the death-mark of an informer—in case he lived long enough to talk. "What's being done about this?" General Hanna asked.

"We're waiting for the State Toxicologist, "Sheriff Matthews replied.

"I can see that. What's being done to apprehend the killer?"

"Some of the boys are down there on the scene taking care of it."

"When I came in they hadn't even set up a police line."

"Albert Fuller went off to get some rope from the fire department, and I reckon he did."

"Did you seal off the bridges?"

"No, Sir."

"Or notify the Columbus Police Department?"

"No, Sir."

Elmer Reese stepped in. "Our law enforcement can handle this."

"Then you damn well better get busy before the killer is out of the county and all the clues mashed down with that crowd milling about the murder scene."

In the hallway outside, John Patterson left his mother's side and came over to General Hanna. His anger, so carefully masked in front of this mother, now blazed on his face. "I don't think they plan to do a damn thing about this," John said, throwing his words toward the emergency room door. "They're going to go through the motions and let it pass and Phenix City will go on like it's always done."

"We're here to see that doesn't happen," General Hanna assured him. "I have orders from the Governor to begin by closing down all gambling joints. We're on our way now."

Down Fourteenth and Dillingham Street the gambling joints, loan companies, and cafes lining both sides of the street to the bridge were quiet, their doors closed, only the gaudy neon, spelling out their names and spilling rainbow colors on the street spoke of the promised pleasures that lay within.

"Pull off here and stay with the car," General Hanna told Pete. "Warren, you come with me."

As they began their patrol of Dillingham Street, hearing what appeared to be slot machines inside the Bama Club, General Hanna banged on the door with his fists.

"Are you bastards gambling in there?"

The door swung open and towering, burly, J. D. Abney, operator of the Bama Club, snarled: "You can't talk to a private citizen that way."

"The hell I can't," Hanna replied. "I didn't come down here to teach

Holding his toe-to-toe position with Abney, General Hanna told Warren: "Go in there and check it out." Immediately, from inside the club and the darkened street outside, a crowd began to form and by the time Warren returned, they were surrounded. Without dropping his eye-lock on Abney, General Hanna asked: "Any gambling going on in there, Warren?"

"No, sir, they're sacking up money."

Abney's face twisted with anger and stepped forward, but it was into the muzzle of an army .45 caliber held by General Hanna's son, Pete, who had seen what was happening and had come forward to defend his father from what seemed to be imminent attack.

"The party's over," General Hanna told the hostile crowd around him. "There'll be no more gambling."

"Sez you and who else, soldier boy?" one hard-eyed tough demanded.

"Me and the State of Alabama," General Hanna replied. "Try it, and I'll put you bastards *under* the jail."

"You ain't the law here."

General Hanna aimed his words like bullets: "Try me."

The gauntlet was down, and the gambling community was ready to meet the challenge.

15

INVESTIGATIONS AND INDICTMENTS

When morning came the governor arrived, anguished by the death of Albert Patterson, inexpressibly angry about the situation in Phenix City, and ready to read the riot act to all the county and city officials, and to Sheriff Matthews and Albert Fuller in particular. The ambush slaying of Albert Patterson had triggered cries of outrage and a torrent of demands from across the state for the governor to take immediate, decisive action.

General Hanna, spit and polish in khakis and combat boots, was waiting for him with a car at the airstrip and threw him a salute.

"What's the situation, Crack?" Gordon Persons asked.

"We've set up headquarters in the National Guard Armory and troops are on their way."

"And the city?"

"A powder keg about to explode. The people are afraid and the police are dawdling around doing nothing, not even following basic police procedure. We're going to have to find out what the hell is going on here, Gordon, and do something about it."

Gordon Persons nodded grimly. "I intend to."

Accompanied by General Hanna, he began an inspection tour of the city and the murder scene, watching workmen scrub the blood stains from the sidewalk where Albert Patterson had fallen dead, looking in the alley where Patterson was shot in his parked car.

At the courthouse, the city and county officials were waiting for the governor as they had been instructed to do. Gordon Persons walked in and pointed an accusing finger at Sheriff Matthews and Albert Fuller.

"Ralph, I want you and Albert to take this for what it is, an ultimatum. This is absolutely the end of the line," he told them. "Gambling and crime will no longer be tolerated in this city in any form whatsoever and I mean *whatsoever*. I'd better not hear of anyone even matching pennies for a stick of gum. General Hanna and the National Guard are here to see to it that Phenix City gets cleaned up and will remain here until it does."

Turning to the city and county officials, the governor told them: "I called General Harper, the commanding general at Fort Benning and asked him to put this entire city off-limits to all military personnel."

General Harper, a World War II combat veteran, was at the Battle of the Bulge, when the Americans were surrounded and the Germans were demanding surrender. It was Harper who delivered General McAuliffe's famous one word response to the Germans: "Nuts."

"There's going to be no more fleecing of soldiers," the governor said, "because I have asked and General Harper has agreed to seal the bridges with military police who will be checking all traffic into and out of the city. The days of Sin City are over!"

Collecting himself and trying to achieve a calmer demeanor, he went next to the Patterson home and talked with Mrs. Patterson, offered his condolences to the family, and spoke privately with John.

"They're not going to find who killed my father," John told the Governor, "because the most likely suspects are the very ones investigating the murder. They're going to cover up and delay and delude."

"Not this time, John," Gordon Persons assured him. "We're going to put the full force of Alabama behind this investigation and General Hanna is here to see that the job gets done."

Hugh Bentley, Hugh Britton, and Howard Pennington waiting with members of the RBA outside the Patterson home, had heard it all before when Hugh Bentley's house was bombed in 1952, when he and Hugh Britton were beaten at the polls, when free and honest elections were promised. This time, with the murder of Albert Patterson, petitions and promises would no longer do.

As the Governor started to leave, Hugh Bentley stepped forward with a list of demands that had been drawn up by the RBA membership.

"Governor, the RBA ..." Hugh Bentley began.

"Not now, Hugh, not now," the governor waved him aside and getting into his car, drove away.

Hugh Bentley turned back to his group, the paper still in his hand. "He wouldn't even listen."

Howard Pennington scowled after the governor's car disappearing in the distance. "We'll send him a registered letter and see to it that the newspapers get a copy."

The explosive reaction came the next morning in the attorney general's office when Si Garrett read the RBA demands laid out in print across the morning papers.

"What in the hell is this?" Si Garrett demanded, as though his young assistant attorney general, Bernard Sykes, could give him the answer. "What in the HELL is this?"

Quiet, methodical, retiring, Bernard Sykes knew from experience that he should only witness his boss' rage and not hazard a reply. Sitting silent and erect behind his desk, he only shook his head and watched Garrett slapping the newspaper he held with the back of his hand as he reiterated the RBA demands: "... that the governor direct the Attorney General to replace Circuit Solicitor Arch Ferrell with the appointment of a special prosecutor to investigate the slaying of Albert Patterson and gather the evidence, that the State Supreme Court order a special grand jury impaneled to hear the evidence, that a special judge be appointed to replace Circuit Judge Julius B. Hicks.'"

Bernard Sykes maintained his silence and waited.

"Don't they know that the powers of the attorney general are such that neither the Governor, nor the Supreme Court nor the Legislature nor any other group of officers can direct the attorney general to do or not to do anything. They've got to come see me directly. Then I will or will not do it."

Bernard Sykes knew it was now time for agreement and he nodded his head up and down.

Assuaged by this affirmation, Garrett stuffed the newspaper in his trash basket and said. "I tell you what, Bernard, I'm going down to Phenix City and straighten this Goddam thing out once and for all."

"Yes, sir."

"People have gone Goddam crazy with this Patterson killing and I'm going to go take charge of the murder investigation myself. You take care of whatever comes into the office here."

"Yes, sir."

Grabbing his briefcase, smashing his hat on his head, with angry strides and flapping coattails, he was gone. He did not, however, arrive in Phenix City until Sunday night, swaggering into the Russell County courthouse past the newsmen lined up on the steps: Ed Strickland from the *Birmingham News*, Rex Thomas from *Associated Press,* Fred Anderson from the *Montgomery Advertiser*, Ray Jenkins from the *Columbus Ledger*, Hershel Crib from the *Columbus Enquirer*, and John Pennington from the *Atlanta Journal*.

Ed Strickland from the *Birmingham News* tried to catch up. "Can you tell us what the situation is now, Mr. Garrett?"

"Not now, Ed. I'm calling a closed-door session. Afterwards I'll have a statement."

With a nod of his head and a crook of his finger, Sheriff Matthews, Mayor Reese, Albert Fuller and Arch Ferrell followed him inside.

For the newsmen waiting on the steps, it was significant that the attorney general himself had come to Phenix City and they speculated among themselves.

"Do you suppose there's been a break in the case?"

"Maybe the killer has been caught and Garrett has come down to make the announcement himself."

"Phenix City never ever caught a killer in two days, not unless they wanted to."

"But this is a big one and the pressure is on."

When Garrett came out of the courthouse, they surged forward with questions.

Garrett held his hand up. "One at a time, boys." He pointed at Ed Strickland.

"Has there been a break in the case?"

Garrett shook his head and pointed to Rex Thomas from the *Associated Press*.

"What's brought you to Phenix City?" Thomas asked.

"As attorney general I am taking full charge of the investigation into the murder of Albert Patterson."

"Do you feel that the local police can't handle it?" Fred Anderson from the *Montgomery Advertiser* asked.

"Certainly not. This is a big and important case. It will be the greatest manhunt in twenty years."

Ray Jenkins from the *Columbus Ledger* stood up. "Do you have a suspect?"

Garrett held up his hand again. "To solve this crime, it will be necessary to clamp a secrecy lid on the investigation and any and all information will have to come through me or my office.

"What about Arch Ferrell?" the *Columbus Enquirer's* Hershel Crib wanted to know. "Are you going to replace him as the RBA has demanded?"

"Absolutely not," Garrett snapped. "Even if I were directed to do so, I would not. Arch Ferrell is one of the best damned solicitors in the state."

John Pennington from the *Atlanta Journal* came forward. "What about the governor? What does he say?"

Garrett smiled smugly and repeated his oft-quoted position. "Let me remind you, gentlemen, the powers of the attorney general are such that neither the Governor, nor the Supreme Court nor the Legislature nor any other group of officers can direct the attorney general to do or not to do anything. They've got to come see me directly. Then I will, or will not, do it."

Satisfied that he had the situation well in hand and under control Garrett, cocksure and confident, left Phenix City on Sunday night.

On Monday, the situation began to unravel again, but for a while on Monday, the anger and outrage expressed by newspapers across the state and nation subsided as last respects were paid to Albert Patterson. In the red brick Trinity Methodist Church where he had long attended, one thousand mourners crowded into the church, filled from floor to ceiling with flowers and expressions of sympathy. Closest to the coffin, covered over with American flag for his service in World War I, was a giant wreath with an illuminated cross from the RBA.

Hugh Bentley, Hugh Britton, Howard Pennington, and members of the RBA, serving as pallbearers, took their place in the church pews behind the family. Mrs. Patterson, frail, dry-eyed and stiff with grief, surrounded by her four sons, John, Maurice, Sam, and Jack, reached over to comfort Patterson's ninety-two year old mother who began weeping as the organ music swelled and filled the church with the hymns that Patterson had loved best.

The funeral services began with four ministers who delivered the eulogies. The white-haired Reverend R. K. Jones who had fought many a battle alongside Patterson and the RBA against the crime and corruption in Phenix City, bent over his Bible and told those gathered in the church: "Albert Patterson was slain because he stood for freedom instead of slavery to the agencies of hell that run this town. Time and again, Albert Patterson, the ministers and the good people of Phenix City appealed to public officials, local and state, for help in stamping out the rackets, and the appeals fell on deaf ears. I know whereof I speak because I was there, and had these officials not failed, Albert Patterson might still be with us today."

"Albert Patterson often quoted Edmund Burke, the English statesman and author who said: 'The only thing necessary for the triumph of evil is that good men do nothing.'"

"As we have seen, there is no limit to what crime and gambling will do. Albert Patterson gave his *life* trying to make a better life for all of us." Raising his voice and a clenched fist, the Reverend White said: "If ever there was a time to stand up and fight to continue his work and end the gambling and crime, it's now!"

When the eulogies were done, a funeral cortege of 100 cars followed the hearse eighty-five miles across Alabama to the country cemetery in Tallapoosa County where Patterson was born. There, under a striped awning in the broiling summer heat, the family and friends listened to last prayers and Albert Patterson was lowered into his grave.

Hugh Bentley was weeping when he found John Patterson after the services. "I would never have believed that the elements of evil in Phenix City would have gone this far," he told John Patterson. "Through it all, I always had faith we would ultimately win."

Red-eyed, with his mouth grimly set in a straight line, John Patterson put a hand on Hugh Bentley's shoulder. "We're going to yet. I've decided to stand for election to the post of attorney general in the Old Man's place and I have pledged myself to carry out his program against crime in Alabama."

Hugh Bentley grasped his hand and shook it vigorously. "That's the best news I've heard since the governor sent in the National Guard. You'll have my compete support as well as that of the RBA."

"I'm going to see to it that his sacrifice was not in vain," John Patterson said solemnly as they walked out of the cemetery.

Back in Birmingham that day the turmoil continued. Jefferson County Circuit Judge Alta King, having heard the rumors of a possible link between the vote fraud in Birmingham and the murder of Albert Patterson in Phenix City, called the Jefferson County Grand Jury before him for special charges.

"Albert Patterson was to have appeared before this inquisitorial body today to bring information he had about the vote fraud tally in Jefferson County. On Friday night he was ambushed and assassinated in one of the most heinous and cowardly crimes in the annals of Alabama history," he told the Grand Jurors.

"Those responsible for the murder of Albert Patterson have flouted the will of the people of Alabama, first, by endeavoring to steal the election from him and when this failed, they ruthlessly took his life ... showing to what extent such lawless elements will go."

"The gravity of this crime strikes at the very vitals of our form of government and is a direct threat to our free elections and to our very way of life, for should we ever lose our freedom of election and the expression of the will of the people at the ballot box, all our other freedoms would soon be lost."

"We should and must do all in our power to pinpoint and bring to justice those who have violated our election laws and to discover, as nearly as possible, the facts on any connection between what happened in Phenix City and the vote stealing in Jefferson County."

The grand jury, still investigating the 600-vote tally change in Lee Porter's favor, had already heard Lamar Reid's testimony naming Si Garrett and Arch Ferrell as the two who had engineered the vote fraud. Charging the grand jury to delve deeper into the matter, Judge King instructed Circuit Solicitor Emmett Perry to bring Si Garrett and Arch Ferrell before the grand jury to tell what they knew.

"We are now awaiting the pleasure of the attorney general," Emmett Perry told Judge King. "He has expressed a desire to make a further statement to the grand jury."

On Wednesday, 23 June, Si Garrett, still confident of his powers as attorney general, arrived for his second appearance before the Jefferson County Grand Jury. After a long and devastating ten and one-half hours of testimony, Si Garrett, hollow-eyed and haggard, emerged from the Grand Jury room. Reporters who had waited outside all day sprang forward.

"Mr. Garrett, can you tell us about the testimony before the Grand Jury?"

Si Garrett, slumped under the weight of his briefcase, shook his head. "I'm leaving the state."

"Why?" the reporters wanted to know.

"I'm turning myself into a psychiatric clinic in Galveston, Texas, for a rest so that I can recover from the Phenix City 'ordeal.'"

Newsmen who had waited all day for a statement from the attorney general were so shocked they stopped taking notes to stare in blank disbelief at this incredible turn of events.

"What about the Patterson investigation? You said you were taking complete charge."

But Garrett got in his car and was gone.

To answer the storm of questions raised by Garrett's abrupt departure from the state, shortly thereafter, Si Garrett's father and personal physician made a joint public announcement which was released to the press by Si Garrett's brother, attorney T. Broox Garrett.

"It became an immediate necessity last week," the statement said, "to return Si Garrett, Attorney General of Alabama, to the John Sealy Hospital in Galveston, Texas, for additional treatment. He was confined to this hospital in August and September 1953, where he was a patient of Dr. Hamilton Ford, psychiatrist."

"About six weeks ago, Dr. Ford and Si Garrett's personal physician recommended that he again enter the hospital for treatment, but hope was maintained by the family that he might improve without hospitalization. Instead, he grew steadily worse."

"Upon his personal physician's advice on Tuesday, 22 June, that Si

Garrett was a very sick man mentally and should be returned at once to the hospital for treatment, the family had him carried on Wednesday night, immediately after he had appeared before the Jefferson County Grand Jury, to the John Sealy Hospital in Galveston for psychiatric treatment."

Arch Ferrell, who had been called to appear before the Jefferson County Grand Jury, never showed up. Instead he issued a prepared statement: "Since this horrible murder, I have sought and received the active assistance of every official investigator known to me and have cooperated with them to the utmost of my physical and mental endurance. I shall continue to do so, unceasingly, until this dirty, brutal, shocking killing has been fully and finally solved."

Not persuaded of the integrity of his effort, the governor appointed young, methodical Bernard Sykes, the assistant in the attorney general's office, to go to Phenix City to conduct the investigation. On arrival, Sykes questioned Ferrell for ten hours, then removed him from the case and directed him to write a report on what action had been taken so far. Next, he removed the investigative offices out of Sheriff Matthews' office and into the Ralston Hotel in Columbus so that the efforts to investigate the Patterson murder were divorced entirely from local authorities.

Mayor Elmer Reese, angered by this suspension of local authority, told the governor that "the Russell County sheriff and the Phenix City police force can handle the Patterson murder if only the National Guard would leave town. They are all over everywhere, raiding everything and in the way."

But the Governor replied: "The Guard will be in Phenix City for a long, long time."

A frenzy of activity began. In Phenix City, on 28 June, the three-man Democratic sub-committee, looking into vote fraud in the 4 May primary in Russell County, resumed their hearings on the charges brought by Jabe Brassell. In Birmingham, the Jefferson County Grand Jury was reeling with its findings. Lamar Reid had been called for his third appearance before the investigative body. On his two previous appearances, Reid had told only part of the truth. This time, Reid told it all beginning with the phone call from Si Garrett on the night of the 1 June runoff election. When he had finished, the Grand Jury, reviewing all the evidence and testimony of witnesses, returned an indictment against Si Garrett, Arch Ferrell, and Lamar Reid for vote fraud in changing the runoff election totals by 600 votes in favor of Lee Porter.

In its final report, the Jefferson County Grand Jury concluded that "we find attorney Lee Porter's campaign for attorney general was financed almost in its entirety by the racketeers of Phenix City."

"We find that the circuit solicitor of Russell County, Arch B. Ferrell, and the attorney general of Alabama, Si Garrett, were in charge of and directing Lee Porter's campaign to be elected to the office of attorney general of Alabama."

"We find these officials directed the spending of thousands of dollars, known by these said officials to have been appropriated by said gamblers and vice lords in an attempt to defeat Albert Patterson and elect Lee Porter. We have taken the appropriate action by indicting these officials."

Concluding their report, the Grand Jury said: "Albert Patterson's murder was the climax of dirty politics, financed by a gang of unlawful men and engaged in by persons with unlawful motives. Lethargy and inaction by the public and by law enforcement agencies set the stage for this horrible murder."

"The army of criminals must be halted."

In the face of this profoundly shocking event, with the sitting attorney general, a circuit solicitor, and a Democratic committee chairman all indicted for vote fraud, the governor found himself doing precisely what the RBA had demanded in the beginning.

His first step was to appoint George C. Johnson, a crack trial attorney known for his eloquence and courtroom flamboyance, as special solicitor to replace Ferrell. Next, at his request, the Alabama Supreme Court ordered the Russell County jury box emptied and a new Blue Ribbon Grand Jury impaneled by veteran Judge Walter B. Jones, appointed to replace Russell County Judge Julius B. Hicks, who was relieved of all duties in circuit criminal court.

Lamar Reid was arrested in Birmingham and Sheriff Matthews, to his regret and dismay, had the unpleasant duty of arresting Arch Ferrell in Phenix City. Both Reid and Ferrell were taken to the Birmingham jail where they were booked, fingerprinted, locked up and later released on bond.

Garrett, still in the psychiatric hospital in Galveston, Texas, waited almost two weeks before returning to Birmingham to face the vote fraud charges against him and to post bond. Under the circumstances with the attorney general under indictment for vote fraud and being treated for psychiatric problems, demands were being made of the governor to replace Si Garrett as attorney general since the real possibility existed that Garrett could come back and take over the investigation, but the governor refused.

"An indictment is nothing but an accusation," Gordon Persons replied. "All men are presumed innocent until declared guilty. No medical board has declared Mr. Garrett insane and he has not been convicted of a crime." "The attorney general is an elected officer under the Alabama Constitution and can only be removed from the office through impeachment for moral turpitude, insanity, and other offenses."

Whereupon Jefferson County Circuit Solicitor Emmett Perry, immediately filed lunacy charges in circuit court against Garrett asking that the court hold a sanity hearing on 9 August to determine if the attorney general of Alabama was insane or of unsound mind.

"Since this defendant is under indictment, it is incumbent upon and the duty of this court," Emmett Perry stated in his formal charges, "to determine as expeditiously as possible the mental condition of the defendant."

"The defendant has been in a hospital for mental patients and himself under observation or treatment as a mental patient in such hospital in a distant city and state, to wit: Galveston, Texas."

"Therefore, it appears that the defendant may enter, as a defense to the indictment herein a plea of insanity or a plea that he is insane or of unsound mind."

"The petitioner is informed that perhaps the defendant will immediately return to said mental hospital in said distant state and be beyond the reach of this court and beyond this jurisdiction and only at great expense and with difficulty, if at all, can the proper careful investigation be instituted and carried out by this court with reference to sanity or insanity."

"Therefore, for the orderly administration of justice, it appears to be necessary that the mental condition of the defendant be determined by a careful investigation instituted by this court, and that this court take such action as provided by law with reference to the custody, care and control of the defendant."

Presiding Judge J. Russell McElroy granted Emmett Perry's petition and set the lunacy hearing for Garrett for 9 August.

Garrett refused comment on the lunacy charges and went instead to consult with his Birmingham attorney, Roderick Beddow, the renowned criminal lawyer who had represented the prosecution in the Fate Leebern murder trial. After an hour in Beddow's office, Garrett, besieged by newsmen, told them: "I am leaving the state again."

"Are you returning to the hospital?"

"No, my family and I are going on vacation."

That night on his way to meet his wife for their vacation he lost control of his car on a narrow Mississippi road, broke his neck, and shattered his elbow. His two children, eight-year-old Silas Garrett IV and four-year-old Pamela, in the car with him, were only slightly injured, but the extent of Garrett's injuries required an extensive stay in the Mississippi hospital, with his family, physician, and attorney refusing to allow any visitors or investigators.

Garrett's latest disaster was only one more of the shocking disclosures that blazed daily in headlines across the newspapers in Birmingham and Columbus, for Hugh Bentley and the RBA had received in the mail a plastic disc recording from a tap on the Hoyt Shepherd's telephone signed by a mysterious "Mr. X" who promised another 200 recordings on the condition that they be played for the press to hear. Hour after hour, the discs spun out the tale of complete political corruption that had begun in 1948: grand juries hand-picked, jurymen intimidated, and verdicts decided before the evidence was even presented, directed by Hoyt Shepherd and involving Albert Fuller.

As newsmen scrambled from one fast breaking story to another, trying to cover all the bases and make sense of all the confusion and accusations, the investigation into the murder of Albert Patterson dragged on with no end in sight. No suspect had been found, no motive officially established.

Behind closed doors, the people of Phenix City speculated among themselves. Patterson, it was agreed, had been killed because of his stand against crime and his pledge to clean up corruption. Some said he had been killed by a hit-man hired by the Phenix City racketeers who stood to lose the most if he took office and carried out his campaign promises. Others argued that this couldn't be so. Patterson had been shot at close range, so close that one of the bullets had wedged between his teeth, and this implied that the killer was no stranger, but someone Patterson recognized and knew, suggesting that the shots may have been fired in anger after an argument. The third most persistent theory was that the killing was tied into the vote fraud, both in Phenix City and in Birmingham. The very day Patterson had made it publicly known that he planned to go before the Grand Jury and tell them all he knew was the day he was shot. That's what did it, the speculators said, the order came down to stop Patterson and kill him if you have to.

Publicly, the people of Phenix City would say nothing because from the moment Patterson was shot, the word had gone out that anyone who talked would do so at their own peril, and an impenetrable silence had fallen on the town. No matter what the townspeople knew about the events that had preceded the murder or what they had seen the night Patterson was shot, no one would talk. In the four weeks that followed Patterson's murder, the silence that had been imposed on the town and the townspeople in Phenix City remained through all the tumultuous events.

Bernard Sykes, who had been hailed by the public and press on his arrival in Phenix City, had, by the middle of July, come under heavy criticism for his lack of progress in the Patterson case. The *Columbus Ledger* in front page editorials was criticizing the conduct of the investigation and appealing to citizens to come forward with what they knew. The *Birmingham News*, in an effort to afford anonymity for informers devised a system of matching numbers so that information could be given without giving one's name. Appeals were being made by Sykes, Special Solicitor George Johnson, and Judge Jones, all appointed by the governor, for citizens to come forward with information.

No one came.

16

GENERAL HANNA AND MARTIAL RULE

As Bernard Sykes was failing in his effort, General Hanna was succeeding in his. From the moment he arrived, General Hanna could see that little was being done by the local law enforcement to apprehend Patterson's killer. On the night of the murder, Sheriff Ralph Matthews, who should have been on the scene conducting the investigation, had instead hung around the hospital chatting with people in the hallway like the proprietor of a country store while a curious crowd trampled through the murder scene smashing down evidence.

Albert Fuller, despite his reputation for fast guns and gunplay, was wearing an empty holster, and for a time had disappeared on some other mission. The next day, they began going through the motions, picking up vagrants and drunks, turning them loose after questioning, conducting raids on gambling establishments that netted almost nothing, waiting it out, as they had always done.

Police Chief Pal Daniel, on the other hand, was like a man walking through a nightmare, paralyzed by the events that engulfed him, staring with haunted eyes that seemed not to see what he looked at nor to hear what was being said, standing on the sidelines while Buddy Jowers took charge and dispatched policemen. Nothing was being done and worse yet, they were *seeing to it* that nothing was being done, masking their misdeeds behind pleasantries and smiles.

Crack Hanna was a man accustomed to accomplishing his mission and the mission wasn't being accomplished. He wasn't being allowed to. As things presently stood, the National Guard did not have the authority to initiate raids or participate in the murder investigation. Their role was to keep the peace and assist the local law enforcement in conducting raids, but not a damn thing was being done either to apprehend Patterson's killer or to effectively close down the gambling operations. Finally, Crack Hanna had seen all he intended to see of cover-ups and concealment.

"Be goddamned if I'm putting up with this kind of crap," General Hanna told Colonel Warren. "I'm going to Montgomery to see the governor."

Storming into the governor's office past the Alabama State Patrol guards posted outside, General Hanna told him: "You've got to do something down there, Gordon. You've got an investigation that is going nowhere and a bunch of outlaw lawmen who are conducting the goddamnedest cover-up I've ever seen and I'll be damned if I'll be party to that. You've got to give me the authority to stop these unlawful acts or get me out of Phenix City."

Gordon Persons was a man under siege. His blood pressure rose as he chafed under criticism and criticism was coming from every quarter. Besides the great outcry of citizens and local press to apprehend Patterson's killer, newspapers across the country had run the story of "Sin City, USA," familiar to more than a million men who been stationed and trained at Fort Benning during the war, giving Phenix City's background of violence, ridiculing its officials for their inability to enforce the law and lamenting that here in America was a city so lawless that no man was safe including the attorney general-elect who was gunned down in the street. It wasn't just the *New York Times* and the big city dailies that had run the story, it was *Time* magazine, *Newsweek*, the *Saturday Evening Post*, and *Look* magazine.

To Gordon Persons' acute embarrassment, after the news media finished with that, then there was the sensational story of the Alabama attorney general, under suspicion of vote fraud, leaving the state to turn himself into a psychiatric hospital. Then the flood of demands that Si Garrett be relieved of his duties. No one knew what Si Garrett might do in his present state, and Gordon Persons figured it was best to leave the situation alone and not provoke him into coming back to the state and taking over the Patterson investigation. There was already trouble enough.

As if ridicule and criticism weren't enough, now there were the threats. Threats against his life as governor of the state, and that of his family, even his teenage daughter, Elizabeth. On Sunday before leaving for church, she had received a phone call saying: "You're next."

To protect his family, he had the Alabama State Patrol guarding the governor's mansion and he himself sat behind his desk in the executive office with a loaded .38 pistol in the drawer ready to use should it become necessary. When he looked up and saw Crack Hanna leaning across his desk with more demands, Gordon Persons was in no mood to be receptive.

Crack Hanna, only five-foot-seven, was built like a bulldog and he had a bulldog's tenacity. Leaning across the desk now, his gray hair so short it was almost shaved, his jaw jutted out, his green eyes locked on his target, he raised his voice to the tone of command.

"Gordon, you can't sit here holed up in the executive office waiting for this thing to solve itself. You've got to take the initiative and make it happen."

Gordon Persons pushed back in his leather chair and with soft hands smoothed back his silky white hair.

"Now, Crack, we've got a virtual armada of Alabama's finest on the scene down there in Phenix City. Bernard Sykes has state investigators, private investigators, and public investigators. George Johnson is there to try the cases as soon as they're made and Walter Jones has been appointed special judge to draw a Blue Ribbon Grand Jury to hear the evidence."

"That's the trouble Gordon. After four weeks of investigation there has not been a shred of hard evidence and there's not going to be so long as local law enforcement runs interference and intimidates witnesses."

"Crack, I've been hearing that same criticism as long as I can remember. A couple of years ago, they even tried to impeach the sheriff, but there was no evidence of wrong-doing and the Supreme Court cleared him completely."

"Well, the Supreme Court was wrong."

The governor drew in a deep exasperated breath at the insistence. "He may not be handling the job like you'd like to see it done, but I've already spoken to them down there. I told them it was the end of the line in Phenix City and I'm satisfied that the sheriff and his deputies are doing the best they can."

"Gordon, there's no use in being a damned fool. These people are into cover-ups, concealment, and unless I miss my guess, conspiracy."

"Conspiracy?" Gordon Persons shook his head. "Crack, you're being way too harsh in your judgment."

General Hanna smashed his wide fist on the desk top. "Goddammit, Gordon, I'm telling you, things down there are much worse than you have ever imagined, and so far, the surface has barely been scratched."

Gordon Persons, no taller than Crack Hanna himself, stood up, walked around his desk and put a hand on Crack Hanna's shoulder.

217

"Crack, do me a favor. Just go do what I asked you to do. Keep the peace."

Crack Hanna took a fresh cigar out of his pocket, bit off the end and spit it across the room. "Gordon, you're a damn fool."

Crack Hanna left the governor's office with no intention of doing what he had been told. He was not about to stand by and watch the charade being carried on by the Phenix City law enforcement and by Albert Fuller in particular. At this stage, it was unclear just how deeply Fuller was involved, the only certainty was that Fuller was one of the key players and that nothing could be accomplished in Phenix City until some one talked. People were afraid to be brought to the courthouse for questioning for fear they would be singled out and shot later. To a man, everyone who had ever tried to solve the situation in Phenix City had been victimized and Crack Hanna had decided he'd be damned under forty feet of hell if it was going to happen under his command and on his watch. Gordon Persons was so absorbed by the politics of the problem and the political cost of what Si Garrett might do that he had lost sight of the mission and was wishfully waiting for the problem to somehow resolve itself while the situation grew steadily worse. It was time to bite the bullet and Crack Hanna had already decided which bullet to bite.

On returning to Phenix City, he chose men from his command and organized his own counter-intelligence team. Sending them out under cover in civilian clothes he told them: "I want you to go and find out what's happening here. Who are the gamblers and where is the gambling equipment being concealed. While you're at it, I want you to find out what happened on the night Patterson was killed, who saw it and what it will take to get them to talk."

To cover his own activities and keep the local law enforcement lulled into complacency, he and the National Guard, as the governor had directed, continued to accompany Chief Deputy Albert Fuller and other members of the local law enforcement on the mock raids that were being staged, raids on isolated farm houses and deserted barns, raids which netted little more than old and worn out gambling equipment that had long since spent its usefulness while his own intelligence team was reporting truck loads of slot machines, roulette wheels and other valuable gaming equipment were being hauled away in the dark of night down other roads.

Standing with General Hanna on a hill in the dark overlooking a dirt road below, Warrant Officer Forney Hughes, one of the intelligence officers, handed him a pair of field glasses.

"Take a look, General. That's a load of equipment leaving the county now."

Following the headlights of the truck as it snaked around the curves on the country road, General Hanna asked: "Do you know who it belongs to?"

"Yes, sir. Our information is that it belongs to Godwin Davis and is on its way out of the county now to his farm across the river in Georgia."

"You know where the farm is located in Georgia?"

"Yes, sir. Near Columbus, in Harris County."

Handing the field glasses back, General Hanna smiled. "Good work, Forney. Keep that truck under surveillance and when the equipment arrives at Davis' farm, see to it that the sheriff of Harris County is informed."

That night, as the gambling equipment was being stored in Godwin Davis' barn, the sheriff of Harris County arrived with a warrant and arrested Davis and his oldest son, Sonny, charging them with possession and storage of illegal gambling equipment.

Continuing his pursuit, General Hanna set his sites on Albert Fuller. Fuller, he knew for a fact, had a number of gambling houses under his protection and was alerting them in advance of every raid and running interference for those hauling gambling equipment out of the county. "That bastard has run us all over the county on wild goose chases and I want him caught dead to rights in his own lies."

When his intelligence team reported that a gambler named Harry LaRue in a white jeep would rendezvous with a truck load of equipment at a country road intersection, General Hanna decided that this would be the opportunity he was seeking. In the sheriff's office that night, he told Fuller: "I have information that a gambler named Harry LaRue is moving gambling equipment."

"Harry LaRue?" Fuller took off his hat and scratched his head. "I don't know no Harry LaRue."

"Then, let's go looking for him."

"Sounds like a waste of time to me."

"I'll be the judge of that."

Pushing himself out of his chair and picking up the keys to his squad car, Fuller shrugged. "Suit yourself."

"It suits me," General Hanna snapped.

Following Fuller, General Hanna in his green Lincoln followed by two jeep-loads of National Guard men pulled into a filling station where Fuller got out and told the attendant, "We're looking for a man named Harry LaRue. You know who he is and where I can find him?"

The attendant looked at Fuller, then over his shoulder at General

Hanna and back at Fuller. "Nope, never heard of him. You might try at that farmhouse down the road. I heard tell there was a new feller that come in down there."

At the farmhouse, Fuller routed a sleepy farmer from his bed.

"We're looking for a man named Harry LaRue."

The farmer shook his head and closed the door.

"There might be a place on the other side of the county, " Fuller was saying, but at that moment over his car radio, General Hanna heard his team give the coordinates for Harry LaRue's location.

Wheeling his car around, General Hanna and the Guard men raced to the specified intersection with Fuller following fast behind. LaRue, in the white jeep was parked by the roadside waiting. As General Hanna and Fuller got out of their cars, LaRue, recognizing Fuller, threw up his hand in greeting. "Albert, how in the hell are you? What are you doing out here?"

General Hanna turned on Fuller without a word. Fuller grinned. "Hell, I didn't know this was the man you were talking about. Why if...."

"Stand aside, Fuller. We're searching these premises now. LaRue, you lead the way."

After a thorough search of the house and outbuildings, General Hanna could find nothing, but as he walked down the driveway, his flashlight caught a narrow path headed toward the woods beside the house.

"What's down there?" he asked LaRue.

"Nothing. Just a path the pigs use when they go down to wallow in water at the creek."

"I want to see it."

"Ain't nothing to it."

"Lead on," General Hanna snapped.

One hundred yards down the path in a clearing they came upon a huge tin barn perfectly sheltered by tall trees.

"What's this?" General Hanna asked.

"Just an abandoned barn."

Running the beam of his flashlight over the outside wall, he caught the electric meter in his circle of light. "Not many abandoned barns have an electric meter with the meter running. Open it up and let's have a look."

Harry LaRue shot a look at Albert Fuller, but Fuller, caught in the lie he had perpetrated, made no response.

Inside the barn was an arena for cock fighting with tiers of seats circled around and on the top tier, a series of doorless stalls with dirty mattresses where prostitutes serviced their clients between events as an added spectator sport. On the floor of the cockfight arena were the gaming tables ready to be moved.

"Call Colonel Warren at headquarters and have him send a truck to pick up this gambling equipment," General Hanna told the guardsmen with him. To Albert Fuller he said: "Take LaRue in and arrest him. I'll be right behind you."

Shortly thereafter, events took another turn when the Civil Service Commission, conducting its own investigation into the voting irregularities in the May 4 primary, fired night police chief Buddy Jowers for his participation at the polls. The territory once shared by Buddy Jowers and Albert Fuller, no longer had Buddy's protection, and three days later, Albert Fuller was in Cobb Memorial Hospital.

"What happened to Fuller?" General Hanna asked Forney Hughes.

"He says he injured his back on a fall from his horse."

"I don't believe that. Go see what you can find out."

Later, Forney Hughes reported. "There's talk in town that Albert Fuller and Buddy Jowers had a falling out over territory. When Buddy got fired, Albert moved in and Buddy gave him a near-death beating. Albert is saying that a fall from his horse injured his back and he can't walk. The talk is that Buddy did it."

Continuing his work with his counter intelligence team, General Hanna began meeting clandestinely in the middle of the night with informers who were willing to talk when privacy and protection were promised. Night after night, information was gathered on the depth of depravity and the extent of the crime and corruption that involved every level of law enforcement in Phenix City and Russell County.

Going to the governor with what he had found, General Hanna told him: "You're going to have to get rid of the law enforcement and declare Martial Law. There are people who can testify to the conditions in Phenix City but they are not willing to come forward under the present conditions. They are afraid of retaliation and they've got good reason to be. If you want the evidence you need to solve that situation down there and get it cleaned up, you're going to have to declare Martial Law."

The governor refused. "Crack, I told you to go down there and keep the peace, keep it quiet and keep the lid on what could become an explosive situation. That's all. I am NOT declaring Martial Law."

General Hanna puffed on his big, black cigar. "Gordon, we're not talking about minor infractions of the law, we're talking about wholesale felonies, crime, and corruption like you wouldn't believe."

"Look, I've got five months left in office. There's no way that I, in five months, can clean up what's been going on down there for the last 100 years."

"Gordon, you can't overlook what's happening. That's tantamount to condoning."

The governor leaned across the desk, his face flamed with restrained anger. "Crack, as the governor of this state, *I* am your commanding officer, and I *order* you to go back to Phenix City and do what you are told."

General Hanna puffed on his cigar again. Through the cloud of smoke drifting between them, he said: "Gordon, I'd hate to have to arrest my own governor, but I will if I have to."

Crack Hanna smashed his cigar in the governor's spotless ash tray, turned on his heel and left the office. He had had all he intended to take of the governor's dawdling and delay. Something was going to have to be done to salvage the situation in Phenix City, and he, *by God*, was going to have to do it, and in the doing, he realized it could cost him his command. Gordon Persons as governor of the state and commanding officer of the National Guard could replace him or relieve him, but if the price of command was standing by and watching a criminal cover-up by local law enforcement making damn fools out of decent men trying to restore justice and law and order, then, by God, they could take the command and shove it up their ass.

Leaving the governor's office, General Hanna made two phone calls, one to Emmett Perry, the hard-hitting Jefferson County Circuit Solicitor who had had the courage to indict Garrett, Ferrell, and Lamar Reid for vote fraud and bring lunacy hearings against Garrett while the governor was still quavering over what Garrett might do. The second phone call was to the executive editor of the *Birmingham Post Herald*.

"We need to talk," General Hanna told them, "about the situation in Phenix City."

At a conference that lasted all night, he laid the facts before them.

"I am convinced," he told them, "that the motive for Patterson's murder is not only tied to the vote fraud in Phenix City and Birmingham, but is tied to the Phenix City crime and corruption and the place to start is confronting the criminals with their crimes. With enough heat somebody will start to buckle and spill their guts."

"The problem, "Emmett Perry said, "is getting the evidence to make the cases."

"No. Our intelligence team has come up with the witnesses. The problem is to get the governor to take the appropriate action to secure the safety of those willing to testify and that can't be done until he gives us the authority to do it by declaring martial law." Emmett Perry, a man with a craggy face and a crew cut, nodded his head. "Then we'd better ask the governor to come tell the Jefferson County Grand Jury why that can't be done."

The editor promised a front page letter to the governor urging action and Emmett Perry added: "I'll bring this information before the Grand Jury in the morning."

The next day, the *Birmingham Post Herald* headlined an "An Open Letter To The Governor" on page one.

"Dear Governor:
Our reporters have been in Phenix City almost constantly since Albert Patterson was murdered the night of June 18.
That was four weeks ago today. And we are convinced of one thing. The murder won't be solved until you exert the full powers of your office toward the solution."

The governor was none too pleased with this public criticism of his handling of the Phenix City situation and even less so with the phone call from Solicitor Emmett Perry inviting him to appear before the Jefferson County Grand Jury. When the governor declined, the foreman of the grand jury took the phone and told him: "If you refuse, we're going to subpoena you."

Three hours later, having traveled the 100 miles from Montgomery to Birmingham, the governor was answering the questions put to him by the grand jury.

Newsmen, alerted to this unusual occurrence, were waiting on the courthouse steps when Gordon Persons emerged from the grand jury room three hours later.

"Tell us what happened, Governor. Are you going to declare Martial Law?"

Hustling into his limousine for his return to Montgomery, Gordon Persons said: "I have no intention of declaring martial law at this time. I will do that when the time is desirable and proper." The Grand Jury, however, recessed for a week to await the governor's decision and a week later, after a trip to Washington, D. C., to consult with President Dwight Eisenhower, F.B.I. Chief J. Edgar Hoover, and constitutional lawyers in Washington, Gordon Persons made his decision and called General Hanna in from Phenix City.

"Okay, Crack, I'm going to give you what you want. At 4:30 this afternoon I am declaring a state of emergency that replaces all elected law enforcement in Phenix City with Martial Rule."

He tossed the Proclamation across his desk and while General Hanna quickly read the authorization, the governor explained: "Unlike Martial Law which is declared during civil riots or disasters, Martial Rule is unprecedented. From what they tell me in Washington, there has never before been a circumstance requiring the replacement of all elected law enforcement."

"That's what we need, Gordon, to get the job done. When we're finished, there won't be a thug left standing. The cleanup will be complete."

Knowing Crack Hanna's tendency for total commitment, Gordon Persons said, "And Crack ..." There was a significant pause in the Governor's voice, "Just take over law enforcement, don't go taking over the investigation of the murder. We've already got somebody on that."

General Hanna returned the Governor's pause with one of his own. "Whatever you say, Gordon, so long as they don't interfere with my mission or my men, but we could damn well get the job done."

"I'm reading the Proclamation at 4:30."

General Hanna looked at his watch. "I'll be back to Phenix City in time to take over."

Crack Hanna was ready to take command. Despite Gordon Person's reluctance and arguments to the contrary, he was certain that Martial Law would have to be declared and when it was, he was ready for it. Leaving the governor's office, he stopped long enough to call Colonel Warren in Phenix City.

"Red Alert. Have the troops stand by to execute Contingency Plan One at 17:30 hours."

In preparing for the possibility of martial law, General Hanna, two days earlier, on 20 July, had instructed Colonel James Brown, a tough combat veteran who had come up through the ranks from master sergeant and known to the troops as "Boxjaw," to prepare a roster of soldiers to be pulled in from summer camp training for duty in Phenix City.

"Boxjaw, I want you to search the records and come up with the best we have in men already trained as jailers, wardens, policemen, and lawyers," General Hanna told him. "We're going to need them all."

Assisted by Lieutenant Jim Roberts, Brown went to Fort McClellan, Alabama, to consult the records of 15,000 men. For his legal advisor, he chose Major Ray Acton, a thirty-three-year old lawyer who was mayor of Homewood, Alabama. With the execution of the Contingency Plan, sixty hand-picked men were loaded onto Army buses at Ft. McClellan, Alabama, headed for Phenix City.

By the time General Hanna reached Phenix City, the troops were combat ready. There was no time to instruct the troops, only to give the order: "Martial Rule is being declared by the Governor in twelve minutes. We are to take over City Hall and the Courthouse. Move out."

In full battle dress in a drizzling gray rain with rifles at the ready, the troops surrounded the Courthouse. As General Hanna and Colonel Warren walked into the sheriff's office, Ralph Matthews and his deputies were sprawled around the office, smoking, laughing and joking.

"Yes, sir, General. What can I do for you?" Matthews grinned.

General Hanna looked at his watch. It was precisely 4:30 P.M. in Montgomery. "At this moment, the Governor is reading the following Proclamation to the citizens of Alabama and it is my duty to so inform you:

> "Whereas, organized crime has for many years existed in Russell County, Alabama, particularly in Phenix City, and a gang of men have conspired and are conspiring to thrive on the systematic exploitation of rights, and the organized lawless activities of this gang continue to hamper the investigation of the murder of Albert Patterson, there exists in this community a state of lawlessness, breach of peace, organized intimidation and fear and a continued imminent danger which the local peace officers are unable or unwilling to subdue:
>
> I, Gordon Persons, as governor of Alabama and commander-in-chief of the Alabama National Guard do hereby proclaim a state of qualified martial law in Russell County.
>
> I further instruct the adjutant general, now on duty with units of the Alabama National Guard in Russell County to take over, assume, supersede and exercise all the activities of the sheriff, deputy sheriffs, the chief of police and all police officers, and until further orders from me, to take and continue to take appropriate measures to suppress the state of lawlessness, intimidation, tumult and fear which reigns in that area."

The jovial smile had slid off Ralph Matthews face, the deputies had stiffened, the atmosphere electrified with tension.

"What does that mean?" Ralph Matthews began.

"That means that you and all your deputies are relieved of your duties. As of this date, Colonel Warren here is appointed Military Sheriff of Russell County."

The attitude of the deputies had gone from surprised to sullen, and Ralph Matthews complained: "I don't see why the Governor felt like he had to go and ..."

225

General Hanna stopped him. "You and your deputies will surrender your badges, guns, gun permits, and squad cars." Pointing at a metal can by the sheriff's desk, he said: " Warren, get that trash basket over there and start collecting them."

As the deputies began unbuckling their gun belts and unpinning their badges from their shirts, General Hanna told Ralph Matthews: "Call in your men on patrol and have them do the same thing."

Remembering Albert Fuller, General Hanna asked: "Where is Chief Deputy Fuller?"

"Still in the hospital in bed," Matthews replied. "You know he had that fall off his horse, "

"Warren, go to the hospital and see to it that Fuller surrenders his badge and gun along with the others."

Leaving Warren in charge, General Hanna walked out of the courthouse and across the street to City Hall where he was joined by Colonel Brown.

"Boxjaw, are your men here?"

"Yes, Sir. Sixty of them. Hand-picked."

"Good. We're going to need them all."

In the police chief's office, Pal Daniel was waiting as he had been instructed to do. Repeating the Proclamation, General Hanna told him: "Call in your men on patrol and have them turn in their badges, their guns, gun permits, and squad cars. As of now, Colonel Brown here is in charge and has been appointed Military Chief of Police."

From Pal Daniel there was no resistance. He moved quickly to carry out the directive, his eyes were full of anxiety, his face full of fear for he remembered only too well what had happened to his father who was the sheriff of Russell County in the cleanup of 1923.

When the takeover was complete General Hanna gathered his troops together in the armory.

"I want to commend you for your action this afternoon," he told them. "What could have been an explosive situation, went off without a hitch. I want to keep it that way."

"The situation here is as serious as combat and is the moral equivalent of war. Thugs and gangs who figure they are above the law have ambushed and killed the attorney general-elect, threatened the Governor of this state, and his family, and have a whole town under siege by intimidation and fear."

"We're going to change all that. I want this mission accomplished without so much as the firing of one shot. Our ammunition is going to be evidence, something the law enforcement in this town has never been able to come up with before."

"When I say evidence, I mean an *avalanche* of evidence that will bury these bastards under the weight of their own misdeeds, misconduct and lawlessness."

"Most of you have served with me before, and you already know that my two pet peeves are the abuse of soldiers and the abuse of women, and that I won't put up with the abuse of either. In this town, it has been the abuse of everybody, by brute force and bloodletting, against the innocent and unprotected, by men who took the law into their own hands and ruled with intimidation and fear. That's going to stop beginning *right now.*"

General Hanna paused, letting his eyes embrace the entire company. "We're going to do everything the law allows. I want everyone of them, no exceptions, hit with every law they've ever violated, so hard and so fast that they'll have no time for masterminding mischief and intimidation, their only concern will be how to save themselves, in other words, an enemy in full retreat."

"Our job here is to restore law and order and the constitutional rights to the people and I mean to see to it that it gets done. If in the doing, any soldier of mine is threatened or harmed, in any way whatsoever, I'll lower the Goddam boom on this town. If a combat situation arises, you are armed and you have been trained to use your weapon. You know what to do, and I expect you to do it."

"Now, as for you legal eagles, " he shot a look at the flock of young lawyers called to active duty to assist in the tangle of legal problems. "I don't want to hear any moaning and groaning and carrying on about 'What if,' or 'Maybe,' I won't stand for any hesitation and hand-wringing. I want this job done and I want it done right. I don't want any cases lost on loop holes or reversals. I want you to make damn sure we stay within the law and if it looks like an action is on the edge of the law or questionable, then I want you to find me a law to get it done."

"Jim Fullan." A smooth-faced, young lieutenant stepped forward. "Yes, Sir?"

"I want you standing right at my shoulder. I don't want to hear a word out of you, but if it looks like I've gone too far on an action, I want you to nudge my elbow and let me know. The rest of you have your orders. Get busy and get it done."

૨ა

Within thirty-two hours of the takeover, the lightning strikes began. At 2:00 A.M. on Saturday, with troops, trucks and equipment, General Hanna led his men to the foot of the Dillingham Bridge and banged on the door of the infamous Bridge Grocery, operated by Head Revel and Godwin Davis' brother, George. When there was no response, General Hanna turned to one of his men: "Hand me that ax."

With several hard, swift blows, he splintered the door and kicked it in. Inside, there was not the smallest pretense of a grocery. Not even a can of beans. Instead, an elaborate setup of gambling equipment, roulette wheels, gaming tables, and billboards for posting the day's lottery winners . The last date posted: Friday, 23 July.

"Be goddamned if they weren't running the lottery right up to this afternoon."

Inside two safes in the office, twenty leather bound ledgers detailed the accounting of the take from the gambling and the lottery.

"All right, men," General Hanna said, "this is the evidence we're looking for. Tag and record every item."

As the men began loading the evidence onto two and one-half ton Army trucks, George Johnson, who had been appointed special solicitor to replace Arch Ferrell and try the cases, told General Hanna: "There's enough evidence here to make a case in forty directions."

General Hanna smiled. "There's going to be more."

At the Bama Club across the street, where General Hanna had had his first confrontation on the night he arrived in Phenix City, J. D. Abney, who ran the club for Hoyt Shepherd and Jimmie Matthews, was taken into custody. Clyde Yarborough, Hoyt Shepherd's old mentor, still holding his handkerchief over his mouth, eaten away by cancer, was arrested at the Yellow Front Cafe. Brass knuckles were found in the Silver Dollar and dynamite in the Eldorado Club run by William Henry Clark.

Waiting Army trucks hauled them off to jail as General Hanna moved over to Fourteenth Street to raid Godwin Davis' Manhattan Cafe. There, behind pink walls, were one-way mirrors, peepholes, sawed-off shot guns, black jacks and an astonishing system of secret passages that linked the Manhattan Club with the Cafe and the Pawnshop, all owned and operated by Godwin Davis and his two sons.

In the pawnshop were the treasures that had been traded at the gambling tables: jewelry, wedding rings, trophies and soldiers' combat boots. Seeing them, General Hanna shook his head sadly. "They even took the boots off the poor bastards' feet."

Working around the clock throughout the weekend, the raids continued. On Sunday night in the sheriff's office, General Hanna received a telephone call.

"General, you're working way too hard in this hard summer heat. I got a truck load of liquor for you and your boys."

"I got all the liquor I can drink," General Hanna replied.

As he slammed down the phone, Jack Warren looked up and asked: "What's that about all the liquor you can drink?"

"Some damn fool wants to bribe me with a truckload of liquor."

Warren's eyes twinkled behind his steel-rimmed glasses. "They know you're serious. They know you're gonna get 'em."

"You're damn right we are. Now how many arrests were made on the weekend raids?"

"We got fifty of them in jail and thirteen truckloads of evidence all piled out in the jail yard."

"There's more out there and I want it all. What about Head Revel, the one who owns the Bridge Grocery?"

"Looks like he's run off to Florida."

"Then issue a fugitive warrant. I want him and I want Godwin Davis."

"Davis," Warren explained, "is at his farm in Hamilton, Georgia. He and his oldest son, Bubber, are due to be tried over there in Harris County in the morning for storing that gambling equipment the sheriff found in their barn."

"Swear out the warrants now. I want them arrested, the minute they set foot back in Russell County."

17

RAIDS AND REVELATIONS

Godwin Davis was sick and tired of trouble. Ever since the divorce trial of his son, Bubber and Gloria Floyd Davis, there had been just one damn thing after another. By the time Head Revel had finished putting the finger on him in open court for running a lottery, the IRS had never given him a moment's peace. They figured $60,000 in unpaid back taxes and put liens on his property and sold his automobiles. Then there was all that trouble over the Patterson killing and having to move equipment out of Russell County in order to save it from the constant raids. He had barely gotten it in his barn at his farm in Georgia when there was the Harris County sheriff with a warrant for his and Bubber's arrest.

It had been a rough day in the Georgia court before Judge T. Hicks Fort, but the verdict was not as bad as it might have been, seven and one-half years probation and a $5,000 fine. Davis paid it off and headed for home in Russell County. He didn't want any more trouble, but trouble was waiting for him the moment he drove up in his drive: National Guardsmen were waiting to take him and Bubber into custody for questioning.

At the Russell County jail standing before Colonel Warren, Godwin Davis, angry and irritable, demanded: "What is this? What in the hell is this?"

"I have orders from General Hanna to pick you and your son up."

"For what?"

"Running a lottery and gambling equipment found on Saturday night's raid at the Manhattan Club."

Godwin Davis, expecting an easy walk-through, reached in his back pocket, pulled out his fat leather wallet and slammed it down on Warren's desk. "All right, let's get this over with. I'm tired and I want to go home. How much is bond?"

"Bond has not been set yet, as the number of charges has not yet been determined. My orders are to hold you for questioning."

"In jail?"

Colonel Warren nodded and motioned to the jailer.

"This is an outrage," Davis shouted. "Get my lawyer on the line, get V. Cecil Curtis and tell him to get the hell over here."

V. Cecil Curtis, the young attorney whose election in the May primary was contested by Jabe Brassell and provoked the Sub-Committee investigation, scurried over to the sheriff's office to arrange for the Davises' bond. He found this could not be done until the next morning when Godwin Davis and his son Bubber were charged with forty-four counts each on running a lottery with bond set at $500 for each count.

"Christ in Heaven!" Davis screamed. "There's never ever been a bond that high in Russell County: $22,000 each! That's $44,000 for the both of us!"

Godwin Davis was absolutely stunned, as were the people of Phenix City. It was almost beyond belief that a gambler of his means and prominence had not only been put in the Russell County jail, but had to remain in jail until bond could be raised. The *Columbus Ledger* and *Birmingham News* recorded this event with banner headlines and photographs of Davis and his son being booked at the county jail.

"That's only the beginning," General Hanna told the reporters who questioned him. "We're going to put them all in jail and we're not going to stop until every pillar of Phenix City's crime castle has been pulled down."

While Godwin Davis remained in jail and V. C. Curtis, scurried to raise the money to release him, General Hanna gave instructions that no straw bonds would be accepted. "I'm not going to have this pledging the same piece of property over and over on every arrest we make. I want good surety bonds taken from the tax assessors records requiring that property pledged is free and clear and twice the assessed amount."

"Property here in Russell County is appraised at about thirty percent of market value. That means, if they're going to get out of jail, they've got to come up with some real money."

Under the newly enforced regulations, Davis' attorney, could not come up with surety bonds for a total of $44,000. In the crunch of this crisis, the gambling community put aside old feuds and hatreds and banded together to help the Davises before the same fate befell them.

Two days later, nineteen signers had pledged enough property to release Bubber Davis. Among those signing the surety bonds were Hoyt Shepherd, his partner, Jimmie Matthews, and Dr. Seth Floyd, whose daughter, Gloria, was still in litigation over child custody in her divorce from Bubber. Looking at the list of signers, General Hanna told his staff: "Study this list and find out what their connections are to the Davises. It will tell us who his friends are and who else is likely linked to the rackets."

While Godwin Davis remained in jail, languishing about his cell in silk shorts and fur-lined bedroom slippers, General Hanna continued the around-the-clock raids and arrests.

"I want the heat kept on and the momentum maintained," he told his staff. "If we're going to get to the bottom of what's going on here, somebody's got to talk."

Three days later, Colonel Warren tapped on General Hanna's door. "There's someone here to see you."

The door opened and Police Chief Pal Daniel walked in. Taking off his hat, he tried to wipe the worst of the worry off his face with the wrinkled white handkerchief he took from his back pocket.

As the jails began to fill up and the mighty began to fall, Pal Daniel, frightened by the prospect of a jail term, became the first of the Phenix City officials to break the silence. He had seen what had happened in the whiskey raids and cleanup of 1923 when his own father, then Sheriff of Russell County, had gone to jail and he could see it coming again, only worse. The crisis in Phenix City had never ever been this critical before, and before he became the victim of what he had been forced to do, Pal Daniel decided to cut out and come clean.

Holding his hat in front of his chest like a shield, he tried to get the words out. "General Hanna, there's something you need to know."

General Hanna leaned back in his chair and watched the worry begin to etch itself back onto Pal Daniel's face as he ran the brim of his battered white straw hat through his hands in a circle.

"All right Chief, let's have it."

"Well, you see, Sir, the way things operated in the Phenix City Police Department ...."

Painfully, Pal Daniel told General Hanna that he had received a "hands-off" policy on the arrest of Phenix City gamblers from higher up. Pressed, he and fourteen Phenix City policeman admitted that it was on orders from Mayor Elmer Reese.

"I don't get to run my police department," Pal Daniel told General Hanna. "Buddy Jowers was the one that done that."

"Buddy Jowers? You mean the night police chief?"

"Yes, sir. He's Mayor Elmer Reese's nephew. Elmer Reese gives the orders and Buddy sees to it that it gets done."

General Hanna looked at Jack Warren. "Go out and pick up Elmer Reese, I want to talk to him."

When Colonel Warren and his deputies returned, he reported: "Elmer Reese has left town."

General Hanna exploded: "Left town!"

"I'm told he went to Birmingham with Arch Ferrell and Sheriff Matthews. There's a meeting down there tomorrow at the Redmont Hotel. The State Democratic Executive Committee is going to vote on voiding the May Primary election in Russell County. Ferrell and Matthews have gone down there to try to save their nominations. Reese, I'm told, went along as an observer to offer his support."

General Hanna rolled his lower lip out, considering the situation. "Elmer Reese may just decide to keep on going like Head Revel did. Go down to Birmingham, arrest him and bring him back."

"On what charge?" Warren asked.

"Willful neglect of duty. Three warrants: allowing the operation of lottery, slot machines, and dice tables."

Reese was asleep in his hotel room in Birmingham when Jack Warren rapped on the door at 3:00 A.M.

"What in the hell do you want?" Reese snarled sleepily as he opened the door and saw Warren.

"I got a warrant for your arrest and orders to bring you back to face charges in Phenix City, so get dressed and let's go."

Two hours later, Reese, angry and indignant, was led into his own jail past a mountain of confiscated gambling machines piled up in the jail yard as evidence.

"That's just some of the gambling equipment you said you couldn't find, " Warren told Reese as he took him into his own jail to be booked, fingerprinted and photographed.

"I don't know why you're picking on me," Reese complained, "if it's for not carrying out the law, you ought to arrest every official in Phenix City."

"Pal Daniel says ... "

"I don't give a damn what he says."

⁂

While Elmer Reese was protesting his charges in Phenix City, Arch Ferrell was protesting his ouster as the Democratic nominee for circuit solicitor and Ralph Matthews' ouster as nominee for sheriff.

The three-man Democratic sub-committee that had investigated Jabe

Brassell's charge of vote fraud and vote buying in the May 4th primary election had recommended in an 800 page report that the full State Democratic Committee meet and declare all the May 4th nominations vacant and void.

"Due to the fraud, corruption, malconduct of elected officials, the casting of illegal ballots and other election violations," the sub-committee reported, "it was impossible to determine which candidate won the election."

On the sub-committee's recommendation, a meeting had been called in Birmingham for 31 July to hear the evidence and decide on appropriate action. Arch Ferrell, standing before the Democratic Executive Committee gathered in the Redmont Hotel in Birmingham, was passionate in his plea.

"I do not know who reached out into the ballot box of Jefferson County or any other county and changed the vote totals," he told them. "What you have heard has been a vicious, outrageous rumor. I grew up in the party of my father and my grandfather," Ferrell said, calling on the record of his relatives. "I, myself, have been a member since 1928, and I direct my future wholly to the Committee and the Democratic Party."

The Committee, however, was not persuaded of Ferrell's integrity or his intentions and struck his nomination, along with that of Sheriff Matthews, V. C. Curtis, and William Belcher, naming Jabe Brassell, who had initiated the inquiry into the vote fraud, to replace Belcher.

Back in Phenix City, Pal Daniel continued to talk. Buddy Jowers, he said, was the satchelman who paid off the voters at the polls and on the night of Patterson's murder Buddy Jowers sent city policemen to warn the gamblers to clear out all their gambling equipment, that the Governor and General Hanna were on the way.

"If you want to know who runs the law enforcement in this town," Pal Daniel said, "it's Buddy Jowers and Albert Fuller. Buddy runs the police department and Albert runs the sheriff's office."

"More than that," Pal Daniel added, "there was a running feud and bad blood between them on payoffs and protection."

Six-foot-six Buddy Jowers , already fired on the first of July by the Civil Service Commission for "voting irregularities" in the May 4th Primary, was brought in for questioning.

Sitting down across the desk from General Hanna, Buddy draped one long leg across the arm of the chair and rolled his cigar to the corner of his mouth. "Were you acting on orders from Mayor Reese to leave the rackets alone?" General Hanna asked.

Buddy, unaccustomed to accounting for his actions, scowled at the question. "I wasn't acting on orders. I was acting on policy. That's the way the police department has always been run. Policy was passed down from one administration to the next."

"What about the competition between the police department and the sheriff's department?" Buddy was asked.

Buddy clamped his cigar in one side of his mouth and leered with the other. "You think I'm scared of Albert Fuller?"

Before a response could be made, Elmer Reese, standing behind Buddy, stepped in and said: "Buddy's not afraid of Albert Fuller, anybody or anything. It was Albert Fuller causing all the trouble. Right before Patterson was killed things had just about reached the boiling point over jurisdiction. The city policemen couldn't get their job done for the sheriff's department. Albert Fuller was taking over, playing favorites, and running things."

❧

General Hanna knew for a fact that Albert Fuller had not been running things lately. Fuller had taken to his bed. Finding refuge in Cobb Memorial Hospital, he had been bedridden since 4 July, when, he said, he had taken a bad fall from his horse. In town, the whispers were that the injuries were not from the horse, but from his arch rival, Buddy Jowers, who had given Fuller a near-death beating.

When the recordings of Hoyt Shepherd's telephone conversations, turned in by Mr. X, were spinning out tales of courthouse control, intrigue and intimidation involving Albert Fuller and Arch Ferrell, both men were questioned by Bernard Sykes. Albert Fuller was questioned for three hours in his hospital room and Arch Ferrell, for ten hours at Sykes' headquarters, but no charges were placed against either of them.

On hearing of Pal Daniel's disclosures, a reporter asked Albert Fuller what he thought of the recent developments to clean up Phenix City, Fuller grinned confidently. "It don't matter what anybody says or what anybody does, Phenix City is a town too tough to tame. It will eventually return to its old ways. It always has and always will."

❧

"The hell it will!" General Hanna exploded when he read of Fuller's remarks in the paper. Whatever the direction of investigation, Albert Fuller always was the center of controversy and General Hanna had had enough of Fuller's arrogance and defiance.

"Warren, what have you got in your file on Fuller?"

"A lot."

"I thought you told me that Hilda Coulter, that little lady from the RBA Auxiliary, had sworn out a warrant against Fuller for his election law violations in the May Primary."

"Yes, sir, six of them."

"Have they been served yet?"

"No, sir."

"Then go serve them."

"I believe he's still in the hospital."

"I don't give a hell if he is. Put him under arrest and put a guard on the door until he makes bond for six counts of violating the election laws."

As Albert Fuller was being arrested and Sheriff Matthews was out trying to raise $4,500 bond money for Fuller, Godwin Davis, after more than a week in jail, was finally being released. Free on a $22,000 surety bond which required twenty-four signatures, he was headed home at last when he was served with another subpoena to appear the next day before the Jefferson County Grand Jury in Birmingham.

Solicitor Emmett Perry, following up the disclosures and discoveries in Phenix City, had subpoenaed Hoyt Shepherd, Jimmie Matthews and Godwin Davis to tell what they knew about the election fraud in the June 1st run-off election.

Godwin Davis had had enough of jails, judges, and questioning and when brought before the Grand Jury in Birmingham, he was uncooperative and belligerent. Solicitor Emmett Perry, after weeks before the Jefferson County Grand Jury, trying to untangle the ties to the vote fraud, had had enough of lies, omissions and evasions, and when Godwin Davis consistently refused to answer the questions put to him by members of the Grand Jury, Emmett Perry hauled him before Circuit Judge Alta King.

"The questions being put to you by the Grand Jury are proper questions," Judge King told Davis, "and if you continue to refuse to answer, you will be held in contempt of this court."

With a sea of trouble, Godwin Davis decided to sell out and told the Grand Jurors the whole sordid story of the assessments made for money to buy the run-off election for Lee Porter. He named names, dates, places and amounts of money. When he finished, Lee Porter, who had, in violation of state law, not reported the gamblers' contributions and had lied before the Grand Jury in earlier testimony, was ruined.

Facing a charge of perjury, Porter then told the Grand Jury how it all began with a telephone call from his old college classmate, Arch Ferrell, who invited him to Birmingham to meet some supporters who wanted to help him win the runoff election.

"Godwin Davis," Porter said, "was introduced to me as a cattleman, and Hoyt Shepherd, as a motel owner, both of whom were interested in defeating Albert Patterson because, they said, he had turned on them."

After hearing Porter's testimony, the Jefferson County Grand Jury, having been in session for two months, in its final report determined that "Lee Porter's unsuccessful campaign was financed by the Phenix City racketeers and directed by Attorney General Si Garrett and Solicitor Arch Ferrell."

৵

In Phenix City, Arch Ferrell was drunk and arrested while driving under the influence. For him, the sky was falling, relieved of his job as circuit solicitor, indicted for vote fraud by the Jefferson County Grand Jury, accused of masterminding the political machine in Phenix City, his nomination voided by the Democratic Committee, and underlings everywhere, buckling under the pressure, spilling their guts.

Arrested by one of the patrolmen in the National Guard, as he skidded his car into the courthouse at 11 A.M., he was brought before Military Police Chief Colonel Brown and his legal assistant, Major Ray Acton, falling down drunk.

"If you're gonna ask me about Albert Patterson, I'm gonna tell you, I didn't kill him, " Ferrell said. "I hated the sonofabitch, but I didn't kill him. When Albert Patterson was shot, I was in my office talking long distance to Si Garrett in Birmingham, and I can prove it, what they're saying isn't so."

"What are 'they' saying?" Ray Acton asked.

"You know very well what they're saying," Ferrell exclaimed, flailing his arms and sinking into the chair beside Ray Acton's desk. "They're saying that Si Garrett and I engineered the election, that we first tried to buy the election, then tried to steal the election, and then when all else failed, they're saying I'm the prime suspect, but I tell you, I did not kill Albert Patterson and I don't know who did."

Ferrell's identifying himself as the prime suspect was the first Ray Acton had heard of this possibility and he let Ferrell continue to talk.

"All of these investigations and interrogations, Sheriff Matthews and Mayor Reese and Buddy Jowers, these are fine men who have done fine jobs."

"What about Albert Fuller?"

"I love Albert Fuller!" he said, pushing himself up out of the chair.

237

"I want to give three cheers for Albert Fuller!"

Stumbling on the carpet, Ferrell fell to the floor, slightly cutting his nose and chin.

"Get him up and take him over to the county jail, " Colonel Brown said. "He needs to be in a cell by himself and we don't have one."

"Where are we going?" Ferrell wanted to know.

"We're going to let you sleep it off," Ray Acton replied.

In Recorder's Court the next morning, Ferrell was fined $100 and had his license revoked. Brought before General Hanna, he asked for a continuance.

"No continuance and no deals," General Hanna told him.

Leaving the courthouse, Ferrell was mobbed by photographers and reporters who called out: "What do you think of the Patterson case?"

"I know nothing about it. On the night Patterson was killed I was talking long distance to the Attorney General in Birmingham," Ferrell replied, repeating what he had said before.

"What does the Attorney General have to say?"

"You'll have to ask him."

But no one was permitted to ask Si Garrett anything. Still in the hospital in Mississippi recovering from the injuries received in his auto accident in July, Si Garrett was seeing no one. "Si's in terrible shape," his attorney, Roderick Beddow, said, "and is allowed visits only by members of his own family." The extent of his infirmities was such that the lunacy hearing brought by Solicitor Emmett Perry had to be delayed.

Delay was an indulgence General Hanna did not intend to entertain. By the end of the first week in August, National Guardsmen had served 2,500 subpoenas on witnesses who were to appear before the Grand Jury when Judge Jones convened the hearings on Monday, 9 August.

Primary among the cases to be heard was that of Red Cook, who was arrested when he came in to sign the bond for his partner, C.W. Franklin.

"You are E.L. Cook?" General Hanna asked. "You are the beer distributor and run the Old Original Barbecue?"

"Yeah, but they call me Red."

"You're under arrest."

"What for?"

"Gambling equipment and paraphernalia gathered on a raid at the Old Original Barbecue. We've been looking for you."

"I been in Florida."

"Well, get ready to open your safe. We want to see what's inside."

"I forgot the combination."

General Hanna looked up at Jack Warren. "Lock him up until his memory improves. If it doesn't, we'll dynamite the safe. In the meantime, have Jim Fullan check the records and see if Mr. Cook here has anything else pending."

As Jack Warren led Cook away, General Hanna asked: "By the way, Cook, why do they call you Red?"

"Because of my eyes," Cook replied. "Drinking made 'em that way."

When Jim Fullan reported his search of the files, he told General Hanna: "He had plenty to drink about. There's a 1950 murder case against him that's never been brought to trial."

"The hell you say!"

"Yes, sir. He killed a man named John Mancil in a bar room brawl, shot and paralyzed another, named William Calvert Rogers, and shot a bystander in the leg."

General Hanna raised his brows and pursed his lips. "All in one shooting?"

"Yes, Sir, and it never came to trial."

"That's the trouble with these bastards," General Hanna said. "They never thought they'd have to pay for anything. If he'd been smart, he'd have gone ahead and run that case through that crooked grand jury and gotten a dismissal while it was rigged with all his friends."

"Well, there's no statute of limitations on Murder One," Jim Fullan said.

"That's right. Book him."

The next day, with a murder charge added to a charge for owning gambling equipment, Red Cook's memory improved and he accompanied General Hanna and the guardsmen to the Old Original Barbecue and opened his safe containing lottery tickets dated as late as 16 June, two days before the murder of Albert Patterson.

In addition to Red Cook, records at the Old Original Barbecue led to the arrest of his partner, C.W. Franklin, who had been foreman of the April 1954 "Screen Door" Grand Jury that could find no evidence of gambling in Phenix City, only a screen door that needed to be replaced in the courthouse. Also arrested on that raid was Ernest Youngblood, operator of the Diamond Horseshoe, who had given Hugh Bentley the beating at the polls in 1952.

After two weeks of raids and arrests, the jails were full of gamblers, gangsters and law-breakers. At Bernard Sykes's press conference on Friday before the convening of the Blue Ribbon Grand Jury on Monday, a reporter asked: "Will you be bringing evidence before the

Grand Jury on the murder of Albert Patterson?"

"No," Bernard Sykes replied.

"Why not?"

"I won't go before the Grand Jury until we have an airtight case."

"There's a rumor going around that you're doing a whitewash," the reporter said. "That the reason the murder investigation is getting no where is because of the officials involved."

"Anyone who knows my reputation," Sykes replied vehemently, "knows I don't whitewash."

"Do you know who killed Albert Patterson?"

"We have some suspects."

"Do you know the motive?"

"There may have been several."

"Was it connected to the vote fraud or was it a personal grudge killing?"

"No comment," Sykes said, gathering up his briefcase and ending the news conference.

Over the weekend, as everyone waited for the opening of the Blue Ribbon Grand Jury on Monday, the tension mounted and the speculation grew on what would happen now that Judge Walter B. Jones, a portrait of stern justice itself, had been appointed to replace Russell County Judge Julius Hicks on the bench.

On Saturday night, General Hanna's phone rang and his aide, Captain Richard Peacock, took the call.

The man on the phone would not give his name. "I have to talk to General Hanna. It's urgent."

General Hanna picked up the phone. "What's the trouble?"

"We talked before," the caller said. "I made you an offer, but you turned it down. Now, we're going to sweeten the pot."

"How's that?"

"A bunch of the boys have gotten up a war chest, $250,000 in cash."

"Is that so?"

"All you got to do is call off your dogs."

"You simple sonofabitch, you think everybody in this world can be bought."

"The boys don't take kindly to what's been happening here. Take some advice, General. Take the money and get the hell out of Phenix City." The caller paused, then added, "Or else."

"Or else what?" General Hanna demanded.

"You might find yourself in the cross hairs of somebody's rifle. The boys start getting reckless when they get riled up."

"All right, Mr. Bastard, you just name it, guns, knives, or chains. I'll

240

meet you anywhere, anytime, any place you say and stomp your sorry guts in the ground."

"The boys don't work by appointment. They pick their own time and their own place."

"I'll be looking for you," General Hanna replied.

The phone clicked, and Richard Peacock who had been listening on the extension, ran into General Hanna's office.

Peacock was aghast. "He threatened to kill you!"

General Hanna laughed. "He damned sure isn't the first and he won't be the last."

"What are you going to do?

"Keep right on until we have every last one of those bastards in jail. There's going to be hell to pay when the Blue Ribbon Grand Jury convenes on Monday and they know it. Judge Walter B. Jones is hell on wheels when it come to seeing that justice is served from the bench."

18

HARVEST OF HELL

Judge Walter B. Jones was an imposing presence. A premier jurist and president of the Alabama Bar Association, his credentials and his attire were impeccable. Arriving for court in a cream colored suit, his bald head shinning under the glare of the overhead lights in the steaming August heat in the courtroom, he was ready to see that respect for the law and justice in the courts be restored.

He had been circuit judge in Montgomery for thirty-four years and took great pride in his Southern heritage and his considerable contribution to upholding the law and protecting the Constitution. His father, Thomas Goode Jones, had twice been governor of Alabama and during his service as a major in the Civil War had carried General Lee's flag to General Grant at the surrender at Appomattox Courthouse in Virginia. At his ancestral home in Montgomery, Judge Jones was something of an institution himself, renowned on the bench for his stern demeanor and evenhanded justice, off the bench for his jovial good humor, his hospitality, his horses and as a raconteur of the first rank.

Judge Jones believed in the Bible, the law, honor, and integrity and had devoted his life to the pursuit and preservation of these things. As president of the Alabama Bible Society, he administered the distribution of 10,000 Bibles each year. As president of the Alabama Bar Association, he had ordered the Grievance Committee to make certain that any lawyers found guilty of misconduct brought to light by the Phenix City cleanup or in the vote fraud investigations be disbarred. It began with Si Garrett, Arch Ferrell, and Lamar Reid, indicted by the Jefferson County Grand Jury for vote fraud, and Lee Porter, charged with perjury, for lying to the Grand Jury concerning the Phenix City gamblers' contribution to his campaign.

"The state bar is not to stand idly by," he told the Grievance

Committee, "and permit members of our honorable and respected profession in Alabama to flagrantly violate the laws of the state, contravene the ethics of our profession, and go unpunished."

"A criminally-minded person without a law license is a threat to the community, but such a person armed with a license to practice law is a deadly menace in that he destroys the confidence of our people in their courts as the instrumentalities for the fair and impartial administration of justice."

"A lawyer must faithfully live up to the requirements and ideals of the profession. When he is honored with high office and is unfaithful to his trust, he is unworthy of membership in our great profession and should pay the penalty of disbarment and expulsion."

When Si Garrett returned from Texas in mid-July to face the vote fraud charges in Birmingham, concern arose that Garrett might decide to remain and take over the investigation. Judge Jones, to protect the evidence that had been gathered, immediately impounded the ballot boxes and made Bernard Sykes custodian of the records.

Appointed by the Alabama Supreme Court as special judge to replace Circuit Court Judge Julius B. Hicks, Jones had arrived in Phenix City a week after the Patterson murder to draw a special Blue Ribbon Grand Jury determined that justice be restored. When he learned of the conditions in Phenix City and was informed that threats were being made to the prospective jurors, he made a public announcement.

"It cannot be and it shall not be that this handful of lawless people and their stooges in this county can overthrow all law, nullify the constitution of the state and make themselves the supreme law of the land. They shall not go unwhipped of justice. Anyone threatening the veniremen for this grand jury will face a felony count and be sentenced to the penitentiary."

On the opening day of court, he greeted General Hanna with a warm handshake and a clap on the back. Smiling, he said: "We're going to strike a blow for victory, Crack. The elusive element has always been the lack of evidence. Now that you and your troops have rounded up the evidence and convinced the witnesses to talk, we're going to see that justice is served."

"We're waiting to see it happen," General Hanna replied. "It's been a long time coming."

"Did you get me that color guard?" Judge Jones asked.

"They're right here, waiting to open court."

"I think it's important that we show the flag and stand on ceremony," Judge Jones said. "I want the grand jurors to see and be reminded of what we stand for."

"I think it's a good idea."

The spectators in the courtroom stood as the military bailiff said: "Oyez! Oyez. Special Criminal Court of Russell County is now in session. The Honorable Walter Jones presiding."

Taking his place behind the bench, Judge Jones stood for the presentation of the colors. As National Guardsmen placed the American flag and the flag of Alabama on each side of the courtroom, the officer in charge said: "God save the United States of America, the State of Alabama and the American flag in Russell County."

After the spectators and grand jurors had settled themselves in their seats, Judge Jones immediately began his charge, addressing himself to the 18 members of the Grand Jury.

"What is to be brought before you for your investigation and consideration is a tragedy bred by crime ... a harvest of hell ... murder, arson, gambling, carnal knowledge, robbery, burglary, vote fraud, misfeasance and malfeasance of those sworn to uphold the law. More tragic yet were those, seeking relief at the bar of justice, who received instead a judicial lynching. *There will be no more judicial lynchings.*"

"I commend to your careful and patient investigation, each and all of the matters here mentioned. Most especially, the court wishes to emphasize the necessity for a full investigation of the cowardly murder of Albert Patterson and to express the hope that his murderer will soon be identified and indicted."

"As to your duties as Grand Jurors, it is proper to state that Grand Jurors are not required, before finding an indictment, to be convinced beyond all reasonable doubt that the accused is guilty of the offense charged against him."

"No such measure of proof is required by law for the finding of an indictment, but, after hearing the testimony brought before you by the State, and twelve or more of you have reasonable cause to believe that a crime has been committed, then you should return an indictment. This is an accusation, in writing, endorsed 'A True Bill' by your foreman. This indictment is authority for the court to put the defendant on trial before a jury of his peers."

Satisfied that the Grand Jurymen had understood his instructions, Judge Jones continued: "The people of Russell County and the State of Alabama owe a great debt of gratitude to the daily and weekly press for the courageous and able manner in which they have brought to light the evil conditions found here. I am aware of the revelations made here recently of organized crime and vice. I am aware of the threats and the fear that grips many."

Looking out over the courtroom, engaging the eyes of those who sat there, he continued: "In speaking to you this morning, let me give a word of assurance concerning freedom from fear. Those who stand for law and decency have no need of fear."

"You need have no fear that the underworld is ever going to ride roughshod over you again.

"You need have no fear that the old days with all their crime and vice will return.

"You need have no fear that your lives, property, and peace of mind will be subject to the caprices of the overlords of organized vice.

"You need have no fear, that there will be any let up in the fight against organized crime.

"Those who should be in a state of fear are those who through the years have nullified and set aside all law here."

In conclusion, Judge Jones acknowledged Hugh Bentley and the members of the RBA by adding: "A word of appreciation should be publicly said from this bench for those who, through long years filled with danger, despite threats, bodily injuries, dynamitings, and arson have fearlessly stood through it all and have done a man's part in trying to bring decency and respect for law and order back to this community. All honor to them for their patience and firm stand."

When the charge was finished, Special Solicitor George Johnson, began the presentation of evidence beginning with the felony cases. The first to be considered was that of Mrs. Nona Faye who had been set afire with an insecticide in an attempted murder by service station operator, William Allred. Mrs. Faye, with a number of fresh bruises on her face, was so fearful of testifying that she fainted when she was called before the Grand Jury.

National Guardsmen on duty outside the jury room to protect the waiting witnesses, picked Mrs. Faye up and revived her. Still too fearful to talk, she was put in protective custody in the jail with guards at the door. That night she took fifteen sleeping pills and had to be taken to the hospital to have her stomach pumped out and two guardsmen walked her throughout the night to wear off the effect.

When Judge Jones heard of Mrs. Faye's hysteria, he was infuriated. "Anyone intimidating witnesses before this court will be subject to a felony charge and serve time in the penitentiary," he announced angrily.

When court convened the next morning, the case of Red Cook, charged with murder, was called. William Calvert Rogers, a witness to the shooting and a victim himself, was wheeled in on a stretcher by two attendants from the local funeral home. Since Cobb Memorial Hospital had no ambulance, the hearse at the funeral home doubled as an ambulance. Rogers, paralyzed from the waist down since the shooting four years before, told the Grand Jurors how he and taxi driver John Mancil got in an argument with Red Cook at his club on a Sunday morning in 1950, how Cook shot and killed John Mancil, wounded Rogers and shot a third man who was on his way to the men's room.

Taken to Cobb Memorial Hospital, Rogers said he was treated for a stomach wound, a fractured left arm, a fractured collar bone and a punctured left lung.

Asked by the Grand Jurors what was done about the shooting, Rogers replied: "Sheriff Matthews came to my hospital room and asked me some questions and said Red Cook would take care of the medical expenses and help support my family."

"Did he?"

"No. He never done nothing after that," Rogers said bitterly. "I wasn't able to work. When my thirteen-year old son needed $27 for school books, he wouldn't even let us have the money for that and my son had to drop out of school because he couldn't pay his expenses."

When Rogers was wheeled away, the call of witnesses continued with Hilda Coulter testifying against Albert Fuller for election fraud in the May 4th primary.

While Solicitor George Johnson was presenting evidence and witnesses before the Grand Jury, General Hanna and his troops were out digging up more. On a routine check by Warrant Officer Forney Hughes for gambling and lottery equipment at the Eldorado Club, the investigation into crime and corruption took a whole new turn.

᠑

Warrant Officer Forney Hughes called Jack Warren at the sheriff's office on 12 August. "I've got to talk to General Hanna. I think I've run up on something."

Hughes a tall, thorough, quiet-spoken investigator was in civilian life an investigator for the railroad and the only one in his National Guard unit who had his son serving in the same unit with him.

Leaving his prisoner outside in his son's custody, Forney walked into General Hanna's office.

"What have you got, Forney?" General Hanna asked.

"I was over checking out the Eldorado Club and learned that Billy Clark, the son of the club's operator, was in violation of his parole."

"Did you pick him up?"

"Yes, sir, but there's more. He was convicted four years ago on a charge of grand larceny and was sentenced to three years in prison, but after sixty days he was released on an order from Judge Julius Hicks allowing him to work on his father's farm. Since his release, he's been working as a bartender in his father's club and has been arrested ten times in four years of probation."

"And never been picked up once?"

"No, sir. His latest arrest was in March of 1954 when he and his eighteen-year old cousin, Harley Tillis, got into a fight with two cotton mill workers from Columbus. Billy Clark was charged with pistol whipping one Roy L. Clark, and his cousin, Tillis, was charged with hitting the other, Bill Dempsey, over the head with a ball-peen hammer resulting in a concussion that required hospitalization."

"Were they arrested?"

"Yes, sir, but they were both released under a $300 bond and when their two victims failed to appear in court, they were advised by a policeman to pay the fine and forget it."

"What was the fine?"

"Clark had to pay $101.50 and his cousin, Harvey Tillis had to pay $26.50."

"Damn! $26.50 for busting a man's head!"

"I got him outside if you want to talk to him."

"Bring him in."

Billy Clark, a young man with a middle-age girth, followed Forney Hughes into General Hanna's office.

"Clark, how is it that you could pistol whip a man for $101.50?"

"That's all they said I owed."

"What brought on this fight, gambling?"

"No, Sir. We ain't had no gambling at the Eldorado since 1950."

"Army intelligence tells me that the Eldorado attracts a lot of the Army trade from Fort Benning. How is it you get the soldier trade with no gambling going on?"

Billy Clark, quick to make some excuse besides the gambling that had landed so many of the operators in jail, said :"We got girls."

"What kind of girls?"

Clark hesitated for a moment. "We got strippers, yes, sir, we got some flashy strippers."

"Forney, get Warrant Officer Ray McFall and check out the strippers. Meanwhile, hold Clark and his cousin Tillis in jail for further investigation. I want to find out what the story is behind Clark and how he could manage ten violations without having his parole revoked."

That afternoon, an order came down from Judge Hicks, revoking Billy Clark's probation and ordering him back to Kilby Prison. When General Hanna learned of this, he said: "Billy Clark is not to be removed from the Russell County Jail except under my signed order. We want to find out what else he knows and who's in such a helluva hurry to get him out of here and back into Kilby."

When word got out that Billy Clark was in jail, anonymous calls began coming into Colonel Warren's office in the sheriff's department. Girls, forced into prostitution, wanted to talk and tell what they knew about the vice-ring, but only with the promise of protection.

General Hanna told his staff: "I'm not interested in locking up these girls unless they need protective custody. What I want is the whoremasters, all of them!"

That night, General Hanna received a call. The woman on the other end of the line spoke in whispers. "I read what you said in the paper, about the whoremasters. I've got to see you. I need some help. They took my daughter."

"Come in to the sheriff's office," General Hanna told her. "I'll wait for you."

"I can't. If someone saw me talking to you, they might harm her."

"All right. Where can I meet you?"

"There's a deserted farm house on Seale Road, about three miles out of town on the left. I'll be there, waiting for you."

As he put down the phone, General Hanna said: "Forney, you and Ray McFall come along with me. We got an informer who wants to talk."

Driving onto the dirt road that led to the farmhouse, General Hanna got out of the car and stood by the headlights.

"Sir, it could be a trap," Forney cautioned. "They see you standing in the light, they might shoot."

"If they do, shoot back," General Hanna said. "That woman won't come out unless she knows who it is."

There was a stir from the bushes around the house and soft steps. "General Hanna?"

General Hanna stepped forward. "Yes?"

A small, pretty woman in her thirties, with a coil of dark hair laying on her shoulder walked out into the light. "I'm Earlene Harper. I'm the one who called."

"You said they took your daughter. Who is 'they' and where did they take her?"

"The night Mr. Patterson was killed and everyone was leaving town, they took her; her name is Sheila Ann and she's only sixteen."

"Who took her?

"Hugh and Jean Kinnard. He was a bartender in Phenix City, they had a stable of girls, and they took them all out of Phenix City because

248

they knew there was going to be trouble."

"Do you know where they took them?"

"I didn't 'til I got this letter from Sheila Ann," she said, handing a small white envelope to General Hanna. "They took 'em all to Aiken, South Carolina where the H-Bomb plant is and set up business there for the plant workers and the soldiers at Fort Gordon."

"I been in the business a long time, as a B-girl, but Sheila Ann hasn't never been involved in anything like that. She's just a kid. Can you get her back?"

"We damn sure can," General Hanna said. "That's a violation of the Mann White Slavery Act, transporting a female across the state line for immoral purposes."

"When?"

"We'll need you to come into police headquarters and file a complaint."

"I'm afraid ..."

"I'll put Warrant Office McFall here in charge and he'll see to it that you get in and out with no trouble," General Hanna assured her.

At police headquarters, Earlene Harper told her story. She and three of her friends had come to Phenix City in 1952 looking for work. The day they arrived, they were arrested and put in jail for "investigation."

We hadn't done nothing," Earlene said. "We had just got into town and as soon as the police saw us, they put us in jail. The next day, a man who identified himself as Glenn Youngblood, came to the jail. He told us he had two night clubs and would get us out of jail if we came to work for him, but ..." Earlene Harper paused, "we refused the circumstances. We stayed in jail three days, and finally the FBI came and couldn't find anything on us and let us go."

After that, Earlene said, she looked for work and could find none, and Glenn Youngblood offered her work again. This time as a B-Girl.

"I had no money and no place to go and the police said if I didn't get work, they'd lock me up again as a vagrant. It was either work for Glenn Youngblood or go back to jail so I went to work. Once I got started, there was no way out. I don't want that to happen to my daughter."

After signing a complaint against the Kinnards, Colonel Brown contacted the South Carolina Law Enforcement Division and two days later, Sheila Ann Harper was located and brought back to Phenix City.

In a signed statement, she told investigating officers that she had first come to Phenix City in 1953 to get her mother out of jail.

"Mother was working in a cafe. This cafe was the Riverside run by Glenn Youngblood. Mother explained a little bit about the place but I didn't know what it was. It was a B-drinking place. I went with my mother every night as I did not have anything else to do. Glenn Youngblood asked me several times to come to work. When he learned I was only sixteen, he said I could still work for him as he had girls younger than me. There was a girl there named Dorothy who had been there since she was twelve. I told him I didn't want to go to work for anyone on the Bridge."

"I heard him tell the other girls what to do. A B-Girl was supposed to get soldiers to buy her a drink. The bartender would serve liquor to the soldier and coke to the B-Girl with just enough liquor on top so he wouldn't get suspicious. The B-Girl was to get him drunk and take him to the gambling room in the back where the cards were marked and the dice were loaded. If the soldier caused trouble, they called the police and had him locked up for drunk and disorderly conduct. Albert Fuller and Buddy Jowers were the ones who came."

"Glenn and various other cafe operators used to meet at the Riverside for jam sessions and talk about how much money they had to pay out for protection and how it was getting higher all the time. Albert Fuller's share was fifty percent of the winnings."

"B-Girls got fifty percent of all the drinks they sold and half of whatever they got rolling soldiers — money, jewelry, cigarette lighters. The bartenders said they didn't care what the girls did as long as they got half."

"Sometimes on payday, a girl would get as many as 75 or 100 drinks a night. When the man who was buying went to the men's room, she'd pour her drink on the floor or else knock it over and have to have another one."

"If the man brought his own bottle, the girls were told to drink it up as soon as they could. They usually poured themselves a whole glass and took it to the bartender. He'd pour it out into a bottle under the bar and then sell it back to the soldier without the soldier ever knowing he was buying back his own liquor. Same way with beer. If a customer didn't finish it all, the bartender poured it back in the bottle, capped it and sold it again."

"If it took too long to get a man drunk or he raised a fuss about something, the bartender put knockout drops in his drink."

In her seven-page statement, Sheila Ann described how her mother later went to work for Glenn's brother, Ernest Youngblood, at the Diamond Horseshoe. Living with her mother in a trailer, with little to do, Sheila Ann kept a notebook and wrote down all the things she saw and heard.

"I wrote about everything I saw just to pass the time," Sheila Ann said. "I had nothing else to do. I went wherever Earlene was working. I drove Ernest Youngblood's car. He always wanted someone to drive him because he was usually drunk. He asked me to sleep with him plenty of times. He said he would open all of the charge accounts I wanted in Columbus and I could have anything I wanted. He said he would give me a car that had been taken from a soldier for his bond. They kept raising the bonds of soldiers to keep them from getting their cars back."

"Once I drove Ernest to his house to get some records that he kept in a strongbox at his house. There were lots of records, five books in all with lists of girls who were prostitutes. When it came time to go, he wouldn't let me leave the house. I called the police, and told them I was at Ernest Youngblood's house, but they never came. Ernest said they wouldn't come, that he could do anything he wanted to."

"I told him about the notebooks I had been writing in, that I had put down everything. He said I'd better get rid of them that it wouldn't be healthy to keep them."

"After the Patterson murder, Ernest asked if I was still writing in those notebooks, I told him there was nothing to write about, and that night I burned them. Everybody was scared and leaving Phenix City. Hugh Kinnard, who was a bartender for Ernest, said he and his wife were going to Aiken, South Carolina, and they would take me with them. I didn't know until I got there what it was for. I wrote a letter to my mother to tell her where I was and what had happened."

When General Hanna read the statements made by Sheila Ann and her mother, he said: "We need you to go before the Grand Jury and testify."

"I'll go," Earlene Harper said, "but I don't want my daughter to go. If they knew where she was and what she had said ..."

Sheila Ann reached over and clasped her mother's hand. "I'll go, Mama, I'll tell them what I saw ... everything."

"We can arrange that her identity will not be known," General Hanna assured her, "and give her protective custody."

Calling in the members of the press who regularly stationed themselves at the courthouse, General Hanna told them: "Boys, I need a favor. We got an important witness we've got to get before the Grand Jury. With the way you boys work, I know it won't be anytime before you know her name, but I'm going to ask you not to disclose it as there is a good deal of danger. If she is identified, she'll likely be killed."

General Hanna, who enjoyed a good rapport with the press, and had been described in the stories they filed as "tough-talking", "two-fisted", "up-front" and "honest with the press," was immediately granted his request, and when Sheila Ann Harper went before the Grand Jury, the next day's newspapers reported: "Mystery Witness Quizzed in Phenix."

As word got out that the B-Girl and Prostitution Ring was being broken and the safety and protection of witnesses was being assured by the National Guard, more than fifty women who had been involved in the vice ring that had operated in Phenix City came forward to tell what they knew.

One shocking revelation after another was brought before the Grand Jury, drawing a portrait of the unbelievable depravity, peonage, payoffs, procurement, and systematic fleecing and mauling of soldiers made possible with knockout drops and mad-dog dope.

On the basis of the testimony of these witnesses, General Hanna ordered the pickup and arrest of all suspects. One of the first to be brought in was thirty-nine year old Rudene Smith and her twenty-two year old son, both charged with procurement for prostitution. Rudene, who began working in Phenix City as a $15 a week bartender branched out into procurement with her son, recruiting farm girls in the country with the promise of finding them work in the city. If a girl resisted prostitution, she was arrested, fingerprinted, mugged and booked for the very thing she was trying to avoid: prostitution. With a record as a prostitute, unable to pay her bond, and threatened with exposure back in her hometown, she was obliged to do the work she had been recruited for. Any reluctance could be changed to willing obedience by the 'housemen' hired to oversee the operation of the whorehouses. Muscle-men were hired to whip or beat them into line and to take care of any customer who became quarrelsome or belligerent.

Girls employed to work at Frank Gullatt's Blue Bonnet Cafe told another shocking story. After being recruited, they were tattooed inside their lower lip for identification. Questioned on the reason for this, one of the girls explained: "So we couldn't run away or get work somewhere else. Anyone hiring a new girl knew to look inside her lip first. If she had a tattoo, then they knew she was one of Frank's."

The reports grew more lurid with the testimony of girls who worked at Cliff Entrekin's Fish Camp where dinner was served downstairs and sex was for sale upstairs, all under the protection of Albert Fuller who witnesses said visited the Fish Camp two or three times a week, and collected his payoffs on Sunday morning.

"I want an arrest warrant for that sonofabitch for bribery," General Hanna told Ray Acton. "Entrekin's Fish Camp was one of the first places raided after Patterson's murder. Naturally, we found no evidence since Albert Fuller led the raid."

While a warrant was being drawn up for Albert Fuller, a dragnet operation resulted in the arrest of other operators implicated in the huge vice ring. One of these was a woman named Fanny Belle Chance, known locally as the Queen of Hearts and co-owner in the Cotton Club with former night police chief Buddy Jowers.

Fanny Belle had come to Phenix City two years before in search of the good life and the fast buck. Beginning as a $14 a week B-Girl, she quickly advanced her ambitions by marrying six men, some of them concurrently, which afforded her a collection of government bonds and monthly allotments from those stationed overseas. Her biggest conquest was adding former night police chief, Buddy Jowers, as one of her suitors. Despite the grave warnings of his uncle, Mayor Elmer Reese, Buddy co-partnered with Fanny Belle the ownership of the Cotton Club with Fanny Belle providing entertainment and Buddy providing protection.

As the vice cases increased, the investigation broadened. A dice factory was discovered where marked cards and loaded dice were manufactured. A college for safe crackers was uncovered where criminals throughout the country came to learn the expertise of quickly and efficiently breaking the combination of a strong box. And then, the rumor of baby sales and an abortion clinic. Louise Malinosky, the forty-five year old wife of a mechanic was arrested and admitted before the Grand Jury that she regularly performed abortions on her dining room table.

"I did it," she told the guardsmen, "to get pin money for whiskey and to help those poor girls in trouble."

With the investigation of the vice ring added to the vote fraud, gambling and murder being investigated by the Blue Ribbon Grand Jury, Special Solicitor George C. Johnson had added three more solicitors to his staff to prepare and try the cases.

"It is hard for the average person to envision the magnitude of this situation," Johnson told newsmen. "The case load put on the trial court as a result of the vice and racket cleanup may make it necessary to have two courts to handle the tremendous volume."

In the face of overwhelming evidence being brought before the Grand Jury, Sheriff Matthews, already relieved of his duties by the declaration of Martial Rule, and under investigation for willful neglect of duty, resigned his office as sheriff, and Lamar Murphy, a Phenix City service station operator, was appointed sheriff by the governor on General Hanna's recommendation.

"Murphy," the governor announced, "will assist the National Guard until such time as elections can be held and a new sheriff elected."

As his legal assistants took down the testimony of the witnesses and evidence piled up, General Hanna ordered the pickup and arrest of all suspects. Hugh Kinnard and his wife, Jean, were arrested and charged with violating the Mann Act. Dressed in shorts and barefoot, twenty-three year old Jean Kinnard cried bitterly as she waited outside the Grand Jury room for questioning. Glenn Youngblood was located and brought to jail and Forney Hughes tracked down Fanny Belle Chance and brought her back to Phenix City for questioning.

Learning that he had been drawn into the inquiry, and that the National Guard was looking for him to answer questions on protecting the rackets, Buddy Jowers left town that night. A fugitive warrant was issued and the last information on Buddy Jowers was that he was somewhere in Mississippi headed West.

❧

In the midst of this depravity discovered by the National Guard, the Phenix City Ministerial Alliance decided that the moment was right to ask a young, but already world-renowned evangelist, Billy Graham, to hold a giant revival in Phenix City. Graham's advance agents arrived in Alabama and received permission from Governor Persons, but when General Hanna heard about it, he promptly canceled Billy Graham's appearance.

"We cannot conduct a full scale investigation with the crowds and confusion this revival would attract. If an appearance by Billy Graham is necessary at this time, let them hold the revival across the river in Columbus."

Both the Governor and the Ministerial Alliance were piqued. Governor Persons popped off a note to General Hanna saying: "Crack, I wish you would have the courtesy to tell me first before countermanding my order and consent."

The ministers maintained a stony silence. Seeing that they were truly hurt by having their opportunity to have a world-renowned evangelist come to their town, General Hanna called a meeting of the Ministerial Alliance to explain the reasons for his abrupt decision.

General Hanna told them: "Now, I believe in talking to the Man Upstairs, and I have done so myself on many occasions, but, Goddammit, the time is not now. We are doing everything we can to clean up the crime and corruption in Phenix City so that you can do the job you've been trying to do all along."

From the rear of the meeting hall, one preacher said, "Amen," this was followed by the applause of the entire company.

"So that you can see what you have been up against, I'll have a

National Guard bus and give you a personally conducted tour of the rats' nests we are trying to clean out."

When it was done, the Ministerial Alliance unanimously voted General Hanna an honorary member. Along with this recognition and approval came an admonishment, a letter from General Hanna's mother, Annie Rebecca, a formidable Southern lady in her eighties, who still kept close watch on her son's activities. She had been following intently the Phenix City developments in the newspapers. One reporter, describing General Hanna's rush from one crisis to another, called him "clear-eyed and cussing."

In the next mail, a letter arrived from Annie Rebecca.

"Dear Walter,
I don't want to hear of your cussing anymore.
Annie Rebecca"

Except for his mother's scolding and the response to his decision to cancel Billy Graham's appearance, his conduct of the cleanup had been overwhelmingly endorsed by the public and the newspapers covering the events. By the end of August, General Hanna and his troops had made a record 204 arrests and had drawn into the investigation the US Treasury Department, the FBI, the Federal Narcotics Agents, and agents from the Federal Alcohol Tax Unit.

Satisfied with the performance of his troops, General Hanna told them: "You're doing an outstanding job, men. We've got an avalanche of evidence and an enemy in full retreat, a solicitor with the guts to prosecute and a judge with the fortitude to see that justice is done."

On Monday, 30 August, the Blue Ribbon Grand Jury, had been in session for three consecutive weeks. It made a partial report of their findings. "The Grand Jury has found so much evidence of lawlessness and corruption that their investigation will have to be broken down in phases, the first phase being the evidence presented on felonies, gambling, and lottery."

With their partial report, the Grand Jury handed down 545 indictments against fifty-nine people, and the hunt was on. The roundup and arrests began.

19

ROUNDUP AND ARRESTS

Hoyt Shepherd did not expect to be arrested. He reminded newsmen that he had gotten out of the gambling business back in 1951 when the federal government required a gambling stamp and had gone respectable. He said he was now growing roses and winning contests for the Christmas decorations outside his house.

"It don't matter what they're saying about me on those disc tape recordings that Mr. X has sent in," Hoyt said. "All that's in the past, said and done, and beyond the statute of limitations."

He and his partner Jimmie Matthews had come to the courthouse to talk about who the National Guard was going to come down on next and to join the crowd waiting to see who would be on the list when the Grand Jury handed down their indictments. Standing at the soft drink machine in the courthouse, laughing and talking with old cohorts, Hoyt didn't notice National Guard officer Captain Elwood Rutlege as he came up to the group.

"You are Hoyt Shepherd?" Captain Rutlege asked.

Hoyt turned up the remains of his soft drink, guzzled it down, and grinned.

"That's right, and this is Jimmie Mathews."

"You are both under arrest."

Hoyt laughed. "Yeah? What for?"

"Four counts of leasing buildings for the purpose of gambling," Captain Rutledge replied, taking Hoyt by the arm. "Come with me."

Hoyt, half-amused, thought it was a joke. In all of the raids that had been made and the tons of equipment that had been confiscated by the National Guard, not so much as one slot machine or lottery ticket had been found to connect him to the rackets. Hoyt was satisfied that what had happened in the past was beyond the statute of limitations, and the

200 taped recordings sent to the RBA by the mysterious "Mr. X," revealing as they were, had demonstrated his influence at the courthouse, but they had been taped six years before in 1948.

"There's not a shred of evidence against me now, linking me to the rackets," he told newsmen, "and there's no way in the world the Grand Jury can indict me because I cashed in all my chips two years ago when the Federal Gambling Stamp was required."

But, like General Hanna, Solicitor George Johnson was determined to see justice done. "We're not going to let Hoyt Shepherd slip through the net," he told his assistant, Conrad Fowler. "Hoyt is in this and has been for years. He's the architect who built the machine and there's got to be a law somewhere that he hasn't figured out how to slip out through."

Days were spent searching the law books until a statute was found. An 1873 "gypsy law" still on the books, designed to prevent gypsy bands and riverboat gamblers from plying their trade during the frontier days, made it a misdemeanor for anyone to rent or lease property for the purpose of gambling. Hoyt and his partner, Jimmie Matthews, owned the buildings that housed the Ritz Cafe, Red Cook's Old Original Barbecue, Clyde Yarbrough's Cafe and the Golden Rule Cafe, and they were taken to jail and locked up on four counts of leasing with bond set at $1,000 on each count.

While Hoyt and Jimmie Matthews were being booked and fingerprinted, City Clerk Jimmie Putnam, Hoyt's partner in a motel, was out gathering signatures for his bond, one of which was Alabama House Representative Ben Cole, who along with Jabe Brassell, had touched off the vote fraud hearing into the May 4th Primary.

Rushing back to the courthouse, Putnam presented the sureties to Colonel Warren who took them to General Hanna. "I can't accept this," General Hanna told Warren after looking at the signatures. "The property listed here has already been pledged on other surety bonds and now exceeds its assessed value."

The gambling community was thoroughly shaken. They couldn't believe that the Kingpin himself had been arrested, and, more stunning yet, was that he was locked up in the Russell County jail with his bond refused. There was little time to reflect on this, however, as the list of those indicted became known. Godwin Davis, his son, and his brother George, already on bond, were indicted on forty-four counts of lottery. Frank Gullatt was indicted for gambling at the Blue Bonnet Cafe. Red Cook was indicted for murder and for gambling. Head Revel, already with a fugitive warrant issued against him, indicted. The list went on and on and the National Guard was everywhere making arrests and jailing those who had been indicted.

While Hoyt waited in jail for Jimmie Putnam to raise his bond, Bernard Sykes called the sheriff's office. "I want Hoyt Shepherd delivered under guard to my headquarters in the Coulter Building to be questioned about the Patterson murder," Sykes said.

More than thirty reporters and photographers from Alabama and Georgia who had followed the chaotic events since the killing of Patterson on 18 June, gathered at the courthouse that day to cover the indictments to be handed down by the Blue Ribbon Grand Jury. Among them: Ed Strickland from the *Birmingham News*, Clark Stallworth of the *Birmingham Post Herald*, Tom Sellers and Ray Jenkins from the *Columbus Ledger*, Bob Ingram from the *Montgomery Advertiser*.

When they learned that Shepherd was being taken in for interrogation, they rushed in a body to follow Shepherd and find out if this meant that there had been a break in the twelve-week old investigation of Patterson's murder.

Watching the throng out in the street, General Hanna told Warren: "I think they're chasing the wrong rabbit. Shepherd has been up to his eyeballs in vice, crime, and vote fraud. He's as crooked as they come and he's managed to slide out of every crime he's ever been associated with, but whoever killed Patterson had to be desperate or dumb or both. And Shepherd's not dumb; he's cunning, crafty, and a gambler. He would have figured the odds—and he would have figured they were too high—that hell would fall on his head for killing the attorney general-elect."

"Who do you think did it then?" Warren asked.

General Hanna shook his head. "I've got some ideas, but not him."

At the Coulter Building the reporters continued their pursuit. "Does this mean there's been a break in the Patterson investigation?" the reporters asked Bernard Sykes.

Tight-lipped, Bernard Sykes characteristically refused comment, but two hours later, when Godwin Davis was brought in for interrogation, the speculation continued.

Godwin Davis came to the courthouse to find out who was on the list of indictments, but when he walked into the sheriff's office, he found that there was a pick-up order for him to be taken to Sykes headquarters for questioning.

When he had finished, he told reporters, "I didn't like Patterson at all, and I admit I contributed to the campaign of the fellow who ran against him, but I didn't kill him and I'm sure none of our crowd did. Hell, look what happened because somebody did kill him." Davis shook his head. "Man, it's plenty rough and getting rougher all the time."

Davis was not the only one complaining. At the courthouse, sixty-nine year old Beechie Howard—better known as Ma Beachie, the most famous cabaret owner in all of Phenix City—had been arrested. Indicted along with the others, she was being booked into the county jail.

Frail, white-haired and bespectacled, wearing her prim signature starched white uniform and a pained look, Ma Beachie complained: "I've been accused of everything, but I'm certainly not guilty. Why, my place was so clean the ladies of the church used to come there for donations."

Left with five children and a grocery store when her husband died thirty years before, Ma had visited New Orleans' night clubs on her second honeymoon and made up her mind to set up one herself when she returned to Phenix City.

At her night club, which she named "Ma Beachie's" for herself, she sat on a high stool in her starched white uniform like a pristine high-priestess and kept a gun at her side in case of trouble, but she liked to indulge in the pretensions that it was as sinless as a Sunday school.

"All I did was provide good clean fun for the soldier boys," Ma explained, "that's why the boys all called me 'Ma' because it was just like home it was so wholesome."

"Ma, what about the slot machines and the strippers?" one of the investigators asked.

"Why those were just exotic dancers," Ma insisted.

The investigator laughed. "Don't try to convince me, Ma. You gotta convince the jury."

With the town still reeling from the dragnet that had brought in almost every gambler in town, two days later a new wave of arrests began when the Grand Jury returned fourteen more indictments. Sheriff Matthews and Mayor Reese were indicted for willful neglect of duty, but more serious than their 'willful neglect' charges which were misdemeanors, were the felony charges the Grand Jury handed down against Albert Fuller and Buddy Jowers: one count each for bribery which on conviction, carried a maximum sentence of ten years in prison. Another felony count of bribery was handed down against H.C. Hardin, operator of the Skyline Club who had offered the bribe.

"Any word on Buddy Jowers?" General Hanna asked Colonel Warren.

"Jowers has been missing since the night Fanny Belle Chance told the Grand Jury about their 'arrangement.' We issued a fugitive warrant for Buddy , but they've found no trace of him yet."

"Tell them to keep looking and go pick up Albert Fuller and bring him in."

Arriving at Albert Fuller's luxurious garage apartment, described as the biggest in Alabama, Colonel Warren found Fuller, dressed in blue silk pajamas, resting in the air-conditioned comfort of his bedroom.

"Albert, you've been indicted on a charge of bribery and it's my duty to arrest you and take you to jail," Warren told him. "Also, Mr. Sykes wants to ask you some questions about the Patterson murder."

"I don't feel like going to jail," Fuller said. "I been in bed three months now from that fall off my horse on the Fourth of July and my doctor says I might have to stay here indefinitely."

"Well, let's just see if he thinks you are too sick to be moved. We got a bed for you in jail."

From Fuller's phone, Colonel Warren placed the call to Fuller's Columbus doctor who said: "I think it might be all right to move him."

Reluctantly, Fuller drew on his red robe and house slippers and allowed himself to be carried into jail by two husky black inmates. "Don't drop me, boys," Fuller cautioned as he was lifted like a sultan in a sedan chair.

At the jail that night Fuller complained of leg pains and when the prison physician, Dr. Seth Floyd, examined him, he recommended that Fuller should be taken to Cobb Memorial Hospital for observation. There, it was determined that it would aggravate Fuller's condition if he were moved around.

When General Hanna received the report, he bit off the end of his cigar, and spit it across the room. "Warren!"

"Yes, Sir."

"I think it's very likely we've got a case of malingering here. Every time Fuller is called in for questioning, he gets too sick to sit up, and the reports I get say he's walking up and down the hospital hall, laughing and talking with the other patients."

"Yes, Sir, that's what we've been told by the guards at the hospital."

"Well, it may be that Mr. Fuller is as disabled as his doctor says he is, but I want a more dependable opinion. I want you to get on the phone and get the Army medics up here to determine the extent of his injuries."

"Yes, Sir."

Counting them off on his fingers, General Hanna said: "I want Colonel Terhume, who is commanding officer of the 109th Evacuation Hospital and an orthopedic surgeon. I want Major Strickland who is an internal specialist, and I want Major Glasgow from the 31st Division who is a radiologist."

"Yes, Sir. Anything else?"

"Send that C-45 National Guard plane down to pick them up."

After spending three and one-half hours with Fuller and studying the new set of x-rays, Colonel Tehume reported that: "Fuller had two fractures of the lumbar vertebrae which have healed completely, a dislocated disc which seems quite painful and no evidence of any other injuries."

"In that case," General Hanna said, "keep him in the hospital and post a guard at his door until he makes bond on the bribery charge."

Back in the sheriff's office, 500 more subpoenas were being served on witnesses to be called before the Grand Jury when they reconvened on 20 September to begin their third phase of investigation, this time into vice and prostitution.

The report was that a key figure would be a former Russell County official, who spent lavishly, keeping more than twenty-nine women as his own in the past three years, and was known to have supported three of them with all their day-to-day needs including homes and fine automobiles.

"Goddam! Twenty-nine women!" General Hanna exclaimed when Colonel Warren gave him the report. "Who are they talking about, Fuller?"

Warren nodded his head.

"If he was keeping up twenty-nine women, he'd need a helluva lot more money than we've found out about so far. Keep digging and see what you can find."

The Grand Jury had just begun listening to witnesses give details on the conditions and prostitution at Cliff Entrekin's Fish Camp when they abruptly stopped their investigation and sent to National Guard headquarters for the sheriff.

In an unprecedented act, Cloyd Tillery, foreman of the Blue Ribbon Grand Jury, directed Colonel Warren as military sheriff of Russell County to arrest H.C. Harden, operator of the Skyline Club, for trying to intimidate a grand jury witness.

"Specifically," the foreman said, "for impeding the justice of a court of the State of Alabama, to wit, the Circuit Court of Russell County."

Harden, already under indictment for gambling and offering a $1500 bribe to Albert Fuller and Buddy Jowers for protection, was arrested and brought to jail again. When his charge was read, Harden said: "I don't know what you're talking about. I don't know what impeding means."

"I'll tell you what it means, Harden, "Colonel Warren said, "it means the Grand Jury is not going to stand for any more tampering and intimidating of witnesses and anybody who tries it is going to end up in jail just like you."

With hell falling on everyone's head, the gambling community put aside old feuds and animosities and came together to support each other in their common trouble. State Representative Ben Cole who had so recently joined suit with Jabe Brassell in the May primary complaint against V. C. Curtis, Hoyt Shepherd's machine candidate, signed the surety bond for Shepherd. Then, he himself was arrested on the same charge of leasing buildings to gamblers. Like Hoyt, he thought he was past the statute of limitations and freely talked about the money he had made from gambling before the federal gambling stamp went into effect. Booked and jailed, the silver-haired State Representative Ben Cole in white shirt and bow tie, sat in his cell playing cards with the inmates while he waited for bond. When he was released, he paid the fine of all his cellmates.

Reporting to General Hanna, Colonel Warren said: "Ben Cole has paid all the fines and emptied the whole cell block."

General Hanna looked at his watch and hooked his thumb toward the stack of warrants waiting to be served. "I'll give you twenty minutes to fill it back up again."

As the Grand Jury continued its investigation and the indictments continued to pile up, Judge Jones announced a special term of criminal court on 4 October to begin dealing with the 559 indictments already handed down by the Grand Jury, and the National Guard was sent out to serve 1500 more subpoenas issued for the cases already docketed.

Judge Julius Hicks, relieved by the Alabama Supreme Court of all connection with the murder investigation and criminal court, had scheduled civil court for the first week in October, but since this was in conflict with Judge Jones' criminal court docket, it was decided that the civil docket would be delayed until the latter part of October and that the special session of criminal court presided over by Judge Jones would begin as scheduled on October 4 with the trial of Red Cook for murder.

Sixty of the seventy-two people already indicted had been picked up and arrested with the remaining twelve still being sought and newsmen asked General Hanna: "Are there going to be anymore sensational arrests?"

"Is there anybody left?" General Hanna smiled. "I thought we had handled everybody involved."

"What about the Patterson investigation?" the newsmen then wanted to know. "It's been fourteen weeks since the murder. When is something going to be done about that?"

General Hanna shook his head. "You'll have to ask Bernard Sykes about that. That's his department."

Posing the question to Bernard Sykes at his news conference that afternoon, newsmen asked: "When will the Patterson case be presented to the Grand Jury?"

"It will be presented as soon as I get it ready," Sykes replied tersely.

"The investigation is now into its fourth month," the newsmen reminded him, "and people want to know."

"I'm aware that the public is becoming impatient due to an apparent lack of progress," Sykes said. "My only answer is to have patience."

Permitting a rare look inside his headquarters, Sykes showed newsmen file cabinets holding interviews with more than 300 people who had been contacted in connection with Patterson's murder and said: "I am satisfied that we are going to solve this homicide before the Grand Jury recesses."

But the newspapers weren't satisfied. The *Columbus Enquirer* reported: "The Patterson murder which sparked the entire cleanup appears to be far removed from consideration by the inquisitorial body. The case is now in its fourth month of probing by the fifteen-man staff of investigators headed by Acting Attorney General Bernard Sykes."

Under the headline: *Will Patterson's Killer Get By With It?*, the *Columbus Ledger* ran a front page editorial reminding its readers that it had been fourteen weeks since Patterson was killed and the killer was still at large. "Will the great state of Alabama allow the killer of Albert Patterson to get by with it?" the editorial asked.

John Patterson, shortly after the murder of his father, had been offered the job of special solicitor by the governor to assist Bernard Sykes in the investigation, but he had declined at the time saying he was needed to take care of family affairs. Later, after having been nominated to fill his father's place as attorney general-elect, he toured the state lecturing on the need to follow his father's policy and stamp out crime. With the electorate firmly behind him, John Patterson now turned to the flagging investigation that in fourteen weeks had not turned up enough substantial evidence to be presented to the Grand Jury.

Continuing its work, the Grand Jury was expected to hand down indictments on its third phase of investigation by the end of September. Judge Jones, with the court calendar set for trials in Russell County Criminal Court to begin 4 October, was ready to begin with the trial of Red Cook. Suddenly, without explanation, the Grand Jury, in mid-session, was recessed.

20

QUASH THE INDICTMENTS

The counterattack had come and the battlefield moved to the courts. Roderick Beddow, considered the most skilled criminal defense attorney in all of Alabama, had been retained by a number of those under indictment. In the face of overwhelming evidence against his clients, Beddow filed a petition to quash all 559 indictments handed down by the Blue Ribbon Grand Jury.

In his best courtroom form, Beddows' heavy bulldog jowls shook with anger. He swept his mane of white hair up and over his massive head, With his beetle eyebrows drawn together, he glared through rimless glasses at his adversaries and declared: "This court is unconstitutional and the jury lists are prejudicially drawn."

In stating his position, Beddow said: "We challenge the Governor's right to send in the militia. We say these raids, seizures, and padlocks are illegal and entirely without authority."

In attacking the validity of the Grand Jury and the indictments against Harden and Abney, Beddow said: "We challenge the action of the Supreme Court's chief justice in displacing Judge Julius B. Hicks, the duly elected circuit judge of Russell County, with the special appointment of Judge Walter B. Jones."

"We charge that the Governor's order of emptying and refilling the jury box was done by a newly appointed commission who chose either members of the RBA or their sympathizers." On behalf of his client, H. C. Harden, charged with gambling, bribery and intimidation of a witness, Beddow asked the Clerk of Court to subpoena the Grand Jury, the Jury Commission, the current RBA president, Howard Pennington, Hugh Bentley, and RBA Auxiliary president Hilda Coulter requiring them to bring the secret membership lists of the RBA to be compared against the names of those drawn for the Grand Jury.

Acting in concert with other defense attorneys, notably Jake Walker, attorney for Red Cook, Beddow filed a petition for a Writ of Mandamus in civil court before Judge Julius B. Hicks stating that with the presently drawn jury lists, his client could not get a fair trial. The petition asked that the Jury Commission empty the jury box and fill it with all males over twenty-one.

Judge Hicks, who had been relieved in June by the Alabama Supreme Court of all official duties concerning the investigation into Patterson's death and the subsequent vice trials, paved the way for Beddow's demands by granting the Writ of Mandamus and ordering the Jury Commission to appear before him to "show cause why this should not be done."

To political observers, this was an effort, on behalf of the gamblers indicted, to regain control of the Grand Jury and the jury lists that had been purged when the cleanup began and to tie up the courts with interminable delays.

Responding quickly to this assault on the court, before the Jury Commission could be subpoenaed, Bernard Sykes, as Acting Attorney General in the absence of Si Garrett, immediately requested Judge Hicks to surrender jurisdiction in the mandamus hearing to Judge Jones. When he refused, Sykes petitioned the Alabama Supreme Court for a Writ of Prohibition asking that Judge Hicks be restrained from any further action.

A rare night session of the justices was attempted, but a quorum could not be obtained and on the following day, the Alabama Supreme Court, invoking the Rule Nisi, ruled that Judge Hicks "should stop and desist all proceedings on the Phenix City dispute or appear before the Supreme Court to present further arguments on why he should handle this issue."

Judge Hicks, failing in his attempt, did not choose to pursue the matter and when asked by the press for his response to the Supreme Court ruling, with a shrug said: "What suits the Supreme Court, suits me."

The defense attorneys, however, did choose to pursue the matter. The trial of Red Cook for the 1950 murder of John Mancil, and the wounding of William Calvert Rogers, paralyzed in the shooting, was the first case on the criminal court docket before Judge Jones. It began, as scheduled on 4 October, with Cook's attorney Jake Walker filing 119 objections charging that there was no authority to appoint Judge Jones as a special judge or to order a special session of Circuit Court or for impaneling a Blue Ribbon Grand Jury to investigate Patterson's murder.

Walker also attacked the order of Bernard Sykes directing Solicitor George Johnson to take over the duties of the regular solicitor, Arch Ferrell. "Such an order," Walker argued, "would have to be done in the name of Attorney General Si Garrett who has left the state."

There were also numerous objections to Martial Rule alleging that this had usurped the office of the sheriff and left him without power. "Because of this and all the other complaints," Walker asserted, "this court was illegally constituted and my client cannot get a fair trial."

After hearing all the grievances, Judge Jones called a recess to study the list and then threw out all 119 objections stating that: "In my judgment, the governor's proclamation of Martial Rule here does not violate the state or federal constitutional statutes." Smashing his gavel down, Judge Jones said sternly, "Now let the trial begin!"

᠔

William Calvert Rogers, wounded and paralyzed by the shooting in Red Cook's club, was wheeled into the courtroom to the witness stand. Lying on a gurney, he told the court what he had told the Grand Jury earlier: that he and taxi driver John Mancil had gotten into an argument with Red Cook on a Sunday morning in his club. Cook turned around, walked back to his office, got a gun and came back and shot him, killed Mancil, and wounded a bystander who was on his way to the men's room, and had never been prosecuted for this.

Cook's defense attorney immediately set out to impeach Rogers' testimony by endeavoring to show that Rogers made a statement at the hospital on the night of the shooting stating that he did not want to prosecute Cook. To support this allegation, Sheriff Matthews was called to the stand.

Under oath, Sheriff Matthews said he had gone to the hospital on the night of the shooting because Rogers thought "he was in a dying condition" and his concern was for the support of his family not for the prosecution of Red Cook.

Rogers denied ever giving a statement that he did not want to prosecute and charged Red Cook with cold-blooded murder. After he was initially treated at Cobb Memorial in Phenix City, Rogers said, "I was transferred to an Atlanta hospital for treatment of a severed spine and Red Cook gave the nurse accompanying me $1,000 in travelers checks to cover expenses."

On the witness stand, Cook used the alibi so often used in a Phenix City shooting. He claimed he shot Mancil and Rogers in self-defense. "During the argument with Mancil and Rogers," Cook said, "Mancil came after me with a knife in one hand and a chair in the other. Then Rogers picked up a chair and there wasn't nothing else to do but to shoot them. I had to defend myself."

"What about the third man who was shot in the leg?"

"I didn't have no quarrel with him. He just got in the way."

Sam H. Pitts, Cook's skinny, bespectacled bouncer who was in the 601 Club that Sunday morning, was called to the stand to testify. He told the court that he was the club's bouncer and that he wore a badge and a gun on his belt, but when questioned about this, he could not remember the shape of the badge or what the badge said.

Under cross examination, the prosecutor asked: "What was your job?"

"My job was to keep order," Pitts replied.

"What did you keep order of?"

"I just kept order in the club."

"Did you guard the crap games?"

"No, sir."

"Did you guard the poker table?"

"No, sir."

"Did you guard the slot machines?"

"No, sir."

"Did you guard the whiskey?"

"No, sir."

"Did you just stroll around with your tin badge on?"

Pitts bobbed his head up and down. "Yes, sir."

"When the shooting started, what did you do?" the prosecutor asked.

"I just stood there by the wall."

"Your boss, Red Cook, said Mancil was after him with a knife, and you just stood there?"

"Yes, sir."

"You didn't try to stop him?

Pitts shrugged. "He wasn't after me."

Although Cook claimed Mancil accosted him with a knife, the knife was never found. Former chief of police Pal Daniel, who investigated the shooting, was called to the stand.

"On the day of the shooting," Pal Daniel said, "we found no marks on Cook's body and his clothes were not torn."

"Did you see a knife anywhere that day?" the prosecutor asked.

"I did not."

"Some of your men investigated, didn't they, Chief?"

"Yes, sir."

"Did they deliver a knife to you?"

"No, sir."

The jury received the case at 4:55 P.M. and at 10:30 P.M. the foreman notified the bailiff that a verdict had been reached. Judge Jones rapped the court to order and said: "Whatever this verdict is, it must be received in absolute silence. We will have no demonstration whatever."

When the jurors were seated, Judge Jones said: "Gentlemen of the jury, have you reached a verdict?"

"We have, your honor," the foreman said, handing it to the Clerk of Court who read: "We, the jury find the defendant, E. L. Cook, guilty of murder in the first degree and fix his penalty at life imprisonment as provided by Alabama law in a first degree murder conviction."

Mrs. Cook, who had sat anxiously through the trial, jumped up and screamed: "Oh, no! God will punish them. God will punish every one of them for this. They would have done the same thing if they were in his place."

Red Cook never changed his expression. He kept chewing gum just as he had done throughout the trial. Mrs. Cook buried her head in the shoulder of a friend sitting beside her. Red Cook went over to comfort her. She was led away and Red Cook was taken into custody by the deputies.

After the Alabama Supreme Court's ruling that Judge Hicks should cease and desist any further efforts in the criminal cases on docket in Russell County, Roderick Beddow's only option on behalf of his client, H.C. Harden, was to file a petition addressed to Judge Jones.

The first of two petitions was a Writ of Mandamus asking that the Jury Commission empty and refill the jury box. Beddow said his plans were to subpoena the entire jury list of 7000 to show that only a small percentage of those qualified had their names put in the jury box.

The second petition, for a change of venue, was filed on behalf of Harden, supported by more than 100 affidavits saying that it would be impossible for him to get a fair and impartial trial before a judge who had been appointed to satisfy one faction, that being the Russell Betterment Association.

Beddow made the further statement that: "It would be unsafe for any man to be tried for the murder of Albert Patterson in this court be he innocent or guilty."

For Judge Jones, Beddow's flamboyance had gone beyond rhetoric to impugning his honor and reputation.

"I would like to state here," Judge Jones stated stiffly, "that I will be glad to place my thirty-four years as circuit judge in Alabama in answer to insinuations set out in the petition."

After hearing arguments on the two petitions by Beddow and

Solicitor George Johnson, who spoke in fiery defense of the court, Judge
Jones ruled against a change of venue on the grounds that: "the law
requires submission of proof that violent action has been threatened
against a defendant before a change of trial site shall be permitted and
no such proof has been submitted."

On the petition to empty the jury box, Judge Jones scheduled a
hearing. Beddow had already subpoenaed 300 of the 7,000 people on
the list. After hearing more than fifty, it was determined that the names
in the jury box had not been prejudicially drawn. In many cases, the
prospective jurors were overage, on active duty stationed elsewhere or
infirmed.

George Johnson made this point clear while examining an elderly
man who had been subpoenaed by Beddow. Standing twelve feet
away, Johnson leaned over the table and said to the witness: "You are
hard of hearing, aren't you?"

The man cupped his hand over his ear and said: "How's that?"

After hearing more than fifty of the people who had been
subpoenaed, Judge Jones denied Beddow's petition for a Writ of
Mandamus to empty the jury box, saying: "The overall testimony of
these witnesses has failed to disclose a pattern of a specifically hand-
picked jury list."

When Harden's trial on gambling charges began two days later,
Beddow and his partner Bob Gwin publicly apologized to Judge Jones
in open court.

"There seems to be some school of thought, rumored about,"
Beddow told Judge Jones, "that we, as counsel for the defendant H. C.
Harden, intended some injury on you. There was no intention on the
part of counsel to attack you or say you could not as a man or judge
give us a fair trial."

"I want to publicly say, and to your honor, that if there has been any
thought in your mind that we intended any personal attack on you and
you were aggrieved by things said, we want to apologize."

Beddow then asked Judge Jones' permission to remove from the
records Harden's petition.

Judge Jones, still stung by the allegations, replied: "The statement
that has just been made by counselor for the defendant Harden is a
statement which in justice and decency should be made."

"Whether intended to have the effect or not, these allegations are
calculated to destroy the confidence of the people in their courts, in their
juries, and in their judges."

"It is regrettable that counsel for Harden should permit their defendant to swear to these petitions when they could have known by any

investigation, the allegations mentioned here were utterly without foundation."

"The court is willing to accept the disclaimers of counsel just made in open court, but it should be stated, that their conduct borders on contempt of court and, of course, the making of the affidavits by Harden and those who assisted him could well result in perjury indictments."

"The court," Judge Jones said with finality, "will let the matter rest with this statement."

Harden, after a day-long legal battle, pleaded guilty to a gambling charge and was sentenced to nine months in prison and a $300 fine.

The courtroom was packed when the case against Hoyt Shepherd and Jimmie Matthews came up next on the docket. Both had pleaded innocent to leasing property for gambling, and spectators squeezed into the hot, sweltering courtroom and sat back ready for a good show and legal fireworks, but when the case was called, Hoyt and Jimmie shocked all the observers by changing their plea.

When asked by the court: "How do you plead?"

Both Hoyt Shepherd and Jimmie Matthews said: "Guilty," and accepted a sentence of ninety days at hard labor and a $1,000 fine. This unexpected turn of events paved the way for a flood of other guilty pleas by lesser gamblers in the hundreds of indictments handed down by the Grand Jury.

❧

While war was being waged in the courtroom, General Hanna had continued his investigation into the connections in racket protection and payoffs and had discovered a different sort of satchelman. Previously, the "satchelman" was the one who dispensed money for corrupt practices and paid off voters, election officials and others whose services or favors were bought. The profile of the new satchelman was the one who arrived with an empty satchel and filled it up with money collected for his services.

The highest profile on this type of activity was Albert Fuller who had already been indicted on one count of bribery for his protection at Harden's Skylark Club. Further investigation indicated that he had been providing protection for a good many more. On the first of October, General Hanna pulled a surprise raid on Fuller's house.

Fuller, lying in bed listening to the World Series on the radio chatted amiably with the National Guard who thoroughly searched his apartment from ceiling to floor. When the drawer to Fuller's bedside table was opened, a handful of amazing documents were found.

Fuller, who had been sitting up smoking, fell back on his pillows and called for a doctor and collapsed. After two shots by the doctor from a hypodermic syringe, Fuller told the investigators: "I'm sick. I don't feel like talking. I need an oxygen tank. I can't breathe."

The papers from Fuller's bedside table were considered explosive and the most electrifying news since the murder of Albert Patterson. They contained a list of 200 names, some with anti-vice affiliations, who had contributed to the Phenix City machine for the last three elections, a handwritten list of gamblers and racketeers with sums of money noted by their names, and pages of names from the voting list with ballot box numbers and sums of money, most frequently, three dollars.

At his headquarters, General Hanna and his staff poured over the papers until 2:00 A.M., calling in various people with knowledge of the voting lists and campaign contributions. Among those called were Hugh Bentley and RBA president Howard Pennington with long years of experience with the voting lists.

When Hugh Bentley arrived, General Hanna shook his hand. "Come on in here, Hugh, I've got a job for you."

Since the night Patterson was killed and the National Guard took over, Hugh Bentley and the other members of the RBA, their leader dead and their efforts all spent, had quietly retreated from the arena and patiently waited in the wings hoping to contribute some needed service.

Hugh Bentley returned General Hanna's warm handshake and said: "We were happy to hear from you, General. We've been waiting to be called."

"Well, on the night all this began you told me to call on you if there was anything you could do. Now we've got something right down your alley. We need your expert help on the jury lists."

Hugh Bentley and Howard Pennington, having spent years fighting the vote fraud in Russell County were able to quickly decipher the notes written on the papers taken from Fuller's apartment. "This is the most incriminating evidence so far," Solicitor Johnson told General Hanna.

After presenting it to the Grand Jury, indictments for ten more counts of bribery were handed down against Fuller, the maximum penalty, 100 years in prison. Responding to this, Fuller told newsmen he would like to take a lie-detector test to clear his name of rumors that he was involved in the Patterson killing.

"I told state investigators three months ago that I was willing to take a lie detector test," Fuller told reporters. "and as soon as my doctor says I am able, I will be glad to even if I have to pay for the ambulance myself to take me there. There's nobody who would like to clear up Mr. Patterson's killing more than me. He was a friend of mine."

When reporters asked Bernard Sykes if he planned a lie detector test for Fuller, Sykes declined comment. Asked about the progress of the murder investigation, he refused again.

"I will not, "Sykes said firmly, "reveal evidence which might give away my case. It's my duty to be cautious."

Pressing Sykes, a newsman said: "We've heard reports of major disagreements among the officers investigating the murder, that some of the officers have threatened to resign because of arguments over the conduct of the probe."

"There have been some honest differences of opinion," Sykes admitted, "but no one has threatened to resign."

John Patterson, who had joined the investigation as a special assistant, told newsmen: "I may not have agreed with everything that has been done, but I'll have to admit there are some good men working on the investigation and I believe the case will soon be solved and brought before the Grand Jury with substantial evidence."

But as the Grand Jury reconvened on 1 November, the *Columbus Ledger* reported the rumor that Sykes had been given an ultimatum of twelve days to present the Patterson murder case. Sykes denied that he had been given an ultimatum or had received pressure from any group or any member of the Patterson family.

"It is not known what course the Grand Jury may take," the *Columbus Ledger* reported, "if it isn't satisfied with Sykes handling of the investigation. Conceivably, the case could change hands for a third time, this time going to Adjutant General Walter J. 'Crack' Hanna, military boss of Russell County under martial rule."

21

FULLER'S BRIBERY CONVICTION

The controversy over Bernard Sykes did not concern General Hanna. He was busy with his own investigation. Pursuing leads into Albert Fuller's past, he continued digging up evidence including the body of Guy Hargett and Clarence Franklin Johns. Hargett, shot five times in a row from his forehead to his belt buckle as he sat in his easy chair in his house in 1949, and Johns, shot thirteen times in the black cemetery in 1950, both killed by Fuller and both killings judged by Arch Ferrell as "line of duty."

With a court order for exhumation, the bodies were dug up in the dark of night, the bullets removed and sent to the State Toxicologist for comparison with the bullets removed from Albert Patterson's body.

All of this persuaded Dave Walden and Wilson McVeigh, already in prison, to tell what they knew about the 1949 killing of Johnny Frank Stringfellow who was doped, shot, and buried in a lime grave. With all the dark secrets from the past being brought to light, they were ready now to testify against Head Revel, Godwin Davis, and Joe Allred who had hired them to kill Stringfellow.

John Patterson, by special appointment from the Governor to assist in the murder investigation, conducted an inquiry into the possibility of reopening the trial, but the killing of Johnny Frank Stringfellow involved the jurisdiction of three states: Alabama, where the crime was commissioned, Georgia, where the lethal dose of drugs was administered, and Florida, where he was shot in the head. Since the moment of death, and thus the site of the crime, could not be established, pursuit of this case had to be abandoned.

"It's like digging volcanic ash," General Hanna told Colonel Warren, "as soon as one layer of the investigation is scraped off, there's another underneath."

In the digging, the case of cab driver Bill Littleton killing Private George Outlaw in 1950 surfaced and extradition papers, signed by Alabama Governor Persons and Georgia Governor Herman Talmadge were filed to bring him back from Georgia to stand trial in Phenix City.

Hoping to trade information for leniency, Bill Littleton told what he swore he would never mention again, what he had seen on the streets of Phenix City at the hour of Patterson's murder.

"No deals," General Hanna told Littleton. "You're going to stand trial for killing that soldier."

Two days later, Littleton's Georgia attorney, Fred New, arrived with a subpoena for General Hanna to appear before a Columbus court challenging his authority and Martial Rule and to bring documents to show where he was authorized to hold his present position.

Fred New charged that the National Guard arrested Littleton in his Hamilton, Georgia, home on a justice of the peace warrant, but Lt. Martin Wieman said a manslaughter warrant was taken to the sheriff of Hamilton who arrested Littleton. Wieman said: "We didn't even go with him to avoid a situation like this." Littleton was given a preliminary hearing in Hamilton and on "a gentleman's agreement" with New, he agreed if extradition papers were returned in five days that Littleton would return to Phenix City to be arrested. When Guard officers returned with the extradition papers, Littleton demanded a new hearing on grounds that the papers were technically incorrect.

"I'm not going to put up with that kind of Goddam crap," General Hanna told Fred New. "Warren! Throw this bastard out in the street."

Colonel Warren began ushering Fred New out of the office and General Hanna snapped: "I said *throw* the bastard out." Two guardsmen then forcibly ejected Fred New out into the street.

On 2 November, the general election in Phenix City was held under the watchful eye of the National Guard with two guardsmen posted at each ballot box to insure that this time there would be no election law violations. Lamar Murphy, who had been temporarily appointed by Governor Persons, was elected sheriff of Russell County, John Patterson won his father's seat as Attorney General and Jim Folsom was elected Governor of Alabama to take office in January.

Jim Folsom's election caused some concern to *Columbus Ledger* editor Bob Brown. Publicly, he urged Folsom to continue the work begun by the cleanup. Privately, it was feared that Folsom, who had vigorously backed Lee Porter against Albert Patterson, would let the investigation die once he was sworn in as Governor of Alabama.

Hugh Bentley, Howard Pennington, and the members of the RBA worried that if the Patterson investigation was not brought before the Grand Jury before the change in administration that the spectacular accomplishments of General Hanna and the National Guard, the grueling work of the Grand Jury, and the courtroom triumphs of George

Johnson and his staff would die stillborn and that the permanent cleanup that he had spent most of his life trying to achieve would die along with it. The greatest urgency lay in finishing what had been begun four months before on the night that Patterson was shot.

By 11 November, the Grand Jury, which had been in almost continuous session since August, filed its fifth report bringing the total number of indictments to 734. This report concerning misconduct in office, recommended that Mayor Elmer Reese, already indicted for "willful neglect," be impeached and then handed down ten more indictments for bribery against Albert Fuller.

Solicitor George Johnson moved to bring Fuller to trial immediately on the first count of bribery concerning Cliff Entrekin's Fish Camp. Entrekin, after his indictment for running a house of prostitution, had disappeared and Fuller, satisfied that his physical infirmities would delay his trial, did not even arrange for counsel.

Trial was set for 16 November and Fuller arrived on a hospital gurney, accompanied by his doctors and his wife, a public health nurse, who sat beside him with her head propped in her hand and mopped his brow with a handkerchief. When Fuller's case was called, Arch Ferrell's brother, Pelham, appearing on behalf of Fuller, asked the court for a continuance of Fuller's case because of the back injuries he had sustained in the 4 July fall from his horse.

George Johnson argued that he would lose his witnesses if the trial were delayed. Many of them, already in fear of their lives, planned to leave the area as soon as they testified. Bonnie Schaply, described by the newspapers as one of the "shapely blond strippers," was so fearful of the threats made against witnesses that she had already tried to kill herself by cutting her throat, arms and legs with a pocket mirror even while being kept in protective custody in jail.

Fuller's Columbus physician was brought in and said what he had said so often before, that it would aggravate Fuller's condition if he were moved from his home.

Judge Jones asked: "How long do you expect this condition to continue?"

"Maybe indefinitely," the doctor answered. "It would aggravate his condition to be moved from his house."

"What then would you do in case his home caught on fire?"

The doctor shrugged. "The best we could."

A second physician, Phenix City Doctor Clyde Knowles was asked: "Is Albert Fuller's condition life threatening?"

"No, but it might prolong his infirmity to move him."

Judge Jones took the arguments under advisement and ruled against a continuance. Fuller's attorneys notified him of the judge's decision and two hours later, Fuller, wearing blue silk pajamas, and covered with a pink sheet, was wheeled to the sheriff's office on a hospital gurney by two hospital attendants to wait for his case to be called.

At 6:30 P.M., in a rare night session, trial began with the calling of the first witness, ex-Sheriff Ralph Matthews, who testified that Fuller had been his chief deputy sheriff and that his salary was $300 per month. Continuing on until 11:00 P.M., three prostitutes, a bartender, and a bouncer from Cliff Entrekin's Fish Camp were called as witnesses.

The first prostitute, a thirty-one year old red-head, whose parents kept her eight children while she worked at Cliff's Fish Camp, testified that the prostitutes paid fifty percent of what they earned to Cliff Entrekin. From his fifty percent, half was paid to Albert Fuller for protection. Later, when Fuller raised the price of his protection, Entrekin told them: "Fuller's protection is choking me to death. You girls are going to have to make up the difference."

"After that, ten percent was deducted from the girls' earnings to pay the increased cost of protection."

"How do you know that this was so?" Solicitor Johnson asked.

"I was the bookkeeper. I made out the pay slips."

"How was Fuller paid?"

"He usually came around on Sunday night to collect. If he didn't, the money was put in an envelope and put in his mail box on Monday morning."

"How do you know this was so?"

"I went with Cliff to Albert's house to deliver it."

"Was he wearing his gun and badge when he came to the Fish Camp?"

"Yes, and sometimes had one of the other deputies with him."

"How much was he paid?" Johnson asked.

"Sometimes $600, sometimes $1300. It depended on how much business we had. Sometimes on payday we had several hundred soldiers."

The second witness, a twenty-two year old prostitute, told the court that she had come to work voluntarily at Cliff's Fish Camp when she was seventeen-years old. Her blind adopted child needed an operation that cost $2,200 and: "I didn't have any way to get up the money so I came to work for Cliff."

Asked to describe the nature of her work at the Fish Camp, she said: "We were entertainers. We worked from 7:00 P.M. until 5:00 A.M. seven days a week. The customer chose which girl he wanted and paid the bartender. The rate was $10 for ten minutes and if there was trouble the bouncer threw him out."

"Cliff had rules," the girl explained. "He fined a girl $10 for being late for work, and $100 for not showing up or going to sleep on the job. This was deducted from the week's pay along with the ten percent for protection."

"After you paid this protection, were you ever raided while working at the Fish Camp?" Johnson asked.

"A couple of times, but Albert said not to worry, that it didn't mean nothing, that Cliff would be along in a few minutes and get us out. Albert said he had to raid every once in a while so that people wouldn't think he was involved."

The raids, payoffs and protection were confirmed by the bartender who collected the money from the girls and the bouncer, an ex-prizefighter, who had witnessed Entrekin paying Fuller off.

Albert Fuller testified in his own defense. Flat on his back on the hospital gurney, Fuller was rolled up to the witness stand, his hands folded across his chest. Pelham Ferrell asked only one question: "Did you receive money from Cliff Entrekin for protection?"

"Not one cent," Fuller said.

In the closing arguments, Solicitor Johnson's bull-horn voice boomed through the courtroom as he shook his finger at Albert Fuller and said: "Here lies the Al Capone of Alabama who wore a tin badge to cover his black heart and used a .38 pistol for guts. He traded on the flesh of women and took money from a poor girl who sold her soul to buy eyesight for her blind child."

Guns and glory gone, Albert Fuller, lying under the pink sheet, trembled at the words, and his wife beside him, mopped the perspiration from his brow.

"This man," Solicitor Johnson said shaking his fist in a rising crescendo, "is a traitor to the State of Alabama and the good people of Russell County. He turned his back on his sworn duty to uphold the law and exploited it instead, and I ask you, gentlemen of the jury, to find him guilty as charged and return the full penalty of the law."

It took the jury one hour and seventeen minutes to return a verdict of guilty. Judge Jones asked Albert Fuller: "Do you know any reason why you should not be sentenced at this time?"

Fuller replied: "No."

"The judgment of this court is to sentence you to seven years in the state penitentiary."

Fuller closed his eyes and made no comment, but his attorneys notified the court they would file for an appeal and Albert Fuller was put under house arrest with bond set at $2500.

As the cleanup continued, Solicitor Johnson, following up on the Grand Jury's recommendation to impeach Elmer Reese, filed an "information," charging that Reese, during his tenure as mayor of Phenix City, condoned the violation of seven sections of the city code, and allowed twenty-two gambling houses to operate "in open and flagrant violation of the law."

The most serious charge was that Reese, as mayor and head of the police department, had allowed Buddy Jowers on the night of 18 June, to dispatch city policemen to notify the gamblers that Albert Patterson had been killed and warn them that raids could be expected in a short time.

Elmer Reese, with twenty days to respond to the "information," chose instead to resign rather than go to trial. In a final public statement at his last city commission meeting, Reese, with tears glistening in his eyes, said: "As I retire into private life, I ask forgiveness for any mistakes I may have made. I have always tried to do my best to carry out my duties to the best of my knowledge and ability."

As his last official act, he called for the commission's vote on his resignation. Sobbing openly, City Clerk Jimmie Putnam was unable to call the role for the vote. The remaining members of the city commission, Dr. Clyde Knowles, who would succeed Reese as mayor and Dr. Seth Floyd accepted Reese's resignation.

Godwin Davis, alarmed by Fuller's conviction and Reese's resignation, was next up for trial. With him and his son each charged with forty-four counts of lottery, Davis was out trying to make a deal. He wanted to trade information, plead guilty to the lottery charge, and take a penitentiary sentence if in turn his son, Sonny, was given probation instead of a prison sentence.

With Godwin Davis, it was not parental concern, but business considerations. When he appealed to Bernard Sykes, Davis told him that he would suffer irreversible business losses if both he and his son were sent to the penitentiary. Sykes turned him down flat, and then Davis, in desperation, sought help from the very people he had for so many years opposed. He went to John Patterson for help.

When that failed, he called Hugh Bentley who was in the midst of conducting an RBA meeting and asked could he bring his appeal before them. The RBA heard Davis out, but no one would speak on his behalf.

Davis and his son, represented by Roderick Beddow, came to trial, despite what had become Beddow's standard 119 objections.

The jury found both Davis and his son guilty after forty-six lottery writers testified to their participation in the Davis' National Lottery which brought in $250,000 a year. Davis was given a two-year penitentiary term to be followed by an eighteen month term by his son.

By the end of November, most of the indictments had been cleared away with guilty pleas, and when the Grand Jury reconvened near the end of November, the long awaited investigation into the murder of Albert Patterson began.

22

Star Witness Slain

Judging from the 100 witnesses who were called to appear before the Grand Jury's investigation into Albert Patterson's murder, newsmen and courthouse observers speculated that the case that Bernard Sykes had worked on for twenty-three weeks would tie the murder to the vote-fraud conspiracy since many of the witnesses waiting to testify had been called for that investigation.

Before the proceedings began, Sykes and Grand Jury Foreman Clyde Tilley met with newspaper, radio, and television representatives and requested that the names and pictures of certain witnesses not be used since it was necessary to protect their identities. The press agreed that only public officials, investigators, and people previously publicly identified with the case would be used.

On the last day of November and the second day of testimony, Bernard Sykes brought his star witness before the Grand Jury. His name was Johnny Frank Griffin, a thirty-five-year old man who had not been without his own troubles. In April 1941, his wife, Bernice Kelley Griffin, had filed an affidavit charging him with bigamy after his marriage to a woman named Conzodie Butler. At the July 1941 term of the Grand Jury, a True Bill was returned charging him with bigamy and he was sentenced to two years in the state penitentiary.

When he filed a request for probation, a Reverend Zebenda appeared on behalf of Griffin and convinced the court that Griffin had seen the light and had been converted and was then living a good life. As a result, Griffin was placed on four years probation.

Immediately after being released, Griffin went to Phenix City and gave his first wife who had filed the affidavit a severe beating. His probation was revoked and he was sent back to the state penitentiary.

On the witness stand, Griffin told the Grand Jury that Friday, 18 June, was a typical Friday evening in Phenix City. At nine o'clock, the streets were still full of weekend shoppers doing their grocery buying, taxi cabs were ferrying soldiers across the Bridge from Fort Benning to honky tonks and cafes, and a Boy Scout meeting at the courthouse had just broken up and Scouts and their families were on their way home.

Johnny Frank Griffin was on his way to work at Smitty's Cafe behind the Coulter Building where Albert Patterson maintained his law office on the second floor.

Parking within a few feet of the Coulter Building, Griffin said he got out of his truck, headed towards Smitty's Cafe and saw Albert Patterson walk from the Coulter Building to his car parked in the alley with a man whom Griffin recognized. As they paused to talk, a second man approached Patterson's car.

As Griffin entered the cafe, he heard gun shots and ran back into the street in time to recognize a man fleeing, the same man he had seen with Patterson at his car.

Twenty-four hours after appearing before the Grand Jury, Johnny Frank Griffin was dead from a knife wound in the throat, his testimony before that secret body sealed forever.

Although he refused the protective custody that Bernard Sykes offered him, he had told one county official: "I've got a feeling they're going to get me. I'm scared."

Griffin had been found as a witness by newly-elected Sheriff Lamar Murphy and John Patterson, independent of the state investigation headed by Sykes. As the afternoon wore on and Griffin grew more anxious and upset, he tried to call Murphy, but he was tied up in court. He went to John Patterson's law office, but Patterson was not there. Obsessed with the idea that someone was going to kill him, he called Murphy again, leaving the message: "I've got to see you." Calling Patterson again he left the message: "I need some help."

Borrowing $4.00 from the cafe where he worked, he wandered down 14th Street, whiling away the time at a service station, a garage, and finally at a grill where he had a bowl of chili and a bottle of beer. Agitated and anxious, Griffin then decided to amble down to Chad's Rose room. It was 6:30 P.M.

On the street corner, at a bus stop, a group of black Boy Scouts, returning from a basketball game at the Mother Mary Mission, were waiting with their Scout Master and an older youth who accompanied them. In passing, Griffin, without provocation, threw out a racial slur and struck sixteen-year old Jerry Washington. Washington whipped out a knife, stabbed Griffin in the throat and ran. Griffin, mortally wounded and bleeding profusely, staggered across the street toward Chad's Rose Room and fell on the sidewalk.

Barbara Parker, a former stripper from Ma Beachie's who had witnessed Griffin provoke the fight, rushed to his side and tried to stop the gush of blood, holding his head in her arms until an ambulance was called.

Major Ray Acton, in his motel room a short distance away, heard the commotion outside, saw the woman holding the bleeding man and ran out to help.

At the hospital, it was assumed that Griffin was just an ordinary knifing victim until his subpoena to appear before the Grand Jury was found in his bloody clothing. Realizing that this was the star witness in the Patterson investigation, Ray Acton immediately notified Bernard Sykes, his assistant, state investigator Maury Smith, and General Hanna.

Like wildfire, word raced around town that the star witness in the Patterson investigation had been knifed. The general supposition was that it was to stop his testimony and a new wave of fear gripped the town and the witnesses who had gone before the Grand Jury.

As Griffin writhed in pain and shock and hospital attendants administered blood transfusions, Bernard Sykes tried to question him on who his attacker was, but Griffin could only babble incoherently calling for Lamar Murphy.

General Hanna called Colonel Brown down to the hospital and told him: "Get on this right away and find out what happened before the town goes into a panic."

When John Patterson arrived at the hospital, he was furious that this had happened to their star witness and angrily told Sykes: "If you've got a case, then the suspect in my father's killing should be arrested immediately. It's dangerous to wait. His continued freedom might endanger other lives."

Sykes refused. "To make an arrest before the Grand Jury hands down an indictment would mean a preliminary hearing that would force the State to present its evidence publicly."

"There's just no excuse for this," Patterson said. "We have looked after Griffin like a baby. Why wasn't he given protective custody?"

"He turned it down," Sykes said, "and we thought it best not to give him an armed guard since he had not been identified with the investigation."

While Griffin's wound was being surgically repaired in the emergency room, Colonel Brown traced Griffin's movements from the time he left Smitty's Cafe at four o'clock and questioned Barbara Parker who told him that she had seen Griffin provoke the fight with a young black man at the bus stop. Three more witnesses were found who corroborated the story.

A short time later, Jerry Washington was located and picked up for interrogation. Griffin, he told the investigators, had come up to him while he was waiting at the bus stop and said: "Draw a white line and don't step over it." When he turned away, Griffin hit him and he struck back with his pocket knife. When he was told that the man he had stabbed was the star witness in the Patterson investigation, he was very upset.

"If I'd known that man was Mr. Patterson's witness," Jerry Washington wept, "I would have let him beat me half to death before I done anything to him."

Reporting back to General Hanna, Colonel Brown told him he was satisfied that the stabbing was in no way related to Griffin's testimony as a witness in the Patterson investigation.

"Unlikely as it may seem," General Hanna told John Patterson, "it was a chance happening. Jerry Washington is just a kid with no criminal record and no ties to the underworld."

Patterson shook his head. "It's a fantastic coincidence that could only happen in Phenix City."

When Griffin returned from surgery, John Patterson asked: "What are his chances for recovery?"

"He's got a chance," the doctors told him. "We'll know more by morning."

To secure Griffin's safety, a guard was put outside his door and Ray Acton was put in charge. Later that night, Griffin's condition worsened and he was taken back to the operating room.

"Get on this scrub suit," the doctors told Ray Acton. "We want you as a witness in surgery."

Ray Acton was surprised. "Witness?"

"As sensitive as this case is, we want to make damn sure we're not accused of malpractice, collusion, or anything else."

Standing on a soft drink box behind the team of doctors, Ray Acton watched as the surgeons worked frantically to save Johnny Frank Griffin's life. Shortly before midnight, when his heart failed, the doctors, in a last desperate effort, opened his chest cavity for open heart massage. Despite their best efforts, Johnny Frank Griffin died and with him died the eye witness testimony in the Patterson slaying.

Even though no fewer than twenty-five people had heard Griffin's testimony before the Grand Jury, it could not be used as evidence before any jury that might try a defendant in the murder case because the defendant, by law, must have the right of cross-examination.

The speculation was that the death of Johnny Frank Griffin would kill the case Sykes had spent five months building, but at a press conference, he told newsmen:

"Johnny Frank Griffin was an important witness, but his testimony was not indispensable. We will continue presenting the evidence before the Grand Jury."

With the star witness gone, James Radius Taylor, the cab driver who had been near the scene the night of the murder, had witnessed a man running away and had taken a vow of silence, could no longer battle with his conscience. Guaranteed his safety by General Hanna and the National Guard, Taylor came forward to testify as did Quinnie Kelley, the courthouse janitor who was standing on the courthouse steps when Patterson was shot.

In prison, Bill Littleton, the cab driver arrested by the National Guard, tried and convicted of the 1950 killing of Private George Outlaw, decided he, too, would testify and tell what he had seen the night Patterson was killed.

The case presented by Sykes traced political intrigue that ended in murder. A call of 100 witnesses began with Mrs. Albert Patterson and included witnesses who had testified before the Jefferson County Grand Jury in the vote tally change, a telephone representative from Southern Bell and two operators, and newsman, Ed Strickland from the *Birmingham News*, Fred Anderson from the *Montgomery Advertiser*, and *Associated Press* reporter Rex Thomas. Former police chief Pal Daniel was brought before the Grand Jury and Hoyt Shepherd and Jimmie Matthews were brought back from Kilby Penitentiary to testify followed by Godwin Davis. Testimony of witnesses went on for ten days ending with John Patterson who told the Grand Jurors that the political scheme to prevent his father's election began in the May Primary when a concerted effort was made to buy the election.

"When this failed and my father won the June runoff election," Patterson said, "then an attempt was made to steal the election by changing the vote totals. After this discovery in Birmingham, the Jefferson County Grand Jury began an investigation. On the day of his ambush murder, Albert Patterson had made known his intention to testify before the Jefferson County Grand Jury to tell what he knew, determined that nothing would stop him. Three bullets did."

At 2:30 P.M. on 9 December, the Grand Jury handed down three indictments. Albert Fuller, Arch Ferrell, and Si Garrett were each identically charged with "unlawfully and with malice aforethought killing and murdering Albert L. Patterson by shooting him with a gun."

Hearing this, Arch Ferrell's younger brother, Pelham, broke into sobs and Governor Gordon Persons that day suffered a heart attack of such severity that family from across the country was called to his bedside, but the indictments took no one by surprise. For months the speculation of courthouse observers and those who had closely followed the case had not been *who* would be indicted but *when*. Even though at the time of the murder Si Garrett was 150 miles away in Birmingham, Alabama law reads that in a conspiracy to commit a felony, the conspirator shares equal guilt with the one who actually commits the felony.

Three days after the murder, when John Patterson was saying that the most likely suspects were the ones investigating the murder, Garrett, on his trip to Phenix City to take charge of the investigation, had startled reporters by providing an alibi for Arch Ferrell before he was a suspect.

"Arch Ferrell couldn't have killed Albert Patterson," Garrett said. "At the time of the murder, he was in his office in the Russell County Courthouse talking long distance to me in my hotel suite in Birmingham when the shots were fired."

Even though records from the telephone company showed that a call had been made between the two numbers, investigators pointed out that what the records did not show was if there was conversation on the line for the thirteen minutes recorded for the call. Or, if the call was made, the phone laid down and the deed done during the thirteen-minute recorded connection.

When Sheriff Lamar Murphy, accompanied by State Patrolman Claude Prier, Colonel Warren, and the National Guard arrived at Fuller's garage apartment to arrest him, Fuller said: "I'm not surprised. I told my wife this morning that I would be indicted."

Fuller was put under house arrest with a list of visitors restricted to immediate family, his physician, his attorneys and his maid. A guard was posted at his door.

Earlier in the day when the indictments were expected, Ferrell had been at the courthouse. He left and returned at 2:00 P.M., went to his office and left thirteen minutes later. When the indictments were handed down and Sheriff Murphy couldn't find him, he drove to Ferrell's home and waited.

When Ferrell arrived, he told him : "I have a warrant for your arrest."

Ashen-faced and in an emotion-laden voice, Ferrell asked: "May I read it?" Then, "Have you told my wife?"

"We spoke to her but did not tell her the nature of the warrant."

"I would like to tell her myself."

Sheriff Murphy nodded, and after a brief word, Ferrell kissed his wife and month-old baby good-bye and accompanied the sheriff and state investigators back to jail where he was booked. His belt and his shoe laces taken from him, Ferrell was put in a cell by himself, the one occupied earlier by Ma Beachie.

Reporters, asking for an interview, were at first refused by Ferrell, and then, he agreed to a written statement. Pale and shaking, he took a reporter's note pad and pencil and repeated what he had said earlier: "I did not kill Albert Patterson. I had nothing to do with the killing of him. I am not a murderer, and I shall be ready to stand trial before a jury of my fellow men."

Within hours of the indictment, Lamar Murphy and two National Guard officers were aboard a National Guard plane with a fugitive warrant signed by Bernard Sykes for the arrest of Si Garrett who was still in the psychiatric hospital in Galveston. On arrival, the Texas sheriff denied service of the fugitive warrant, requiring a certified copy of the indictment charging Garrett with the murder of Albert Patterson. General Hanna immediately dispatched a National Guard plane to deliver the required document which paved the way for the extradition of Garrett from Texas back to Alabama for trial.

Garrett, wearing green pajamas and a stubble of beard, showed no emotion as a Texas deputy read the warrant.

"Does that mean I am under arrest?" Garrett asked.

"Yes," the deputy replied.

But Garrett's Texas attorney said: "Mr. Garrett will resist any attempt to take him back to Alabama before he is able to leave the hospital of his own free will."

At the psychiatric clinic, his physician said: "Mr. Garrett's condition is such at this time that he must remain in the hospital for an indefinite period of time and upon his discharge, he will return to Alabama."

Meanwhile, in Phenix City, Hugh Bentley and the RBA were cheering and congratulating all of those involved in the cleanup. The Blue Ribbon Grand Jury made its final report after having handed down a total of 749 True Bills against 152 people for violation of 46 separate statutes. General Hanna and the National Guard were finishing up their mop-up operations on what newspapers were calling 'the world's biggest dry-cleaning job.'

The Youngblood brothers, Ernest and Glenn, whose gambling and prostitution enterprises were brought to light by Sheila Ann Harper, were captured in a fishing camp in Florida by Forney Hughes.

"We planned to come back to face trial," Ernest Youngblood told him, "when we got up money for bond."

"Well, you're going back now," Forney said. "We have a fugitive warrant and you're under arrest."

Asked if they would waive extradition, the Youngbloods agreed, but Glenn insisted that his wife, who was with him, be allowed to accompany him. General Hanna agreed and three National Guard soldiers were flown down to convoy the Youngbloods, their three cars and one pickup truck back to Phenix City to face trial.

The dragnet was closing and the list of arrests read like a roster of all those who had participated in Phenix City's vast underground of sin and vice. In the last set of indictments handed down by the Blue Ribbon Grand Jury, there was yet one more shocking and sensational revelation.

Evidence uncovered by the National Guard into what General Hanna called "the baby sale racket" had gone before the Grand Jury and socially prominent Dr. Seth Floyd, father of Gloria Floyd Davis and long time member of the City Commission, and his wife Alice, were indicted and arrested on three warrants charging that they did "unlawfully and without license from the State Department of Welfare in Alabama advertise and induce parents to give up their children for adoption."

The case of the young unwed mother, represented by Albert Patterson, charging that her child had been taken from her at birth by Mrs. Floyd was still before the courts and had been investigated by the National Guard.

Louise Malinoski, who claimed she helped poor girls in trouble by performing abortions on her dining room table, was charged with running an abortion clinic, convicted and sentenced to thirty months in prison.

The attempt to capture Head Revel, wanted on a fugitive warrant for multiple gambling violations at the Bridge Grocery, was a near miss. Since his disappearance the night Patterson was killed, numerous efforts had been made to locate him. Finally, in December, Forney Hughes had tracked him to the Miami area where he was running a restaurant. Informants revealed where Revel was living and as Forney Hughes and Richard Peacock were entering the front door, Revel burst through the back and disappeared again.

Buddy Jowers, also wanted on a fugitive warrant, was finally located in Odessa, Texas, through telephone calls to relatives back in Phenix City. When he was arrested, Jowers, tired of running and thirty pounds lighter, said: "I'm glad it's over. I spent six months living in a cabin and once I almost panicked when I was stopped for a routine traffic violation."

MacDonald Gallion, Governor Person's special representative in the Patterson case, accompanied National Guard soldiers to make the arrest. On the return trip, the plane developed mechanical trouble and was forced to land in Mississippi. After being repaired, the weather prevented take-off and the remaining 200 miles of the trip was made by car. Arriving in Phenix City at 1:00 A.M., Buddy Jowers was booked and arrested on the bribery indictment that had been returned against him and Albert Fuller for the protection they afforded H. C. Harden's Skylark Cafe.

Questioned on what he knew about the Albert Patterson slaying that had brought murder indictments against Fuller, Ferrell and Garrett, Buddy said: "There ain't a man living that can run fast enough to catch me and make me talk about that. That's the quickest way I know to get killed."

Albert Fuller, it was reported, had been threatened shortly after his arrest on the indictment for Patterson's murder and General Hanna had had him transferred by ambulance to Kilby prison hospital.

"For safe-keeping," General Hanna said.

Shortly thereafter, Fuller's lawyers on a writ of habeas corpus were able to arrange a $12,500 bond for his release. Sykes agreed to this as well as a similar bond for a similar amount to release Ferrell since a habeas corpus hearing would require the State to present evidence they chose to save for the trial.

As December was ending, the biggest clean-up team ever assembled in Phenix City was breaking up and heading home. George Johnson and his staff had gotten convictions or pleas of guilty on eighty cases and there were handshakes all around as they packed up their law books, records and files to return home. Judge Jones was handing out plaudits to the Grand Jury, and Bernard Sykes, now called "a steady plugger" by the press, was returning to his office in Montgomery.

As the Phenix City investigations and vice and vote fraud trials were ending and the year was coming to a close, Governor-elect Jim Folsom made a stunning announcement. General Hanna, he said, would, at the beginning of his administration, be replaced as commanding general of the National Guard, by his friend and political supporter, William D. Partlow, a colonel in the National Guard.

Hugh Bentley and the RBA were outraged and up in arms about this deliberate attempt by Folsom to publicly embarrass a battle-proven major general by replacing him with a less experienced political appointee.

"Dirty, scheming, low-down politics is what it is," Bentley said. "Until General Hanna got here law enforcement could never ever come up with enough evidence to bring anybody to trial for anything. General Hanna and the National Guard filled up the jail, the jail yard and the courts. Now they're going to get him for putting the truth on trial."

"It's time for the RBA to start a petition and get this thing stopped," Bentley told General Hanna.

A wintry smile swept General Hanna's face. "Hell, Hugh, you know how it is when you get in a fight. It'll always cost you something, a busted lip, a bloody nose, maybe some broken bones. In a fight, nobody comes out unscathed. What's important is, was it worth it? And you and I both know the answer to that."

"But look at what it cost you."

General Hanna's granite jaw was set. "The price of the purchase was worth it. Phenix City is rid of the gangsters who have run this town for 100 years and you have the free elections you've always worked for. And," he pulled open a desk drawer and lifted out a large file box of cards, "it isn't likely that this will happen here again. The whoremasters won't have the police helping them anymore."

"What's that?"

"It's a jammed-packed file of the photos and fingerprints of all the little girls forced into prostitution by the police, some as young as twelve-years old. We found it right here in the sheriff's office."

"I'm grateful for that," Hugh Bentley said, "but the opportunity is there for you to protest Folsom's appointment and win the controversy."

"I know that, Hugh. In fact, I've had a number of prominent Alabama lawyers volunteer their services for free, but we've done the job here we were sent to do. Order has been restored, justice has been done, a new administration in Phenix City has been installed. Now it is up to the courts to deal with the accused and bring them to the bar of justice. After six months of duty away from their homes, families and jobs, my men have done their duty and are ready to go home."

However, before Martial Rule ended and the troops returned home, General Hanna had a medal struck and awarded to each man for his service. Jack Warren, who, with General Hanna, was the first to arrive in Phenix City on the night of the murder, was the last of the cleanup crew to leave. There was no band, no fanfare, no farewell.

"It's a disgrace," Hugh Bentley said, "after all the National Guard was able to accomplish under General Hanna's unchallenged integrity and fearless leadership."

On the last day of December, the *Birmingham News* posed the big unanswered question in the minds of all who had been involved in the Herculean effort to clean up Phenix City. *What about Garrett? And what action will he take following his release from the psychiatric hospital in Galveston?*

Will Garrett return to testify in his own behalf in the murder case and the vote fraud case, both pending against him?

Will he claim not guilty by reason of insanity at the time both incidents occurred?

Or, will he claim his constitutional rights to immunity on the grounds that it might incriminate him?

Ferrell's attorneys, arguing for a continuance on both cases, said Garrett's testimony was necessary to Ferrell's defense, and Roderick Beddow, representing Garrett said: "Si Garrett has expressed his willingness to testify in both cases when he is well, but there is no way to estimate when that will be as his doctors have reported that he is growing progressively more depressed."

Fighting the motion for a continuance, Solicitor Emmett Perry, who had brought the vote fraud charges against Garrett, Ferrell, and Lamar Reid before the Jefferson County Grand Jury and would represent the State at trial objected: "We will never get to trial on any of these cases until the men who stand accused see fit. They're passing the buck, from one to the other and back again."

Complicating Garrett's return to face trial was the petition for a lunacy hearing filed before Judge Wheeler by Emmett Perry in July when Garrett returned from the psychiatric hospital to be arrested on the vote fraud indictment in Birmingham. Before Judge Wheeler could schedule the hearing, Garrett had broken his neck in an automobile accident on his way to Mississippi and the hearing was delayed.

In the meantime, Garrett's attorney, Roderick Beddow, contended in briefs before the Supreme Court that Judge Wheeler did not have the authority to order the lunacy hearing because Garrett was not in confinement when the lunacy hearing was ordered. Garrett came within the narrow confines of an 1867 statute which provided that "even though a person is in confinement when proceedings are begun, the judge loses jurisdiction to proceed if thereafter such person shall have been released from confinement."

On the basis of the 1867 statute, the Supreme Court ruled that Judge Wheeler did not have jurisdiction, and threw out the petition for a lunacy hearing.

"I have no quarrel with the High Court," Perry said, "only with the inadequacy of the present Alabama law written in 1867. We now have no definite knowledge as to what Mr. Garrett's mental condition actually is. He may plead sane or insane at his own disposal."

While the wrangling over Garrett continued, a judge was chosen to hear the trials of Albert Fuller and Arch Ferrell, both charged with the murder of Albert Patterson.

Judge Jones, after six months presiding over the trials in Phenix

City, asked to be relieved to catch up with the workload of important decisions in his own office that had accumulated in his absence, and the Alabama Supreme Court appointed Judge J. Russell McElroy, an expert and author of a text on evidence, to replace him as trial judge in the Patterson murder case.

At an arraignment hearing before Judge McElroy, both Albert Fuller and Arch Ferrell formally pleaded not guilty to the murder charge.

On 17 January 1955, the administration changed. Jim Folsom became governor of Alabama and John Patterson became the state attorney general. Heading the prosecution as attorney general, John Patterson pressed for an early court date in January. Defense attorney Roderick Beddow, still arguing for a delay because of Si Garrett's continued confinement at the psychiatric clinic in Texas, insisted that the trial be postponed.

Over objections of both the prosecution and defense attorneys, Judge McElroy set the murder trial date for 14 February and granted the defense a change of venue to move the trials to Birmingham with ex-Marine Cecil Deason appointed as special prosecutor to try the cases.

Arch Ferrell, still facing the vote fraud trial before Judge Wheeler in Birmingham had been granted a continuance from 10 January to 7 February. With the murder trials set for 14 February and the determination not yet made on which defendant would be tried first, Ferrell's attorney, George Rogers, was able to have the vote fraud trial delayed until 7 March with Judge Wheeler's stern warning: "This is a date beyond which I will not go."

In a ruling before the trial, Judge McElroy granted the right of secrecy to state witnesses, ruling that their identity could be kept secret until the day of the trial and when trial began on 14 February 1955, the State chose to try Albert Fuller first in what was being called the most sensational trial since the 1931 Scottsboro Boys' Trial.

23

THE TRIALS: CONVICTION/ACQUITTAL

When the trial began, Albert Fuller, now fully ambulatory and flashily dressed in a brown suit and cowboy hat, was light-hearted, laughing and joking with reporters, certain he would be acquitted. His alibi was that he was at the Russell County jail talking with Sheriff Ralph Matthews in a back room when the murder was committed. Witnesses called by the State told a different story, and the burden was on the State to prove that what Albert Fuller claimed was not true.

In examining the prospective jurors, Judge McElroy's primary question was: "Do you believe in conviction on circumstantial evidence?"

"Many people have the idea that circumstantial evidence is weak evidence," Judge McElroy said. "This is not necessarily true. The State can present a powerfully strong case on circumstantial evidence, just as it can produce a powerfully weak case on eye-witness evidence. Circumstantial evidence," he explained, "does not mean weak evidence."

Solicitor Cecil Deason called witnesses for the state, establishing the time and circumstances of Albert Patterson's slaying on the night of 18 June. Patterson's friend, Leland Jones, the last to see him alive, told of seeing the lights on in Patterson's upstairs office at approximately 8:30 P.M. and stopping by to ask him to join him for dinner. Furniture movers taking office equipment out of a second floor office in the Coulter Building, told of hearing Patterson clump down the stairs on his cane at 9:00 P.M.

So that the jury could understand the location of buildings and the placement of witnesses at this point in time, Deason had a map board brought in showing the intersection of 14th Street and Fifth Avenue in Phenix City where the Russell County Courthouse faces the Post Office building across 14th Street. Behind the Post Office, he pointed out the

Coulter Building on Fifth Avenue where Patterson was coming down the steps of his second floor office; the Russell County Courthouse, where Arch Ferrell, in his second floor office said he was talking long distance to Si Garrett in Birmingham, and behind the courthouse, the Russell County jail where Albert Fuller claimed he was in conversation with Sheriff Matthews.

The State then called Phenix City cab driver, Bill Littleton, who had been brought back from Kilby Prison to testify in the Patterson murder case after his December 1954 conviction for the 1950 killing of Private George Outlaw. Solicitor Deason for the State asked Littleton to tell the court of his whereabouts on the night of 18 June 1954.

Littleton told them that he was then employed by the Co-op Cab Company, and on that night he had picked up a young girl at the corner of 12th and Broad Street and delivered her to Idle Hour Park.

"I proceeded down Fifth Avenue in the direction of the Coulter Building where Mr. Patterson had his office," Littleton said, "and as I passed the Coulter Building I saw Albert Fuller and Arch Ferrell standing in front of that building."

"And approximately what time was that?" Deason asked.

"About 8:50 P.M."

"And then what happened?"

"I tooted my horn and threw up my hand in greeting and Mr. Ferrell threw up his hand returning the greeting."

After that, Littleton said, he returned to Choppy's Drive-In in Columbus where he had a date with his girl friend, waitress Virginia Lange. It was while he was talking to her and her boss that he mentioned seeing both Fuller and Ferrell in front of the Coulter Building.

"When I heard what had happened, that Mr. Patterson had been shot, I was afraid of what might happen if someone knew what I had seen and I never mentioned it again until late December—just before Christmas—when I contacted Mr. Bernard Sykes and Solicitor Deason from prison."

Deason then called Columbus cab driver James Radius Taylor who was both a worried and a reluctant witness. Shortly before the trial began, while under subpoena, he disappeared and was rumored to have left for Mexico with three soldiers. After several days of searching, he was found in South Georgia saying he was on his way back to Phenix City from Florida after having taken a fare down there.

On the witness stand he testified: "On the night of 18 June 1954, I picked up a fare in Columbus, an army lieutenant who wanted to go to Chad's Rose Room. We had stopped for a traffic light at the corner of

293

Fifth Avenue and 14th Street in Phenix City when we heard three shots ring out, and the lieutenant said: 'We must be in Phenix City now.'"

"And what time was this?" Deason asked.

"Shortly after nine o'clock," Taylor replied.

"And then what happened?"

"The light turned green and as I proceeded on down 14th Street, I saw Albert Fuller run out between some buildings toward a car parked parallel to the curb with the right door open. Fuller jumped in and the car took off down 14th Street. After that, I heard about what happened to Mr. Patterson on my car radio. When the dispatcher asked: 'Who did it?', before I could catch myself, I said: 'Albert Fuller.' After that, I was so scared, I went straight home and never opened my mouth once until the star witness, Johnny Frank Griffin, got murdered and then I figured I had to speak up."

The third eye witness called was courthouse custodian Quinnie Kelley who, at 9:00 P.M. that night, was closing up the courthouse after a Boy Scout Court of Honor meeting. At 9:05 P.M., as he was locking the courthouse door, he looked at his watch and as he did, he heard three shots fired in the direction of the Coulter Building. Seconds later, he saw Arch Ferrell running down a pathway behind the Post Office toward the courthouse.

To amplify the testimony of these three witnesses, the State brought out its surprise witness: a thirty-year-old construction worker Cecil Padgett, who, accompanied by his wife, had come to Phenix City on the night of 18 June looking for a movie to see. Padgett told the jury that he parked his car on Fifth Avenue, directly across the street from the alley where Patterson's car was parked. "While my wife waited in the car," he said, "I walked across the street to the Palace Theater to see what was playing. When I saw that the movie being shown was one we had already seen, I walked back to the car and just as I got there, I heard three shots fired."

"And what did you do then?" Solicitor Deason asked.

"I looked back toward the sound of the shots in time to see Albert Fuller and a man I believe to be Arch Ferrell run from the scene and disappear," Padgett replied.

Absolute silence fell on the courtroom, but Albert Fuller, who had smiled faintly throughout Padgett's testimony, chuckled when Padgett told of seeing him with Arch Ferrell fleeing the scene.

Although the bullets that killed Patterson had been retrieved from his body by the coroner, the gun used in the killing had never been found and the State contended that Patterson's killer was someone who was known to him since he was shot at such close range. The State toxicologist testified that the gun used to shoot Patterson was held only an inch away from his face and the bullets that killed him were the type used in police work, unusual in that all three bullets were of a different type.

Warrant Officer Ray McFall testified that a collection of guns and an assortment of bullets, similar to the three removed from Patterson's body, were taken from Albert Fuller's home.

Hugh Bentley and Howard Pennington told the jury that when Fuller, long known by everyone in Russell County for his display of guns and gunplay, arrived at the hospital shortly after the murder, he incredibly was wearing no gun, only an empty holster. A photograph, taken by the *Columbus Ledger*, of Fuller wearing no gun at the scene of the homicide investigation, was then introduced in evidence.

Roderick Beddow, with all the might, skill, and ferocity that had made his reputation as the foremost criminal defense lawyer in Alabama, attacked the testimony given on behalf of the State setting his sites on the four eyewitnesses who had placed Fuller and Ferrell on the scene. His most intense attack was on the damaging testimony of Cecil Padgett but Padgett never wavered from what he had seen the night of the murder.

Trying to impeach Padgett as a witness, Beddow brought out Padgett's financial indebtedness and accused him of seeking the $10,000 reward as his motive for testifying against Fuller and Ferrell.

"Isn't it true that you are in deep financial trouble?" Beddow demanded.

Padgett, a father of four with a workman's rough hands and sunburned face, stirred uneasily in the witness chair. "I've had some trouble."

"Tell the court what you do for a living."

"I'm a foreman on a construction site."

"And what do they pay you for this job?"

"One hundred dollars a month."

"And your take home pay?"

"About $87."

"And you have a wife and four children to look after?"

"Yes, sir."

"And then your daddy got sick and stayed sick a long time?"

Padgett's face clouded. "My daddy died."

"And the bills ran up and you ran out of money."

Padgett caught his breath.

Beddow continued: "You needed money so bad you had to borrow $20 to pay your back rent, didn't you?"

Padgett struggled with the accusations.

"You needed money so bad you even pawned your pistol, didn't you?"

Padgett nodded wordlessly.

"And at Christmas time you sold the children's wagon, didn't you?"

Unable to withstand anymore, Padgett burst into tears, left the witness stand and ran sobbing from the courtroom.

Rapping for order, Judge McElroy said: "That will be all. The court will take a brief recess."

When court resumed, Padgett was persuaded to take his place on the witness stand again. Beddow, fearing a boomerang of sympathy from the jury immediately abandoned his grueling line of questions about Padgett's personal failures and finances.

Fuller took the stand in his own defense and Roderick Beddow in a booming voice demanded: "Face this jury, Mr. Fuller, and tell those men sitting there. Did you kill Albert Patterson?"

Albert Fuller turned toward the jury and in a strong, firm voice said: "I did not kill Mr. Patterson and I do not know who did. Mr. Patterson was a personal friend of mine. I supported him in his run for attorney general."

"Did you vote for him?"

"No, sir, but I encouraged others at the poll to do so and because of that I took a good deal of criticism at the courthouse."

"Tell the court where you were on the night of June 18 when Mr. Patterson was killed."

Fuller described in detail his earlier visit that day to a fitness club in Columbus, coming home to change his shirt, then going to the Sunny Lane Cafe for a beer and at 7:30 P.M. to the Steak House Cafe where he ate dinner.

"After that," Fuller said, "I went to the jail and talked with Sheriff Matthews and the deputies. Some of 'em were getting ready to go on a raid and we just shot the bull 'til they left."

"What time was that?" Beddow asked.

"Somewhere along about 8:30 or 9:00. Then a couple of the deputies left for the raid, Deputy Johnny Dees went out to Smitty's Grill for ice cream and Sheriff Matthews and I went back to one of the jailer's bedrooms for a private talk."

"When did you learn that Mr. Patterson had been shot?"

"Not 'til Johnny Dees came running back to tell us."

On the witness stand, Sheriff Matthews confirmed Albert Fuller's alibi stating that he was talking with Fuller in the jail at the time of the murder. Eight other deputies were called and each swore that the time and the circumstances as outlined by Fuller and Sheriff Matthews were true.

In rebuttal, the members of the RBA testified enmass. Hugh Bentley, Hugh Britton, Howard Pennington, Hilda Coulter, and Bernice Bentley all testified that Albert Fuller and Sheriff Matthews were of bad character and not to be believed under oath.

The trial lasted for twenty-six days; forty-four witnesses were called by the State, forty-six witnesses by the defense. In the closing arguments, Cecil Deason asked for the death penalty and Roderick Beddow, declaring his client innocent, asked for acquittal, "Because," he said, "if Albert Fuller is convicted, the real assassin will go free forever and a day."

At 3:37 P.M. on 12 March 1955, the jury, after deliberating for six hours and fifty minutes, notified Judge McElroy that they had reached a verdict. Before allowing the jury to return, Judge McElroy ordered everyone out of the courtroom to be searched for deadly weapons.

❧

Thirty deputies, policemen, and bailiffs were stationed at strategic points around the courtroom, along the aisles, the doorways and around the balcony railing. Ten deputies and police officers surrounded Fuller for the reading of the verdict, one of whom was Jack Warren, back on duty in his civilian job as a police lieutenant on the Birmingham police force.

Fuller, amused by all the courtroom preparation, winked at the press and smiled at the grim-looking deputies and policemen as Judge McElroy cautioned the courtroom: "If you have ever behaved, do so now."

The foreman of the jury stepped forward and in a loud, firm voice before a courtroom packed with 300 people said: "We, the jury, find the defendant guilty of murder in the first degree and fix his sentence at life imprisonment as charged in the indictment."

Fuller, fully expecting an acquittal, sank back in his chair, stunned. The smiling confidence he had maintained throughout the trial was gone. His face paled but he never lost his composure.

Roderick Beddow immediately announced that he would appeal the verdict and when newsmen pressed in to ask Fuller his reaction, Fuller, still believing in the power of those who could help him, said: "It's all right. I'm still innocent."

❧

As Fuller was being taken away to jail, in a sixth floor courtroom upstairs, the trial of Arch Ferrell on the vote fraud charges in Jefferson County was just ending.

The trial, which had lasted for fifteen days, began with Emmett Perry, prosecutor for the State, laying the groundwork for Ferrell's trial by introducing the official records where the Jefferson County vote totals in Birmingham had been changed. *Birmingham News* reporter Ed Strickland told of the discovery of the change and Democratic Executive Committee Chairman, Ben Ray, verified the discrepancy.

Lee Porter, already under a perjury indictment for failure to report his campaign contributions from Phenix City gamblers, was brought to the stand and told of the meeting at the Redmont Hotel in Birmingham arranged by Arch Ferrell with Hoyt Shepherd, Jimmie Matthews and Godwin Davis to discuss campaign finances and their contribution of $23,000 to support his campaign to defeat Albert Patterson.

Still reluctant to give the details, Porter finally admitted: "I considered it a fact that Arch Ferrell got the money for me."

Lamar Reid, indicted along with Ferrell and Garrett on the vote fraud, waived his rights as a defendant to testify, telling the jury the details of the vote tally change. Ferrell, he said, assured him there was no need to worry about the 600 vote change because any committee formed to investigate vote fraud charges would not investigate the tally sheets.

"He assured me that it was the right thing to do," Reid said, "that every political faction was behind it, and Mr. Folsom was going to close the transaction."

Mrs. Lee Porter, called as a witness, testified that she and her husband had been called to the meeting at the Molton Hotel, described by Reid, and that Arch Ferrell insisted that she thank Lamar Reid for what he had done.

Mrs. Porter told the jury: "I said 'Arch, I already told Si Garrett I am grateful for everything you and Si have done, but I will not do anything dishonest.'"

Mrs. Porter said Ferrell told her he was disappointed in her. "I'm not asking you to ask Lamar to do anything he has not already done. He has already changed the figures for your husband."

Arch Ferrell, having pleaded innocent to all charges, did not take the stand in his own defense. Instead, his attorney countered with a parade of twenty-eight character witnesses to establish that Ferrell was a man of political integrity and family prominence, a man whom they all swore was of good character and worthy of belief under oath.

It took the jury just one hour and twenty-eight minutes during which time they also had their supper, to vote acquittal. Arch Ferrell, grim and silent throughout the trial, was now jubilant, vigorously shaking his attorney's hand and walking from the courtroom arm in arm with his wife and his brother, ringed with smiles.

Emmett Perry, profoundly shocked by the verdict, when asked by the press for a comment said: "Ask the jury why they turned a guilty man loose. Arch Ferrell offered to plead guilty before the trial started if we recommended a fine without imprisonment."

After a conference with several attorneys, including John Patterson, who was opposed to any compromise, the decision was made to let the case run its course before a jury.

Judge Wheeler who had heard the case shared the shock of the verdict and made the comment: "Some of the jurors in my court did not do the duty their oath required."

The prosecution saw Ferrell's acquittal in the vote fraud case as damaging to his trial for murder which was scheduled to begin a month later on 18 April. When it did, George Rogers, in a pretrial hearing before Judge McElroy who would hear the case, brought eleven lawyers and fifty affidavits attesting to the belief that on the basis of Solicitor Emmett Perry and Judge Wheeler's remark and the extensive press coverage that the case had received that it would be impossible for Arch Ferrell to receive a fair and impartial trial and he filed a motion for an indefinite postponement.

Judge McElroy took it under advisement and postponed a decision until he questioned the 208 prospective jurors who had been called for duty. Satisfied that the thirty-six veniremen required for trial could be obtained, Judge McElroy denied Rogers' motion for an indefinite postponement and trial began as scheduled on 18 April.

Solicitor Deason began by reading the charge in the indictment, that "Arch B. Ferrell did willfully and maliciously and with malice aforethought kill and murder Albert Patterson on the night of 18 June 1954." In his opening statement he told the jury: "The State will prove beyond a reasonable doubt and a moral certainty that Arch B. Ferrell is guilty of committing this crime."

Following the same pattern, with much of the same evidence and many of the same witnesses as called in Albert Fuller's trial for murder, Solicitor Deason began by establishing where Arch Ferrell was on the night of 18 June and the events leading up to the murder. Cab driver Bill Littleton, James Radius Taylor and Quinnie Kelley were called again to testify to the time and what they had seen. As in Albert Fuller's trial, Cecil Padgett told the jury that he had seen Fuller and a man he believed to be Ferrell running from the scene shortly after the shots were fired.

Ferrell denied being there. On the night of the murder, Ferrell said he had driven from his home, several miles away on Seale Road, to the Post Office, which was across the street from the Courthouse where he had a second floor office. After picking up his mail, he moved his car behind the courthouse and went upstairs to his office, arriving there at approximately 8:30 P.M. He then made a number of telephone calls in an effort to locate Si Garrett, several of them to Frank Long. A call, made at 8:57, located Frank Long with Si Garrett at the Redmont Hotel in Birmingham and lasted until 9:01. A second call to Si Garrett's suite was placed at 9:02 and lasted until 9:15, during which time he said he was talking with Garrett.

The district manager for Southern Bell said the company had no way of verifying if the calls logged were actually made from Ferrell's office phone to Si Garrett's hotel room or if the calls were made from another number and charged to Ferrell's phone. Neither would the records prove that a person was talking all of the time specified.

"The long distance operator," the Bell representative said, "does not customarily cut in to check on a call unless the call lasts for an unusually long time."

Asked if he had heard the sirens as the police and ambulance raced to the Coulter Building, Ferrell said he could not recall any as it was not unusual for sirens to be blowing around the courthouse.

Turning to the conditions of open gambling in Phenix City prior to the runoff election, Ferrell said that he was not aware that there was any open gambling, and his attorney, George Rogers, insisted that it was not his job to clean up vice and gambling. "That responsibility belongs to the police and the sheriff's department." Ferrell's job as circuit solicitor, Rogers said, was to try the cases brought to him by the law enforcement officials.

Deason asked: "Did you see the Russell County Courthouse yard filled with gambling equipment that was seized by the National Guard after Patterson's death?"

Ferrell replied: "I saw that a large number of gambling devices were brought in."

"But you knew nothing about open gambling in Phenix City?"

"No, sir."

Deason then dropped his bombshell. He handed Ferrell a small slip of paper that had been taken from Ferrell's wallet on an earlier search. The paper listed a number of names including Hoyt Shepherd, Jimmie Matthews, Godwin Davis, J.D. Abney, Frank Gullatt, Red Cook, Albert

Fuller, and Head Revel, each with a number written by his name.

Ferrell said he did not know what the numbers meant, that the slip of paper Deason was showing him was a copy of a paper he had found in the Redmont Hotel when the gamblers turned over $18,000 to help Lee Porter in his campaign against Patterson.

Deason asked: "Where did you find it?"

"I believe it was on a table."

"Were you present there with Hoyt Shepherd, Jimmie Matthews, and Godwin Davis?"

"I believe they were there."

"Did you ask them what these numbers meant?"

"Yes, but they didn't know."

"Why did you write it down?"

"I was mainly curious."

Ferrell said he copied the list of names and figures down and kept them in his wallet.

"Was this a list of contributors to Lee Porter's campaign with the amount in thousands noted by the side?"

"I don't know."

"Godwin Davis' name is there with a '5' beside it. You say he is a farmer?"

"He has farmed extensively for the last few years."

"Do you know what kind of business Head Revel is in?"

"I believe he is connected with the Bridge Grocery."

"Did you know he was a professional gambler?"

"I don't know that."

"Have you ever been in the Bridge Grocery?"

"Some time ago to use the telephone."

"Did you ever see any groceries in the Bridge Grocery?"

"No, I just noticed the phone."

"Do you mean to say that you went in the Bridge Grocery and did not see any gambling equipment?"

"I did not."

Godwin Davis was called to testify and told of the meeting at the Redmont Hotel where arrangements were made to supply money for Porter's campaign to defeat Patterson.

Ferrell admitted going to the Redmont Hotel to introduce Lee Porter to Shepherd, Matthews, and Davis whom he called a farmer, but denied any part of making the arrangements for money.

Deason then presented his surprise witness, Solicitor Kenneth Cooper from the 28th judicial circuit in Bay Minette who told of a meeting of all solicitors in Montgomery called by Si Garrett who said he wanted to discuss the recent Supreme Court ruling on segregation. Cooper testified that Arch Ferrell, sitting at the head table, got up and said he wanted to say a few words and then for fifteen to twenty minutes he cursed Albert Patterson.

Cooper quoted Ferrell as saying: "That goddamned son-of-a-bitch Albert Patterson is not going to take the attorney general's office."

"Ferrell," Cooper said, "told the meeting of solicitors that they should all go on record for Lee Porter because he and Si Garrett were going to go up and down the state and see that Patterson did not become attorney general."

In response, Ferrell said, "I don't believe I said that. I recall saying that I was going to work as hard as I could to see that my friend and classmate, Mr. Porter, was elected. I asked all present to support Mr. Porter as strong as they could."

"On two occasions, after the murder of Mr. Patterson, it has been testified in this court by four newsmen that you stated in their presence that you hated Albert Patterson and that you were glad he was dead."

"There were some things about him I didn't like, but I don't believe I said that."

"You worked for Porter during the campaign and Patterson was leading, and you came to Birmingham at the request of Silas Garrett who was then the attorney general."

"Yes, sir."

"What conversation did you have with Si Garrett and Lamar Reid about a vote change?"

"Mr. Deason, I don't recall that there was any talk of changing the votes."

"Do you remember when Mr. Garrett mentioned a 2,000 vote change to you and you said that was a little too rough, that you like to do things smoothly?"

"I don't recall any conversation about 2,000 votes."

"What was said about changing the vote?"

"I did not hear anything said about changing the vote."

"Didn't you call up Mrs. Porter and tell her you wanted her to thank Lamar Reid for what he had done for her husband, that he changed 600 votes?"

"No, sir, I know I did not make that statement."

"You were a solicitor when the attorney general of Alabama told you Lamar Reid had changed 600 votes in the election, weren't you?"

"He didn't tell me Lamar Reid did it."

"Did you report it to the law enforcement authorities in Jefferson County?"

"No, sir."

At the close of the cross examination, Deason returned to direct testimony Ferrell had given concerning his movements on the night of the murder.

"Now, Mr. Ferrell, you said that while you were in your office with the windows open, you heard no sirens."

"Not that I can recall."

"When you left your office at approximately 9:15 P.M. and went to your car parked behind the post office, you said that you noticed no commotion near the Coulter Building a half block away?"

"No sir."

"You saw no one from the time you left your office until you arrived at Huckabee's Store near your home."

"Not that I recall."

"What time did you arrive at Huckabee's?"

"About 9:30."

"And it was at Huckabee's in the TV room that you first learned of Albert Patterson's murder?"

"That is correct."

Ferrell's defense attorney George Rogers claimed the prosecution witnesses, Bill Littleton and James Radius Taylor, placing Ferrell on the scene the night of the murder were motivated by promises of leniency and Cecil Padgett, by the $10,000 reward that had been offered for the arrest and conviction of Patterson's slayer. He reserved his most stinging accusations for Quinnie Kelley, who alone had identified Arch Ferrell as the man running away from the scene back toward the courthouse at the hour that Patterson was killed.

In interminable and repetitive detail, he questioned Quinnie Kelley over and over about where he was on the courthouse steps, which step, how many, which one he was standing on when he heard the shots fired. Rogers took him to the map board showing the downtown area.

"Now, Quinnie, the scale of this map is one foot to one-sixteenth of an inch." Turning to Judge McElroy on the bench, Rogers said: "Isn't that right, Judge?"

"Yes, that is correct," Judge McElroy replied.

"All right, Quinnie, you come here with me and look at this map and show me where you were and how far away you were."

"I can't figure no one-sixteenth, Mr. Rogers, all I know is what I seen, and I seen Mr. Ferrell running toward the courthouse right after I heard them three shots."

"Now, Quinnie, you had a falling out with Mr. Ferrell sometime before, didn't you?"

"No, sir, I ain't never fell out with him or anybody."

"Isn't it true that in your capacity as custodian of the courthouse that you sought permission to carry a gun?"

"With all that goes on around here, I asked to carry a gun. Yes, sir."

"And Mr. Ferrell opposed your having a permit to carry a gun, didn't he?"

"I don't know a thing about that, Mr. Rogers," Quinnie Kelley replied.

"And isn't it true that you were having trouble keeping the kids from playing on the courthouse grass?"

"Yes, sir, but..."

"And isn't it true that Mr. Ferrell refused you that permit because he was afraid you might lose your temper and shoot the children?"

"No, sir," Quinnie Kelley protested, "ain't none of that so."

"And isn't it true that because you were refused a permit, you hold a grudge against Arch Ferrell, and you've been told that if you testify against him that you'll be made a deputy and given a gun?"

"No, sir, ain't none of that so."

"And that's why you waited four months before you came forward to testify?"

"Mr. Rogers, I didn't come forward because I was worried what would happen to me if I did and sure enough it did."

"Worried? What do you mean worried?"

"After I come forward and testified last month in the case against Albert Fuller, my brother, who is a minister, got a call from Ralph McKinney. He's the scoutmaster who held the Court of Honor that night at the courthouse. McKinney told my brother to tell me that I was in trouble and I wouldn't live long if I kept on talking."

Seeing that Quinnie Kelley was ravaged by the heat in the courtroom and the relentless grilling, Judge McElroy rapped his gavel and told the jury: "Gentlemen, we will take a recess for about fifteen minutes. You may retire to the jury room."

When the time had passed and the jury returned, Judge McElroy turned to Arch Ferrell's defense attorney and said: "All right, Mr. Rogers, you may proceed with the cross examination."

Approaching Quinnie Kelley in the witness chair, Rogers now used formal address and assumed an icy matter. "Now, Mr. Kelley, I believe you told us you saw Arch Ferrell nearly every day and every night."

"Yes, sir, I did."

"He has a one-man office down there in the courthouse, doesn't he?"

"Yes, sir."

"He doesn't have any secretary, does he?"

"No, I ain't seen nare'un there."

"He has to do all his own work."

Cecil Deason for the State objected: "We object to what he has to do."

The court sustained the objection, Rogers reserved the exception and continued: "It wasn't unusual for Mr. Ferrell to be in his office at night, was it?"

"No, sir."

"So if it was a usual thing for Mr. Ferrell to be at the courthouse at night, it could have been somebody else you saw running down there near the Post Office toward the courthouse that night after the shots rang out."

"No, sir. it was Mr. Ferrell. I seen him," Quinnie Kelley insisted.

"How can you be sure?" Rogers demanded. "It was dark that night. Trees shadow the sidewalk and there's a high hedge around the Post Office that's higher than your head, isn't it?"

"I don't know about that hedge, Mr. Rogers, I ain't never walked up against it."

"Do you mean to tell me, Mr. Kelley, from where you were standing on the courthouse steps you could see so clearly and in such detail?"

"Yes, sir."

"How far *can* you see, Mr. Kelley?"

Quinnie Kelley scratched his head, paused for a moment to reflect and then said: "I can see the moon. How far is that?"

Exasperated, Rogers told Judge McElroy: "I want to reserve this witness for further cross examination."

Judge McElroy rapped his gavel and said: "The witness is excused."

Ralph McKinney, the Scoutmaster who had conducted the Boy Scout Court of Honor at the courthouse, named by Quinnie Kelley as the one who threatened him, was next called to testify. On the stand, he denied calling Quinnie Kelley's brother and denied making threats that Quinnie Kelley wouldn't live long if he continued to talk.

When the final arguments began, George Rogers, in a humble tone of voice, praised Solicitor Deason's ability to sway a jury and regretted that he himself lacked this skill.

"However," he reminded the jury: "You took an oath before serving as jurors that you would give a fair trial to this defendant, his family, his attorneys and the State. It was because you promised to do this that you were chosen for this jury. I want to remind you now that Arch Ferrell is covered up with the cloak of innocence until you gentlemen find beyond a reasonable doubt, and a moral certainty that he is guilty."

"So let's take the window dressing off this case the State has presented. Let's take the vote fraud thing away and boil it down to its bare essentials, the testimony of three witnesses: Bill Littleton, Cecil Padgett and Quinnie Kelley."

Dismissing the testimony of all three witnesses, Rogers blamed politics for Ferrell's indictment and ended by saying that: "Arch Ferrell is no more guilty of this charge than any one of you sitting on this jury."

Rising to begin his closing argument, Solicitor Deason said: "The defense attorney, Mr. Rogers, would have you believe that everybody in this case is lying but his own client. Arch Ferrell's alibi is that he was talking on the phone to Si Garrett, but nobody but Arch Ferrell has testified that he was talking on the phone with Si Garrett when Patterson was killed. Arch Ferrell could have made the call, put down the receiver, walked over and killed Albert Patterson in about two minutes and returned to talk over the phone. The defense makes light of the vote fraud in the attorney general election, but the fact is, gentlemen of the jury, that the vote fraud is the guts of this case. A man doesn't just go out and kill without a reason. Hate was the motive and Arch Ferrell has convicted himself with his own words.

"You've heard for yourself the expressions of hatred Arch Ferrell made witnessed by three members of the press, saying that he hated that 'goddamned son of a bitch' Albert Patterson. And, at a state solicitors' meeting in Montgomery called by Si Garrett, he told the gathering that he and Si Garrett were going to travel up and down the state to make sure Albert Patterson never became attorney general."

Solicitor Deason traced the line of testimony and concluded his closing argument by telling the jury: "Albert Fuller and Arch Ferrell killed Albert Patterson, each for his own reason. Albert Patterson had sworn to rid Phenix City of vice and gambling and that would have put Albert Fuller out of business. Albert Patterson also swore to reveal the perpetrators of the vote fraud, and that was imminent danger and political suicide for Arch Ferrell. I don't know which one pulled the trigger, but both Albert Fuller and Arch Ferrell were there. One was just as guilty as the other."

Pointing at Ferrell, Pearson said, "The state of Alabama has met its burden of proof, gentlemen, and has proven beyond a reasonable doubt and to a moral certainty that this man is guilty as charged with killing Albert Patterson. Justice in this case deserves and demands that you sentence this defendant to death in the electric chair."

After deliberating for nine and one-half hours, when the jury returned, they prefaced their verdict by saying that during this trial, they had had few privileges and many privations. "We have studied this case and we have prayed over it. We render our verdict with no apologies anyone."

"And what is that verdict?" Judge McElroy asked.

"We find the defendant, Arch Ferrell, not guilty."

A gasp arose from the courtroom and eight deputies surrounded Ferrell, his wife and attorneys and immediately escorted them to Judge McElroy's chambers. When Ferrell came out, he read a statement he had written for the press: "Twelve courageous and honest men have confirmed my innocence which I personally have always known. I am deeply grateful for the justice I have received."

Afterwards, Ferrell, his wife, attorneys, and Sheriff Matthews went to visit Fuller in jail on an upper floor. A county official, witnessing the visit reported that Fuller, when told of the verdict, was stunned and could not believe that a jury had acquitted Arch Ferrell.

Ray Jenkins, the young reporter assigned by the *Columbus Ledger* to cover the Phenix City story on the night the murder was committed had followed the story through to its end. He asked a disappointed John Patterson what he thought of the verdict. "No man," Patterson said, "is acquitted at the bar of his own conscience."

≥❧

In Phenix City, the gambling was gone and the racketeers were in jail. Out of the hundreds of convictions in the vice and vote fraud trials, not a single case was overturned in appeals.

Across the river, there was great rejoicing in the *Columbus Ledger* office when Robert Brown and his staff of reporters won that newspaper the 1955 Pulitzer Prize for their reporting of the Phenix City story and the political assassination of Albert Patterson, a story that was front page news for an entire year, requiring the transmission of 20,000 words a day to cover the trials in Birmingham.

Albert Fuller appealed his conviction on the grounds of new evidence not available at the time of trial, that being Arch Ferrell's willingness to testify, after his counsel's refusal to let him testify at the original trial. The Alabama Supreme Court, however, denied this appeal pointing out that Ferrell was in the courthouse available for subpoena, and Fuller served seven years before being paroled.

While working as a parolee, he fell on his head from a ten-foot ladder, and after nine months and several operations, he died in Phenix City. Part of his sentence had been that he could never ever go to Phenix City again. At the last, as he was dying, the court, by special permission, allowed him to return to Phenix City where he had once reigned supreme.

Arch Ferrell, acquitted in both the vote fraud and murder trials, was disbarred by the Alabama Bar Association. Several months after the death of Albert Fuller, he was reinstated and resumed his law practice in Phenix City.

Lamar Reid, indicted in Jefferson County along with Arch Ferrell and Si Garrett for vote fraud in changing the vote totals, pleaded nolo contendre, was fined $500, sentenced to six months at hard labor and given a one year probation.

Charges against Si Garrett lingered in the courts for nine years. With Roderick Beddow as his counsel, the legal maneuvering over Garrett's sanity and whether the state could require him to be subjected to a mental exam was finally abandoned by then-Attorney General Richmond Flowers who said prosecution would be futile since many witnesses were dead. Shortly thereafter, Garrett died and the Phenix City story became history.

EPILOGUE

In Montgomery, Albert Patterson stands on the north side of Alabama's capitol, commemorated in marble, the fatal date of 18 June 1954, carved beneath his lame left foot supported by his cane. This was done during the administration of his son, John, who after taking his father's place as attorney general, won the gubernatorial race over George Wallace and was elected governor of Alabama.

Hugh Bentley was guardian of the legacy that was left from those tumultuous times and was ever vigilant that the condition that had existed before did not return or begin again. In 1955, he was the subject of the Ralph Edwards' network TV program, *This Is Your Life*, which honored citizens for extraordinary accomplishment in their community.

"There was another extraordinary accomplishment in our community," Hugh Bentley said later, "really, a near-miracle. Red Cook, whose devilment I had known since childhood, found Jesus in jail. A lot of folks said, criminals always claim they find Jesus in jail, but Red really did. He turned his life completely around. He began by helping the prison chaplain, later became assistant chaplain, and when he was paroled, he continued his work by ministering to the inmates in prison."

Before he died on 13 April 1984, Hugh Bentley, a dedicated religious man, accomplished an extraordinary and signal event himself—fifty years of teaching Sunday School to the children in his church in Phenix City, and a lifetime of struggling for justice and keeping the Faith.

"My earliest memory," Hugh Bentley said, "was my Mama standing up for right against my Daddy's indifference over the crime and criminal ways in Phenix City. To this hour, I can remember her shielding me against his anger and taking us children to live outside the corruption he tolerated. Fighting for the right to raise children in a decent community was Mama's legacy to me, and I felt obliged to pass that legacy on to my own children and those who came after."

Always mindful of the fact that he was the seventh son and the Biblical importance of this, Hugh Bentley bore this responsibility all his life. "I never wanted to do what I had to do when Phenix City was so bad," he said, a month before he died. "I begged God not to make the burden mine. I had a home and a family to protect, but when I saw my home blown up and my family spared I knew that the destiny was mine, that all my life, the things that had happened had pointed me in this direction. Then, when Mr. Patterson was killed, I was lost, and I asked God to send us some help, and he gave us a mighty sword, he sent General Hanna and the National Guard."

What Hugh Bentley had hoped to do, what Albert Patterson had tried to do, and what General Hanna was able to do, along with a virtual armada of Alabama's finest in the investigative and legal fields was at last accomplished. The cleanup of Phenix City was final and complete and has remained so since that time. In November 1983, this event was marked by Jane Gullatt, the Mayor of Phenix City, who had been a school girl when Albert Patterson was murdered and Martial Rule declared. In a commemorative ceremony and in appreciation for the restoration of the citizens' constitutional rights, Mayor Gullatt, amidst banners and bunting, presented the keys to the city to General Hanna and his staff for their part in breaking the strangle-hold of crime and corruption that had held Phenix City in its grip for 120 years.

At 83, Crack Hanna, impatient with old war wounds that forced him to the use of a cane, was still the warrior general, dauntlessly getting about, going to his office every day, attending to the business of Hanna Steel as chairman of the board. Talking with Hugh Bentley that day of the commemoration, remembering Phenix City and all that had happened there, his eyes lit up.

"It was a helluva fight and I'd do it again tomorrow if I had to. We can't sit by and let criminals, cutthroats, and whoremasters take over our towns and communities. If we have to fight the bastards, then I say, let's fight. We have to protect our freedoms."

CAST OF CHARACTERS

Abney, J.D.: Hostile operator of the Bama Club; General Hanna's first encounter on patrol in Phenix City.

Acton, Ray: National Guard major who witnessed repair surgery on Johnny Frank Griffin. Legal advisor to Col. Brown.

Allred, Joe: Arranged meeting with Walden and McVeigh; charged, along with Revel and Godwin Davis, for the murder of Johnny Frank Stringfellow.

Archer, Patricia Ann: Dave Walden's wife of one week who was killed by Walden and McVeigh in 1944 and whose remains were recovered from Okefenokee Swamp in 1948.

Beachie, Ma: Grandmotherly proprietor of Ma Beachie's night club; arrested.

Beck, Sam: Liquor runner with Pete Hargett, 1949.

Beddow, Roderick: Flamboyant Birmingham attorney hired by Donald Leebern to assist State in prosecuting Hoyt Shepherd in 1946 Fate Leebern trial; represented gamblers' interests in 1954 cleanup, attempted to quash 600 indictments. Defense attorney for Fuller and Si Garrett in Patterson murder trial.

Belcher, William: Attorney for Hoyt Shepherd in Fate Leebern trial.

Benefield, Johnny: Ace Phenix City safe-cracker.

Bentley, Hugh: Moral leader who grew up with crime and corruption in Phenix city, led crusade against gamblers, formed RBA in 1951 with Albert Patterson, house blown up in 1952, publicly beaten at polls in 1952, initiated impeachment proceedings against Sheriff Matthews in 1953; persuaded Patterson to run for attorney-general in 1954.

Bentley, Calvin: Hugh's father who provided bond for gamblers.

Bentley, Minnie: Hugh's mother, who moved out of his father's house with her seven sons in 1912 because of effects of crime and corruption on her children.

Bentley, Bernice: Hugh's wife, who was inside dynamited house.

Bentley, Hughbo: Hugh's son, also beaten at polls.

Bentley, Truman: Hugh's son, also inside dynamited house.

Borders, A. S.: 1946 Circuit Solicitor who tried Leebern case.

Brassell, Jabe: Attorney for Hoyt Shepherd in 1946 Leebern trial; his complaint caused Democratic Sub-Committee investigation into 1954 primary vote fraud.

Brassell, Bowen: Jabe's son, Juvenile Court Judge who testified at Sub-Committee hearings.

Britton, Hugh: ally and close friend of Hugh Bentley. Known as "Two Hughs" they began fight against gamblers.

Burch, Shannon: Russell County Sheriff 1946, made probate judge in 1947 shake-up.

Brown, Col. James: National Guard officer who brought troops to Phenix City for Martial Rule. General Hanna's Military Police Chief under Martial Rule.

Brown, Robert: *Columbus Ledger* editor who assigned reporters to cover criticizing lack of progress in Patterson case.

Brown, Roberts: Speaker of the Alabama House of Representatives, attorney for RBA in impeachment proceedings against Sheriff Matthews, whose house was set afire in 1953.

Chance, Fanny Belle: Proprietor of Cotton Club with night police chief, Buddy Jowers; known as "Queen of Hearts."

Chestnutt, Dewey: Phenix City police officer who pocketed the gun in the investigation of Fate Leebern.

Clark, Billy: Parolee arrested by W/O Forney Hughes, leading to discovery of prostitution racket.

Clark, Roy: Mill worker who was beaten by Billy Clark.

Cobb, Homer: Mayor of Phenix City who allowed gambling to save the city from receivership during Depression; hounded by Hugh Bentley and his mother, Miss Minnie, for allowing gambling.

Cole, Ben: State representative from Phenix City, defeated with Brassell in 1954 primary; arrested by General Hanna for leasing buildings for gambling.

Cook, E. L. "Red": Phenix City gambler who grew up with Hugh Bentley, operated the Old Original Barbecue lottery, arrested by General Hanna, tried and convicted of 1950 murder of John Mancil.

Cook, Grady: Fed. Alcohol Tax officer in the 1949 Guy Hargett case.

Cook, Eugene: Ga. Attorney General during 1949 border war.

Coulter, Hilda: Phenix City housewife who organized RBA Auxiliary; charged Albert Fuller with vote fraud in 1954 primary election. Testified at murder trial.

Curtis, V. C.: Phenix City attorney who won and was challenged by Jabe Brassell in 1954 race for seat in Alabama House of Representatives, provoking Sub-Committee investigation.

Daniel, Pal M.: Phenix City Police chief, the first official to break silence, telling General Hanna of "hands-off" policy on gamblers ordered by Mayor Elmer Reese' nephew, night police chief, Buddy Jowers.

Davis, Godwin Sr.: Gambler, slot machine king, indicted in 1948 for murder of Johnny Frank Stringfellow; lottery empire was revealed in 1950 divorce of his son, Bubber, and Gloria Floyd Davis. Jailed by General Hanna on forty-four counts of lottery; first gamble to break silence, revealing financing of 1954 machine candidate.

Davis, Godwin, Jr. "Sonny": Godwin's son, charged with forty-four counts of lottery.

Davis, William Robert "Bubber": Godwin's son whose divorce from Gloria Floyd Davis revealed gambling empire.

Davis, George: Godwin's brother who became a partner with Head Revel in the Metropolitan Lottery operated at the Bridge Grocery, after Revel and

Godwin Davis split up following the Stringfellow affair.

Davis, Gloria Floyd: Daughter-in-law; divorce testimony revealed gambling empire.

Deason, Cecil, Solicitor: Specially appointed solicitor to prosecute Fuller and Ferrell in the murder of Albert Patterson.

Dees, Johnny: Russell County jailer on night Patterson was slain.

Dempsey, Bill: Mill worker; another of Billy Clark's victims.

Drinkard, John: Driver for Governor Jim Folsom, called to testify.

East, John: Witness against Red Cook at Sub-Committee Hearing.

Eisenhower, Dwight D.: President of US in 1954, consulted by Governor Persons on martial rule.

Entrekin, Cliff: Operated brothel at notorious Cliff's Fish Camp; testimony of his girls convicted Albert Fuller of bribery.

Faye, Nona: First witness in cleanup, set afire by William Allred.

Ferrell, Arch: attorney for Hoyt Shepherd in Fate Leebern trial; after 1947 recircuiting, appointed Russell County Circuit Solicitor. Relieved of duties by Governor after 1954 Patterson slaying. Indicted by Jefferson County Grand Jury along with Attorney General Si Garrett and Lamar Reid in 1954 vote tally change in Birmingham. Acquitted. Indicted by Russell County Blue Ribbon Grand Jury for murder of Albert Patterson. Acquitted. Disbarred by Alabama Bar Association 1955; reinstated, 1969.

Ferrell, A. S. His father, assistant Russell County Solicitor before recircuiting abolished his job.

Ferrell, Pelham: His bother; an attorney who represented Albert Fuller in bribery charge.

Floyd, Dr. Ashby: Revered Phenix City physician and long time member of Phenix City Commission who served as judge of Recorder Court when Grady Shepherd was arrested for murder of Fate Leebern.

Floyd, Dr. Seth: His son, father of Gloria Floyd Davis; indicted and arrested along with his wife, Alice, for baby sales discovered by General Hanna.

Floyd, Alice: His wife, charged by unwed mother in 1951 for what Albert Patterson called "traffic in human lives."

Folsom, Jim: Governor of Alabama, 1946-1950, 1955-1959; supported Machine candidate, Lee Porter against Albert Patterson in 1954 attorney general race. Replaced General Hanna as Adjutant General on taking office in 1955.

Foster, Floyd: Poll-watcher who testified at Sub-Committee Investigation that Buddy Jowers was satchel man paying off at polls.

Franklin, C. W.: Foreman of Russell County 1954 Screen Door Grand Jury.

Fuller, Albert: Russell County Deputy Sheriff, who began in 1944 as deputy under Sheriff Ralph Matthews; killed Guy Hargett in 1949, Clarence Franklin Johns in 1950; chief rival of Phenix city night police chief, Buddy Jowers; rose to power with protection and prostitution rackets; indicted and convicted on vote fraud; convicted and sentenced to seven-year prison sentence for bribery in Russell County; indicted and convicted of murder of Albert Patterson.

Died from fall after parole.

Fuller, Mrs. H. E.: Protested Volunteer Police Force.

Fullan, Lt. Jim: National Guard legal advisor to General Hanna.

Gallion, MacDonald: Lost in three-way 1954 primary for attorney general, threw his support to Patterson, was later named as Special counsel to report to Governor on Patterson murder investigation.

Garrett, Silas M. III: Alabama Attorney General 1954, supported Machine candidate Lee Porter against Albert Patterson in 1954 race for attorney general; testified before Jefferson County Grand Jury concerning June 1954 vote tally change in Birmingham; left state and turned himself into Texas psychiatric clinic; lunacy charges against him filed by Jefferson County Grand Jury for vote fraud. Indicted by Russell county Blue Ribbon Grand Jury for murder of Albert Patterson. Represented by Roderick Beddow, case dismissed in 1963 by Attorney General Richmond Flowers.

Garrett, Broox and Watrous T.: His brothers, also attorneys.

Gordon, Clyde: Accomplice to Clarence Franklin Johns in 1950 Manhattan Cafe holdup, killed in getaway car.

Gowers, O.T.: Judge in 1949 Stringfellow case.

Graham, Billy: Evangelist denied invitation by General Hanna.

Griffin, Johnny Frank: Witness in Patterson case; killed by Jerry Washington in 1954.

Gullatt, C. L.: Phenix City Commissioner with Homer Cobb since 1931.

Gullatt, Frank: Ran Blue Bonnet Cafe, tattooed lips of prostitutes.

Gunter, Charles: Member of RBA.

Gwin, Robert: Co-counsel with Roderick Beddow for Albert Fuller.

Hanna, Major General Walter J.: The Warrior general responsible for the cleanup of Phenix City. Denied service in World War I because of his age, he later rose through the ranks in the National Guard from private to major general, earning the name "Crack" for his proficiency with bayonet and rifle. Serving in World War II as a commander of a regimental combat team in savage jungle warfare he earned military history's highest ratio of enemy killed for unit losses. Appointed Alabama Adjutant General under Governor Gordon Persons in 1950, he forced the decision for Martial Rule, relieved Russell County Sheriff Matthews and Police Chief Pal Daniel in take-over; gathered evidence measured in tons, toppling crime syndicate and resulting in the return of 747 True Bills from the Blue Ribbon Grand Jury. Uncovered gambling, prostitution, abortion clinic, peonage, baby sales, college for safe-crackers.

Hanna, Vera: Crack's wife who received call from Governor Persons.

Hanna, Pete: Crack's son who drove him to Phenix City the night Patterson was killed.

Hancock, Elzie: Legendary tracker and revenue officer, assisted Sheriff Howell in 1948 Stringfellow case, arrested in 1949 Border War.

Hargett, Guy: Liquor runner, shot five times in raid by Albert Fuller and Ben Scroggins in 1949 raid.

Hargett, Pete: Guy's brother, arrested in 1949 raid.

Harper, Earlene: B-girl who tipped General Hanna on violations of Mann Act by Hugh and Jean Kinnard involving her daughter.

Harper, Sheila Ann: Earlene's daughter who recorded Phenix City events in her notebook; warned by Ernest Youngblood.

Harper, Joseph H.: Commanding General at Fort Benning who declared Phenix City off-limits during cleanup.

Harris, J. D.: Russell County Deputy, defense witness in Leebern trial, appointed to City Commission 1947, elected mayor in 1950 following death of Homer Cobb, succeeded by Otis Taff.

Hicks, Julius B.: Defense attorney for Hoyt Shepherd in Leebern trial. Machine appointed Circuit Judge when Russell County was recircuited in 1947; relieved by the Alabama Supreme Court in June 1954 of all official duties concerning Patterson murder investigation.

Howell, E. F.: Sheriff of Muscogee County, who discovered murder of Johnny Frank Stringfellow and Patricia Ann Archer in Flordia in 1948.

Hughes, Forney: National Guard Warrant Officer who uncovered prostitution ring during Martial Rule.

Jenkins, Ray: Reporter for *Columbus Ledger*, attacked at polls in 1952 election, covered Fuller and Ferrell trials in Birmingham.

Johns, Clarence Franklin: Shot thirteen times by Fuller and ABC agent Ben Scroggins in cemetery after 1950 holdup of Manhattan Cafe.

Johnson, Carlton: Managing Editor of *Columbus Ledger*.

Johnson, George: Appointed Special Solicitor to bring evidence before Blue Ribbon Grand Jury; achieved record eighty convictions.

Jones, Rev. R. K.: Member of Ministerial Alliance.

Jones, Walter B.: Premiere jurist, president of Alabama Bar Association, appointed Special Circuit Judge by Alabama Supreme Court for cleanup vice trials.

Jowers, Buddy: Phenix city night police chief, nephew of Elmer Reese, shared protection racket with Albert Fuller; partner in Cotton Club with Fanny B. Chance.

Kefauver, Estes: US Senator, investigating 1950 organized crime.

Kelley, Quinnie: Russell County courthouse janitor, a principal witness in Ferrell and Fuller murder trials.

King, Alta: Jefferson County Circuit Judge who ordered investigation into tie between vote fraud in Birmingham & Patterson's murder in special charge to Grand Jury.

LaRue, Harry: owner of cock-fights, apprehended by General Hanna; provided first hard evidence of Albert Fuller's duplicity.

Leebern, Fayette "Fate": Hoyt Shepherd's gambling rival, killed at victory celebration for Elmer Reese in 1946 at Southern Manor night club.

Littleton, Bill: Cab driver charged with 1949 death of Pvt. George Outlaw; a principal witness against Fuller in Patterson murder.

Long, Frank: Head Alabama League of Young Democrats, whose name was used by Attorney General Si Garrett for code.

Luttrell, John: Supported and assisted Hugh Bentley in RBA.

Mancil, John: Killed in shoot-out at 602 Club by Red Cook in 1950.

Matthews, Ralph: Russell County Sheriff, relieved of all duties by General Hanna; indicted by blue Ribbon Grand Jury for "willful neglect of duty."

Matthews, Jimmie: Partner of Hoyt Shepherd.

Mayhall, Roy: Judge during Sub-Committee investigation into Brassell's vote fraud charge in May 1954 primary.

McFall, Ray: Warrant Officer, investigator on General Hanna's staff.

McElroy, J. Russell: Expert on evidence, appointed by Alabama Supreme Court as trial judge for 1955 Fuller and Ferrell murder trials; granted change of venue from Phenix City to Birmingham.

McVeigh, Wilson: Hired by Revel, Davis, and Allred to kill Johnny Frank Stringfellow in 1944. Repudiated confession in 1948; convicted and sentenced to two life sentences for murder of Stringfellow and Dave Walden's wife, Patricia Ann Archer.

Murphy, Lamar: Appointed sheriff of Russell County to replace Ralph Matthews; working with John Patterson, discovered key witness, Cecil Padgett, who replaced murdered Johnny Frank Griffin.

Newton, Reuben: Attorney whose trial Albert Patterson attended in Montgomery on 18 June 1954 when Patterson announced he would testify before Jefferson County Grand Jury.

Outlaw, George: Army private killed by cab driver Bill Littleton in 1949 who was brought to trial by General Hanna in 1954.

Padgett, Cecil: Key witness who gave unshakable evidence in Patterson murder trial discovered by Sheriff Lamar Murphy and John Patterson.

Patterson, Albert Love: Represented Hoyt Shepherd in 1946 at the Leebern trial; elected state senator in 1946, supported bill to recircuit Russell County as 26th District in 1947; represented Head Revel in the Johnny Frank Stringfellow murder trial in 1948. Defeated in race for lieutenant governor in 1950; represented Gloria Floyd Davis in divorce from Godwin Davis' son Bubber in 1950 which established open gambling in Phenix City; joined Hugh Bentley in 1951 Russell Betterment Association as legal adviser; represented unwed mother in 1951 in litigation against Mrs. Alice Floyd charging traffic in human beings; co-counsel in impeachment proceedings against Sheriff Ralph Matthews in 1953; won attorney general elect against Machine candidate Lee Porter in 1954; assassinated 18 June 1954, before taking office.

Patterson, Louise: Albert's wife who testified before Blue Ribbon Grand Jury and was a witness at Fuller and Ferrell murder trial.

Patterson, John: Albert's son and law partner who pursued prosecution of his father's killers; elected attorney general in his place in 1954; elected Governor of Alabama in 1958, erected memorial statue to his father on capitol grounds in Montgomery.

Patton, General George C.: Trained World War II troops at Ft. Benning; publicly threatened to mash Phenix City flat.

Pennington, Howard: Joined Hugh Bentley in RBA, elected RBA president in 1954; campaigned with Albert Patterson in race for attorney general; notified Democratic Executive Committee about vote discrepancy.

Perry, Emmett: Jefferson County Solicitor who brought vote tally change before Jefferson County Grand Jury in Birmingham; sought lunacy hearing for Attorney General Silas Garrett; prosecutor in Ferrell vote fraud trial in 1955.

Persons, Gordon: Governor of Alabama, 1950-1954, petitioned by Hugh Bentley for State assistance in 1950 Minister's War; declared Martial Rule on General Hanna's insistence in 1954.

Porter, Lee: Attorney who lost race for attorney general against Silas Garrett in 1950; Machine candidate who accepted gambler contributions to run against Albert Patterson for attorney general in 1954; charged with perjury in 1955 for lying to grand jury.

Porter, Martha: Lee's wife who testified in Ferrell vote fraud trial.

Prier, Claude: Alabama State Patrolman, worked as investigator on Patterson murder; provided information to General Hanna.

Randall, Harry B.: Russell County Judge for Grady Shepherd's commitment hearing; later charged for signing criminal bond for Albert Fuller.

Ray, Ben: Chairman Democratic Executive Committee, ordered probe into vote fraud in Phenix City and vote change in Birmingham.

Ray, Lee B.: Defense witness for Hoyt Shepherd in 1946 Leebern trial, made bodyguard for Shepherd, served on Spring 1954 Screen Door Grand Jury.

Reid, Lamar: Young attorney persuaded by Attorney General Si Garrett to change 1954 vote totals in Jefferson County; his testimony before Jefferson County Grand Jury brought charges against Garrett and Ferrell.

Revel, C. O. (Head): Arrived in Phenix City during the depression, built gambling empire; charged in 1948 with Godwin Davis for murder of Johnny Frank Stringfellow; operated Metropolitan Lottery at Bridge Grocery with Godwin Davis' brother, George. Fled Phenix City after Patterson's slaying.

Revel, Nora: Head's wife, shot Mabel Yarborough in January 1948.

Reese, Elmer: Phenix City Mayor, Hoyt Shepherd's candidate elected to City Commission in 1946; Machine mayor who succeeded Otis Taff, 1953-1954; charged and arrested for criminal neglect in office during 1954 cleanup, resigned during Martial Rule to avoid prosecution.

Rogers, George: Attorney who represented and won acquittal for Arch Ferrell in vote fraud and murder trial.

Rogers, William Calvert: Paralyzed victim shot by Red Cook in 1950; prosecution witness in 1954 Red Cook murder trial.

Robertson, Anne: *Columbus Ledger* photographer, who photographed Hugh Bentley and Hugh Britton beaten at polls in 1952 (see dust-jacket of this book).

Rosenthal, Albert: Attorney who was Birmingham campaign manager for Albert Patterson and brought vote change fraud to Jefferson County Solicitor Emmett Perry for investigation before Grand Jury.

Roye, Edna: Fate Leebern's young companion on night he was shot at Southern Manor night club, 16 September 1946; prosecution witness at Hoyt Shepherd trial.

Sanders, Leon: Phenix City policeman who warned John Patterson of danger to his father before assassination.

Satterfield, E.E.: Georgia Revenue Agent arrested with Elzie Hancock during 1949 Georgia-Alabama Border War.

Sellers, Tom: *Columbus Ledger's* veteran reporter attacked at polls in 1952 election.

Scroggins, Ben: Alcohol Tax Unit Agent, involved in 1949 shooting of guy Hargett, and who, with Albert Fuller, shot Clarence Franklin Johns thirteen times in cemetery.

Shepherd, Hoyt: Phenix City's kingpin gambler and political boss who arrived penniless in Phenix City during the Depression, schooled in gambling by Clyde Yarborough; charged with 1946 murder of Fate Leebern; engineered Phenix City political Machine and recircuiting Russell County as 26th District.

Shepherd, Grady: Hoyt's younger brother who admitted killing Fate Leebern.

Simms, Leroy: AP bureau chief who received tip on 1954 vote fraud.

Smith, Rev. Roland A.: Militant member of Ministerial Alliance who joined Hugh Bentley in 1950 Minister's War and angered Governor with criticism.

Smith, Roy: Phenix City Attorney who defended Hoyt and Grady Shepherd in 1946, represented Bubber Davis in 1950 divorce trial.

Stewart, Otis: Floor manager at Southern Manor night club who disappeared after 1946 shooting of Fate Leebern.

Strickland, Ed: *Birmingham News* veteran political reporter who with Leroy Sims discovered vote tally change in Birmingham; learned first of Albert Patterson's assassination; covered cleanup from beginning to end.

Stringfellow, Johnny Frank: A soldier used as undercover agent on 1944 Federal liquor case against Godwin Davis, Head Revel, and Joe Allred; killed in 1944 on contract by Wilson McVeigh and Dave Walden; remains discovered in 1948.

Sowell, Dr. W.L.: Performed autopsy on Patterson and testified at trial.

Sykes, Bernard: Assistant Attorney General, appointed by Gov. Persons to replace Att. Gen. Si Garrett, to investigate Patterson murder.

Taff, Otis: Defeated by Elmer Reese in 1946 election for City Commissioner; appointed City Commissioner in 1947 when City commissioners were expanded from three to five members; became mayor in 1953 after death of J.D. Harris; as mayor, declared state of emergency in law enforcement and sanctioned Volunteer Police Force; removed from office when city government reverted back to three members.

Taylor, James Radius: Cab driver who witnessed the suspects running from Patterson murder scene; key witness in Fuller and Ferrell trial.

Tillis, Harley: With cousin Billy Clark, was charged with beating cotton mill worker.

Thornhill, Ralph: Russell County coroner investigated killings of Hargett and Johns.

Unwed Mother: Represented by Albert Patterson, attempting to reclaim child.

Walden, Dave: Hired with Wilson McVeigh in 1944 by Godwin Davis, Head Revel, and Joe Allred to kill Johnny Frank Stringfellow; also killed his wife of one week, Patricia Ann Archer. Convicted, sentenced to two life terms.

Warren, Col. Jack: Chief aide to General Hanna, named Russell County Sheriff under Martial Rule.

Washington, Jerry: Sixteen-year old black man who killed Patterson witness, Johnny Frank Griffin, in November 1954.

White, Rev. J.R.G.: Retired Baptist minister who denounced "gangster circuit" at 1951 town meeting following bombing of Hugh Bentley's house.

White, Bruce: Law partner and brother-in-law of Lamar Reid.

Williamson, Roy: Informant who revealed details on Johnny Frank Stringfellow murder to Muscogee County Sheriff Howell in 1948.

Yarborough, Clyde: Mentor of Hoyt Shepherd who taught him tricks of gambling trade; pocketed evidence used in Fate Leebern trial.

Yarborough, Mabel: Clyde's wife, shot in 1948 by Head Revel's wife, Nora.

Youngblood, Ernest: Vice lord who operated prostitute pickup at Diamond Horseshoe; warned apprehended and arrested in Florida by National Guard Officer Forney Hughes; fined in 1952 for beating Hugh Bentley at polls.

Youngblood, Glen: Brother to Ernest who operated Riverside Cafe where soldiers were rolled and drugged; apprehended and arrested along with his brother by Forney Hughes; brought back to Phenix City for prosecution.

AUTHOR'S NOTES AND RESEARCH

To witness the triumph of good over evil is pure elixir to the human spirit for the restitution of justice long-delayed. Such a story...a true story...is *The Tragedy and the Triumph of Phenix City, Alabama.*

I have had the privilege as an author to write about two carriages of justice: *Murder In Coweta County,* a story of due process achieved against unimaginable odds by an honorable, determined Southern sheriff who believed in even-handed justice. Rich or poor, white or black, there were no exceptions. This story of Coweta County Sheriff Lamar Potts was filmed as a CBS-TV Movie-of-the-Week and received the ninth highest rating for a made-for-TV-movie that year, 1983.

A producer for CBS asked me to find another such story. There were many stories, but none entirely supported by legal documents, which was a requirement. Later, I remembered a story about Albert Patterson, an elected law-enforcement official who was gunned down in the streets of Phenix City, Alabama, before taking office in 1954. I knew little about the story because at that time in 1954, I was living in San Francisco where my husband was stationed at the Presidio.

Starting out for the details of the Phenix City story, I went to my good friend, George T. Smith, who was at that time serving as a Justice on the Georgia Supreme Court. He, of course, knew all the details of the story, and from his office, he called his friend, Richard L. "Red" Jones, a Justice on the Alabama Supreme Court, explained my mission, and solicited his help in locating participants in the year-long search for Albert Patterson's assassins and final solution of the Phenix City story. Through Justice Jones, I met Major General "Crack" Hanna who called in all his staff during the 1954 cleanup and had them tell me their tasks and their stories. Following this, he gave me all his official documents and private papers concerning the clean-up of Phenix City. Then he took me to Montgomery to meet ex-governor John Patterson, the son of the slain attorney general-elect. As with General Hanna, Governor Patterson made his papers available to me and assured me of his approval and full support for the undertaking of this project. He contacted Dr. Ed Bridges, archivist for the Alabama Archives and State History Department, and requested that all material relevant to this case be made available to me. When I arrived, his staff had collected a wire grocery basket full of documents and books concerning the case.

Having contacted most of the participants in the cleanup, I went to Phenix City to find out how the tragedy all began and to talk to the man who was the catalyst and moral leader of this crusade to end violence and restore decency and honest elections to this infamous town. His name was Hugh Bentley.

In the fall of 1983, my son, Dr. David J. Dukes, and I drove to Phenix City to interview Hugh Bentley. The interview lasted for seven and one-half hours. Hugh Bentley was a man with total recall. He remembered *everything* from early childhood to conversations reported here with direct quotes. He not only remembered, he had supporting documents, tagged and dated like courtroom evidence, covering his dining room, living room, study and the walls of his house. Seven and one-half hours later, walking out the door, Hugh Bentley was still talking so we scheduled another interview. For Hugh Bentley, the cleanup of Phenix City had been a life work and a Holy War. He died of a heart attack the following spring, but his son Truman is the archivist of his collection and his documents and holds them as a sacred trust. There are no footnotes or citations on the chapter about Hugh Bentley. I simply told the story that was told to me with total documentation. Any scholar, however, seeking further research on Hugh Bentley should contact Truman Bentley in Phenix City, Alabama. Truman will be glad to oblige.

The Phenix City Story, a book compiled from newspaper columns written by Birminghan reporters Ed Strickland and Gene Wortsman, was another valuable guide for locating dates and sources on previous murders and criminal events in Phenix City.

Beyond personal interviews and private papers, the greatest source of reliable information was found in the *Columbus Ledger* and the *Columbus Enquirer;* the *Birmingham News* and the *Birmingham Post Herald.* "The Phenix City Story", as the press labeled it, was front page, in-depth news for an entire year. Invaluable background stories on previous Phenix City events were run as sidebars in all of these four newspapers. The *Columbus Ledger* along with the Alabama National Guard, under the command of General Walter J."Crack" Hanna, spearheaded the campaign to cleanup Phenix City and bring Albert Patterson's assassins to justice. For their outstanding efforts in pursuing the story and keeping it alive and front-page news for a year, the *Columbus Ledger* was awarded the 1955 Pulitzer Prize.

The last great source of information was the Alabama Archives and State History Department. There will be found the legal documents, the affidavits, and the unsworn testimony of Attorney General Silas Garrett before the Jefferson County Grand Jury, and the trial transcripts. It was from these documents in the testimony that the direct quotations were taken to write the narrative as it happened.

A great many people contributed their time, effort and expertise to the telling of this long-ago brave story. A great many helped in preparing the manuscript for publication. Joe Williams and Jana White's efforts were above and beyond. I am grateful and indebted to them for their contribution to this important story of courage. Courage inspires courage, and these lessons from the past strengthen our purpose today and give us courage for the challenges we now face.

Margaret Anne Barnes
2002

THE MURDERS THAT MADE A DIFFERENCE:

1940: Secretary of War Henry Stimson, after inspecting the Army's classified record of Ft. Benning soldiers who had been beaten, robbed, maimed and murdered, declared: "Phenix City, Alabama is the wickedest city in America."

General George Patton, outraged by the assaults on his soldiers, publicly threatens to take his tanks across the river and mash Phenix City flat.

1944: 21Sept, 1944: Johnny Frank Stringfellow killed by Dave Walden and Johnny McVeigh on $1000 contract for Godwin Davis, Sr. Head Ravel, and Joe Allred. Stringfellow was a witness against these three for a violation of the alcoholic tax law
<> PC/ES p-133 <> Stringfellow's bones found in shallow lime grave ten miles from St. Augustine, Florida in 1948.

1946: 16Sept, 1946: Hoyt Shepherd kills Fayette Leeburn/ hires every lawyer including Albert Patterson, for defense: Roderick Beddow

1948: Johnny Frank Stringfellow discovered. Patterson/ Ravel

1949: 3Mar1949: Albert Fuller kills Guy Hargett. <> PC/ES p-136>
    CE: 10Nov1950

1949: 12Nov1949: Cab driver, Bill Littleton kills Pvt. George Outlaw

1950: 6Aug1950: Red Cook kills John Mancil and paralyzes Wm Rogers

1950: 25Sept1950 Clarence Franklin Johns killed by Fuller and ABC Agent Ben Scroggins in graveyard. Shot 13 times in self-defense. Johns took cash in stickup from Godwin Davis' Manhattan Café. Money never recovered. Caused Davis hatred of Fuller <> PC/ES p-139<>

Phenix City   CHAPTER OUTLINES

Research: following outline/ dates based on reports from:

Columbus Ledger (CE) Columbus Enquirer (CE)
Birmingham News (BN) Birmingham Post Herald (BPH)
The Phenix City Story by Ed Strickland (PC/ES)
Documentation: All dates cited/ xeroxed and on file

Chapter 2: Hugh Bentley (1916/1923)
1912: Minnie Bentley leaves home w/ 7 sons Historical background: 1833
Frontier town
1915: Alabama Prohibition Law: WTCU/ Anti-Saloon League
1916: First Attempted Clean-up/ Hugo Black/ Whiskey Creek
1917: World War I: Homer Cobb/ Patterson/ Hanna
1923: Second Attempted Cleanup/ Officials jailed
1929: Depression/ Boll Weevil/ Shepherd/ Revel arrives
1932: Receivership: Homer Cobb makes deal with gangsters
1938: Lottery: Collapse of Ritz Café kills 24 people
1941: World War II/ Crime increase/ Fort Benning

Chapter 3: Hoyt Shepherd 1944-1946
1. Hoyt Shepherd becomes Kingpin/ Gambling Czar
2. Returning veterans/ Albert Fuller/ Arch Ferrell
3. Loose law enforcement: Ralph Mathews/ Buddy Jowers
4. Hugh Bentley becomes moral leader/ political activist
5. Chicago convention 1946: Bentley returns committed
6. Election Day: 16Sept, 1946: Machine wins
7. Victory celebration for Elmer Reese
8. Bentley threatened/ Leeburn killed

Chapter 4: Fayette Leeburn Murder
1946
Monday: September 16, 1946: Leeburn killed. Grady shepherd arrested
Tuesday: September 17, 1946: Clyde Yarborough turns in knife to Sheriff
Wednesday: September 18, 1946: Pal Daniel locates Hoyt and Jimmie
Mathews
Thursday: September 19, 1946: Grady waives preliminary hearing
Friday: September 20, 1946: Leeburn unaware

Sunday: September 22, 1946: Columbus Ledger Editorial/ Scores Police
Monday: September 23, 1946: Hoyt and Jimmie Mathews arrested
Tuesday: September 24, 1946: Attys ask preliminary hearing/ Hoyt and
Jimmie
Wednesday: September 25, 1946: 23 witnesses to testify
Thursday: September 26, 1946: State not ready/ Free on $7500 bond
Friday: September 27, 946: Permit to exhume Leeburn
Sunday: September 29, 1946: Leeburn case goes to Grand Jury Monday
Monday: September 30,1946: Judge warns jurors against threats
Tuesday: October 1, 1946: Grand jury indicts Hoyt and Grady
Friday: October 4,1946: Hoyt and Grady arraigned/ severance granted
Sunday: October 6, 1946: Shepherds face trial on Tuesday
Monday: October 7, 1946: Selection of the jury
Tuesday: October 8, 1946: Severance/ Hoyt pleads not guilty
Wednesday: October 9, 1946: Witnesses: Jeanette Mercer/ Clyde
Yarborough
Thursday: October 10, 1946: Defense and prosecution summations
Friday: October 11, 1946: Jury acquits Hoyt
Sunday: October 13, 1946: Grady's trial is set for November 11, 1946

November 11, 1946: Trial continued until March 1947. Missing witnesses.
Case dead docketed.

Chapter 5: Johnny Frank Stringfellow Murder

1948: April: Johnny Frank Stringfellow murder discovered. Patterson
fights extradition of head Revel Florida.
>References: BN: 14Nov54 Es: wrap-up
>*CL: 18Sep54: Tom Sellers*
>ES/ PC: p-133-136: confession: p-133
>CL: 9April48: Davis arrested
>CL: 11April48: Revel/ Allred: murder charge
>CL: 19April48: Grand jury indicts revel/ Davis/ Allred

- Tom Sellers' story is essentially the same as Ed Strickland's
14Nov54 story except that Sellers says on p-12 pgr # 3 that
Stringfellow's role as informant was discovered when a letter he
had addressed to US Treasury agents fell out of his pocket and
into the hands of a Phenix City hoodlum. This explains how
Davis, Revel and Allred knew whom to contract for. They likely

also had information that Stringfellow was a friend of McVeigh's.

12Oct44: Trial set for Godwin Davis; head Revel, Joe Allred Liquor conspiracy postponed. Government witnesses Johnny Frank Stringdellow missing.

21Sept44: Johnny Frank Stringfellow killed by Dave Walden and Wilson McVeigh. Contracted by Davis, Revel, and Allred for $1000.

30Jan48: Nora Revel shoots Mabel Yarbrough CL: 30Jan48

March 48: Tennessee convict Roy Williamson tells Columbus friend who reports killing to Columbus authorities. Walden and McVeigh apprehended, arrested, confess, lead police to grave. Confess killing Walden's wife, Patricia Ann Archer at same time, burying her in Okefenokee Swamp. Swamp dragged, body not found.

8April48: Godwin Davis, Homer Blakely arrested on murder warrant by GBI agent Elzie Hancock in Hamilton, Georgia. Jailed in Ben Hill County jail in Fitzgerald.

11April48: Head Revel, Joe Allred charged with murder.

12April48: Ben Hill Grand Jury indicts Davis, Revel, and Allred for murder.

18April48: Revel and Allred surrender to Russell County authorities, post $5,000 surety bond each, pending extradition proceedings.

19April48: Chief Deputy Sheriff Albert Fuller says Revel and Allred will fight extradition. Albert Patterson hired to fight Revel's extradition charges. Loses.

29Jan49: McVeigh conviceted/guilty w/mercy. Appeals to Sup Ct.

12May49: Judgment confirmed/ All justices concur.

Chapter 6: Albert Fuller: 1949/1950

1949: 3Mar49:Albert Fuller kills Guy Hargett. PC/ES p-136
CE:10Nov54 (exhumed by Gen Hanna)

1949: Cab Driver Bill Littleton kills Soldier Pvt. George Outlaw.
CL:25Oct54 (extradited from Georgia by Gen Hanna)

1950: Red Cook kills John Mancil/ Paralyzes Wm. Calvert Rogers BN: 3Aug54: Arrested by Gen Hanna.

1950: 25Sept, 1950: Clarence Franklin Johns killed by Fuller and ABC Agent Ben Scroggins in the graveyard. Shot 13 times in self- defense. Johns took cash in stick-up from Godwin Davis' Manhattan Café.

Money never recovered. This caused Davis hatred of Fuller. <> PC/ ES p-139<> BN: November 10,54: (exhumed by Gen Hanna)

1949:

29Jan, 1949: McVeigh by Ben Hill jury/ Appeals Super Ct
24Feb, 1949: A/J: Ga. Revenue Agents (Hancock) arrested by Pc
28Feb, 1949: Albert Fuller kills Guy Hargett CL: March 4, 1949 <Also:
    BN * 20Oct, 1954: p-29 c-7 case reopened
    BPH: * 10,Nov 1954: p-1 Bullets removed
    *BN: 10,Nov 1954; p-3: Bodies exhumed
12May, 1949: Ala Supreme Court Affirms Mcveighs Judgment
1949: John Patterson joins father's law firm
1949: Buddy Jowers made night police chief
6July49: Ferrell made depart commander of American Legion
12Nov49: Bill Littleton kills Pvt. George Outlaw
        See BN: October 25, 54: p-7 c-5/8
        Includes: Sykes appoints Borders to replace Ferrell
2Dec49: Minnie Bentley dies

1950

9Jan50: Revel: Manhattan Heist with Clarence F. Johns
6May50: Patterson defeated for Lt. Gov. by James Allan <BN: June 19,
    54>
< SatEvePost: October 20, 50 p-29>
6Aug50: Red Cock kills John Mancil
8Aug50: Carlton Johnson named city Editor of CL
24Aug50: Mayor Homer Cobb dies of heart attack

Chapter 7: Gloria Floyd Davis

Sept50: Political struggle: Roy Greene beats Bentley 2-1
2Sept50: Fuller kills Clarence Franklin Johns BN: October 2, 54 p-29
September50: Ferrell resigns Am Legion to seek re-election
20Oct50: Gloria Floyd Davis divorce trial begins
31Oct50: Patterson motion for IRS and balance sheets
3Nov50: Rackets revealed/ Revel testifies
6Nov50: CL: Ferrell promises arrests/ citizen request Kafauver
6Nov50: Roy Smith motion to annul Davis marriage

13Nov50: Revel/4 Davises fined $500 gambling
--Judge Hicks grants annulment/ Patterson appeals SupCt

Chapter 8: Ministers' War On Rackets/ RBA

1Mar51: Supreme Court Reverses Hicks decision
26April51:Rehearing denied
<>PC/ES: Bentley organization/ fear church surrender to rackets
1May51: CL: Clergymen call State Investigation a Farce
2May51: CL: Ministers discover 48 slots in Ala Revenue records DCP: P-39
6May51:AJ: Bill Diehl: Ministers ask Gov/ State investigation. Rackets
    alerted/sell soft drinks. Gov's investigator reports "one isolated case"
    Rev. Ronald Smith calls investigation "Farce." Calls on local
    Government
7May51: CL: meeting on PC Taxes/ Hugh Bentley/ Rev. Roland Smith
8May51: CL: Petition Against Taxes
9May51: CL: Gov Persons Pledges Clean-up: " My own way"
10May51: CL: Bentley Criticism Angers Grand Jury
14May51 CL: Ministers Renew pledge to clean-up PC
15May51: CL: ministers invite PC Commission to Church Services
29May51: CL: Ministers Harris Wants Goodwill tour of City
May51: PC/Es: JC/C survey: 80% graduating class "Bug"
6June51: US C/C awards PC JC/C award on church work
8Sept51: CL: Ministers petition Sheriff Mathews/ stop gambling DCP P-
    240: Ministers warned
21Oct51: Ministers appear before RC Grand Jury PC/ ES P-188
25Oct51: RBA formed DCP P-45
31Oct51: CL: Bentley Heads Anti-Vice
1Nov51: Federal Stamp for gambling/ ES/PC: P-56/ DCP P-46
ES:P-211: Shepherd offers Bentley deal P-77: Kefauver/Stamps

1952

9Jan52: House bombed 12:22 a.m. (DP/C: P-47)

Chapter 9: Bombing/ Beatiing/ Burning

9Jan52: Gov. Persons inspects. "No Stone." (DP/C P-48) Garrett/
    Daniel/ Mathews inspect (CL: 9Jan52)

<>No dates: Russell Betterment Auxiliary formed. 15 women. Bernice Britton, president. Hilda Coulter.

23Jan52: Ferrell dares RBA to impeach/ sister slaps (BN)

25Jan52: Rumor machine accesses Bentley of bombing his own house. (CL: 25Jan52)

24Feb52: Arsonist sets Patterson's office afire (CL: 25Feb52)

14Mar52: Reporter Tom Sellers Accompanies Hilda Coulter and auxiliary members demanding honest election to J.D. Harris' office/ also Chairmen Dem. Exec. Com. CL: 14Mar52 (Also DP/ C P-57)

6May52: Election Day: Bentley/ HughBo/ Britton beaten at polls

CL: 6May52: Sellers/ Jenkins/Anne Robertson (Photo)

(See also: DP/C P-60-61)

1Jul52: RBA represented by Ala. Speaker of the house Roberts Brown (Opelika) files impeachment of sheriff Mathews (CL: 1Jul52, See Also: DP/C: P-64)

23Oct52: Roberts Brown (Opelika) house burned. $12,000 damage

CL: 31Oct52 (See Also: DP/C: P-65) Chief of Opelika Police Floyd Mann sees connection.

<> 21Dec52: BN: P-2 C-5: Fred Taylor: Gen. Hanna possible candidate for Governor/ spurred by Eisenhower/ Warrior Generals<>

Chapter 10: Rise Of Albert Fuller/ Volunteer Police Force

April53: Mayor J.D. Harris dies. Taff named mayor pro-tem

28April53: Taff declares: "State of Emergency" <>see DPC<> Organizes 25-member

Volunteer Police Force Taff clean-up opposed by Reese and A.L. Gullatt <>See BN: July 4,54 A-2 and A-3 ES<>

7May53: Jabe Brassell/ Ben Cole introduce bill (general legislation/ no advertisement) to revert from 5 to 3 members/ City Commission CL: 7May53 (DP/C: P-70)

<>Brassel injunction to stop Taff's Gestapo brought by Mrs. H.E. Fuller. Judge Hicks grants injunction. <> See: BN July 4,54 A-02 ES<>

8June53: Trial of Sheriff Mathews before Ala. Supreme Court. CL: 8June53 (also DP/C P-66): Ft. Benning Investigator: Gambling/26 places

Howard Pennington: school children and gambling

Mathews: "No open gambling/his term or before"

40 character witnesses/ including Garrett.

13June53: Supreme Court unanimously acquits Mathews. Acknowledges "unsavory reputation of P/C." CL: 15June53 (also: DP/C P-6)

11Aug53: Circuit Judge Hicks rules 5-man City Commission unconstitutionally devised in 1947. Taff and Leonard Coulter lose seats. A.L. Gullatt and Elmer Reese remain. Dr. Seth Floyd added as third member.
Sept53: Elmer Reese elected Mayor of Phenix City

1954

Chronological Outline For Chapters 11-13:
Feb54: Gen Hanna dedicates Phenix City Armory
April54: "Screen Door" Grand Jury   < find date/ report>
4May54: Primary Election: Vote Frauds charged
15May54: Brassell/Cole file vote fraud charges.
1June54: Runoff Election: Patterson by 854 votes
3June54: Hearing before 3-man Subcommittee in Russell adjourns as judge Hicks issues
Writ of Prohibition
4June54: Garrett persuades Lamar Reid
6June54: Birmingham News discovers vote tally alteration
10June54: Patterson confirmed winner in state canvas
11June54: Alabama Supreme Court reverses Prohibition Writ
14June54: PC Hearings resume. 4 days testimony/ 35 witnesses
17June54: Hearings adjourn. Prior subcommittee commitments.
18June54:Garrett testifies before Jeff/ Co Grand Jury
Patterson: to testify and tell all.
    9 p.m: Patterson killed in Phenix City

Chronological Outlines For Chapters 14-25:

June 1954:

*18June54: Patterson killed/ Gov sends Gen Hanna
* 19June54: Gov Inspects: Delivers Ultimatum
+   Gen Hanna Orders Gambling stopped
+   65 Guardsmen Arrive to Patrol: NGR
+   Guard Helicopter/ L-19 Patrol County: NGR
+   Benning CG Orders PC "Off-Limits"
*20June54: Garrett Arrives PC "to take charge"
Will Not Replace Ferrell: "Best Solicitor"
Routes Shepherd/ Mathews 5 a.m.
Takes Ferrell's .38 BN: 3July54

* 21June54: Judge Alta King: Special Charge to J/C G/J:
Possible tie: Vote Fraud/ Murder BN: P-1 C-6
+ Guard Arrests Red Cook on Gambling: $40,000 Eq.
* 22June54: John Patterson: "Most Likely Suspects"
+ Guard Raids: Police Ineffective/ No Suspects
+ Gen Hanna to Montgomery: BN: 23June54: P-3
* 23June54: Garrett testifies 10 _ hours. Leaves State.
+ Ferrell issues prepared statement: CE P-2

* 24June54 Gov. appoints Bernard Sykes to replace Garrett.

* 25June54: Arch Ferrell removed from office.
+ Judge Jones replaces RC Judge Hicks
+ No Leads-Sykes Appeals for Information
*26June54: John Patterson files for Atty Gen
+ Guard seizes gambling eq. /fills jail yard

* 27June54: John Has Father's Records: CE: P-1: C/ Johnson

*28June54: Sub-Com resumes 4May Primary Vote Fraud PC

* 29June54: Family Says Si Very Sick Mentally CE: P-8 C-4
        BPH: Garrett's Father/ Doctor Report
+   Lee Porter 3 Hrs before J/C G/J

*30June54: Garrett, Ferrell, Reid indicted by J/C G/J:
Vote Fraud. Reid/ Ferrell Arrested.
+ Judge Jones arrives PC to empanel Blue Ribbon Grand Jury   <>
  check this date<>

July 1954:

*1July54: Buddy Jowers fired by Civil Serivice: Vote Buying

CSC vote 2 to 1: Mayor Reese Dissenting CL:P-1

+ MacDonald Gallion appointed Special Counsel for Governor.
* 2July54: George Johnson named Special Prospector.
+ Godwin Davis, Sr: $60,000 tax lien

*July 3,54: Hugh Bentley receives first wiretaps.

* 4July54: Albert Fuller injured "on fall from horse."

* 5July54: Ferrell relieved of all duties.
*6July54: Russell country Jury Commission Resigns.
+   C.W. Franklin charged with gambling equipment..
*8July54: RBA receives 200 wiretaps.
*9July54: Ferrell quizzed 10 hours by Sykes.
*10July54: MacDonald Gallion's wife threatened.
*11July54: <> Gen Hanna Demands Gov Declare Martial Law
* 12July54: Garrett returns from Texas. Posts Bond. Emmett Perry files
    lunacy charges.
* 13July54: Judge Jones makes Sykes custodian of records.
* 14July54: Garrett breaks neck in auto collision.
* 15July54: Gov Persons before Jefferson County Grand Jury three hours.
    Demands Martial Law.
* 16July54: Sub committee says void Russell County elections. 8 days
    testimony:
800 pages.
  + 31July54 set to nominate candidates by Dem. Com.

* 17July54: Sykes replaces Joe Smelley as Chief Investigator.
* 18July54: 800 all-night prayer meeting/ Phenix City.
* 19July54: Judge Jones draws 50 venire men.
* 21July54: Judge Jones empanels Blue Ribbon Grand Jury.
      +   Recesses til 9August54: NO EVIDENCE
* 22July54: Governor Declares Martial Rule: Gen Hanna takes charge:
    Strips Sheriff and Police Chief.
* 24July54: Gen Hanna leads round-the-clock raids.
* 25July54: 50 Jailed over weekend.
* 26July54: Godwin Davis jailed after release from Harris Co.
*27July54: Fuller questioned 3 hours in hospital.
* 29July54: Pal Daniel tells "lay-off" orders.
* 29July54: Conrad Fowler added as R/C Solicitor.
* 30July54: Guard raids Mayor Reese's house.
* 31July54: 3 a.m.: Reese arrested in Birmingham Hotel.
  + Dem. Ex. Com. meets at Redmont: B'ham
  + Voids Ferrell/ Mathews nomination
  + Ferrell protests

August 1954:

    * 1Aug54: Report of Jowers Warning Gamblers
    * 2Aug54: Fuller arrested: 6 counts/violating election laws.

+ Godwin Davis released from RC jail
* 3Aug54: Godwin Davis testifies before Jefferson County Grand Jury. Discloses $22,000 gift: Porter
+ Gen Hanna arrests Red Cook: Lottery: Old Barbecue.
* 4Aug54: Ferrell arrested DUI: Guard interrogates: Ray Acton
+ Final Report: Jeff Co Grand Jury: Ferrell directed/ Mob financed Porter.
+ Cook charged with murder of John Mancil
    *5Aug54: Gen Hanna: Guard Raids Pile Up Evidence
    + Safe Cracker to break safe.
    + Arrests: Ernest Youngblood/ C.W. Franklin.
    * 5Aug,4: BN: P-27: "Gen Hanna Inspires Men with Crusading Spirit"
    * 6Aug54: 2500 subpoenas.
    * 7Aug54: Guard Raids Shepherd/ Mathews Houses: Warren/ Brown
Reese offers to resign.

* 9Aug54: Russell County Grand Jury Convenes: Judge Jones: Harvest of Hell: 18 witnesses.
+ Mrs. Bell takes overdose. File photo.
*10Aug54: Hilda Coulter accuses Fuller
+ Red Cock victim (Wm. Calvert Rogers) Testifies.
+ FBI enters case on civil rights-jail cook.
*11Aug54: George Davis arrested: 53 counts: lottery
* 12Aug54: Turning point: Billy Clark arrested. Probation revoked. Prostitution racket. BN: P-12 C-1 Also: 13Aug54: BN : P-1 C-2/3 Clancy Lake.
*13Aug54: Gen Hanna Predicts vice empire end 10 days.
+ Mother scolds for profanity.
* 14Aug54: Billy Clark's probation officer investigated.
* 15Aug54: Guard quizzes B-girls
* 16Aug54: Evidence draws in FBI/ Narcotics Tax<>
* 17Aug54: Rolling Soldiers/ Mad Dog Dope: BN: P-8
+ Gen Hanna inspects Summer Encampment
*17Aug54: Guard sets trap: B-girl Ring
* 18Aug54: Earlene Harper arrested <> Check Date<>
* 18Aug54: BN: P-2 C-6: Billy Clark first break in B-Girl
* 19Aug54: Grand Jury recesses for solicitors to catch up
*20Aug54: Mystery witness before RC/GJ <Shelia Ann Harper>
*21Aug54: Kinnards arrested: Violating Mann Act

* 22Aug54: Rudene Smith/ son arrested: enticing females
* 23Aug54: Sheriff Mathews resigns/ Hanna recommends Murphy<>
* 24Aug54: Blue Ribbon Café: Frank Gullatt: Tattoos
*25Aug54: Billy Graham to come to Phenix City
* 26Aug54: Mrs.Malinoski admits abortion ring
+ Fanny Belle Testifies before RC/GJ
* 27Aug54: Buddy Jowers leaves town
 + Factory for marked cards/loaded dice
    *28Aug54:   CL: P-1: Guard Links Queen of Hearts/Jowers
       +   Gov. Persons Approves Billy Graham visits
   * 29Aug54:   Gen Hanna Disapproves Billy Graham visit
       +   CL: P-C3: Col. Warren bio/ feature.
   * 30Aug54:   Blue Ribbon Grand Jury: 545 True Bills against 59.

   * 31Aug54:   Guard makes record 204 arrests in August

SEPTEMBER 54: ARRESTS AND ROUND-UPS:

   * 1Aug54:   Gen Hanna has 34 in custody/including Ma Beechie
   * 2Sept54:   Shepherd and Matthews jailed on 4 counts
   * 2Sept54:   Fuller arrested taken to jail on chair
* 3Sept54: Grand Jury indicts Reese and Sheriff Matthews for "willful neglect of duties"
*Fuller (in Hospital) indicted for taking bribe.
*Frank Gullatt indicted/gambling equipment
*4Sept54: Red Cook released on $32,500 bond/ 45 signatures
Guard arrests 47 of those indicted 30Aug54.
* 5Sept54:   George Davis released on $ 27,500: 55 lottery
* 6Sept54: Mrs. Malinoski first on trial in Opelika
+ Fuller refused bond. "Held for Investigation"
* 7Sept54: Mrs.Malinoski convicted/ 30 mos. jail $2001 fine
* 9Sept54: Gen Hanna flies in Army medics to examine Fuller
* 10Sept54: Gen Hanna: Fuller: 2 back fractures/vertebrae
* 11Sept54: Fuller makes bond. Guards removed.
* 11Sept54: Attys lose: Garrett Sanity Hearing Set 1Oct54
* 11Sept54: Judge Jones to announce Vice Trials date
   * 12Sept54:   Dragnet for Revel and Buddy Jowers <> June
   * 13Sept54:   Judge Jones: Special Criminal Court: 4Oct54
   * 13Sept54:   Ben Cole jailed: 5 warrants
 + Russell Court's longest session –123 cases

*13Sept54: Col Warren speaks to Ministerial Alliance
*15Sept54: Gen Hanna Takes Ministerial Tour: Eyes Opened
* 17Sept54: Sykes orders Reese: Election list for city commission primary
20Sept54
+ Garrett lawyers to ask Supreme Ct to quash lunacy
*18Sept54: Dave Walden/ Johnny McVeigh willing to testify
*19Sept54: Grand Jury to return to Eye Vote Fraud
* 20Sept54: 500 subpoenas returned
* 20Sept54: Ben Scroggins jailed for beating Negro
*20Sept54: National Guard guards city election
*27Sept54: Grand Jury Hears Girl Trade Testimony
+ Supreme Court upholds Garrett's vote Fraud
+ Judge Wheeler ordered to show cause: lunacy
* 29Sept4: Grand Jury unexpectedly recesses: 6Oct54
+Murder theories: Clarke Stallworth; BN: C-3 bf
 +Harden arrested for intimidation
* 30Sept54:   Gen Hanna's remarks to postpone Red Cook
 +Gwinn's move to void indictments
Check date: Judge Hicks issues Writ of Prohibition

Chapter 19: Roundup And Arrests

    *1Oct54:   Beddow seeks secret RBA files
    *1Oct54:   Gen Hanna: Surprise 3-hour raid on Fuller
              + Explosive papers: Fuller collapses
    *3Oct54:   Defense plans to quash 559 indictments
    *4Oct54:   Judge Jones throws out 119 objections
+ Hicks issues Writ of Mandamus: empty jury box
    *5Oct54   Red Cook Trial begins
    * 6Oct54: Battle before High Court: Sykes asks Writ of Prohibition to
    prevent Hicks hearing/ Rare night session of Supreme Court
+ Red Cook convicted 10:40 p.m.: Life
    *7Oct54:   High Court Rule Nisi: Hicks/cease and desist.
    *8Oct54:   Fuller served 10 Warrants: bribery
    * 9Oct54:   Beddow's bid to tie up court: 7000 subpoenas
    *10Oct54:   Argument to attack legality of PC Jury
+ National Guard: PC payoffs/satchel men
    * 11Oct54:   Judge Jones denies Venue/ Rebukes Beddow
    * 12Oct54:   Harden pleads guilty: 9 months/ $300 fine
    * 13Oct54:   Judge Wheeler responds to Garrett lunacy

* 14Oct54:   Beddow and Gwin apologize
* Shepherd and Matthews plead guilty
* Johnny Benefield trial: burglary
* List of guilty pleas
    * 15Oct54:   Grand Jury Recesses til 1Nov54 to allow time
    * 17Oct54:   Fuller Becoming Central Character BN-B-2 Sparrow
    * 19Oct54:   Gen Hanna: Shooting of Clarence Franklin Johns
    * 25Oct54:   Bill Littleton extradited from Georgia
    * 26-31Oct54: Transfer from 1Oct54 file

November 1954:

CL:	* 1Nov54:	Sykes given Ultimatum
CL:	* 2Nov54:	Sykes Denies Ultimatum
BN:	* 3Nov54:	Ferrell/Randall jailed
BN:	* 4Nov54:	Davis wants to deal
BN:	* 5Nov54:	Grand Jury Probes $30,000 vote steal <> Jeff Co?
BPH:	*6Nov54:	Shepherd ordered to talk
CL:	* 7Nov54:	Illegal arrest: Littleton
CL:	* 9Nov54:	Guard Exhumes Hargett-also BN
BN:	*10Nov54:	Johns exhumed/Gen Hanna
CL:	*11Nov54:	3rd Exhumation/ Gen Hanna
BPH:	*11Nov54:	Youngbloods/ McVeigh arrested/ Florida
BPH:	*12Nov54:	PC Grand Jury Recommends: Impeach Reese
CL:	*12Nov54:	Guard Ejects New: to arrest Hanna
BN:	*14Nov54:	Cons May Break Stringfellow Murder
BN:	*15Nov54:	Fuller to Stand Trial: Bribery
BPH:	*16Nov54:	Fuller Bribes/Benefield sentence <CL>
BN:	*16Nov54:	Vice Girls saw Bribes/ Fuller Flat on Back
BN/CL:	*17Nov54:	Fuller Convicted/ Bribery: 7 years <BPH>
BN:	*17Nov54:	117 Reasons: Davis
BPH:	*18Nov54:	Davis Jr. Delays Trials
BPH:	*19Nov54:	State Moves to Impeach Reese
BPH:	* 20Nov54:	Davis Jr. Guilty
CL:	*27Nov54:	23rd Week Since Murder
BPH:	* 27Nov54:	McMurdo And House Return B'ham
BPH:	*30Nov54:	1st Murder testimony/25 G/J Witnesses
BN:	*30Nov54:	Cook/ Clark Guilty/ Queen of Hearts
BN:	*30Nov54:	Shepherd/ Matthews go to prison Photo:C.W.
Franklin		

December 1954:
BN: * 1Dec54:   Ben Cole Guilty
Aaron Smith Not Guilty
Si Garrett Sanity Test Ordered
BN: *2Dec54:   George Davis sentenced 18 months
BN: *2Dec54:   Reese Resigns
BN: *3Dec54:   Judge Jones:Ala. Bar to file disbarment: for
   Reid/ Ferrell/   Garrett
BN: *3Dec54:   Johnny Frank Griffin Slain 2Dec54
BPH: *4Dec54:   Patterson witness slain
Evidence to convict Patterson killer
Patterson calls for Immediate Arrests
BN: *5Dec54:   E/S: Slaying Won't Ruin Case
BN: *6Dec54:   Ferrell/Fuller Plead Guilty in P/C vote Fraud/
   Fined $200/$250
BN: *7Dec54:   State to Tie Conspiracy to Patterson Davis Jr.
   Jury Deadlocked
BPH: *8Dec54:   James Wilson McVeigh (Hilltop House) 1st
   bawrdy house operator convicted
BPH: *9Dec54:   Gov. Persons has heart attack
BPH: *9Dec54:   Racket Kingdom Falls: Sheriff Matthews pleads
   guilty
Davis Sr. and Jr.: $2500 fine each
SR: 2 yrs hard labor/ Jr: 1 yr. hard labor
CE: *9Dec54:   Grand Jury Indicts Ferrell/ Fuller
BN: *10Dec54:   Ferrell Denies Guilt
                  Third Party to be Arrested
                  Shots That Snuffed Out Patterson's life
BPH: *10Dec54:   Ferrell/Fuller Charged on 9Dec54
                  Grand Jury Time Table
                  Sykes Steady Plugger
                  P-2: Vice Empire Falls
* Ferrell's Big Break
* Fuller's Gold-Plated Gun
BPH: * 11Dec54:   No Bond Sought/Ferrell in Jail
CE: *11Dec54:   Special Grand Jury Dismissed: 25 Weeks
BN: *12Dec54:   Biggest Dry Cleaning Job: Gen Hanna
AJ:*12Dec54:   749 Indictments Against 152/ GJ:54 Days
BN: *13Dec54:   Fugitive warrant for Garrett
BPH: *13Dec54:   Arrest of Garrett/ Guard plane

BPH:	* 14Dec54:	Garrett to Fight Extradition
BN:	*14Dec54:	Fuller Moved to Kilby: Gen Hanna
BN:	*15Dec54:	Porter Indicted/ Arrested: Perjury
BN:	*16Dec54:	High Court Ends Garrett Lunacy
BPH:	* 17Dec54:	Ferrell Free on Bond: $ 12,500
BPH:	*18Dec54:	Fuller Released on $12,500 Bond
CE:	*19Dec54:	Fuller Denies Life Threats
BN:	* 22Dec54:	Dr. Seth Floyd Arrested: Baby Sales
CE:	*23Dec54:	Dr. Floyd/Wife Arrested: Baby Sales
BPH:	*23Dec54;	Judge McElroy to Hear Murder Trials
CE:	*27Dec54:	Geo Johnson: 80 convictions
	*Benefield Quizzed	
BN:	*28Dec54:	Ferrell/ Fuller Trials Set 14Feb55
CE:	* 28Dec54:	First Hearing set 31Jan55
BPH:	* 31Dec54:	Ferrell Vote Fraud 7Feb55: Amid Disputes
BN:	* 31Dec54:	Garrett May Play Big Role
CE:	* 31Dec54:	Gen Hanna Decorates National Guard

1955:   TRIALS:

14Feb55:   Albert Fuller: Murder
 8Mar55:   Arch Ferrell: Vote Fraud: Jefferson County
18April55:   Arch Ferrell: Murder

Reference For Trials 1955

All Reports From *Columbus Ledger*[1]

Albert Fuller: For Murder:

Columbus Ledger-	February 1955
Sun 13 Feb55:	State Granted Right of Witness
P-1 C-4	Secrecy

Mon NF 14Feb55:	Local Cab Driver Sought As Missing Key Witness (Taylor)
P-1 C-6	
Cont: P-2 C-5	"Trial"

Tues NF: 15Feb55:	Albert Fuller Will Be Tried First
P-1 C-7-8	Selection of Jury Near Wind-up
cont. P-11 C-3-4-5	"Trials"

Wed NF: 16Feb55:	Patterson Widow Relates Tragedy At (Formal Opening) of Fuller Trial
P-1 C-1-2-3	
Cont. P-2 C-3	"Trial"

Thurs NF: 17Feb55	Witness Saw Man Flee From Murder Scene
P-1 C-5-6,	
Cont: P-8 C-1-8,	"Trial"
P-9 C-1-8	"Trial"

Fri NF: 18Feb55	Fatal Revolver Slug Fired Inch
P-1 C-6-7-8	From Patterson's Mouth
Cont:	

Sat NF: 19Feb55	Witness Says He Saw Fuller Near Scene of Slaying After Shots
P-1 C-1-2	
Cont:	

---

[1] Key: NF= Night Final/ bf= Below Fold.

Sun. CE/CL: 20Feb55:   Taylor Says Fuller Dashed to Bushes
P-1 C-4-5   'Minute' After Shot

Mon NF: 21Feb55:   Cabbie Says 3 Tires Ripped After He Put
P-1 C-1-2   fingeron Ex-Deputy
Cont: P-21 C-3-4-5-6   "Trial"

Tues CL: 22Feb55:   Witness Says Fuller Wore No Gun

Wed NF: 23Feb55   Witness Tells of Car Speeding
P-1 C-7-8   Toward Jail Shortly After Killing
Cont: P-9 C1-4   Trials?<> Ray Jenkins Wrap-up   P-16-
17-18   Testimony of 9th Day

Thurs NF: 24Feb55   Janitor Says Ferrell Fled Alley
P-1 C-7-8   Seconds After Shots (Quinnie
Cont. P-11 C-3-4   Kelly) <> Trial? <> Testimony
P-20-21-22-30   (Quinnie Kelly/ Padgett)

Fri NF 25Feb55:   Witness Puts Fuller-Ferrell/Patterson
P-1 C-7-8   Together in Alleyway
Cont P-2 C-5-6   "Trial"
P-1 C-7   Beddow Admits Witness a Surprise
P-9-10-11   Testimony: Quinnie Kelly/Padgett

Sat NF: 26Feb55   State Concludes After Wife Supports
P-1 C-5-6   Padgett Testimony
Cont P-5   "Testimony"

Sun CE/CL: 27Feb55:   Fuller Battery Visits Phenix City To
P-1 C-7   Stage Defense
Cont A-2 C-1-8   "Defense"

Mon CL. <?> 28Feb55   Nine Convicts Called to Testify For
P-1 C-4   Fuller
Cont. P-10   "Fuller"

Columbus Ledger   March 1955

Tues NF: 1Mar55   Defense Aims Attack at Padgett
P-1 C-7-8   Testimony: Hits Cabbies' Stories
Cont. P-2 C-7-8   "Trial"

P-11 C-1-2-3-4-5-6	Trial Testimony
Wed NF: 2Mar55:	Padgett Cracks Up Under Heavy Grilling/
P-1 C-7-8	Weeps Leaves Witness Stand
Cont: P	Trial Testimony
FERRELL:	
NF: 2Mar55	Judge Denies Delay for Ferrell
P-1 C-1-2	Vote Fraud Trial/Set 7Mar55
Thurs NF: 3Mar55	Alibi Witness Places Fuller Within
P-1 C-7-8	Jail at time of Shooting (Phillips)
Cont: P-12 C-3-4	"Trials"
P-20 C-1-8	Today's Testimony
P-38 C-1-8	Trial Testimony
P-41 C-5-6	Trial Testimony
P-44 C-1-5	Trial Testimony
FERRELL:	Judge Denies Delay in Vote Fraud
NF: 3Mar55	
P-1 C-5-6 bf	
Fri NF: 4Mar55	Mistrial Motion Filed AS Case Nears
P-1 C-7-8	Close: Hint Mystery Witness
Cont: P-2 C-2-3	"Trial"
P-16 C-18	Today's Testimony
P-17 C-1-8	Trial Testimony
P-18 C-1-8	Yesterday's Testimony
P-18 C-3-4 bf	Padgett Once Fired Witness Who Testifies
	on Bad Name
Sat NF: 5Mar55	Fuller Tells Court He Can't
P-1 C-7-8	Remember Bribery Conviction
Cont: P-3 C-1-8	"Fuller Tells His Story"
P-1 C-5-6 bf	Atmosphere Tense as Fuller Testifies
P-5 C-1-8	Ex-Sheriff Matthews Backs Fuller
Cont: P-10 C-1-2-3	Trial Testimony
Sun CE/CL 6Mar55:	Fuller Denies Slaying; Falters on Three
P-1 C-4	Points
Cont: A-2 C-3-4-5	

P-1 C-3-4-5   Jury Will Soon Deliberate Conflicting Trial
                                Testimony
Section C: Fuller On Stand in Own Defense
P-8-9-10 C-1-8-   (Repeat of Sat 5Mar55 testimony)
Section D: Witnesses Tranton And East Rebuttal for
P-6 C-3-4   State

Mon NF: 7Mar55   Defense Witness Says He Wouldn't Believe
P-1 C-7-8   Fuller Under Oath
Cont P-10 C-6-7   "Trial"
P-8 C-1-6   Trial of Fuller Nears End

FERRELL: Last Try Fails to Delay Trial
NF: 7Mar55:   (For Ferrell)
P-1 C-3-4   "Ferrell"
Cont P-10 C-5

Tues NF: 8Mar55   Witness Blasts Hole in Phillips Testimony/
P-1 C-7-8   State Rests Rebuttal
Cont P-2 C-4-5   "Fuller"
P-10 C-3-8   Testimony:
P-11 C-1-8   Mrs.Oakley (Rebutts Phillips)
P-16 C-1-5   Hilda Coulter (clerk of jury com)
P-17 C-1-8   Pennington
P-19 C- 1-8   McMurdo
P-20 C-1-2

FERRELL: Defense Objections Slow Ferrell
NF: Mar8,55:   Vote Fraud Case
P-1 C-1-2-3-4 bf   "Tally"
Cont: P-2 C-5

Wed NF: 9Mar55:   State Starts Closing Arguments
P-1 C-7-8   As Defense Winds Up Testimony
Cont: P-2 C-1-2-3-4   "Fuller"
P-10 C-1-8   Patrolman First Defense Witness
P-11 C-1-6   Trial Testimony
P-12 <?>   Character Witnesses
P-17 C-1-8
P-18 C-1-8
P-19 C-1-8

FERRELL:
NF: 9Mar55:   Reid Involves "Mr. Folsom"
Cont: P-1 C-1-2   "Ferrell"

Thurs NF: 10Mar55   Jurymen May Receive Fuller Case
P-1 C-7-8   Tonight; Defense/State Close
Cont: P-10 C-5-6-7   "Fuller"
P-22 C-1-2-3-4   Last Word of Testimony
P-22 C-5-6-7-8   Defense Presents Case Summation
P-23 C-1-8   Defense Summary (Buddow)
P-24 C-1-4   Deason Sums Up Prosecution Case
p-24 C-1-3 <?>   Defense Summary
P-26 C-1-3   State Summary

Columbus Ledger Night Final 10mar55 Cont.

FERRELL:
NF: 10Mar55   State Finishes Case Against
P-1 C-3-4-5   Ferrell
P-1 C-3-4-5   "Ferrell:" <>Right Page?<>
P-1 C-7-8 bf   Reid Draws Oberservation of Garrett/Ferrell

Fri NF: 11Mar55   Fuller Guilty
P-1 C-1-2
Cont.: P-2 C-3-4-5-6   "Fuller"
P-1 C-4-5-6   Judge McElroy Salutes Jury
Cont.   "Jury"
P-12 C-1-3   Deason Asks Death Sentence
P-12 C-6-7-8   Mrs. Porter Outlines Meetings
Photo   Broox Garrett at Trial

FERRELL: Ferrell Trial Ends
NF: 11Mar55:   Goes to Jury Today
P-1 C-1-2-3
Cont.: P-2 C-2 C-1-2-3   <> Ferrell?<> End Night Final

Sat 12Mar55: No Night Final   Fuller Convictedd of Murder
P-1 C-1-2   Jury's Verdict 3:37 p.m.
Cont. P-12 C-1-2   26 Day Trial
Ferrell:
CL: 12Mar55:   Ferrell Acquitted in Vote Case
P-1 C-1-2   Verdict Caught Newsmen/Surprise

Cont: P-12 C-6   "Ferrell"

Sun CE/CL 13Mar55   McElroy's Remark Re: Case
P-1 C-3-4-5-6
Cont: P-11 C-2-3-4-5-6-7-8
P-11 C-1   Taylor Discounts Threat on Life But goes Armed

Columbus Ledger April 1955

CL Wed 13Ap55:   Rogers Delays Postponement
P-13 C-1   Request of Trial
                        *Will ask indefinite postponement
                        *Statements: Judge Wheeler to Grand Jury
                        4May55. Perry: "a miscarriage of justice in
                        Ferrell vote fraud"

CL: Fri 15Ap55:   Court Recesses Ferrell Action To
P-1 C-7   Delay Trial
Cont P-2 C-5-6-7   Rogers Called 11 lawyers/ had 50 affidavits:
                         Ferrrell: no fair trial

CL: Sat 16Ap55   Deason Says Ferrell Can Fair Trial
P-1 C-4-5

CE/CL Sun 17Ap55:   Ferrell Going to Trial
A-1 C-6-7   Hoping for late Delay
Cont A-2 C-5   "Ferrell"

Columbus Ledger – April 1955 — NIGHT FINAL RESUMES:

NF: Mon18Ap55:   Selection Seen Today of Ferrell
P-1 C-7-8   Trial Jury Unless Delay Granted
Cont; P-2 C-5-6   (Judge McElroy Quizzes Jurrors)
P-1 C-1-2-3   Witness Reported Threatened Again
                        (Quinnie Kelly Threatened)

CL: Tues 19Ap55:   State Flies Subpoenas to Godwin
P-1 C-7-8   Davis Sr/James Radius Taylor
Cont P-2 C-5-6-7-8   "Ferrell"
P-1 C-1-2   Source Says- Second Witness Threatened
                        (Emory Powell)

NF: Wed 20Ap55;	State Builds Motive by Attempting
P-1 C-7-8	Link of Arch/Vice Ring
	* Defense Says Not His Duty To
	Stop Vice
Cont P-2 C-3-4-5-6	"Ferrell"
P-2 C-4	400 Witnesses Called
P-10 C-1-2	Testimony Begins in Ferrell Trial
	Mrs. Patterson on Stand
P-10 C-3-4-5	Ferrell Courtroom Casual Before Tense
	Trial begins

NF: Thurs 21Ap 55:	Mistrial Looms After Man Says " Hang
P-1 C-7-8	Him" To a Friend on Jury
P-7 C-1-8	Kirkland is First State's Witness
	(Saw Ferrell park his car at courthouse:
	8:25-8:45 18June54)
P-8 C-3 (only)	Second Day's Testimony (Littleton)
P-21 C-1-8	The First Testimony
	Early Testimony Parallels First Days of
	Fuller Trial

Columbus Ledger – April 1955 — Night Final

NF Fri 22Ap55:	Witness Says Ferrell Told Group
P-1 C-7-8	Patterson Wouldn't Take Office
Cont P-2 C-5	"Trial"
P-6 C-1-2-3	Trial Testimony: Sanders on Stand As Trial
	Resumes
P-6 C-5-6-7-8	Farmer's Remark Throws Ferrell
w/photo	Trial in Turmoil

NF: Sat 23Ap55	Godwin Davis Spills Info on
P-1 C-7-8	Contributions to Defeat Pat's Son
Cont P-2 C-5-6-7	"Trial"
P-7 C-1-8	Saturday's Testimony:
	Sowell Relates Autopsy Details
	(includes: Davis Testimony)
w/Photo:	E.J. Peoples (Witness Threatened)
Sunday CE/CL	Missing on This Microfilm:
CL/CE 24Ap55:	Red Porter/Reid
A-7 A-10	Trial Testimony

NF: Mon 25Ap 55   Intense Grilling Fails to Shake
P-1 C-7-8   Padgett's Murder Night Story
Cont P-2 C-4-5   "Trial"
P-3 C-1-2-3-4   Reid/ Mrs. Porter Quizzed
                      Questions Follow Vote Fraud Lines

NF: Tues 26Ap55:   State Resting Case; Defense Giving
P-1 C-7-8   Kelly Rugged Examination
Cont P-2 C-5-6-7   "Trial"
P-14 C-2-8   Testimony: Photographs of Coulter
                     Buildings Are Shown/ Reporters
                     Testify
C-2-3:   Strickland
C-3-4:   Wortsman
C-5:   Kelly
C-6:   Padgett
C-7:   Residential/ Burch
C-8:   Rex Thomas/ AP Montgomery

NF:Wed 27Ap55:   Witnessess Boomering As Defense
P-1 C-7-8   Attacks Quinnie Kelley Story
P-2 C-3-4-5   "Trial"
P-10 C-1-8   Trial Testimony
                    Defense Opens Case:Scout Tells
                    Seeing Court House Janitor
P-11 C-1-8   Trial Testimony: Kelly:
                    (Cross- Exam by Rogers)

NF: Thurs 28Ap55:   Defense Pounds Hard to Discredit
P-1 C-7-8   Padgett on Death Night Story
P-2 C-3-4   "Ferrell"
P-22 C-3-4-5-6-7-8 Witness throws doubt
                    Defense Attacks Padgett Story
P-23 C-1-8   Trial Testimony
P-23 C-5 Begins   Sanders/Lenoir
                    Wednesday's Testimony
P-24 C-3-4-5-6   Trial Testimony
                    Mrs. Bentley/ McKinney

Columbus Ledger — April 1955 — Night Final:

NF: Fri 29Ap55:   Defense Plans Close Of Case

P-1 C-7-8	Tomorrow/ Arch May not Testify
Cont P-2 C-3-4-5-6-7-8	
P-21 C-1-6	Kelley takes Stand 3rd Time
P-22 C-1-8	Trial Testimony
P-22 C-3 Begins	Thursday's Testimony
P-22 C-8 Last pg.	McElroy ruled that Garrett's name not be used in arguments to jury.
CL: 30Ap55:	Arch Ferrell Takes Stand Swears He Did not MURDER A.L. Patterson
NF: Sat 30Ap55:	Defense Rests- Ferrell is Under Fire
P-1 C-7-8	Over Three Hours
Above Masthead:	Verbatim Report of Arch Ferrell's Testimony
P-9 C-	Testimony of Mrs. Ferrell
P-14 C-	

Columbus Ledger May 1955

CE/CL Sun 1May55:	State Says Bell List Refutes
P-1 C-4	Ferrell Calls
Cont. A-2 C-4-5-	"Ferrell"
Sec: C-8 C-1-8	Ferrell on Stand in Own Defense
Sec: C-9 C-1-8	Trial Testimony
Sec: C-12 C-1-8	Trial Testimony
NF: Mon 2May55:	Sick Juror Causes Court Recess
P-1 C-7-8	Until Tomorrow Morning
Cont P-2 C-5	"Trial"
P-2 C-3-4	Mrs. Porter Only Witness
NF: Tues 3May55:	Jury Will Get Case Before
P-1 C-7	Nightfall; State Urges Death
Cont P-17 C-3	
P-17 C-1-2	Deason Asks Jury for Death Penalty
Wed 4May55:	FERRELL NOT GUILTY
P-12 C-	Deason's Opening Argument
P-12 C-6-7-8	Closing Argument
P-13	Defense Summation
P-14 C-1-3	Defense Argument (Redden)
P-14 C-3-8	Defense Argument (Rogers)

Additional Sources

Law Enforcement Interviews:

Major General Walter J. "Crack" Hanna
Lt. General James A. Mickle
Colonel James "Boxjaw" Brown
Lt. Colonel Jack Warren
Major Ray Acton
Captain Richard A. Peacock
Lieutenant James M. Fullan, Jr.
Warrant Officer George J. Stacy, Jr.
Alabama State Patrol Investigator Claude Prier
Justice George T. Smith, Georgia Supreme Court
Justice Richard L. "Red" Jones, Alabama Supreme Court
Judge J. Russell McElroy
Governor John Patterson
Georgia Revenue Agent Elzie Hancock

In Phenix City, Alabama:

Hugh Bentley, RBA President
Bernice Bentley, his wife
Truman Bentley, his son
John Luttrell, RBA activist
Howard Pennington, RBA activist
Hilda Coulter, Head of RBA Auxiliary

Press Interviews on File:

Columbus Ledger reporter Ray Jenkins, Editorial page editor, *The Evening Sun*, Baltimore 1985
Columbus Enquirer photographer Ann Robertson
Columbus Ledger/ Columbus Enquirer Archives
Columbus Ledger/ Columbus Enquirer Editorial Page Editor Billy Winn
Columbus Ledger reporter Richard Hyatt
Columbus Ledger columnist Beverly Greer
Columbus Ledger/ Columbus Enquirer staff reporters
The Birmingham News reporter Ed Strickland, Montgomery, AL

Associated Press reporter Gene Wortsman, Anniston, AL
Montgomery Advertiser reporter Bob Ingram, Montgomery, AL
Atlanta Journal-Constitution editor Jim Minter
Atlanta Journal reporter Bill Diele
Newnan Times-Herald publisher Billy Thomasson; editor Mary Ann
Thomasson; reporter Winston Skinner, Newnan, GA

Historical Research on File:

Dr. Floyd Watkins, Professor Emeritus Southern Literature, Emory
University, Atlanta GA 1984-1999
Linda Matthews, head, Woodruff Library Special Collections, Emory
University, Atlanta GA 1983-1993
Joyce LeMont, head, Hoole Library Special Collections, University of
Alabama, Tuscaloosa, AL 1983-1993
Barbara Loar, head, DeKalb County Library, Decatur, GA 1983-1993

Primary Materials on File:

Columbus Ledger/Columbus Enquirer daily newspapers 1954-1955
Birmingham News daily newspapers 1954-1955
Birmingham Post-Herald daily newspapers 1954-1955
Baltimore Evening Sun editorial, Ray Jenkins, 1984
Montgomery Advertiser daily newspapers 1954-1956
Atlanta Journal/Atlanta Constitution microfilm 1954-1955
Newnan Times-Herald daily newspapers 1954-1955
New York Times index 1954-1955
Columbus Ledger, Bill Winn, editorial, February 23, 1999, A-6
    Richard Hyatt, feature, February 19, 1999, A-11
    Richard Hyatt, feature, February 21, 1999, B-1
    Richard Hyatt, feature, May 18, 1999, B-1
Newnan Times-Herald, Winston Skinner, feature, February 21, 1999
    Winston Skinner, May 18, 1999, P-1
The Phenix City Story, Ed Strickland and Gene Wortsman, Vulcan Press
    Birmingham, AL 1955
Documented Phenix City Story, Roland J. Page, Doctoral Thesis, Florida
State University, 1966

Periodicals on File:

Alabama Journal, June 18, 1959, 2-E

Atlanta Journal/ Constitution, January 10, 1999. L10
Atlanta Magazine, March 1999
The American City, Honors Award, February, 1956 126, 127
Guideposts, Ray Jenkins, 1959
Life Magazine, October 4,1954, 49
Look Magazine, October 5, 1954, 33-37
McCall's Magazine, September 1955, 52, 54, 56, 62, 66
Newsweek, August 2, 1954, 19-20
Newsweek, December 27, 1954, 18
Newsweek, October 5, 1959, 31
Parade, January 11, 1965, 40-45
Reader's Digest, December 1955, 71-75
The Reporter, February 24, 1955, 22-27
Time Magazine, June 28, 1954, 22
The Saturday Evening Post, November 27, 1954, 20-21, 60, 62-64
The Saturday Evening Post, January 8, 1955, 6

Exhibits on File:

Ralph Edwards, CBS-TV "This is Your Life Hugh Bentley," 1955
Unpublished photographs: Alabama National Guard, 1954
        Columbus Ledger: Attack on Hugh Bentley et al
Unpublished File: Mug Shots of girls forced into prostitution

Correspondence and Personal Papers on File:

General Walter J. Hanna
Governor John Patterson
Ed Strickland
Hugh Bentley
John Luttrell
Attorney Kenneth Henson

Justice George T. Smith
Dr. Floyd Watkins
Dr. Linda Matthews
Bernice Bentley

James Fullan